A SMARTER, GREENER GRID

Forging Environmental Progress through Smart Energy Policies and Technologies

Kevin B. Jones and David Zoppo

Energy Resources, Technology, and Policy
Benjamin K. Sovacool, Series Editor

🌐 PRAEGER

AN IMPRINT OF ABC-CLIO, LLC
Santa Barbara, California • Denver, Colorado • Oxford, England

Library of Congress Cataloging-in-Publication Data

Jones, Kevin B.
  A smarter, greener grid : forging environmental progress through smart policies and technologies / Kevin B. Jones and David Zoppo.
      pages cm. — (Energy resources, technology, and policy)
   ISBN 978-1-4408-3070-9 (hardback) — ISBN 978-1-4408-3071-6 (e-book) 1. Energy policy—United States. 2. Environmental policy—United States. 3. Smart power grids—United States. 4. Electric power distribution—United States. I. Zoppo, David. II. Title.
   HD9502.U52J659 2014
   333.793'20973—dc23   2014001561

ISBN: 978-1-4408-3070-9
EISBN: 978-1-4408-3071-6

18 17 16 15 14   2 3 4 5

This book is also available on the World Wide Web as an eBook.
Visit www.abc-clio.com for details.

Praeger
An Imprint of ABC-CLIO, LLC

ABC-CLIO, LLC
130 Cremona Drive, P.O. Box 1911
Santa Barbara, California 93116-1911

This book is printed on acid-free paper ∞
Manufactured in the United States of America

CONTENTS

SERIES FOREWORD

As societies around the world grapple with a changing climate, competition over scarce energy reserves, growing collective energy insecurity, and massive fluctuations in the price and affordability of energy services, what could be more important than a book series which analyzes the interaction between society and the energy sector? The Energy Resources, Technology, and Policy book series at Praeger/ABC-CLIO does this, and it explores topics as diverse as energy reserves, fuels, resources, and socio-technical systems on the one hand, and policymaking, behavioral change, and the complexities of human energy end-use and consumption on the other.

Apart from investigating state-of-the-art innovations in the energy sector and illustrating the ways in which energy development is fragilely balanced with environmental protection, the series also meets a demand for clear, unbiased information on energy and the environment. Books emerging from the series are intended for an audience of professionals, upper-division undergraduates, graduate students, and faculty in such fields as engineering, public affairs, global studies, ecology, geography, environmental studies, business and management, and energy policy.

Books in the series take an investigative approach to global and at times local energy issues, showing how problems arise when energy policies and technological development supersede environmental priorities but also demonstrating cases in which activism and sensitive policies have worked with energy developers to find solutions. The titles in the series offer global perspectives on contemporary energy sources, the connected technologies, and international policy responses, showing what has been done to develop safe, secure, affordable, and efficient forms of energy that can continue to power the world without destroying the environment or human communities.

The series ultimately shows the progress of energy developers and environmental advocates toward sustainable resolutions. For that, I hope the pages to come excite and challenge you as much as they have me.

Benjamin K. Sovacool
Series Editor

FOREWORD

Benjamin K. Sovacool

There is almost no question that we as a society can use electricity and energy more intelligently and that we need "smarter" electricity grids. Conventional electric grids have simple or unsophisticated meters, have flat or inflexible pricing, and are built according to the hub-and-spoke model of centralized supply. They offer little to no storage, cannot handle intermittent renewable sources well, and use only a minimal amount of information technology. Smart grids, by contrast, have advanced net metering or smart meters, allow dynamic pricing that changes, and are built to accommodate distributed generation. They can incorporate various types of storage (batteries, appliances, cars), are friendlier to wind turbines and solar panels, and utilize large-scale digital networking and feedback.[1]

In fact, smarter grids improve energy efficiency and enable customers and consumers to use energy more prudently in a variety of ways. Smart controls and communication technologies enhance the efficiency of home appliances, whereas smarter electricity pricing can incentivize more sustainable patterns of energy consumption on the scale of neighborhoods and even countries.

Industry players and policymakers have looked closely at the reliability and economic benefits of the smart grid, often citing its environmental benefits as an afterthought. Although this book acknowledges those benefits, it takes a hard look at the environmental, economic, and social promise of the smart grid in the United States. It provides lay readers with a concise and accessible introduction to the components of the modern electricity industry, while explaining how the smart grid can fundamentally change those components to make the electricity business greener and smarter. It is comprehensive in its treatment of the smart grid's environmental and climate attributes, and it provides readers with a balanced, unbiased assessment of the benefits and drawbacks of smart grid technologies.

A *Smarter, Greener Grid* does all of this by exploring six cutting-edge case studies of the smart grid in practice: Sacramento Municipal Utility District's SmartSacramento program in California, the Salt River Project in Arizona, Commonwealth Edison's Smart Grid Innovation Corridor in Chicago, San Diego Gas & Electric's smart grid program, Central Vermont Public Service's SmartPower, and the Pecan Street Project in Texas. For each of these cases, the book investigates the following:

1. What is the pathway for environmental improvement?
2. What progress do the case studies demonstrate in these areas?
3. What policies are necessary to ensure we achieve the environmental promise?

Following this discussion, the authors present a policy roadmap to address how to implement a smart grid that expands the effectiveness of energy efficiency and demand response programs, more fully deploys electric vehicles, better integrates distributed clean generation, and fully "greens" the grid through distribution automation. The book, in short, is essential reading for those concerned with energy policy, law, and technology.

NOTE

1. William J. Mitchell, Christopher E. Borroni-Bird, and Lawrence D. Burns, *Reinventing the Automobile: Personal Urban Mobility for the 21st Century* (Cambridge: MIT Press, 2010), 126.

ACKNOWLEDGMENTS

The Smart Grid Project at Vermont Law School's Institute for Energy and the Environment (IEE) began in the fall of 2010. This book is very much a multiyear work product of the many smart grid project team members who were students and faculty at VLS. The Institute for Energy and the Environment works on real energy law and policy problems, focusing on laws and policies that benefit the environment. Given this focus, the last three to four years have been an appropriate time to explore how smart energy technologies and policies can best lead to a greener grid. This has been a fun but challenging question, leading to many avenues for exploration.

Our research project began by looking at six very different organizations and how they were implementing smart grid technologies. In particular, we wanted to study how their policies and technologies could benefit the climate. We also recognized that maintaining the privacy of customer data was integral to the success of the smart grid. Accordingly, we decided to develop a model privacy policy for utility customer smart grid data.

In 2010, we began by selecting the organizations we were going to study. Matthew Stern (J.D./Master of Environmental Law and Policy [M.E.L.P.] 2011) and Colin Hagan (J.D. 2012) were the first team volunteers. Matt was the lead researcher on the Salt River Project case study and performed some of our early research on demand response and the smart grid. Matt currently practices energy law in Vermont. Colin Hagan was the lead researcher on our Central Vermont Public Service case study and was one of the coauthors of our smart grid privacy policy. During his second year, Colin also participated in our research on legal and regulatory policy issues surrounding the smart grid. Colin is practicing energy and commercial law in Vermont. Rebecca Wigg (M.E.L.P. 2011) was a lead researcher on our Pecan Street case study and served as our smart grid fellow for a year following graduation. Becky has left her imprint on a lot of the work we have done. She currently works for the Regulatory Assistance Project. Christine Breen (J.D./M.E.L.P. 2011) was also a lead researcher on our Pecan Street case study and performed some early research on renewable energy policy. Christine now practices energy law in Colorado. Chris Cooper (J.D. 2013) was a lead researcher on our Commonwealth Edison case study, worked as our first smart grid fellow, and also authored a book on the sun and coauthored a book on energy megaprojects while at the IEE. Kari Twaite (J.D. 2012) did research on distributed generation before she went to Yale on a joint degree program. Kari now practices environmental law in Washington, D.C. Allie Silverman (J.D./M.E.L.P. 2012) was also one of our initial team members. Allie was the lead researcher on our Sacramento Municipal Utility District case study and researched some of the broader environmental benefits of the smart grid. Allie works on climate law and policy in Washington, D.C. During the summer of 2011, Shauna Thompson (M.E.L.P. 2011) joined the team and worked with us on developing a smart grid policy seminar. Shauna has returned to California to work on energy and environmental policy. Zhen Zhang, a global energy fellow at IEE, provided early research assistance to our project, including research on U.S. and European Union policies. Zhen currently works for the California Public Utility Commission.

During the fall of 2011, our second-year team included Katie Thomas (J.D./M.E.L.P. 2013), who was the lead researcher on our San Diego Gas & Electric case study and coauthored our smart grid privacy policy. In November, Katie and Colin were invited to present our privacy policy to the Legal Seminar of the American Public Power Association. Their work was met with rave reviews, including one commentator who noted that many of the practicing lawyers at the meeting could not have shown as much poise as Katie and Colin, who were then second- and third-year law students. Katie will begin her legal career as an associate with a Washington, D.C., firm that represents municipal and cooperative utilities. Graham Jesmer (J.D. 2013) led the research on distributed energy technologies and worked with us until the spring of 2013, when he left for a semester-in-practice with the New York Public Service Commission. He is currently employed there. Meredith Crafton (J.D./M.E.L.P. 2012) worked with us on how the smart grid enhances energy efficiency. Meredith, a former world jump rope champion, now works as a staff attorney at Hanford Challenge in Washington State. Shannon Clarke joined the fall 2011 team and researched demand response policy. She is also responsible for coming up with the idea that the smart grid "democratizes" demand response. Coauthor David Zoppo (J.D. 2013) joined the team in the fall of 2011 and rejoined us the following year following a semester-in-practice in Hawaii. In addition to helping write this book, David's research focused on electric vehicles and the smart grid.

Our third year of research began in the fall of 2012. Joining our returning members were Chris Supino (L.L.M. in Environmental Law 2013), Christopher Casey (J.D./M.E.L.P. 2013) and Mindy Blank (M.E.L.P. 2013). Chris Supino, an Energy Fellow at the IEE, worked on legal and regulatory issues facing the smart grid and drafted an update to our smart grid data privacy policy before graduating and heading off to the Midwest to practice energy law. Chris Casey researched energy efficiency and the smart grid, and some of his published work is cited in the book. Following graduation, Chris headed to the Northwest to begin his career in energy law and policy. Mindy Blank worked on electric vehicle policy during her year with us and left us to work in Europe on sustainability and international smart grid policy issues with the International Energy Agency. Speaking of Europe, the 2013–2014 team plans to refocus our research on smart grid implementation in the European Union. Our new team members, Stephanie Gardner (M.E.L.P. 2014), Jonathan Hart (Master of Energy Regulation and Law [M.E.R.L.] 2014), Achyut Sherestha (M.E.R.L. 2014), and Jonathan Blansfield (J.D. 2014), are researching and writing about how the EU is using the smart grid to benefit the climate. We must also acknowledge honorary smart grid team members Abi Barnes (J.D. 2015) and Nick Rossi (J.D. 2014), who worked with us during the summer of 2013, providing much needed editorial assistance.

Any research project going on this long needs a sponsor. In that regard, we want to acknowledge the excellent support provided by the U.S. Department of Energy's Office of Electric Delivery and Reliability. We have greatly benefited from the DOE's support and we appreciate the feedback that we have received from Lawrence Mansueti, Joseph Paladino, and others. Our smart grid project has also been managed under the DOE's National Energy Technology Laboratory (NETL), and so we also thank our NETL project manager, Ryan Watson. Ryan has been a tremendous positive influence on our work, and we thank him for his helpful insight and collaboration. We expect big things from Ryan in the future as he pursues his doctor of law degree in energy law part-time in West Virginia while working with NETL. We also must note that our work with the Department of Energy would never have gotten underway without the support of Vermont congressman Peter Welch. Congressman Welch is a good friend of Vermont Law School and a strong advocate for energy efficiency, and we appreciate the support that he and his staff have provided. We would also like to thank his chief of staff, Bob Rogan, and former staff member Mary Sprayregan, who tells us it wouldn't have happened without her. So thanks, Mary!

We also could not have completed this project without the support of our case study participants, and thus we would like to acknowledge the collaborative support from the staff of the Salt River Project, San Diego Gas & Electric, Commonwealth Edison, the Pecan Street Project, Central Vermont Public Service (now Green Mountain Power), and the Sacramento Municipal Utility District.

We would like to thank some key people who keep the good things happening at VLS and IEE. A big thanks to President and Dean Marc Mihaly, Vice Dean of Faculty Mark Latham, Melissa Scanlan, Director of the Environmental Law Center, and Michael Dworkin, Director of the Institute for Energy and the Environment for creating this opportunity at VLS. A special thanks to Dean Mihaly for helping introduce solar photovoltaic and electric vehicle charging stations on campus, which certainly makes the Vermont Law School feel smarter and greener. And last, but most important, we would like to thank our IEE coordinator, Jenny Thomas. As everyone in the greater VLS community knows, when you need some support or assistance you can always count on Jenny. Only Jenny knows how many times her creative problem solving has rescued us from unknown calamities. Thanks, Jenny!

Finally, the material in this book is based upon work supported by the Department of Energy under Award Number DE-OE0000446.

1

INTRODUCTION
The Digital Energy Revolution

Over the past half-century, the evolution of information technology has given rise to a new world order. Whereas people used to write letters, send telegrams, or make telephone calls to communicate over long distances, they can now do so almost instantaneously through Internet-based platforms like Skype or Facebook. Whereas companies used to do business on paper and over the telephone, and often had to use staff to manufacture goods, manage operations, track inventory, conduct deals with clients and vendors, or market products to consumers, they can now employ a variety of computer software and technologies to automate, streamline, and execute (in real time) these same tasks. Even the entertainment industry has undergone drastic change: Whereas people used to go to record stores to purchase CDs, cassettes, or vinyls, they can now purchase music, movies, and television series with only an iPod, an iTunes account, and an Internet connection. In short, breakthroughs in information technology have made a wealth of information available to nearly all of Western civilization. As a result, the pace of everything—communication, business, entertainment—has quickened.

The American electric power sector is an exception to this trend.[1] Although the industry saw rapid growth and increasing efficiencies essentially through the 1960s,[2] it has yet to fully leverage information technology in the way that other sectors of society and the economy have. In many parts of the country, the electricity grid is more of an antique, mechanical superstructure than it is a modernized, automated, and digital machine. About one-fifth of the power plants in America's generation fleet are more than fifty years old, and much of the nation's high-voltage transmission network was designed for an era when there was very little

I

interstate commerce in electricity.[3] And although many innovative technologies have become available over the last three decades, the electric power sector spends less than 1 percent of total revenues on research and development,[4] whereas other major industries spend as much as 3 percent.[5] In terms of harnessing the potential of information technologies, the electric power sector lags behind the rest of the economy.

This is where the smart grid comes in. The smart grid provides an opportunity to revolutionize the electricity industry in the same way that information technology has revolutionized the rest of the modern economy. The smart grid is an information technology architecture that permits two-way communication between the electricity grid and anything connected to it.[6] In this way, the smart grid is not a single, discreet technology that utilities can simply install and forget. Rather, it is an amalgamation of technologies that essentially create an Internet-like system on the grid, allowing grid operators, utilities, competitive service providers, and customers to share information.[7] This information sharing enables utilities and operators to manage the grid more efficiently and allows consumers to make more informed decisions regarding their electricity consumption. When applied properly, smart grid technologies have the potential to improve reliability, strengthen grid security, reduce costs, increase efficiency, and meaningfully decrease the environmental footprint of the electric power industry.

This last point is especially important. Among industry players and policymakers, smart grid technologies have typically been viewed as a means to improve grid reliability and reduce costs. Smart grid technologies can undoubtedly achieve both of these goals, which are important in and of themselves. And utilities have focused on the reliability and economic aspects of smart grid investments because they need to justify these expenses to government regulators, who will ultimately determine whether these costs may be recovered through customer rates.

But in this discussion of economics and reliability, we must not lose sight of the important environmental benefits that the smart grid can create. In particular, the smart grid provides a cost-effective means of addressing one of the most pressing environmental problems of the twenty-first century: climate change. Anthropogenic greenhouse gas emissions, particularly from the electric power sector, are a major cause of global climate change.[8] Although the smart grid is not a panacea to stopping climate change, it can contribute to a meaningful reduction in greenhouse gas emissions within the electric power sector. Investing in smart grid technology today is a down payment on tomorrow's environment.

Granted, smart grid technology is not enough. A truly smart grid requires smart energy policies. The environmental potential of the smart grid is meaningless if industry and government do nothing to harness that potential. There have been some early indications that policymakers at the state and federal level recognize the potential of smart grid technologies. Through the American Recovery and Reinvestment Act of 2009, the Department of Energy (DOE) invested $3.4 billion—matched by $8 billion in private funds—to upgrade the electricity grid with smart technologies.[9] In California, the state legislature passed a bill requiring regulated utilities to develop smart grid implementation plans that will, among other things, "significantly reduce the total environmental footprint of the current electric generation and delivery system in California."[10] California utilities have responded to this legislation by developing innovative smart grid deployment plans that seek to reduce the state's overall greenhouse gas emissions. Although these developments represent an important step forward, they are far overdue. Additional leadership from industry and government is needed—at both state and national levels—to fully leverage the environmental benefits of smart grid technologies.

OVERVIEW OF THE ELECTRIC POWER INDUSTRY

When waking up in the morning, most people probably take it for granted that, when they flip a switch, the lights will go on. They start their coffee makers or plug in their cell phones without giving much thought to where or how the electricity that powers these devices is produced and delivered. In fact, the business of generating, transmitting, and delivering electricity is enormously complex. With over $600 billion in physical assets and annual sales of over $260 billion, the electric power sector is the nation's largest industry.[11] There are more than nine thousand power plants throughout the United States, producing electricity that is transmitted over nearly 300,000 miles of transmission lines and 5.5 million miles of distribution lines.[12] America's electricity infrastructure is literally the largest machine in the entire country. Although this machine has worked well in providing power to millions of Americans for the last century, it has historically faced a number of unique challenges that have made it woefully inefficient.

The electricity power industry is divided into three sectors: generation, transmission, and distribution. The generation sector is where utilities and independent power producers (that is, generators not owned by retail service utilities) produce electricity. Unfortunately, the actual production of power is both environmentally harmful and highly inefficient. The fossil-fuel resources that create electricity—namely, coal and natural gas—are extracted through processes such as strip mining, surface mining, mountain top removal, and hydrofracking. These extraction techniques have been associated with potentially toxic by-products, as well as air and water pollution, soil erosion, and massive land disturbances.[13] Moreover, the actual production of electricity is a highly inefficient process. A typical fossil-fuel power plant is only about 33 percent efficient—that is, only one out of every three units of fuel actually goes toward producing electricity, while the rest are lost as waste heat.[14]

After it is produced at a generating plant, electricity is sent across miles of high-voltage transmission lines. However, as in the generation sector, a significant amount of energy is lost when electricity is transmitted over long distances: Transmission lines typically lose 3 to 7 percent of the electricity they carry.[15] Another issue in the transmission sector is storage—or the lack thereof. Unlike most goods, electricity cannot be efficiently stored in large quantities, and so generators, grid operators, and utilities must ensure that at any given moment there is enough electricity flowing to the grid to satisfy demand. Demand, however, varies depending on the time of day—and time of year—so utilities rely on "intermediate plants" and "peaking plants" to produce electricity when demand increases beyond the capacity of base-load plants. Because intermediate and peaking plants operate less frequently, and because they are generally more expensive to run, utilities must spread the costs to operate those plants over fewer units of production, which drives up the price of electricity to consumers. In this way, our inability to economically store electricity at some point along the transmission network drives up the costs of production—and thus, overall electricity rates.

Once the electricity gets closer to population centers, utility substations "step down" the voltage and transmit it across their distribution network directly to customers. The major obstacle to efficiency in the distribution sector is pricing. Unlike most goods, the retail price of electricity often does not reflect the cost of production. As you probably know from looking at your utility bill, electricity is often priced to consumers at a flat rate. But as mentioned, the cost of providing electricity varies on both a daily and a seasonal basis. That is, it costs a utility more to provide power during rush hour as opposed to the witching hour, but a utility will often price power at the same rate despite these fluctuations. Thus customers have no incentive to reduce their consumption or shift that consumption to more cost-effective times of day.

ENVIRONMENTAL BENEFITS OF THE SMART GRID

Smart grid technologies and smart energy policies can help correct many of these inefficiencies and, in so doing, mitigate many of the electric power sector's negative environmental externalities. Indeed, although America's electricity infrastructure has drastically raised standards of living and improved economic productivity over the last century, these gains have come at a significant cost to the environment.

One of the main benefits to implementing smart grid technologies is decreased carbon dioxide (CO_2) emissions. The electric power sector is the largest—and one of the fastest growing—sources of CO_2 emissions in the United States. This is primarily because of our heavy dependence on fossil fuels, which account for about 70 percent of the nation's net electricity generation.[16] As a result, CO_2 emissions from the electric power sector make up a third of the American economy's total greenhouse gas (GHG) emissions and about 8 percent of global CO_2 emissions.[17] Moreover, the electric power sector is also a significant source of other harmful air pollutants that pose a risk to human health and the environment, independent of climate change.

The consequences of failing to reign in the nation's CO_2 emissions are potentially catastrophic. Anthropogenic GHG emissions contribute significantly to the modern climate change phenomenon. When released into the atmosphere from cars, power plants, and other fossil-fuel combustion activities, these gases create a "greenhouse effect," trapping heat that is radiated from the earth's surface and creating a net warming effect. Although the greenhouse effect is a naturally occurring phenomenon, the atmospheric concentration of GHGs has increased drastically since 1750 and, based on data from ice-core samples, far exceeds the natural range over the last 650,000 years.[18] Changes in land-use patterns have also contributed to an increase in atmospheric GHG concentrations: The world's forests are "carbon sinks" that absorb CO_2, but they are quickly being cleared for lumber and agricultural cultivation. Together, these trends (increased concentration of GHGs in the atmosphere and changes in land-use patterns) have helped raise global average surface temperatures and global average sea levels.[19] A vast majority of the world's climatologists have concluded that anthropogenic GHG emissions are "very likely" contributing to global climate change.[20]

Despite the scientific consensus on the *existence* of global climate change, there is great uncertainty about the severity of its *consequences*.[21] Recent data shows that between 1998 and 2013, global surface temperatures remained flat, despite the fact that the world added almost one hundred billion tons of GHGs in the first decade of the new millennium.[22] This suggests that the earth's climate is perhaps more resilient to climate change than scientists originally suspected. Nonetheless, both scientific research and recent human experience indicate that the effects of climate change, though unknown, could be enormous.

For one thing, climate change has had—and is expected to continue having—a significant impact on freshwater resources and low-lying islands and coastal regions. Average ocean temperatures have increased since 1961, and the extent of annual Arctic sea ice has shrunk by almost 3 percent per decade since 1978, with larger decreases in the summer.[23] If these trends persist, sea levels could rise an additional sixty centimeters by 2100,[24] which could increase the severity and frequency of storms and flooding in coastal communities. Farther inland, rising surface temperatures have caused glaciers and mountainous snowpack to recede significantly.[25] Regions that depend on glacial melt and snowmelt for fresh water could experience water shortages, disruptions in hydropower potential, and extreme variations in the seasonal flow of rivers and streams.

Climate change is also very likely to increase the frequency and intensity of extreme weather events—such as hurricanes, floods, droughts, and heat waves—which could degrade or forever change entire ecosystems, disrupt or stunt productivity in fisheries and agriculture, and cause enormous destruction to human life and property. Indeed, the extreme weather patterns that global warming could produce will increase the vulnerability of communities throughout the globe to weather-related disasters, and especially those in the developing world.[26] Small island states in the Pacific are particularly at risk, as sea-level rise could threaten their very existence. Moreover, although recent North American superstorms—such as Hurricanes Katrina and Rita in 2005, Hurricane Irene in 2012, and Hurricane Sandy in 2013—cannot be conclusively tied to climate change, they demonstrate that even the most developed parts of the world remain vulnerable to extreme weather events. The nation—indeed, the world—will have to learn to cope with more of these destructive events as climate change progresses.

In addition to greenhouse gas emissions, the electric power sector also produces several other harmful air pollutants, such as sulfur dioxide (SO_2), nitrous oxides (NO_X), and particulate matter, which pose risks to human health and the environment. Coal and natural gas power plants, for example, are a significant source of NO_X and SO_2.[27] When released into the atmosphere, these pollutants transform into sulfuric acid (H_2SO_4) and nitric acid (HNO_3), which fall as acid rain and snow. Acid precipitation, of course, has devastating effects on the environment. It destroys forest habitats, detrimentally alters the composition of soil, degrades the health of fish and aquatic habitats, and harms waterfowl and riparian bird species by killing off or contaminating the fish and insects on which they feed.[28] NO_X and SO_2 are also precursors to ozone (O_3) and particulate matter (PM), both of which can cause and/or aggravate respiratory and cardiovascular diseases such as asthma, bronchitis, and nonfatal heart attacks.[29] Ozone also reduces photosynthetic activity in plant life, which negatively affects crop yields in the agricultural sector.[30] Finally, coal plants are a significant source of mercury, a hazardous air pollutant that can deposit onto land and water bodies and become "methylmercury . . . a highly toxic, more bioavailable form that magnifies in the aquatic food chain," creating dangers for humans and other animals alike.[31]

The obvious question is, what can the smart grid do to solve these problems? The answer is that the smart grid can mitigate the environmental harms of our current system of electricity production. It does this in two ways. First, the smart grid will make the electric power sector more efficient, such that generators will be able to burn fewer fossil fuels while still providing the same quality of service to customers. Of course, every unit of avoided fossil-fuel combustion "carries an associated reduction in air emissions, including nitrogen oxides, sodium dioxide, volatile organic compounds (VOCs), other criteria air pollutants, and most significantly, greenhouse gases."[32] By improving energy efficiency and demand response programs, smart grid technologies will enable utilities and customers to manage energy production and consumption in a more efficient manner.

Second, the smart grid will help integrate cleaner, more environmentally friendly fuels and technologies into the American energy portfolio, which will displace fossil-fuel combustion as a source of electricity. In particular, smart grid technologies can help integrate renewable resources and electric vehicles (EVs) into the American energy portfolio. Renewables and electric vehicles will help reduce GHG and air pollutant emissions, help utilities meet their respective state renewable portfolio standards (RPS), and provide customers with greater access to clean, renewable energy.[33]

The smart grid is therefore critical not only to updating the nation's aging electricity infrastructure but also to reducing emissions of both CO_2 and other harmful pollutants.[34] The Pacific Northwest National Laboratory (PNNL) estimates that, if smart grid technologies are fully deployed across the country in the next two decades, the electric power sector could reduce both energy use and carbon emissions by 12 percent of what they are projected to be in 2030.[35] Likewise, the Electric Power Research Institute (EPRI) estimates that smart grid technologies could curtail retail electricity sales by 1.3 to 4.8 percent in 2030.[36] This translates into a decrease of 2.7 to 9.5 percent of projected CO_2 emissions.[37]

Granted, achieving these emissions reductions depends on a number of important assumptions which vary between studies. For instance, PNNL

Table 1.1 PNNL Projections: Energy Savings and Carbon Reductions from Deploying Smart Grid Technologies

Pathway	Percent Reduction in Energy Use in 2030	KWh/Year Saved	Percent Reduction in U.S. Carbon Emissions in 2030	Metric Tons/Year Saved
Energy Efficiency & Conservation	7.0%	366,000,000,000	7.0%	217,000,000
Demand Response	0.04%	2,000,000,000	0.03%	1,000,000
Electric Vehicles	3.0%	139,000,000,000	3.0%	82,000,000
Distributed Generation, Renewables & Storage	0.02%	1,000,000,000	0.02%	1,000,000
Distribution Optimization & CVR	2.0%	99,000,000,000	2.0%	59,000,000
Total	12.1%	607,000,000,000	12.1%	360,000,000

Note: The numbers in this table represent reductions in energy use and emissions relative to what they are otherwise projected to be in 2030.

Source: PNNL.

assumes that, by 2030, every utility in the country will have fully deployed smart grid technologies throughout its service territory, while EPRI assumes significantly lower market penetration rates for smart grid technologies.[38] EPRI's study also factors in changes to the nation's energy portfolio over the next twenty years, assuming "more aggressive implementations of renewables, nuclear, and advanced coal with greater efficiency and carbon capture and sequestration by 2030."[39] The PNNL study does not take into account any such changes in calculating the direct benefits of the smart grid; it does, however, account for "indirect benefits" of smart grid technologies. Instead of translating into energy and emission reductions, these indirect benefits "reduce capital and/or operational costs that can then be reinvested in the deployment of energy efficiency programs or . . . renewables to provide reductions."[40] If the indirect benefits from the PNNL study are taken into account, then expected energy usage and carbon emissions decrease by an additional 6 percent, for a combined reduction of 18 percent in direct and indirect savings.

It is important to note that because many smart grid technologies and programs are still in their infancy, preliminary estimates of potential CO_2 savings are highly uncertain. Thus the degree of CO_2 emissions reductions that the electric power sector would actually achieve depends on the extent to which these assumptions prove correct. Despite these uncertainties, the smart grid holds tremendous potential to reduce energy consumption and GHG emissions in the electric power sector. In particular, this book identifies five pathways by which the smart grid can leverage digital information technology to improve the efficiency of the electric power sector and thereby reduce its overall environmental footprint. This introduction will briefly describe these pathways.

ENERGY EFFICIENCY AND CONSERVATION

Energy efficiency refers to receiving the same or better level of energy services using less actual energy. For example, a consumer might install a light bulb that provides the same amount of light, but by using less energy. The consumer does not have to sacrifice comfort for energy savings. Energy conservation, on the other hand, refers to achieving energy savings by "reducing the level of energy services."[41] So rather than install a more efficient light bulb, a consumer might simply use the lights less often. Together, the energy savings from efficiency and conservation programs translate into reduced emissions, thereby reducing the environmental footprint of the electric power industry.

Smart meters and other advanced metering infrastructure (AMI) are critical to increasing both efficiency and conservation in the electric power sector because they enable consumers, the grid, and the utilities to better communicate with one another. Smart meters measure customer electricity consumption instantaneously, can store this data at fifteen-minute (or more frequent) intervals, and can transmit that data to both the customer and the utility as needed.[42] This provides utilities, third-party energy service companies, and customers with more frequent—and more detailed—information regarding the customer's energy use. It is this information exchange that enables the smart grid to promote greater end-use energy efficiency investments. The idea is that, by making customer electricity consumption more precise and transparent, utilities and customers will have the ability—and the incentive—to reduce long-term energy consumption through energy efficiency and conservation.

Emissions reductions from these energy efficiency and conservation measures could be significant. PNNL estimates that smart grid technologies could reduce energy consumption and electricity-related CO_2 emissions by 7 percent in 2030.[43] EPRI's estimate is more conservative. It projects that the energy efficiency benefits of smart grid technologies will reduce energy consumption and electricity-related CO_2 emissions by about 4 percent.[44] Of course, the accuracy of these estimates will depend on the extent to which utilities and consumers leverage data provided by smart grid technologies.

DEMAND RESPONSE

Demand response refers to a temporal shift in energy consumption as a result of market or reliability concerns. Demand response is nothing new in the electric power sector. A variety of demand response programs have existed for several decades, but they typically have been limited to large commercial and industrial customers. Generally speaking, these programs send price signals to customers to discourage electricity consumption during peak hours (when demand is at its highest) and to incentivize consumption during nonpeak hours (when demand is lower). Successful demand response programs reduce peak load to the point that the utility need not turn on peaking plants, which are generally less efficient, more expensive, and burn "dirty" fossil fuels. These programs reduce utility costs and emissions and defer the need to construct additional new generation.

As a result of enhanced communication between consumers and utilities, the smart grid can "democratize" demand response so that it may be applied not only to large customers but also to small commercial and residential customers. Smart meters will be critical to the success of these expanded demand response programs. Smart meters and advanced metering infrastructure facilitate two-way communication between the utility and the customer, such that utilities can control a customer's appliances and directly curtail customer consumption. Smart meters and AMI will also enable utilities to implement rate structures that discourage on-peak consumption, thereby shifting consumption to off-peak hours (this is known as "load shifting").

Granted, load shifting will not necessarily reduce energy use or emissions. Rather, demand response simply shifts energy consumption to another time, when the costs and emissions created may be lower. Accordingly, demand response may have little potential to reduce overall emissions and energy consumption. PNNL, for instance, estimates that total energy savings and carbon reductions associated with demand response may be quite small: By 2030, demand response programs could reduce electricity consumption by .04 percent and expected CO_2 emissions by .03 percent.[45] Likewise, EPRI estimates that, with smart grid technologies, demand response programs could yield energy savings equivalent to .09 percent of total retail electricity sales in 2030.[46] These projections are consistent with historical data, which shows that over the last ten years, energy savings from demand response programs averaged about .03 percent of total retail electricity sales.[47]

This does not mean that we should completely write off demand response as a means of achieving environmental improvements. Although demand response has not historically put a large dent in overall electricity consumption, it has consistently produced positive peak load reductions with relatively little investment. And as more renewable resources are deployed, the carbon footprint of base-load and/or off-peak generation will likely shrink. In this way, demand response represents a cost-effective means of reducing emissions from the electric power sector.

ELECTRIC VEHICLES

Smart grid technologies can also facilitate more widespread adoption of electric vehicles, which will reduce American dependence on foreign oil and the transportation sector's carbon footprint. This is largely because an electric vehicle's battery-powered electric motor is far and away more efficient than a conventional gasoline-powered internal combustion engine. Even when electric vehicles are powered by electricity from a "dirty" resource—such as coal or natural gas—they still present a more efficient and more environmentally friendly means of transportation than a traditional automobile. A study conducted by EPRI and the Natural Resources Defense Council indicates that electric vehicles produce 28 to 67 percent less GHG emissions than comparable conventional vehicles.[48] Moreover, the fuel costs for electric vehicles would actually be lower than fuel costs for a conventional automobile.[49] Electrifying the transportation sector would therefore benefit America's economy and its environment.

The smart grid can help integrate electric vehicles into the American economy by providing appropriate price signals for when consumers should charge those vehicles. The PNNL study argues that the electric power industry could support electrification of up to 70 percent of the American light-duty vehicle fleet without having to build additional generation or transmission assets.[50] Charging times and locations, however, would have to be carefully managed so that consumers do not charge their vehicles during peak hours. This is where the smart grid comes in. Consumers who install charging stations at their homes could essentially have a "smart meter" for their car, which would provide price signals for when the vehicle should be charged. If consumers heeded these price signals, utilities would not have to build additional generation and transmission to meet demand from EVs. Rather, the utility could meet this demand by utilizing existing capacity in a more efficient manner—that is, during nonpeak periods.

If charging times are properly managed, electric vehicles could be a boon for the environment and increase the efficiency of the electric grid. PNNL estimates that electrifying the transportation sector and implementing "smart charging" behaviors could reduce energy-related CO_2 emissions by about 3 percent in 2030.[51] EPRI is more conservative, asserting that the CO_2 reductions attributable to smart grid technologies would be on the order of 0.4 to 2.7 percent of emissions levels in 2030.[52] Of course, encouraging electric vehicle adoption is not solely an issue for the electricity industry. Wider adoption of electric vehicles is constrained by a number of important factors, including the cost and efficiency of battery technology and the current lack of charging infrastructure. Overcoming these obstacles and deploying electric vehicles on a large scale will require not only the smart grid but also a concerted effort from policymakers, the auto industry, and the electricity sector.

DISTRIBUTED GENERATION, RENEWABLES, AND STORAGE

Historically, utilities have tried to take advantage of economies of scale by building large, central generating stations to supply power to customers. The power produced at these stations is sent across transmission lines at high voltage, then stepped down at substations and delivered to customers across the utility's distribution network. In the last two decades, however, utilities, independent power producers, and individual customers have developed small-scale generating units on the *distribution* network (i.e., closer to the point of consumption). For example, a homeowner who installs solar panels or wind turbines on his property would be considered a small-scale generator. When the homeowner generates more energy than his home consumes, this energy is sent to the grid. This redistributed energy is called "distributed generation" (DG) because it is generated on the distribution side—rather than the generation side—of the electrical grid. Distributed generation is usually fueled by renewable energy, such as wind or solar, but it can also take the form of combined heat and power (CHP) plants, which capture waste heat from electricity production or other industrial processes and use it to warm other buildings or facilities.

Distributed generation—and renewable resources in general—create several challenges for utilities. First, when a customer with a distributed generation resource produces more electricity than it can consume, some energy flows back on to the utility's distribution network. This reverse flow of energy can place great strain on distribution lines—some of which were not designed for dual-direction energy flow—negatively affecting system reliability (i.e., could lead to an outage). Second, renewable resources are inherently intermittent, producing electricity only when the wind blows or when the sun shines. These variances pose a challenge for utilities because they must constantly maintain supply to match demand at any given time. Greater levels of intermittent and variable resources challenge a utility's ability to maintain this constant balancing act.

Smart grid technologies can help address both these problems. A utility can install technologies that regulate the voltage of electricity on distribution lines surrounding distributed resources.[53] Some utilities are even looking into deploying technologies that would store excess power until it is needed. As far as intermittency is concerned, the smart grid's advanced communication and control technologies enable a utility to better manage the intermittency and unpredictability of renewable energy sources. Essentially, the smart grid will provide utilities with tools to plan for and accommodate the intermittent nature of renewable resources.

From an environmental standpoint, renewable and distributed generation is desirable because it can displace dirtier, fossil-fuel capacity. Distributed generation can also eliminate the need for new transmission and distribution facilities, as distributed resources are located (by definition) closer to the point of consumption. If renewables are to occupy a larger share of the energy portfolio at the distribution level, smart grid technologies will be critical to managing renewable intermittency.

DISTRIBUTION OPTIMIZATION AND CONSERVATION VOLTAGE REDUCTION

The lack of two-way communication technology in the electric distribution system forces utilities to operate with little on-the-ground intelligence on customer-level system voltage. To understand why this intelligence is important for utilities, it is necessary to first grasp a few fundamentals regarding the physical properties of electricity.

Utilities deliver electric power (measured in watts) to customers, and the amount of power delivered is a product of its current (measured in amperes) and voltage (measured in volts). To understand these terms, it is useful to compare the electric grid to a system of water pipes. Current is like the flow rate of water through the pipes, whereas voltage is the water pressure. And just as water pressure drops when water moves farther along a pipe, so too does electricity lose voltage as it moves from the distribution substation along the distribution network to homes and businesses. In fact, utilities will increase the voltage of electricity at the substation (up to around 126 volts), knowing that it will eventually drop to appropriate levels (between 114 and 120 volts) once it reaches the customer.[54]

But increasing voltage also increases the amount of electricity that consumers use. For this reason, many have argued that utilities should "conserve voltage" by reducing voltage levels at the substation, which would reduce overall energy consumption. The problem is that if the utility reduces voltage too much, customers could see a loss in power quality at their homes and businesses.[55] For example, when the efficiency of induction motors in various appliances goes down, these motors will compensate for the loss in voltage by drawing extra current from the grid, negating any potential energy savings.[56]

Smart grid technologies provide a remedy for this problem because advanced meters and sensors can provide detailed information about customer-end voltage levels. These technologies enable utilities to more precisely control voltage along the distribution network and thereby optimize energy savings. The use of smart grid technology to better manage voltage levels and save energy is known as "conservation voltage reduction." Utilities using advanced meters to measure voltage levels at the point of consumption can then use other technologies to automatically monitor and maintain voltage at a minimum level, which optimizes energy savings.[57] These technologies require little capital investment, and therefore represent a cost-effective means of improving utilities' operational efficiency. Indeed, PNNL estimates that conservation voltage reduction could reduce electricity consumption and energy-related CO_2 emissions by 2 percent in 2030.[58]

In subsequent chapters, we will explore in greater detail the smart grid's five pathways to environmental improvement. These chapters will use research from six case studies to describe how utilities are utilizing each pathway to reduce greenhouse gas emissions. The research for these case studies was compiled between 2009 and 2010. Our team of researchers interviewed representatives from six utilities across the country—three investor-owned utilities (IOUs), one municipal utility, one public power entity, and one demonstration project—to assess how they were deploying smart grid technologies relative to each pathway. These chapters also suggest policies and practices that governments and utilities should adopt to fully leverage the potential environmental benefits of each pathway. Such technology has the potential to not only upgrade the nation's aging electric infrastructure but also provide for greater carbon reduction in the electricity sector. For the health of our planet and our people, it is critical that utilities and policymakers act to realize this potential.

2

LEGAL AND REGULATORY ISSUES

Although this is a book about how a smarter electric grid will lead to a significantly greener electric grid, this policy debate would be incomplete without discussing other key legal, regulatory, and policy issues that have arisen during the transition from the traditional grid to the smart grid. The electricity industry is highly regulated, and for the country to achieve the full environmental promise of a smarter electric grid, it must successfully address these other significant policy issues. The other legal and regulatory issues that we have encountered in our case study analysis include

- regulatory cost recovery,
- customer data privacy,
- health concerns with wireless smart meters,
- low-income concerns, and
- technology policy.

We don't profess to fully address all of these policy issues here, nor do we claim that we have identified an exhaustive list, but we do find value in sharing our insight on how these legal and regulatory issues are critical to successfully implementing the smart grid.

COST RECOVERY POLICY

Modernizing the grid is a capital-intensive undertaking. The Electric Power Research Institute estimates that it will cost $338–$476 billion (or $17–$24 billion per year over the next twenty years) to fully deploy smart grid technologies across the country.[1] Each utility will try to recover these costs through the rates that it charges to customers, but before it can do so, the utility must receive approval from state regulators. This process is known as "cost recovery," and it is rooted in a theory of regulation—often referred to as the "cost of service" theory—that has predominated in the electric utility sector for more than a century. To understand how cost recovery works, it is useful to first understand a little bit about the nature and history of the electric power sector.

The electric power sector began developing in earnest around the turn of the nineteenth century, after Thomas Edison invented the first practicable incandescent light bulb. Initially, the industry operated much like any other industry of the day, with firms competing for customers and profits in an unregulated, "free-market" setting. As time passed, however, many within the industry and government realized that this was a highly inefficient market structure. The electricity sector, after all, is a capital-intensive industry; it requires utilities to build generation plants, substations, power lines, and other specialized equipment to deliver electricity to customers. So when multiple utilities compete for customers in the same locale, there are enormous redundancies in capital infrastructure: Each builds its own plant and power line to serve its own customers. Moreover, the utilities fight among themselves for both capital—which is expensive (i.e., interest rates are high) because of the industry's atmosphere of "severe competition"—and customers.[2] With only a fraction of a locality's total customers, each utility must spread the cost of its capital investments over a smaller and smaller customer base. Together, these factors drive up prices for everyone.

What industry players and policymakers began to realize was that a single firm could supply retail electricity services more efficiently than a multitude of competing firms. In economics-speak, they realized that the electricity sector is characterized by a "natural monopoly." A natural monopoly occurs when a product or service can be supplied at the least cost by a single firm, as opposed to two or more firms. In the electricity sector, where fixed capital costs are high, it makes sense for a single utility to control the local market because it can reduce costs through economies of scale. That is, with a monopoly, the utility can effectively spread out its capital costs over a larger customer base and reduce customers' average costs since a proportionate increase in inputs yields more than a proportionate increase in outputs.

As a result of this economic reality, utilities actually began to lobby state legislatures for heavier regulation. Except for a handful of states that have been partially deregulated, the regulatory system that developed at that time largely persists to this day. Under this system, the state grants the utility an exclusive franchise—a monopoly—over a given territory, and in return, the utility agrees to have its rates and activities regulated by the state. In these states, electric distribution utilities must receive state approval for virtually anything they do—constructing additional power plants, building additional lines, or investing in smart grid technology. Most important for our purposes, if the utility wants to recover the costs associated with these investments through its retail rates, the state must give its approval. Generally speaking, regulators will only allow the utility to recover the costs of a given investment if this investment was "prudent"—that is, if it created sufficient benefits for ratepayers. Utilities are allowed the opportunity to recover the costs of all prudent investments, plus a reasonable "rate of return" on net investments in capital assets.

Of course, discussion of electricity regulation would be incomplete without addressing the issue of deregulation. In about fifteen states, the traditional regulatory paradigm has given way to deregulation (or "restructuring"). The premise of deregulation is that allowing customers to choose where they get their power from (often referred to as "retail choice") will lower prices for all ratepayers. To achieve this goal, most state legislatures passed laws requiring incumbent utilities to divest themselves of their generation assets, either by transferring those assets to non-utility affiliates or by selling them outright to new firms. The idea was to give independent generators access to the retail market. Accordingly, in deregulated states, the utility no longer receives a return on investment on generation assets. Rather, its primary function is to operate, maintain, and deliver power through the local distribution network to retail customers. The transmission and distribution systems remain subject to rate of return regulation.

This regulatory paradigm is critical when addressing cost recovery for smart grid investments. In order for utilities to recover the costs of smart grid investments they will have to present a positive business case for those investments. In theory, this should not be a very difficult task. EPRI estimates that the benefits of smart grid investments could be anywhere from 2.8 to 6.0 times greater than the costs of those investments. Although this book focuses on the environmental benefits, smart grid technologies will also improve the reliability of the grid, as well as the efficiency of electric utility operations. In particular, utilities can use AMI to both remotely read customer meters and to initiate and disconnect service, eliminating the need to send personnel and their vehicles to each customer address. Smart grid technologies, through improved outage management systems, can also vastly improve the reliability of the grid by reducing the number and duration of outages. The annual cost of power disturbances to the American economy ranges from $119 to $188 billion per year.[3] Utilities can install various sensors, intelligent electronic devices, and other information technology infrastructure on transmission lines and substations; on the distribution side, utilities can deploy similar technologies to reduce line losses and to instantaneously communicate information regarding the location of an outage as well as the customers affected.[4] Collectively, these technologies improve reliability and system performance by monitoring grid conditions in real time and relaying data to grid operators, who can correct problems before they fully materialize.[5] Thus, in addition to the environmental benefits, utilities can make a strong business case for smart grid technologies based on the increased operational efficiencies.

HOW COST RECOVERY WORKS IN PRACTICE

When utilities get cost recovery approval associated with smart grid deployment is almost as critical an issue as *whether* they can recover those investments. Most utilities would prefer to receive advanced approval for smart grid investments, as this increases their financial security. Regulatory commissions, however, generally do not approve investments in utility plants and equipment until such time as the investments are "used and useful"—that is, fully implemented and operating. Accordingly, all investments made by a utility present some level of cost recovery risk until the investments are complete and the costs have been approved for rate recovery. Some states, through legislation or regulation, implement advance policy guidance in order to facilitate investment consistent with state policy goals. For example, in California the state legislature passed a bill directing the utility commission to set guidelines for the California investor-owned electric corporations to move forward with smart grid deployment plans.[6] While legislative and regulatory smart grid policy paves the way for utility cost recovery, financial risk remains until the specific costs are approved for rate recovery.

Once investments in smart grid technology are completed and are eligible to be deemed "used and useful," utilities will need to seek recovery of the costs, either through new rate proceedings or through some formula rate mechanism. In states such as California and Vermont, where there are clear state policies, this cost recovery process has been largely noncontroversial and implementation has remained on schedule. In Vermont, the Public Service Board agreed in advance that AMI investments made as part of an approved implementation plan would be treated as if they are economically used and useful.[7] Accordingly, utilities in Vermont do not appear to face significant regulatory barriers to cost recovery. The Public Service Board has balanced flexibility for investments in fast-developing technology with measures to ensure that decisions about major investments are prudent.[8]

Other states do not have clear direction—such as implementation plan requirements—for their smart grid policies. In these jurisdictions, utility regulators likely will evaluate whether an investment was prudent, including an evaluation of the business case for the technology, during the rate recovery process. For example, a utility commission could refuse to allow a utility to recover some portion of the cost of an AMI system if it was found to not be cost effective. A lack of clarity on cost recovery procedure for AMI investments could delay rollout of the technology. Utilities will be reluctant to make an investment if they believe that state regulators will not allow full recovery of those investments. Smart grid investments present an unusually risky situation for utilities, given that the digital technology central to AMI could be expected to have a shorter life than current electro-mechanical meter equipment. Both the rapid change in digital technology, creating technological obsolescence, and a perceived shorter operational life of this equipment suggests that smart grid investments may face an increased cost recovery risk compared to the current equipment.

POLICY HOPSCOTCH: THE COMMONWEALTH EDISON EXPERIENCE

In contrast to the experience in California and Vermont, the experience of Commonwealth Edison (ComEd) in Illinois could easily be deemed one of the most dysfunctional cost recovery odysseys in recent memory, and thus it is worth a closer examination. Cost recovery policy in Illinois has traversed chasms between the utility, the state regulator (the Illinois Commerce Commission [ICC]), the courts, the legislature, and the governor's office and back again in a seemingly endless loop of policy hopscotch. Although there is a long history of effective cost recovery policy in Illinois, ComEd has faced greater regulatory and political hurdles when attempting to recover costs ever since the state began experimenting with deregulation.

In the late 1990s, Illinois initiated the transition to a deregulated electricity generation market, which was designed to encourage competition, expand customer choice, and reduce energy costs. The Illinois General Assembly passed the Electric Service Customer Choice and Rate Relief Law of 1997, ordering most Illinois utilities (including ComEd) to divest their generation assets and give their customers the option of purchasing generation from other suppliers. ComEd would still be responsible for delivering this electricity to its customers over its distribution network, but the customer would be purchasing that electricity from third-party suppliers that were independent of the utility itself. The idea was that allowing consumers to choose where their electricity comes from would both offer increased customer choice and the opportunity for lower costs. The law also reduced residential electricity prices by 20 percent by the year 2001 and froze that rate until 2007 while the state's utilities developed a competitive market for obtaining their electricity.

Unfortunately, deregulation did not proceed as regulators had anticipated. As the end of the rate freeze approached in 2006, a fully competitive electricity market threatened residential customers with rate increases of nearly 33 percent, sparking a public outcry against deregulation and a spirited debate among state legislators about whether to extend the rate freeze for several more years while they decided whether to suspend the deregulation experiment altogether. ComEd responded that such an extension likely would bankrupt the company.[9] In 2007, as part of a compromise, ComEd devised a new rate plan that allowed customers to defer payment of any increases in the delivery portion of their electricity bills, subject to about 3 percent interest on any unpaid portion. The experience, however, left many Illinois ratepayers wary of price hikes.[10]

In the midst of all this controversy surrounding the deregulation of electricity markets in Illinois, ComEd was beginning to roll out AMI and other smart grid technology. Accordingly, in June 2009, ComEd filed a petition with the ICC to raise its rates so it could recover the costs of its AMI pilot program from ratepayers.[11] Later that year, the ICC issued an order approving ComEd's AMI pilot program, including a special rate rider that would allow ComEd to recover most of the program's costs.[12] The special rider was meant to act as a mechanism for recovering the costs of system modernization projects likely to occur between its general rate cases and allowed ComEd to recover those costs without having to go through a full-blown rate case. ComEd and others believed that the rider method of cost recovery was essential to accelerate deployment of smart grid technologies and leverage federal funding of smart grid demonstration projects.[13] Other stakeholders, however, worried that nontraditional cost recovery methods would shift the risk of smart grid investments from utilities to ratepayers and lead to substantially higher monthly energy bills.[14]

As a result of these concerns, several stakeholders, including the Illinois attorney general and the Citizens Utility Board (a consumer advocate), appealed the ICC's approval of the special rider mechanism to the Illinois Appellate Court. On September 30, 2010, a unanimous three-judge panel of the Second District rejected the ICC's approval of the AMI rider on the grounds that it violated the state's prohibition on single-issue rate making.[15] The court held that the ICC had discretion to approve a rider mechanism to recover costs if (1) they were imposed on the utility by external circumstances over which the utility had no control and (2) the cost does not affect the utility's rate of return. The court found that the AMI rider did not meet these criteria since the expenses related to AMI and the adoption of smart grid technologies generally were not unexpected and ComEd was pursuing the program precisely because the increased costs would be more than offset by corresponding savings. Since ComEd historically recouped the costs of distribution improvement through traditional rate making, the court found no reason that ComEd's smart grid expenses should be treated differently.[16]

Of course, this order did not mean that ComEd could not recover the costs associated with its AMI pilot program. Rather, the company would now have to initiate a formal rate case—an expensive and time-consuming endeavor—to recover these costs. And in May 2011, after a traditional rate case was concluded, the ICC ultimately allowed ComEd to recover many of the AMI pilot costs.[17] This experience, however, motivated the utility to lobby hard in favor of House Bill 14/Senate Bill 1652, bills in the state legislature that would change the nature of smart grid cost recovery in Illinois. The legislation would lay the groundwork for rolling out smart grid in Illinois, while capping customer rate increases at 2.5 percent per year. Under the proposal, ComEd's profit margin is limited to 10.25 percent, and the current ICC review process of eleven and a half months would be replaced with a quicker rate review process defined in the legislation.[18] Although the bill passed both houses of the Illinois legislature, Governor Quinn vetoed the legislation. Intense lobbying on behalf of affected utilities, however, convinced the legislature to overturn the veto, and the Energy Infrastructure Modernization Act (EIMA) became law in October 2011.[19]

The saga does not end there. The EIMA established policies and goals for rollout of smart grid technology, called for utilities to make the investments necessary to achieve them, defined investment timetables and performance metrics to measure that achievement, and provided the means to fund those investments.[20] On April 23, 2012, ComEd requested that the ICC approve its Smart Grid Advanced Metering Infrastructure Deployment Plan (AMI Plan), as required by the EIMA. ComEd's AMI Plan provided that, over a ten-year period, ComEd would invest in AMI sufficient to cover its entire service territory. According to ComEd's updated business case, the present value of the total benefits of the AMI Plan exceeded the present value of the total costs of the plan and would therefore be cost beneficial. ComEd anticipated that, as filed, the plan would allow it to recover the reasonable costs it incurred in implementing the AMI Plan, including the costs of retired meters.

In the following months, the ICC issued two orders that had important implications for ComEd's AMI Plan. In May, the ICC issued an order on

ComEd's formula rate tariff, which determines the specific level of cost recovery for smart grid infrastructure investments, among other things. In this formula rate order, the ICC cut customer rates by approximately $179 million. This was over four times what ComEd had proposed for a rate decrease. The ICC's changes to the formula rate plan addressed issues such as the recovery of pension assets and did not directly involve the recovery of costs from the AMI Plan.

Nonetheless, ComEd requested a rehearing of the formula rate order so that the ICC could reconsider its decision. Then, in June, the ICC approved (with minor modifications) ComEd's AMI Plan. The ICC found that the ComEd AMI Plan met the conditions of the EIMA and was cost beneficial. The ICC's modifications to the plan included adopting additional tracking measures and a requirement that ComEd work with the Smart Grid Advisory Council and other stakeholders to explore how to maximize adoption of dynamic pricing rates, including a time-of-use rate. Although ComEd was undoubtedly glad to have its AMI Plan approved, the rate formula order significantly lowered the utility's rates, which significantly lowered revenues, jeopardizing the extent to which ComEd would be able to fund that plan.

Accordingly, in July ComEd filed a petition for the ICC to rehear the AMI order. ComEd sought a rehearing on three aspects of the order. First and foremost, it essentially argued that, in light of the fact that the ICC cut its rates by $179 million, it could no longer afford to make the investments called for in its AMI Plan.[21] Second, ComEd noted that it had been "forced to delay the AMI deployment originally scheduled for 2012" and would have to reconsider participating in the structure created by EIMA.[22] Finally, ComEd argued that, even if the ICC revised its formula rate order and agreed to less of a cut in customer rates, ComEd would still need to revise its AMI deployment schedule "to account for the delays that have occurred as a result of the uncertainty."[23] If the formula rate order is not revised, according to ComEd, the schedule will require "more sweeping changes" including the possibility of "withdrawing from EIMA altogether."

In October, the ICC granted ComEd some measure of relief from this predicament when it issued its order on rehearing in ComEd's formula rate tariff. The order set rates through the end of 2012 and represented a $133 million reduction in revenue, but this still provided ComEd with approximately $35 million in additional revenue compared to the ICC's previous order.[24] Following the ICC order, ComEd announced in a news release that "because the ICC is not fully funding the grid deployment program, ComEd is forced to make modifications to its program to align the deployment of key infrastructure with the ICC decision. ComEd must delay installation of additional smart meters until 2015."[25] In its news release, ComEd stated that the ICC's decision will result in the under-recovery of revenues by nearly $100 million per year starting in 2014. The loss of these revenues will cause the delay of more than $2.3 billion in customer savings and the creation of two thousand jobs. ComEd also appealed the rate order in court on a variety of technical rate issues.

Interestingly, the dispute between the ICC and ComEd is not di-rectly about the merits of the costs of the smart grid infrastructure build-out (which were determined by the EIMA and approved by the ICC order on ComEd's implementation plan), but mostly about how ComEd is allowed to calculate its return on the investments in the for-mula rate. Specifically, the ICC and ComEd dispute how infrastructure investment balances are calculated, to which a rate of return is applied, and, additionally, the interest rate applied to annual adjustments to those investment balances. As acknowledged by the ICC, another part of the controversy is that

> the rate setting process put in place by the [EIMA] . . . is quite different from the traditional rate setting process known by the Commission. Although some aspects of traditional ratemak-ing . . . are still applicable, the input data, the formula rate itself, and the reconciliation practice specified in the Act do not fit neatly into the traditional ratemaking paradigm. Each of the parties argues that the new provisions support their position. . . . While some claim to know what was intended when [the EIMA was] . . . enacted, the Commission is not bound by the views of a few as to what the statute requires. The record in this case warrants the finding that the lan-guage used in the statute leaves room for interpretation by the Commission.[26]

Essentially, in the EIMA, the Illinois legislature laid out in significant detail how the ICC is to treat these smart grid infrastructure costs, and it did so in a manner that was not consistent with previous ICC policy. As a result, the commission and various parties believe that the legislature left some discretion with the ICC. The fact that there is significant tension on intended cost recovery of smart grid investments is highlighted in the comments of Jonathan Feipel, the ICC's executive director. According to the *Chicago Tribune*, Feipel stated that the legislature's "resolution was hyper-specific" and amounted to the legislature taking over the ICC's role as regulator.[27] These are unusually critical words by a regulator toward a legislature, since that legislative body determines the ICC's statutory authority.

While the public may have been tiring of the political back and forth, ComEd was still at least a hop, skip, and a jump from policy resolution. In March 2013, the legislature passed Senate Bill 9, which resolved a subset of ComEd's rate issues and would open the door for smart meter installation resuming in late 2013, but instead Governor Quinn in May, again, decided to veto the ComEd supported legislation. Similar to the previous time around, Quinn's veto was again overturned by the legislature later that month. On June 6, 2013, a ComEd press release signaled the end of this phase of the cost recovery odyssey by noting in now conciliatory terms that the ICC had issued an order that would finally allow ComEd to begin expedited smart meter deployment, although installations will continue through 2021. Governor Quinn was less positive, calling the legislature's action a "very disturbing process" through which a utility sought relief in the legislature over a dispute with its regulator.[28] ComEd continues to pursue the unresolved rate issues in the court while it simultaneously moves forward with smart meter implementation.

THE POLICY EXPRESS: CALIFORNIA AND SAN DIEGO GAS & ELECTRIC

If Illinois serves as an example of how *not* to roll out smart grid technology, California serves as a model for policy leadership in smart grid deployment. In 2008, the California state legislature took an important step forward and passed Senate Bill 17, which required its investor-owned electric corporations, including its large investor-owned utilities—including Pacific Gas and Electric (PG&E), San Diego Gas & Electric (SDG&E), and Southern California Edison (SCE)—to submit plans to the California Public Utilities Commission (CPUC) to implement smart grid technologies into their service territories.[29] The goal of this legislation was "to modernize the state's electrical transmission and distribution system to maintain safe, reliable, efficient, and secure electrical service."[30] The CPUC would then "determine the requirements for a Smart Grid Deployment Plan consistent with the policies set forth in [Senate Bill 17] and federal law."[31] The CPUC required California IOUs to file smart grid deployment plans by July 1, 2011, and outlined the content required in those plans.

Specifically, the CPUC decision clarified areas of focus for the major utilities in California:[32]

a. Create a self-healing and resilient grid.
b. Empower consumers to actively participate in operations of the grid.
c. Resist attack.

d. Provide a higher quality of power and avoid outages, saving money.

e. Accommodate all generation and storage options.

f. Enable electricity markets to flourish.

g. Run the grid more efficiently.

h. Enable penetration of intermittent power generation sources.

i. Create a platform for deployment of a wide range of energy technologies and management services.

j. Enable and support the sale of demand response, energy efficiency, distributed generation, and storage into wholesale energy markets as a resource, on equal footing with traditional generation resources.

k. Significantly reduce the total environmental footprint of the current electric generation and delivery system in California.[33]

A leading reason why SDG&E and the other IOUs have been able to organize such comprehensive smart grid plans is because the state of California gave such clear guidance for the CPUC to follow. California's legislation allowed the commission to create an environment in which utilities can be relatively sure they will recover the costs of their smart grid investments. Senate Bill 17 is a comprehensive law that set clear expectations and smart grid goals.[34] Then the CPUC gave clear guidelines for what was expected from the IOUs in their smart grid deployment plans.[35] SDG&E established goals for 2015 and 2020 completion in its smart grid deployment plan filing with the CPUC.[36]

PUBLIC POWER AND SMART GRID INVESTMENT

Two of our other case studies, the Salt River Project (SRP) in Arizona and the Sacramento Municipal Utility District (SMUD) in California, demonstrate that public power utilities have a very positive experience with cost recovery of smart grid investments. The public power organizations in these states are not subject to rate review by state utility commissions due to their ownership arrangement, management structure, and nuances of state law. The fact that public power utilities are not-for-profit companies owned and controlled for the benefit of their customers removes some of the public mistrust that was clearly prevalent in the ComEd case.[37] Although state utility commissions do not regulate either utility, they are still subject to market forces and other legislative restrictions and requirements created by state legislature. Public power utilities may have a different process for recovering the costs of investments in the smart grid than most for-profit utilities, but they still benefit from clear state and federal policy leadership. This is especially true when it comes to funding. The federal American Recovery and Reinvestment Act (ARRA) allocated

$4.5 billion to fund federal smart grid programs.[38] The SRP received $56.9 million in ARRA for smart meter infrastructure.[39] SMUD received $19.2 million in ARRA and California Energy Commission grants, which partially funded smart grid-related research and demonstration projects.[40] The SRP and SMUD cases demonstrate that public power utilities, which have differing regulatory incentives from investor-owned utilities, have had strong success in gaining approval for smart grid investments from their customer-focused boards.

Ensuring that rates are both just and reasonable suggests that utilities implementing new technologies, such as smart grid investments, should bear some performance risk in order to ensure that they have sufficient incentive to exceed poor or mediocre performance. On the other hand, regulatory risk should not be seen as a disincentive to invest in cost-effective technologies. No matter how positive the business case, utilities will not have the incentive to invest in capital intensive technologies if they don't believe they are likely to earn a competitive rate of return on their invested capital. While there has been significant progress in installing AMI and other smart grid technologies, in many jurisdictions across the country, either the business case has not yet been made or there is insufficient regulatory policy certainty. Electric customers and the environment will not receive the full benefits from a smart electric grid without clear and functioning regulatory cost recovery policies.

CUSTOMER DATA PRIVACY

The average smart meter–connected home generates from 750 to 3,000 points of data a month.[41] Some of these data points include information about consumer habits, electricity use, or other personally identifiable information.[42] Not surprisingly, privacy concerns have attracted the attention of consumers and regulators alike. According to Martin Pollock of Siemens Energy, an arm of the German engineering giant, "We, Siemens, have the technology to record it (energy consumption) every minute, second, microsecond, more or less live. . . . From that we can infer how many people are in the house, what they do, whether they're upstairs, downstairs, do you have a dog, when do you habitually get up, when did you get up this morning, when do you have a shower: masses of private data."[43] Utilities, which need access to this information to maximize the smart grid's potential for delivering energy savings and improving grid reliability, and the smart grid technology industry, which stands to profit on the sale of its technology and associated services, have long recognized the challenge that customer privacy concerns present to their business model. Indeed, many of those familiar with these industries recognize that to ensure customer privacy, collection of energy use data will require government oversight.[44]

Smart grid customer data privacy concerns are not new to the federal government. The U.S. Environmental Protection Agency (EPA) has previously noted that there are significant privacy risks associated with collecting large amounts of energy use data.[45] The Department of Energy has sought public comments on several questions regarding utility and third-party access to smart grid data, as well as relevant privacy policies.[46] Most recently, in 2012, the Obama administration released a report titled "A Framework for Protecting Privacy and Promoting Innovation in the Global Digital Economy," which specifically finds that privacy principles are important to smart grid development.[47]

Although smart grid technologies pose their own legitimate privacy concerns, privacy problems in other industries are perhaps unfairly being attributed to utilities in the electricity sector. Certainly, these problems can provide important lessons for utilities as they implement smart grid technology. But customer opinions on privacy issues related to smart grid technology have largely been informed by their experience in other sectors (social networking, e-mail, etc.). One rarely opens a newspaper without hearing about privacy concerns levied at Google, Facebook, or other companies that keep our private information on file.[48] In particular, several high-profile breaches of data security have brought attention to privacy in the Internet and financial services industries.[49] Breaches in these industries demonstrate the importance of privacy to customers and the challenges of protecting privacy. Historically, utilities generally have been good stewards of the data they collect. Many utilities, however, recognize that the additional data required by advanced metering technology poses new challenges. Addressing these challenges up front can help avoid delays and reduce customer opposition and, potentially, regulatory disapproval.

OVERVIEW OF PRIVACY PRINCIPLES

There are numerous privacy principles that can help protect smart grid data. Privacy principles from other industries that handle and store sensitive information have also provided insight into how utilities can best protect consumer electricity data. Drawing in part on lessons from other industries, regulators and other interested parties have developed privacy principles tailored to the needs and particularities of the electric utility industry.

The Federal Trade Commission (FTC) has developed the Fair Information Practice Principles,[50] which are based on a synthesis of studies about how businesses collect and use personal information. Several utilities, smart grid hardware manufacturers, and service providers have indicated support for applying these principles in the smart grid context.[51] Key principles include notice and awareness, choice and consent, access and participation, integrity and security, and enforcement and redress.[52]

Notice to customers is the most fundamental privacy principle.[53] Utilities must inform customers what type of information is collected, how it is likely to be used, and with whom it will be shared. Utilities should also inform customers how they intend to maintain the confidentiality of this information. In some cases, customers may want to share information with third parties who provide non-utility energy services. The utility should provide adequate notice to customers to inform them of the consequences of sharing their smart data with third parties. Notifying customers of these practices helps them make informed decisions about what information to disclose. Indeed, given predictions about how smart grid technology could expose individuals' daily activities, transparent notice could help minimize any skepticism and allay customers' fears.

Choice and consent are also "widely-accepted core principle[s]" of data collection and use.[54] Utilities should empower consumers with the ability to choose how their information will be used and stored to control the risk that this data will be misused. Utilities need to use the data they collect to provide electric service to their customers and to ensure that such service is reliable and cost effective. Aside from any valid business uses necessary to provide reliable and cost-effective electric service, utilities should give customers the option to share or withhold third-party access to their data. In upholding this principle, the California legislature specifically empowered electric customers to choose to disclose their data to certain third parties and to prohibit utilities from encouraging their customers to disclose data without their consent.[55]

"Access" is a related principle. Customers should have the choice to access their own electric-use data to take advantage of the insights it can provide on energy-saving opportunities. Generally, the term "access" refers to a customer's opportunity to view data about herself for purposes of contesting a bill or obtaining other necessary information. In the smart grid context, customers may need to access their own data or authorize a third party to access that data so it can be presented on in-home displays, smart appliances, and other smart grid-enabled devices. After a customer gives consent to share the data with a particular third party, utilities should be released from liability for disclosure or misuse of data. At that point, liability for data misuse shifts to the third party with whom the customer is sharing data.

The last two principles address data security and redress. To be useful to the customer, data must be accurate and safe. Methods of keeping data secure include adopting appropriate cyber-security protocols and taking reasonable steps to use information safely. All utilities should have a plan for redressing customer concerns and a contingency plan for how to fix problems and data breaches, should they occur.

Various proposals have emerged to address data access and security with regard to electricity-use data and other utility-held personal information. Perhaps most notably, Ann Cavoukian[56] has developed Privacy by Design, a set of principles designed to embed privacy protections into smart grid programs.[57] More recently, Vermont Law School's Institute for Energy and the Environment (IEE) developed a set of principles for customer data privacy and then used these principles to develop a model data privacy policy for utility smart grid customers.[58] Privacy principles advocated by the IEE include the following:

1. Make privacy the default setting.
2. Provide complete privacy protection.
3. Know the law regarding public disclosure in your state.
4. Only store and provide access to necessary information.
5. Obtain written consent before disclosing to most third parties.
6. Educate customers about the implications of sharing data with third parties.
7. Notify customers when data is disclosed.
8. Develop a plan for contingencies.
9. Make the privacy policy accessible to customers.

Release of data to third parties is an area of particular concern. Privacy regulations often address a utility's disclosure of data to contractors. Utilities are typically permitted to disclose customer energy-use data to contractors that assist in providing electricity services to customers, but such disclosures are often subject to contractual privacy protections in the agreement between the utility and the contractor. Some states require utilities to include in these contracts clauses that protect the privacy of customer data. These regulations often forbid contractors from storing more data than is necessary for business purposes or limit who within the contractors' organization can access data. Disclosure of electricity-use data to third parties not under contract with the utility can present more complicated concerns. Regulations often exempt utilities from liability related to a third party's misuse of electricity data that has been released based on a customer's consent.

One of the most important privacy-related duties for utilities is educating the customer about the risks and dangers associated with sharing their electric use data with third parties. The utility will strive to protect its customers' data, but the vendors may not have the same goals and standards for data privacy. The worst thing that could happen is for a customer to think that the utility is implying that a third party—which is typically not subject to the same level of public oversight as the utility—will have the same security protections the utility does. In the best-case scenario, the utility will only share data at the customer's request. In this case, the customer should be made aware that the third-party vendor is not part of the utility and thus is not subject to all the same privacy requirements as the utility. In particular, the customer should be notified that this third party might release the customer data to other parties or fail to adequately protect it from theft.

The Green Button Initiative, a White House-inspired but industry-led initiative to give customers access to their own data, while important in creating access for third parties and promoting innovation in services, also presents some challenges for protecting customer data. The Green Button's ease of use could create opportunities for customers to unwittingly provide access to their data to parties that have less than honorable intentions. This is where the importance of customer education about third-party release comes in. While educating customers about the risks from release of data to third parties is important, it is more difficult to advise customers on how they should know if they can trust a third party. Promising initiatives that can help in this area are privacy seal programs such as TRUSTe, which can be found on websites that have agreed to adhere to various privacy policies. Certifying that a customer can trust a particular third party because it has agreed to follow well-defined policies is a big step in the right direction in protecting customer data that is shared with third parties.

STATE LEADERSHIP ON DATA PRIVACY

Numerous states have statutes or regulations that specifically address customer data privacy. In particular, California and Colorado have led the way in addressing the privacy issue. In Colorado, the Public Utilities Commission has adopted rules prohibiting utilities from disclosing data regarding electricity use and personally identifiable data to third parties without the customer's consent.[59] Colorado also requires utilities to notify customers of the type of information that is available for disclosure to the customer or third parties.[60] In addition, it requires annual notice of the utility's privacy policy and information about how electricity-use data can reveal customer habits.[61] Recognizing the utility's need for this data, Colorado's rules authorize a utility to disclose certain data without notifying the customer if the data is used by a third party for a contracted service and the third party maintains data security procedures at least as protective as the utility's.[62] Finally, Colorado exempts utilities from liability for the use of electricity data shared with a third party with a customer's consent.[63]

In California, both the legislature and the CPUC have implemented comprehensive policies governing access to personally identifiable information and smart grid data. In February 2010, the CPUC requested comments on the privacy implications of smart grid technology. Several consumer advocates and technology companies responded. A few months later, the legislature passed a bill expanding privacy protections to electricity-use data in anticipation of smart grid rollouts across California.[64] Meanwhile, the CPUC ordered utilities implementing smart grid programs to file deployment plans.[65] The deployment plans were required to include a vision statement "that addresses how the plan will enable consumers to capture the benefits of a wide range of energy technologies and energy management products and services, while protecting the privacy of consumers."[66] The CPUC wanted utilities to address privacy concerns "explicitly at the planning stage" of the project.[67] Indeed, the CPUC made clear that it would not order utilities to provide access to authorized third parties before rules were in place that were "consistent with . . . the general public interest, and state privacy rules."[68]

California's smart grid privacy statute attempts to balance the utility's legitimate need for access to the data with the consumers' interest in personal privacy. The statute applies to electricity-use data, including personally identifiable data such as the customer's name, account number, or address.[69] It prohibits utilities from sharing data with any third party unless the customer has consented or the disclosure is required or specifically authorized by law.[70] In addition, the law prohibits utilities from selling electricity-use data or using incentives to encourage customers to share their electricity-use data.[71] On the other hand, the law allows utilities to share electricity-use data with third parties for operational needs, demand response, or other business needs.[72] Utilities also may aggregate anonymous electricity-use data "for analysis, reporting, or program management," as long as all identifiable information has been removed.[73] Finally, the law releases utilities from responsibility for electricity-use data that customers have authorized to be shared with third parties that are not contractors of the utility,[74] but utilities must maintain "reasonable security procedures and practices" to protect consumers' data from unauthorized use.[75]

In 2011, the CPUC adopted rules to implement the requirements of the privacy statute.[76] The detailed rules require utilities to publish a privacy policy and comprehensive notice regarding access, collection, storage, use, and disclosure of meter data and identifiable information, unless that information is used for the "primary purposes" of billing, operational needs, demand response or efficiency, or complying with state or federal law.[77] This notice must be concise and easy to understand.[78] In general, the rules guarantee customers access to information regarding how the utility collects, stores, and discloses data, unless that data is used for primary purposes. They require utilities to give customers information about how to dispute any data or limit or revoke authorization to share data not used for a primary business purpose. Further, the rules require that utilities contractually bind third-party contractors to equally protective privacy policies and practices, provide notice of breach of data security, create a process for addressing complaints, and conduct periodic audits.

California's consent and notice requirements do not apply to data collection and disclosure for billing, operational requirements, legally required disclosures, or demand response planning. Further, the rules provide an exception for disclosures to emergency responders when an imminent risk to human health is present. Finally, the rules limit utilities' liability for disclosures that are made to third parties who are not contractors and to whom the customer has authorized disclosure. These provisions help balance requirements for utilities with protection and flexibility for the utilities. In addition, the utilities' access to information is balanced with customers' privacy interests.

Since the legislation's enactment and the CPUC's order, San Diego Gas & Electric has partnered with Privacy by Design to ensure that its Dynamic Pricing Project adequately protects customer data.[79] As part of SDG&E's dynamic pricing option, it adopted an approach that it hopes will embed privacy and security "at the earliest stages of system decision-making and will thus become incorporated into all aspects of design."[80] This approach applies the FTC's Fair Information Practice Principles and the seven principles of Privacy by Design.[81] The efforts SDG&E has undertaken include appointing a chief customer privacy officer to oversee an interdepartmental privacy team,[82] using technological applications to limit employees' access to customer data to "a strict need-to-know basis,"[83] and contractually obligating vendors and service providers to observe numerous privacy policies and security protocols.[84]

Various means have been proposed for protecting individual data in ways other than prohibiting its release to third parties. It has been argued that removing personally identifiable data (for example, name, account number, or social security number) from the customer data would appropriately mask the confidentiality of the end user, although there is evidence from other industries that even masked individual data can be combined with other sources of data to effectively reveal the identity of the end user. Others have proposed data aggregation as a means to mask the individual data. Various rules of thumb have evolved in terms of what is acceptable, such as a sufficient number of similarly situated customers or perhaps aggregating the data at no less than the town or city level. Unfortunately, data aggregation can defeat the purpose of releasing individual customer information in the first place, which is to learn about individual customer habits and how you might influence them to save energy. In some jurisdictions the competing public goals of governmental transparency and individual privacy come in conflict. In other regions, public records laws require some governmental agencies, such as municipal and state power authorities, to publicly disclose customer information. These situations require a careful balancing of public interest in disclosure versus individual customer data privacy.

Utilities have experience managing and protecting customer data, so resolving customer data privacy concerns should be a policy hurdle they are prepared to overcome. Smart meters and the associated infrastructure allow utilities to collect a greater volume of more granular data, but the policy issues have not dramatically changed. Third parties will become increasingly interested in smart meter data, and utilities must be prepared to protect customer privacy. Clear legislative and state regulatory policy promoting customer privacy is the necessary starting point. Within this framework, utilities that provide clear and transparent privacy policies, and directly engage their customers on these policies prior to implementing a smart meter rollout, will experience broader customer acceptance and smoother success in smart grid implementation.

HEALTH CONCERNS FROM SMART METER RADIO FREQUENCY RADIATION

Another significant public challenge to smart grid technology deployment is the concern that radio frequency radiation (RFR) emitted by wireless smart meters results in negative health effects. As we discuss in chapter 3, smart meters must share data with a broader utility network predominantly through power-line carrier technology (wired meters) or through radio frequency (RF) via a mesh network (wireless meters). Wireless meters are the predominant form of meter being deployed across the United States. Thus the public concern with RFR has largely arisen with the wireless smart meters and the RFR that they emit.

RFR is a form of electromagnetic radiation. There are two types of electromagnetic radiation: ionizing (e.g., x-rays, radon, and cosmic rays) and non-ionizing (e.g., RFR and extremely low frequency or power frequency).[85] The FCC limits the amount of RFR that can be emitted from any device, establishing maximum exposure limits to prevent thermal effects of RFR based on the number of microwatts per square centimeter (μW/cm^2). In particular, FCC standards provide that a member of the public cannot be exposed to more than 610 μW/cm^2.[86] The Vermont Department of Health found that RFR levels from a smart meter on the exterior wall of a residence ranged from 50 to 140 μW/cm^2.[87] Since meters are usually placed on the outside of a residence, the study noted that "measurements at distances of three feet or more away from the smart meter were at or near background [levels]."[88] At the same time, the Vermont study found that RFR emissions from a mobile phone are about 490 μW/cm^2. Similarly, a study by the state of California reported the following key findings:

1. Wireless smart meters, when installed and properly maintained, result in much smaller levels of radio frequency exposure than many existing common household electronic devices, particularly cell phones and microwave ovens.
2. The current FCC standard provides adequate factor of safety against known thermally induced health effects of existing common household electronic devices and smart meters.
3. To date, scientific studies have not identified or confirmed negative health effects from potential nonthermal impacts of RF emissions such as those produce by existing common household electronic devices and smart meters.
4. Not enough is currently known about potential nonthermal effects of radio frequency emission to identify or recommend additional standard for such effects.[89]

In addition to these findings, it's important to note that smart meters only emit RFR intermittently for the few seconds it takes to relay data to the utility. And although smart meters have the capability to record and store customer usage data every five to fifteen minutes, it is likely that the meter will transmit this data on a less frequent basis—perhaps every few hours or only a few times a day. Thus smart meters will not be constantly emitting RFR. Government health and science organizations in Vermont and California have both found that the FCC limits on RFR are more than sufficient to regulate smart meters.[90]

POLICY RESPONSE: CUSTOMER OPT-OUT

Although state regulators generally have not concluded that RFR from wireless smart meters poses any public health threat, a number of states have begun to adopt policies that allow customers opposed to wireless smart meters to opt-out of their installation. Generally, opt-out policies allow a customer to refuse installation of the wireless smart meter by simply notifying the utility of their decision. Depending on the state policy, opting out could mean either that the customer keeps her existing analog meter or that she receives a smart meter that has its RF signal turned off. A smart meter with the RF signal turned off could still allow a customer to take part in dynamic pricing programs, but the data would need to be downloaded by a meter technician on site. Given that refusing a wireless smart meter results in ongoing utility costs for meter reading, many utilities have been allowed to charge a customer more for the privilege of opting out. For example, in California, PG&E has been allowed to charge seventy-five dollars per request plus an ongoing fee of ten dollars per month, and customers only have the option of either accepting a wireless smart meter or keeping an analog meter.[91] Customers enrolled in the CPUC's low-income program (California Alternate Rates for Energy) electing to opt-out will be assessed an initial fee of ten dollars and a monthly charge of five dollars.[92] By contrast, in the late hours of the legislative session in 2012, the Vermont legislature tacked on a provision to an energy bill prohibiting utilities from charging an opt-out fee and requiring them to remove smart meters without a charge. At this time, Vermont is the only state that has mandated no opt-out fee. To date, feedback from across the country suggests that the voluntary opt-out rate has generally been very low at well less than 1 percent of customers.

Utilities have demonstrated that smart meter deployment can result in both improvements in customer reliability and long-term cost savings, so allowing a customer to refuse the installation of a smart meter sets a unique precedent in electric utility policy. Given the strong opposition from a passionate group of customers, both legislatures and state commissions have been willing to support this policy to reduce the public policy tension arising from concern with this technology. Requiring customers to pay cost-based fees for opting out provides a reasonable balance for allowing a customer to refuse this technology. Allowing a customer to choose the option to keep an analog, rather than a digital meter (with the RF signal disabled), prevents a small group of customers from benefiting from dynamic pricing and other services.

LOW-INCOME ISSUES

Nationally, consumer advocates are keeping an eye on smart grid investments. This is because deploying smart grid technologies will not only change rate designs but also require utilities to recoup their investment through customer rates. Consumer advocates want to be sure that the costs are allocated justly and do not negatively impact low-income customers. As noted in this chapter, investment in a smart grid is a very capital intensive process and utilities will collect a significant amount of their costs in the future, so it is important to ensure that the benefits are both real and spread fairly among all customers. Mary Healey, the president of the National Association of State Utility Consumer Advocates (NASUCA), argues that regulators should put the risks of smart grid investments primarily on the utility's investors rather than the customers, who do not have the power to choose one way or the other whether to deploy these technologies.[93]

Consumer advocates have raised a number of specific concerns regarding new policies following smart meter deployment. One such concern is that dynamic pricing alternatives, such as time-of-use rates, can serve as an additional cost to customers who must use electricity during peak hours and are unable to shift this use. Stay-at-home parents with young children, the elderly, and customers receiving at-home medical care are examples of people who could be potentially harmed if dynamic pricing was mandated for all electricity-use customers.

A second concern is that the smart grid automates customer disconnections centrally from a utility office. Before smart meters were in place, a utility would have to physically go to a residence to turn off the electricity in the case of nonpayment, which meant that a human being had to knock on the customer's door and notify that person that their service was to be disconnected. This human contact has been seen as an important safeguard that provides additional security to disadvantaged populations. With advanced metering in place, a utility has the technical capability to remotely connect and disconnect utility service and would presumably want to do so without the door knock requirement in order to forego the cost of an employee and truck visiting the residence. Before a utility can use this new capability, they would need to receive regulatory approval to ensure that the customer was notified a sufficient amount of time in advance of the disconnection. Some consumer advocates would prefer the utilities continue this door knock requirement prior to disconnecting service, which (from a utility perspective) would reduce the cost effectiveness of smart meter installation.

A third concern consumer advocates have is educating low-income customers about the benefits of the smart grid in an effort to help them understand the ways that the smart grid can save them money. Consumer advocates request that utilities use specialized marketing to reach out to and educate customers who are least likely to understand (or try to understand) how dynamic pricing can work. Consumer advocates are also concerned with privacy, security, interoperability, and health concerns, all of which are addressed in this chapter. As noted previously, California has reduced wireless smart meter opt-out fees for low-income customers.

One report by the Smart Grid Consumer Collaborative titled "Spotlight on Low Income Consumers" found that low-income consumers have a lower awareness of the smart grid than the general population and that these consumers communicate in different ways: 42 percent of them don't use the Internet and only one in five own a smart phone. The report did find that low-income consumers are as likely as the general population to participate in time-of-use rates and perceive that they can save money on these programs. The report concluded that there was a need for more effective outreach, including customized communications, but that all classes of customers were receptive to participating in dynamic pricing programs.[94] Ongoing consumer behavior studies and other evaluations of dynamic pricing implementation should be followed carefully to identify and resolve any challenges for low-income participation.

THE SMART GRID AND TECHNOLOGY POLICY

The development and implementation of a smart electric grid requires a number of fundamental technical changes to what is already a complex electricity infrastructure. As discussed in chapter 1, the electricity industry is essentially faced with bringing the digital energy revolution to the electric grid. The technologies that utilities deploy need to be interoperable and must not become obsolete after they are deployed. Utilities also need to ensure that the communications network that overlays the electricity grid has wireless capabilities. In addition to implementing these complex technology solutions, which must interact seamlessly and with a level of reliability that is significantly greater than what may be the standard in other industries, a number of significant policy changes are also required. Smart grid technology interoperability standards and the availability of wireless spectrum are two policy areas that require continued federal policy focus and coordination. It is also important that federal and state governments fund research and development projects and demonstration programs that improve upon current technologies.

TECHNOLOGY STANDARDS FOR INTEROPERABILITY

A significant piece of the smart grid puzzle that is essential for success is common interoperability standards. Interoperability means that "two [or more] different systems or components [are able] to communicate, share, and use information that has been exchanged without need for custom integrations or end user intervention."[95] The Holy Grail of interoperability is embodied in a plug-and-play system, in which a component intended for either the customer or utility side of the meter is plugged into the system and can automatically and intelligently communicate with the system. You plug it in and it plays, without any additional engineering or fuss involved. Practically speaking, electric utilities, home appliance manufacturers, grid component technology manufacturers, and consumers all need one system that is compatible everywhere. Essentially, smart grid technologies must interact with each other as seamlessly as individual appliances interact with wall sockets. Everywhere you go within the United States, you are sure to find electric outlets that are compatible with various electric appliances because there is an interoperability standard. You don't have to have a different adapter for everything—at least, not until you cross international borders (or try to charge the mobile phones in your household). The smart grid needs this kind of fundamental similarity as well.

On the customer side of the meter, interoperability is important because a lot of the expected benefits of the smart grid are based on customers' ability to use their smart appliances, in-home displays, and smart phone apps in any utility's service territory. For customers to actually decrease their electricity consumption, they should be able to purchase an electricity usage monitoring device and know that it will work in their home without worrying about whether the interoperability standards their utility uses are the same or different than those used by the company that sells the device. The customers' experience is paramount. The smart grid benefits are only possible if customers support the investments being made with their money and then choose to participate in the programs and use the technologies.

Interoperability is essential to help decrease cost and increase practicable usage of smart grid technologies well into the future. Common interoperability standards can also increase incentives for customer adoption of demand response programs. Instituting standards for reliability and interoperability will also help utilities improve future system performance and reduce the risk of future regulatory disallowance of costs from lack of system performance.[96] This is the major concern for most utilities—today's expensive smart grid investments must be compatible with tomorrow's technology. Moreover, efforts to advance interoperability should also help "'prosumers' (those that both produce and consume energy)"[97] connect to the grid more easily. This will make it easier for a utility's customers to install distributed generation (e.g., solar panels or a wind turbine). Although there is significant effort focused on these challenges, there are still murmurs in the field that technologies are not working together or need assistance from a good field engineer to ensure that projects succeed.

As important as interoperability standards are, there is no federal jurisdiction to require them right now. Neither the Energy Policy Act of 2005 nor the Energy Independence and Security Act of 2007 (EISA) give the Federal Energy Regulatory Commission (FERC) jurisdiction to create a uniform set of interoperability standards. The EISA did require the National Institute of Standards and Technology (NIST) to create standards for smart grid implementation. These standards are not, however, mandatory because the EISA empowered FERC through a rule-making proceeding to adopt such standards and protocols as necessary on a purely advisory basis.

The National Institute of Standards and Technology, following its mandate in the EISA, offers advisory standards for interoperability in the smart grid.[98] The NIST is a government organization that sets all kinds of national standards; for instance, the institute decides exactly how much weight really equals a pound. Accordingly, the NIST is an appropriate agency to set standards in the smart grid area as well. It has already suggested certain cyber security and privacy standards for operating the smart grid. NIST works closely with the Smart Grid Interoperability Panel (SGIP), an independent, member-funded organization that engages smart grid stakeholders to accelerate standards harmonization and advance interoperability. There is a tremendous amount of time and energy being invested by industry stakeholders through this collaborative (albeit voluntary) effort.

ACCESS TO BROADBAND

Optimizing the benefits of smart grid technology requires transmitting enormous amounts of information. In particular, utility metering will embrace a more granular approach to collecting and transmitting energy information on a regular and timely basis.[99] As previously discussed, since there is no utility data network in place between the customer and the utility data center, the smart grid requires the development of a completely new two-way communications network. Although some of this communications network will include utilizing a new fiber optic network, many utilities are choosing to use wireless technologies to complete the communication path to the customer. The volume of data transmitted over such networks could potentially constrain communication resources, but developing and taking advantage of broadband resources can provide the capacity for utilities to meet their communication needs in a cost-effective manner. New state and federal policy changes would be helpful to expand and provide access to broadband resources.

In 2009, the American Recovery and Reinvestment Act called for the Federal Communication Commission to produce a national broadband plan. Congress directed the commission to include a plan for using broadband in "advancing . . . energy independence and efficiency."[100] Published in 2010, the National Broadband Plan specifically addressed opportunities for broadband and smart grid.[101] The plan recognizes that broadband will help maximize the benefits of the smart grid because "pervasive Internet connectivity brings innovative competitors, technologies and business models to energy management systems."[102] Its vision is "to build a modern grid that enables energy efficiency and the widespread use of both renewable power and plug-in electric vehicles, reducing the country's dependence on fossil fuels and foreign oil."[103]

The plan identifies two specific barriers to using broadband to expand smart grid opportunities. First, the plan notes that while utilities in the United States already rely on broadband networks, they typically use private and narrowband[104] networks.[105] The plan further notes that none of the experts who have estimated the capacity requirements of the smart grid predict that sufficient narrowband capacity exists to meet the needs of the smart grid.[106] In order to meet their needs, several large utilities have made plans to develop private wireless broadband networks.[107]

In part, this choice is due to the lack of commercial broadband resources that perfectly mirror utility service territories and the need for utilities to have highly reliable and stable communications infrastructure.[108] In the face of utilities' obligation to adhere to strict reliability standards, the "rapid emergence and integration of numerous new smart grid components" has led to some skepticism about using commercial broadband systems for smart grid projects.[109] One recent report found "somewhat widespread agreement" that using commercial broadband networks would not meet reliability standards.[110] For example, utilities typically require more reliable or extensive backup power access for their networks than commercial broadband providers do.[111] In addition, utilities worry that they will not receive priority service in emergencies or periods of congestion, although utilities could make contractual agreements for guaranteed priority service.[112]

Perhaps more fundamentally, utilities face disincentives for using commercial networks because cost of service ratemaking creates an incentive for infrastructure investments. Electric utilities are regulated as natural monopolies—the utility provides universal access to all customers at a reasonable price in exchange for receiving a virtually guaranteed return on their investments.[113] Traditional forms of cost of service ratemaking discourage collaboration between smart grid projects and commercial broadband networks because the utilities are rewarded for assets in their rate base and would not earn a rate of return for leased access to commercial broadband capacity.[114] That is, if a utility installs and operates its own broadband network, most state regulators would allow it to earn a return on its investment rather than just pass an operating expense through its retail rates. The plan and other observers agree that differences in regulatory paradigms for utilities and broadband service providers lead to incongruous economic interests and incentives.[115] To some, these differences "appear to be intractable because they stem from divergent regulatory paradigms that have fostered fundamentally different approaches to issues of elementary importance to grid modernization."[116]

Second, the report identifies regulatory uncertainty as one factor "slowing utility decision-making and stifling the development of some smart grid applications on commercial networks."[117] In particular, the plan points to uncertainty about how the critical infrastructure protection (CIP) security of the North American Electric Reliability Corporation (NERC) will apply to smart grid communication networks.[118] CIP standards provide risk controls for "critical assets" in the country's electricity infrastructure. NERC's CIP standards apply to the bulk power system and utility-owned and -operated assets, while many smart grid projects are distribution focused and will include customer-owned displays and network hardware.[119] To remove all doubt, the plan recommends that NERC clarify the CIP's affect on these "customer-side" smart grid technologies. Despite NERC's significant recent activity regarding cyber security for critical assets, it remains unclear how these CIP standards will affect smart grid applications.

The National Broadband Plan also identifies solutions to compensate for the nation's lack of broadband capacity. For example, the plan recommends allowing utilities to have some limited access to public safety networks, which also provide "universal coverage and a resilient and redundant network." Additionally, the plan identifies important needed areas that need research, including an examination of examining the reliability and resiliency of commercial broadband networks and a review, with the Department of Energy, of utilities' communication needs and the types of networks that are suitable for their use. The plan further suggests identifying a single, dedicated band for smart grid networks.[120]

Finally, the National Broadband Plan seeks to balance access and privacy. It recommends that utility commissions require utilities to provide customers with access to smart grid data.[121] Furthermore, it suggests that FERC provide model regulations for data access and control and that the federal government establish privacy and access regulations if states do not issue them within a reasonable time.[122]

Some states, such as Vermont, have also developed creative solutions to remedy the lack of broadband access. In 2011, Green Mountain Power (GMP)[123] and the Vermont Telephone Company (VTEL) launched one of the first statewide collaborations between smart grid and broadband. Using VTEL's 4G "Long Term Evolution" (LTE) broadband network, the partnership will meet the utility's communication needs and help expand broadband into areas of the state where it would not otherwise exist. Demonstrating the need for reliable communication service, GMP is using a phased approach, beginning with a backhaul network of existing fiber, cellular, and landline telecommunications infrastructure until VTEL develops the new network.[124] In the end, this collaboration has the potential to provide cost savings and additional functionality for the utility's smart grid project. GMP estimates that it will save 40 percent on the cost of developing a wireless network, while allowing VTEL to serve a 20–25 percent larger area than previously estimated.[125]

However, this experience provides a glimpse at some of the challenges associated with using broadband technology to support smart grid deployment. First, this collaboration was only possible because VTEL had fortuitously acquired spectrum previously independent of this project. Second, both GMP and VTEL had access to separate sources of federal funding. Vermont governor Peter Shumlin also understood the opportunity that could arise from this collaboration, and he provided the policy leadership to forge an agreement. As a result, all of the pieces were present for GMP and VTEL to build a joint network that would serve both the state's goal to expand broadband to underserved areas and to support a statewide smart grid rollout. If modernizing the electric grid into a smart grid truly is a federal policy priority, then more coordinated federal communication policy and electric grid modernization policy is necessary to remove risk and uncertainty.

3

SUPERCHARGING ENERGY EFFICIENCY

As with many regional conflicts of the era, the 1973 Arab-Israeli War between Israel, Egypt, and Syria had implications beyond the Middle East.[1] The United States and the Soviet Union, constantly jockeying for an advantage over one another in their global Cold War chess match, quickly took sides: the former aiding Israel and the latter aligning with Syria and Egypt. The United States' support for Israel during this conflict did not go unnoticed by Arab member states of the Organization of Petroleum Exporting Countries (OPEC), which quickly announced that it would cut oil production by 5 percent per month until Israel withdrew from Sinai, Gaza, the West Bank, and the Golan Heights.[2] The sudden contraction in global supply created massive oil shortages in Western economies and caused oil prices to soar. This oil shock exacerbated existing inflationary trends in the American economy and helped contribute to a twenty-one-month recession—the worst the country had seen in the post-World War II era.[3]

The 1973 oil shocks were a rude awakening for the American public. Consumers throughout the country waited in long lines as gas stations rationed fuel, and businesses saw a dramatic increase in operating costs, as the price of bringing goods to market sharply increased. But the oil shocks were more than an inconvenience: They demonstrated how America's oil dependency could be used as a weapon against it. Suddenly, improving energy efficiency and conservation became a national priority—and not just in the automotive sector, which was (and still is) heavily dependent on oil, but in the electricity sector as well.[4] In an effort to reduce overall energy consumption, utilities began implementing demand-side energy conservation and efficiency programs. By and large, these programs have achieved their intended goal. Prior to 1973, national electricity consumption grew, on average, by about 6.25 percent per year. Since then, it has grown by less than 2 percent per year.[5] This is due in no small part to energy efficiency programs, which have achieved significant—and increasing— energy savings year after year.[6] This trend will continue, as savings from efficiency programs are expected to increase from 0.5 percent of total demand in 2010 to as much as 8.2 percent in 2030.[7]

Moreover, energy efficiency programs are perhaps the most cost-effective means of meeting the country's electricity demand. Utilities have essentially two ways of meeting consumer energy needs: build additional supply or try to reduce demand. Recent history demonstrates that the latter is the cheaper approach. Between 2002 and 2011, utilities have spent about 3.8 cents for every kilowatt-hour of energy they save through energy efficiency and demand response programs.[8] According to government data, the next-cheapest means of meeting that demand would be to construct an advanced combined cycle natural gas plant, which (depending on the market price of natural gas) could provide energy at a cost of about 6.5 cents per kilowatt-hour.[9] So in terms of meeting consumer demand, it's actually more cost effective for utilities to invest in energy efficiency programs than it is for them to build generation resources.

Energy efficiency programs are also an important tool for combating climate change and other environmental challenges. Because these programs reduce overall end-use electricity consumption, they provide a means of meeting demand without any corresponding increase in energy use or emissions. That is, energy efficiency programs effectively act as an additional "resource" in a utility's energy portfolio because they displace the need for utilities to construct additional generation or burn additional fossil fuels.[10] These programs have historically helped reduce emissions of carbon dioxide, nitrous oxides, sulfur dioxide, and particulate matter from the electricity sector.[11] Perhaps most important, energy efficiency produces persistent savings: Once a consumer or a business invests in energy efficient equipment, they can realize those savings year after year, throughout the life of the equipment.

The smart grid can boost energy efficiency programs, reducing energy use and emissions in the electricity sector. Smart meters will be especially important. These devices will be critical for providing consumers with feedback on their energy use, allowing them to make smarter energy use decisions. Likewise, utilities can use data collected by these devices to identify customers who have a high potential to reduce energy use through energy efficiency and energy conservation, and to educate those customers on approaches that they can take to reduce consumption. The bottom line is that smart meters and associated AMI technology are critical to providing people and utilities with information so that they can make smarter and more environmentally conscious decisions about their energy use.

BASIC CONCEPTS IN EFFICIENCY

It is important to understand the distinction between energy efficiency, energy conservation, and demand response. Energy efficiency refers to receiving the same or better level of energy services using less actual energy. For instance, when a consumer purchases an energy-efficient air conditioner, her house stays just as cool as it did with her old air conditioner—the only difference is she's using less energy to achieve the same level of comfort. By contrast, energy conservation is when consumers reduce energy use by "reducing the level of energy services."[12] So instead of purchasing a new energy-efficient air conditioner, a consumer would simply use her existing air conditioner *less*. In this way, energy conservation requires consumers to sacrifice some degree of comfort. Finally, demand response— often referred to as load shifting or load control—does not necessarily reduce energy use. Rather, it defers use to different times of the day, which reduces peak demand and overall costs. Although energy efficiency, energy conservation, and demand response are different concepts, they are all directed toward the same objective: reducing end-use energy consumption (it is for this reason that these concepts are often collectively referred to as "demand-side management," or DSM).

Efforts to promote energy efficiency and conservation are not unique to the electricity sector. For example, the auto industry is constantly improving the design of cars to achieve higher average vehicle mileage standards. Local and state governments have recently been revising building codes to incentivize more efficient construction and retrofitting of buildings and homes. In addition to utilities themselves, there are other government and third-party organizations that conduct energy and weatherization audits on residences and businesses throughout the country. Appliance manufacturers are constantly improving the efficiency of consumer products, seeking certification from government programs like Energy Star. Entities in various industrial sectors have endeavored to improve the efficiency of their production processes, whether in response to government incentives or in an effort to reduce overall costs. Energy efficiency is a common trend throughout the American economy.[13]

In the electricity sector, however, there are generally two methods of improving energy efficiency: supply-side programs or demand-side management. Supply-side programs focus on improving operational efficiencies on the utility's side of the customer meter. For example, a utility might build more efficient generating units, improve the efficiency of existing units, or deploy technologies that reduce energy losses that occur when electricity is transmitted across the transmission and distribution network. Demand-side management focuses on improving efficiencies on the customer's side of the meter.[14] Generally speaking, these "downstream savings" are more important than energy savings that occur farther up the energy supply chain.[15] This is because demand-side energy savings reduce "compounding losses" that otherwise would have occurred in each stage of the energy supply chain.[16] When a consumer invests in a more efficient light bulb—or boiler, or refrigerator, or whatever—the utility saves not only the excess energy that would have been actually *used* to power the device but also all of the energy that would have been lost in producing and transmitting it. Indeed, for every unit of avoided consumption at the consumer end, the utility can save an extra one to two additional units of energy that would have otherwise been lost in the production and distribution chain, upstream of the consumer[17] (some studies conclude that this ratio is closer to 1:10).[18]

But if the very objective of energy efficiency programs is to reduce consumption, it seems counterintuitive to suggest that a utility would want to implement such a program. Efficiency runs against the utility's profit motive. If consumers are using less electricity, that means utilities are earning less revenue. There are few—if any—businesses that would want to reduce demand for their own products. What makes utilities any different?

For one thing, energy efficiency programs represent one of the most cost-effective ways of meeting consumer demand. As discussed above, demand-side management programs can act as a resource for meeting consumer demand—they provide the same services as a coal or natural gas combustion unit, but at a lower cost.[19] Moreover, because these programs create important environmental benefits, they also generate goodwill for utilities in the eyes of the public. Implementing energy efficiency can therefore improve the utility's reputation. Historically, however, these incentives have not proven strong enough to encourage utilities to vigorously adopt energy efficiency programs. In response, government regulators have employed a device known as "decoupling" to further incentivize utilities to adopt energy efficiency programs.

To understand how decoupling corrects this disincentive, it is useful to first understand how utilities set their rates and earn a profit. In every jurisdiction in the United States, local distribution utilities (which deliver power directly to customers) must have their retail electricity rates approved by government regulators.[20] Most regulators follow the "cost of service" theory of regulation, which provides that rates should be set at a level that allows the utility to recover its costs plus a reasonable rate of return on its net investment in capital assets. Typically, the regulator will examine historical data on the utility's costs and sales, and use that data to project what the utility's costs and sales will be in the current year. The regulator then adds the utility's total expected costs to its allowed return on investment to arrive at a "revenue requirement." It then divides this figure by the utility's total expected sales to arrive at the appropriate retail rate.[21]

Of course, in reality, the utility's sales will not always be consistent with the regulator's forecast during the rate case. If actual sales exceed the regulator's projection, then the utility likely earns an extra profit that is over and above its revenue requirement. By contrast, if actual sales are lower than the regulator's projection, the utility will earn less profit and—if the drop in sales is large enough—may not even earn enough revenue to cover its costs. For obvious reasons, the utility would prefer the former to the latter. It therefore has an inherent disincentive to encourage energy efficiency among its customers. Decoupling corrects this disincentive by essentially separating (decoupling) the utility's cost recovery from the amount of electricity that it sells.[22] Once sales are actually known, regulators will adjust or "true-up" utility rates so that the utility can collect its revenue requirement based on actual sales.[23] If actual sales are above the forecast, then regulators will reduce rates in the following period; if actual sales are less than forecast, then regulators will increase the utility's rates to make up for the shortfall.[24]

TRADITIONAL ENERGY EFFICIENCY PROGRAMS

Utility energy efficiency programs have historically taken on several forms. At the outset of these programs in the 1970s, utilities would simply provide generalized information to consumers through workshops, flyers, and educational pamphlets. Some utilities even provided consumers with loans to make necessary investments.[25] Then in the 1980s, states began requiring utilities to develop "integrated resource plans"—essentially forward-looking strategies in which utilities would assess how to meet consumer demand in the future. Under these plans, utilities had to conduct a cost-benefit analysis, considering everything from constructing additional generation to improving their transmission and distribution networks to demand-side management. Because of the cost effectiveness of energy efficiency programs, utilities began to devote more resources to these programs. They began sending out staffers to customers to provide specific recommendations and cost estimates for energy efficiency investments.[26] It was also during this time that utilities began offering rebates to customers who purchased and installed energy efficient equipment.[27] By the 1990s, utilities were targeting not only residential customers, but large-scale industrial and commercial customers as well, helping them identify, finance, and install comprehensive packages of [demand-side management] measures."[28]

Today, utilities have continued with and expanded upon these efforts. Some utilities run energy audits on customer homes and businesses and install low-cost equipment themselves.[29] Other utilities have broadened their focus and have banded together to create "market transformation programs." Rather than focusing on encouraging energy efficient behaviors among individual consumers, these programs move up the distribution chain and encourage manufacturers to produce more energy efficient devices.[30] The "golden carrot" super energy efficient refrigerator program of the 1990s is an example. Twenty-five utilities pledged $30.7 million to incentivize refrigerator manufacturers to build an energy efficient, CFC-free refrigerator. The manufacturer that could achieve the most savings "would receive guaranteed rebates for selling the super-efficient refrigerators in the participating utilities' service areas."[31] Whirlpool ended up winning the contest, but for a variety of reasons, it sold far fewer of the energy efficient refrigerators than it produced.[32] This program, however, encouraged manufacturers to improve upon Whirlpool's design and is credited as "bringing together many different groups, particularly public utilities and manufacturers, to work toward the goal of transforming a market."[33]

The deregulation of the electricity sector has caused some utilities to cut back on DSM spending, as they are no longer responsible for planning for the customer's long-term energy supply needs in a competitive market. Many argue that, in deregulated markets, third-party companies that are not affiliated with the utility are better suited to administer these programs. Some state governments remedied this problem by imposing an additional charge—often referred to as a public benefits charge—on retail sales of electricity in their jurisdiction. The proceeds from this fund go to funding energy efficiency, renewable energy, and low-income assistance programs in the state.[34]

ADVANCED METER INFRASTRUCTURE

Smart meters, in-home displays, and other advanced metering infrastructure will all be critical to improving the effectiveness of energy efficiency programs. Together, these technologies create a web of infrastructure that permits two-way communication between the utility and the customer. Conceptually, we can compare AMI systems to an inverted pyramid. The individual household smart meters and home area networks (HANs) are at the base. Data from these devices is relayed through a series of networks—often referred to as neighborhood area networks (NANs) or wide-area networks (WANs)—and then to the utility control center, where all the data from individual consumers is collected, aggregated, and analyzed.[35] The utility can then send data back down through the pyramid to individual consumers. At this point, each individual utility is developing its own AMI, and as a result, there is much variety in how these communication networks actually operate. To date no standardized system or architecture has emerged, although several organizations have attempted to develop a common framework that can be used by all.[36] Despite the diversity of systems that have been developed, we describe the basics of AMI below.

Smart meters have been described as the smart grid's "fundamental enabling technology" because, unlike mechanical, analog meters, smart meters can record and store granular data on energy and relay data back and forth between the utility and the consumer.[37] These metering systems record data at hourly[38] (or more frequent) intervals and transmit that data on a daily (or more frequent) basis through a communications network and back to the utility.[39] For this reason, smart meters have capabilities that traditional meters do not. For instance, smart meters allow utilities to automatically record and access customer energy consumption (as opposed to sending out meter readers and their vehicles every month), to send price signals to customers, and to provide enhanced information and feedback to customers on their energy use.[40] Customers can view this information through in-home displays or Internet portals on the utility's website. In this way, smart meters provide customers with the information that they need to make informed and intelligent decisions about their energy use.

Smart meters provide a whole host of other services that will improve utilities' operational efficiencies. These devices can provide improved "net metering" services for customers who install small, distributed generation on their property (e.g., a wind turbine or solar panels) and want to sell electricity back to the grid. If the home and the generator have separate meters, utilities will be able to calculate how much electricity the customer consumes, how much electricity the generator produces, and how much electricity fed back into the grid. Smart meters will also facilitate new options such as "prepay" services for electricity. Finally, these devices allow utilities to automatically turn power on or off for a given customer and help utilities monitor and prevent energy theft.

The communications network beyond the smart meter, over which data is transmitted between utilities and customers, could take on various forms. One type of architecture, often referred to as power-line carrier (PLC) or broadband over power line (BPL), would essentially allow utilities to simultaneously transmit both data and electricity over power lines.

This is referred to as a "wired" smart meter network.[41] The technology is not new, as utilities have used power lines for many decades as a means of transmitting data (albeit in small quantities).[42] Because power is distributed to every electrical outlet in the household, such a system would enable consumers and utilities to control the amount of electricity that each household device consumes. The problem is that transmission and distribution networks were not designed for carrying high quantities of data, and the design of these systems varies by jurisdiction, making standardization of any communications infrastructure difficult.[43] Moreover, the signal that travels across these systems tends to attenuate as distance increases, which would require utilities to install boosters to maintain signal strength.[44] This would increase the costs of deploying such a system. Finally, the signal would be transmitted to households through the closest transformer. There are typically four to eight households that draw electricity from a single, low-voltage transformer; accordingly, these households would have to share bandwidth, which could create problems related to congestion, interference, and privacy.[45]

Utilities can also use wireless networks to transmit data to and from a customer's smart meter. This appears to be the preferred approach for most utilities that have installed AMI.[46] Wireless AMI can be configured in a number of ways. Many utilities use private radio frequency mesh networks at the customer and neighborhood level and then use other broadband wireless options (3G, 4G LTE, and WiMax) to transmit data from the neighborhood back to the utility substation. At that point, data is relayed over the utility's fiber optic network back to the utility headquarters and data center.[47] In telecommunications lingo, the RF mesh network is a "point-to-point" network in which signals from one "node" (in this case, a smart meter on a customer's property) can be relayed to another node, until it returns to a data "hub."[48] The smart meters contain an RF chip that allows the two-way communication with the network.[49] Mesh networks are low cost, but they have less bandwidth (i.e., they carry less data) and higher latency (they don't react as fast) relative to other network configurations.[50]

It's important to note that these communication technologies are not mutually exclusive. A single utility may utilize several of these technologies throughout their AMI. San Diego Gas & Electric, for instance, will likely use a mix of technologies to support its smart grid applications, "including Wi-Fi, WiMAX, LTE cellular and to a smaller extent, propriety RF solutions."[51] Each utility's choice of technology will ultimately depend on how it balances cost, coverage, reliability, and security.[52]

Most smart meters are also capable of including a second wireless communications chip for the home area networks. These chips also offer a variety of different communication technologies such as Zigbee or WiFi.[53] HANs connect the smart meter to "smart" appliances and in-home displays in the consumer's home. The HAN serves as a communications portal through which consumers can control the energy consumption of individual devices throughout their home. This technology allows consumers to set preferences such that, if the utility sends a certain price signal to the smart meter, certain devices (e.g., air conditioners or dryers) will automatically turn off or defer consumption to a later time.[54]

THE SMART GRID AND ENERGY EFFICIENCY

Historically, energy efficiency programs have been all about providing consumers with information on how to make intelligent decisions regarding energy use. Utilities have distributed information to consumers on energy efficient appliances and devices, have helped conduct energy audits and provide individual customers with specific recommendations as to how to reduce energy use, and have marketed rebate and loan programs to customers who invest in energy efficient technologies. The smart grid can supercharge these programs by providing customers, as well as their efficiency providers and new customer applications, with more granular and detailed information. This will enable customers to make more informed energy choices. Utilities can also use this information to identify households or businesses with the greatest potential for energy savings, to provide more targeted energy efficiency marketing campaigns, and to conduct more intensive program evaluation.

CUSTOMER FEEDBACK AND THE CONSERVATION EFFECT

The most important aspect of the smart grid in terms of energy efficiency is its ability to provide more detailed feedback to customers on their energy use. The goal of feedback is to overcome energy invisibility—the separation of human behavior from energy use. A positive benefit of overcoming energy invisibility through feedback is known as the "conservation effect": Once consumers can see how much energy they use, they are likely to take steps to reduce that consumption. The conservation effect is evident among those who own automobiles like the Toyota Prius, which provides drivers with real-time data on their vehicle's fuel economy. Studies have shown that these drivers modify their driving habits (such as by letting up on the accelerator) to improve their vehicle's energy efficiency.

Similarly, smart meters and applications that record and display data on energy consumption "enable consumers to become active managers of

their own energy . . . use."[55] Indeed, studies have shown that, when consumers receive near-term feedback on their energy use, they are more
likely to reduce energy consumption. In one study from as far back as the
1970s, a group of households were provided with a meter that showed
electricity use in cents per hour. Over a period of eleven months, these
households consumed 12 percent less electricity than the control group,
which had no such meter.[56] A more recent study compared the energy
savings from real-time, residential feedback pilot projects across the globe
and found that households reduced their electricity consumption—by 0 to
19.5 percent, with an average savings of 3.6 percent.[57] Other programs
have produced savings in excess of 20 percent of usual household consumption,[58] although there are some studies that have not found any link
between feedback on energy use and energy savings.[59]

Of course, it is not enough that utilities simply provide customers with
cold, hard numbers on their energy use. Changing individual consumption
patterns is about more than providing consumers with information—it's
about changing behavior. There is an element of social psychology that
needs to be taken into account when designing these programs. Research
suggests that customer feedback is most effective when it is coupled with
persuasive rhetoric that links efficiency to results that most people would
consider normatively "good"—such as environmental improvements,
financial savings, or self-reliance.[60] Utilities must not only present the customer with information, but must also "market" energy efficiency in a
commercially attractive way. All this is to say that customer feedback must
be presented in a manner and at a time that is most likely to change behavior. Information is not enough—persuasion and timing are also crucial
to maximizing savings.

In this vein, there are many ways in which utilities could deliver customer feedback to consumers, and some are more effective than others.
One form of feedback, known as "enhanced billing," provides consumers
with comparative information on their energy use in their monthly billing
statement. Such a statement usually compares the customer's energy use for
that month with her historical energy use, or it might assess the customer's
energy use relative to similarly situated households.[61] These feedback programs are low cost and have produced average annual energy savings of
about 3.8 percent per household.[62] This method of feedback, however, is
somewhat limited by the fact that the consumer receives the information
long after the actual consumption has occurred. Moreover, the data is often
not detailed enough to inform the consumer of how she is using electricity
and where savings might be realized.

Real-time feedback—which provides consumers with information about
their energy use almost contemporaneously with consumption—is much

more effective at changing consumer behaviors. Studies have shown that real-time feedback on household energy use can produce average annual energy savings of 9.2 percent per household. When that data is disaggregated to the appliance level—showing consumers how much electricity each of their household devices is consuming—average annual energy savings spike to almost 12 percent per household.[63] All of this suggests that there is an ideal format in which customer feedback should be presented to consumers; generally, it should be based on actual usage data, provided on as frequent a basis as possible, be as detailed and disaggregated as possible, and provide social and historical comparisons by which customers can assess their energy use.[64]

Practically speaking, there are two technologies that utilities can use to present data on energy use to consumers: in-home displays and web presentment. The former may not always be cost effective. Early studies suggest that, although consumers will initially utilize an in-home display to gauge their consumption, the technology quickly becomes obsolete. After initially using the in-home display and learning how much energy individual appliances consume, consumers no longer need the displays. Accordingly, there is some concern that the life cycle of this expensive technology is no more than ninety days "from the kitchen counter to the kitchen drawer."

Web presentment, on the other hand, is a more lasting and lower cost means of providing consumers with feedback on their energy use. After installing smart meters, most utilities utilize meter data management systems to download customer consumption data onto servers that present this data through various graphic interfaces on the utility's website. This allows utilities to display highly detailed data on various time scales, and gives customers the ability to compare usage to other factors such as temperature. Other options include utilizing rate comparators to see if other rates that the utility offers may be more cost effective for a given customer based on historic usage. Data presented on the Internet is often delayed as much as a day, compared to the immediate feedback from an in-home display.

Combining web presentment with additional feedback such as "customer insights" via regular email alerts has been found by some utilities to enhance customer feedback. These customer insights might compare current usage to a budget or past billing periods. If the customer has established a budget, these notifications could warn the customer when he or she is going to exceed that budget. They could also inform the customer of important weather information that could affect energy usage. Finally, utilities can also make consumption data available on smart phones and other mobile devices, providing consumers with a portable and convenient means of accessing energy use information and controlling consumption.

In practice, some utilities have applied these principles in a variety of unique settings. In Arizona, the Salt River Project—one of the United States' largest public power utilities—runs a prepay program called M-Power. The SRP has been running M-Power since 1993, and it has grown to be the largest prepay electricity program in the nation (130,000 participating customers).[65] The program utilizes smart cards, in-home displays, payment kiosks, and a prepay meter. Customers can purchase power at designated kiosks in SRP's service territory by loading credit in one-dollar increments on a smart card. Swiping the card on the in-home display then downloads the credits from the smart card, and the consumer can use electricity until the credits run out. The in-home display then communicates with the smart meter to provide the consumer with certain information, including

- the current retail rate of the electricity;
- the amount that the household has spent on electricity during that day, the previous day, the previous month, and the previous year; and
- how much money the consumer has left on her prepay account.[66]

Not only are customers extremely satisfied with M-Power (83 to 96 percent of customers report being "satisfied or very satisfied"), but they also save a significant amount of energy: Customers on the M-Power program use about 12 percent less electricity than those who are served by SRP's standard residential program, despite the fact that both groups pay the same nominal rate for electricity.[67] Although the program is technically not an application of smart grid technology (because there is no two-way communication between the consumer and the utility), it demonstrates how effective customer feedback is at reducing overall energy use.[68] M-Power has demonstrated that if you provide customers with both timely information and the ability to control their usage, customers will respond with significant energy savings. The program has proven that prepay electric service can result in both satisfied customers and a greener grid.

San Diego Gas & Electric has been another utility leader in developing programs and partnerships to explore ways that smart grid technology can enhance energy efficiency. It was the first utility that committed to the White House to utilize the Green Button Initiative and give customers timely access to their energy data with the click of a button.[69] Green Button allows customers to download their data directly to their computer and includes a second option to authorize third parties direct access to customer data through a standard interface. The Green Button was developed as a consensus-based standard with the collaboration of the National Institute of Standards and Technology. SDG&E's website provides links to a growing list of energy applications that are available to use with Green Button data.

San Diego Gas & Electric has also launched several initiatives to take advantage of social media. Perhaps its most innovative efforts are its current behavioral and social networking pilots with Opower and Simple Energy. Opower was founded in 2007 and runs behavior-based efficiency programs. The SDG&E pilot included a group of twenty thousand customers in the Opower Home Energy Reports program. Customers in Opower's program are entered into the program by default and have the option to opt-out. Opower's experience is that this opt-out system motivates consumers to participate in the program, which provides consumers with information about their energy use as well as ways in which they can make their home more efficient. Each paper report includes

- information on the customer's home energy consumption, relative to homes that are nearby and similar in size;
- progress tracking on energy use changes over time and across seasons; and
- ideas on how to save energy, including information on the rebates and other special programs.

San Diego Gas & Electric has also partnered with Simple Energy to create a number of social gaming experiences to encourage customers to save energy. One such event was called the "Biggest Energy Saver Contest," in which "approximately 200 participants were selected to pit their energy efficiency skills against one another, sharing their results daily online through a social gaming application and monitoring their savings in real-time through home energy management devices provided by SDG&E."[70] These new behavioral-focused energy efficiency companies are bringing significant innovation, which when combined with enhanced smart grid data is supercharging utility energy efficiency programs.

Finally, SDG&E is also leveraging mobile technology so that consumers can monitor and control energy use on the go. San Diego Gas & Electric has partnered with Alarm.com, which sells programmable thermostats and operates a successful Internet-based home security platform. Alarm.com allows customers to control their thermostats through a web portal or through mobile devices. These customers receive notices from SDG&E on high-demand days ("event days") and can log onto Alarm.com's platform to program their thermostat accordingly.[71] In the future, interactive, smart phone energy management capabilities such as this will become more popular and more important for consumers to maximize energy savings.

The available research indicates that providing customers with feedback on their energy use not only benefits those customers individually, but also the economy as a whole. The Pacific Northwest National Laboratory estimates that by 2030, customer information and feedback systems could reduce overall electricity consumption and carbon emissions by 3 percent relative to projected levels.[72] Likewise, the American Council on an Energy Efficient Economy estimates that customer feedback programs could reduce electricity consumption by anywhere from 1.8 to 9.4 percent, relative to projected levels in 2030. On a macroeconomic level these programs could save $1.63 to $7.70 for every dollar that utilities spend implementing them.[73]

As time goes on, utilities and policymakers will understand more about how to provide information to consumers in the most effective way. An important component of the Department of Energy's smart grid investment grants (SGIGs) is a partnership with nine SGIG award recipients who are conducting consumer behavior studies to examine the acceptance, retention, and response of consumers involved in time-based rate programs that include advanced metering infrastructure and customer systems, such as in-home displays and programmable communicating thermostats. The studies combine a variety of rate treatments, technologies, and information feedback mechanisms to gather data on the most successful combination of technologies and rate strategies. Over 150,000 customers are participating in these voluntary studies. These studies are an opportunity to advance the electricity industry's understanding of consumer behavior through the application of statistically rigorous experimental methods and will provide valuable information on how best to combine smart technologies and smart policies in order to achieve greater benefits.[74]

UTILITY FEEDBACK

Smart meter data will provide benefits not only to consumers but also to utilities. In particular, feedback on customer energy use can help utilities develop more effective and more targeted energy efficiency programs. Traditional meters simply provide utilities with information on a customer's monthly energy use. These meters cannot discern when during the day that use occurs or which appliances within the home are using the most energy. However, smart meters can provide data on such a detailed level that, over time, utilities can actually determine the purpose for which the electricity is being used—cooling, heating, and the like.[75] In fact, using advanced analytic techniques, analysts can map meter data to a specific device—a space heater, a water heater, an air conditioner, and so on.[76] As smart devices become more popular, it will be easier and easier for utilities to determine which devices in the home are using the most amount of energy. Privacy concerns aside, giving utilities access to such granular data along with the appropriate analytical tools promotes energy efficiency because it enables utilities to "identify customers with significant energy saving opportunities" and to recommend energy efficient devices or appliances to those customers.[77] In other words, smart meter data along with some advanced analytics can function as a "check engine light" to the utility and customer to inform them that some systems are underperforming before that underperformance imposes a significant cost.

Utilities could also use data from similarly situated homes to establish trends or baselines for energy usage in a given type of structure; extrapolating from this data, the utility could then "target homes that have greater-than average potential to benefit from energy-efficiency improvements."[78] Utilities can compare buildings of similar ages, similar sizes, or in areas that have similar weather and climactic patterns to determine what the average level of energy use is for that type of structure. They can then promote energy efficiency solutions to those customers, offering them rebates or loans to make the investments. As smart appliances become more popular, utilities will be able to drill down to the appliance level and recommend distinct devices or services to homes that are underperforming.

Finally, utilities can also use smart grid technologies to improve their measurement and verification (M&V) of the energy savings that efficiency programs produce. Generally speaking, utilities must compare energy use prior to implementation of the efficiency measure with energy use after the retrofit to determine how much savings has occurred. Typically, utilities measure and verify energy savings through controlled tests that compare energy consumption with or without the energy efficient device.[79] They then combine these savings with an estimate of how often the device would be used and extrapolate savings from there. Alternatively, the utility may compare customer bills and energy use before and after adopting an efficiency measure to calculate savings. Finally, the utility may conduct short-term metering, installing meters that monitor the energy savings of a given retrofit over a short period of time and extrapolating the savings from there.[80] With the smart grid, smart meters and other devices could monitor energy savings in real time and relay that data back to the utility. This would not only reduce the cost of traditional M&V efforts but also provide more reliable and accurate data about energy savings that result from energy efficiency investments, especially for large commercial and industrial customers that require more sophisticated M&V systems.[81]

RECOMMISSIONING FOR COMMERCIAL AND INDUSTRIAL CUSTOMERS

Smart meter data is especially valuable for customers in the commercial and industrial sectors, who typically purchase large equipment that uses a significant amount of energy. When this equipment is originally installed, building managers commission the equipment—that is, calibrate it to work under a certain set of circumstances and parameters. They must take into account how often the equipment is to be used, how many people are going to be using it, and other environmental factors, such as weather.[82] Chillers, boilers, cooling towers, HVAC systems, economizers, and heat pumps are all examples of technologies that have to be commissioned when they are installed.[83] Over time, "changes in operational requirements . . . tend to render initial equipment settings sub-optimal for operational efficiency as well as for energy efficiency. As a result, re-commissioning is important to ensure the best equipment performance."[84] Recommissioning is usually a timely and tedious process.

But with smart grid technologies, industrial and commercial facilities could *continuously commission* their equipment to ensure that it is operating at an environmentally optimal level.[85] Smart grid technologies can monitor the equipment's performance and notify either the utility or the customer when that equipment is "not performing to nameplate efficiency specifications."[86] Some technologies may be able to detect faults and problems with the equipment, so that facility managers can diagnose and address problems before they become serious and require costly repairs.[87] By improving the commissioning and recommissioning process, smart grid technologies can further reduce energy use and carbon emissions from the electricity sector.

CONCLUSION

Energy efficiency programs gained traction at a time when there was an energy crisis in the United States. Today, the country faces a similar dilemma. The great recession of 2008 caused significant economic upheaval, putting pressure on both consumers and businesses to cut expenses whenever possible. At the same time, the country still needs to find a way to meet its energy needs in a manner that conserves natural resources, promotes economic growth, and seriously confronts the climate change crisis.

Improving energy efficiency in the electric power sector can help achieve all of these objectives. Energy efficiency investments are one of the most cost-effective, environmentally friendly ways for utilities to meet demand while cutting back on emissions. Such investments also help individual households and businesses cut down on expenses. With more detailed and relevant information, customers across all sectors—residential, commercial, and industrial—can make more intelligent decisions about their energy use. The smart grid is critical for this purpose. Smart grid technologies can supercharge energy efficiency efforts, providing consumers with more accurate and timely information about their energy use. Utilities can leverage these technologies to improve their energy efficiency programs, maximize energy savings, and reduce carbon dioxide emissions.

4

DEMOCRATIZING DEMAND RESPONSE

Electric utilities have utilized demand response (DR) and load control for over seventy years, but following the 1973 oil shocks, it became increasingly popular. Unlike energy efficiency, demand response—also referred to as load shifting or load control—does not necessarily reduce total energy consumption. Rather, demand response is intended to reduce overall peak demand (and the associated costs that come with it) by shifting energy use away from peak hours to off-peak hours. Peak demand (or peak load) is the maximum total demand on the system during a given period of time. Peak demand fluctuations may occur on daily, monthly, seasonal, and yearly cycles. Demand response, energy conservation, and energy efficiency are all different means of reducing the timing or amount of electricity consumption, but they are often collectively referred to as demand-side management.

There are three classic forms of load management: peak clipping, valley filling, and load shifting. Peak clipping is focused on reducing the system peak load and has traditionally been achieved by using direct load control (DLC), which occurs when the utility or a "third-party aggregator" reduces electricity consumption by directly controlling customer appliances. The customer gives the utility or third-party authority to reduce or shut off electricity consumption of these appliances during peak hours. Valley filling involves shifting electricity consumption to off-peak hours and traditionally has been achieved by practices such as thermal energy storage for water or space heating. Finally, load shifting is just what the name suggests—shifting load from on-peak to off-peak periods. Load shifting includes storage water heating or time-of-use pricing programs for services such as electric vehicle charging.[1]

Three Classic Forms of Load Management

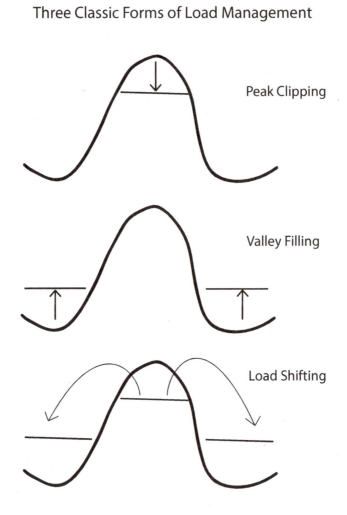

Peak Clipping

Valley Filling

Load Shifting

The Energy Policy Act of 1992[2] contained provisions advocating both demand-side management and integrated resource planning (IRP). Also known as "least-cost planning," IRP is an energy planning process that many utilities use. It requires utilities to consider a variety of ways of meeting energy demand, including supply-side resources (e.g., constructing additional generation) and demand-side resources (e.g., energy efficiency or load shifting). The process begins with a range of projections for future electricity demand. Then, potential supply and demand resources are developed for meeting the future resource needs. These alternatives are then evaluated to determine what mix of resources can produce enough energy to meet demand at the least cost. Often, environmental externalities—that is, the environmental cost of producing electricity, which is usually not fully reflected in the market price for electricity—are quantified and explicitly included when evaluating a given resource decision.[3] More recently, demand response has been identified by the White House as a key action necessary for achieving the twenty-first-century grid: "Federal, state, and local officials should strive to reduce the generation costs associated with providing power to consumers or wholesale providers during periods of peak demand and encourage participation in demand management programs. Innovative rate designs will be more feasible as smart grid technologies become more widely available."[4]

THE DEMOCRATIZATION OF DEMAND RESPONSE

Energy efficiency advocates have consistently argued that it is both cheaper for ratepayers and better for the environment to save energy rather than build new power plants. Although this view has been widely accepted over the last few decades, historically, demand response has played a minor role in the balancing of electrical demand and supply. How could the benefits of demand response be widely recognized but rarely utilized? Traditionally, the problem has been that the utility industry has faced a number of technological and policy hurdles to widespread utilization of demand response. Utilities have had insufficient information about real-time customer demand and provided inadequate price signals to customers regarding the cost of that demand. Although demand response can be applied to all classes of customers (industrial, commercial, and residential), only larger commercial and industrial customers have historically had the metering technology necessary to implement DR programs. Utilities have required larger commercial and industrial customers to have demand meters that can measure their maximum consumption during a given hour. In addition to being billed for their monthly energy usage (kWh), these customers are also billed demand charges (kW), which provided an incentive to reduce peak demand. Demand meter technology goes back to 1894, when Arthur Wright of Brighton, England, first demonstrated them to Samuel Insull. "Unlike other meters," notes Maury Klein, "Wright's version recorded not only how much electricity a customer used but also when he used it and the maximum level of his use."[5] Because it has generally been cost prohibitive for utilities to deploy these meters to smaller customers, only commercial and industrial customers could justify the expense. More recently, prior to digital smart meters being installed, utilities with time-of-use rates have utilized mechanical equipment to reduce peak demand; for example, some utilities have used timers that disconnect water heaters during on-peak times and reconnected them during off-peak times.

These challenges have resulted in a disconnect between what most residential and commercial customers pay for electricity and what it costs utilities to produce it. In fact, although the wholesale price of electricity can be volatile during peak load periods, utilities have historically priced energy delivered to their customers at flat average rates, which do not change for months or even years. Flat retail rates are inefficient because they result in both higher system costs and higher customer bills than if rates reflected the utility's marginal cost. In this case, marginal cost is what it would cost a utility to produce one additional unit of electricity at a given point in time. Obviously, a utility's marginal cost during peak hours is higher than the utility's cost during nonpeak hours because it costs the utility more to purchase or produce electricity during the former than it does during the latter. The mismatch between the variable whole-sale cost of electricity and the relatively constant retail price charged for electrical service has meant that utilities often send incorrect price signals to peak-time users, rather than incenting more efficient electricity consumption.

The installation of smart meters and associated AMI technology can bring the benefits of the digital energy revolution to all customers. In this way, the smart grid can democratize demand response. These technological changes result in the transformation of demand response from its traditional framework to the new smart grid framework. The traditional framework included the following attributes:

- Utility control
- Limited customer options
- Incentive-based programs

With the advent of smart meters and AMI, the new smart grid model advanced the framework to include the following:

- Access for all customers
- Enhanced customer choice
- Dynamic pricing alternatives

BENEFITS FROM MODERN DEMAND RESPONSE PROGRAMS

Modern demand response provides three types of benefits: economic efficiency, system reliability, and environmental benefits. The economic benefits are created because demand response can lower wholesale energy and

The Smart Grid Has Democratized DR
Expanding Access to All Customers

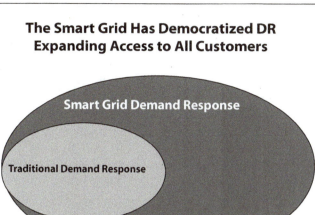

ancillary service prices. When demand response resources participate in wholesale electricity markets, they can reduce peak demand, displacing the need for higher priced peaking generation resources and thereby reducing both peak energy and ancillary service prices. Moreover, as demand response resources are used more and more over time, they can reduce overall peak demand, meaning that utilities can forego constructing costly new peaking generation.[6]

Demand response also benefits system reliability by providing a more orderly means of reducing load during an electric system emergency. As previously discussed, electricity is the only significant energy source that cannot be easily stored. This means that electricity must be produced and consumed at the same instant. Of course, residences and businesses constantly turn on and off appliances and commercial processes, so load is constantly changing. To maintain the voltage and frequency on the system, generation resources (sometimes located great distances from the load centers) must follow the load as it ramps up and down. But at times, since the electric grid is driven by customer demand, the system operator may encounter a shortage of supply. In these instances, the operator may first try to reduce the voltage on the electrical system, which will in turn reduce the amount of electricity that it must supply to the grid. However, if the voltage drops below acceptable limits, the grid will not fail gracefully, and cascading blackouts will occur. Thus, as a last resort, the operator must shed customer load in a controlled manner to keep the system in balance—or there will be a much larger uncontrolled wide-reaching blackout.

Historically, emergency demand response programs began at the utility level with voluntary interruptible load tariffs. Industrial and commercial electric customers received rate discounts for offering to reduce load during these system emergencies. Utilities would contact the customers and request that they reduce their demand (interrupt their load) for a certain number of hours. Customers were usually not required to accept these requests, but if they refused to reduce their load, they would face some sort of financial penalty. Since then, the Federal Energy Regulatory Commission has encouraged utilities in various regions of the countries to form independent system operators (ISOs) and regional transmission organizations (RTOs). The utilities cede operational control (not ownership) of their transmission assets to the ISO/RTO. The ISO/RTO is then responsible for managing power flows over its respective regional grid. It organizes and operates wholesale markets in a given region and maintain reliability by ensuring that there are enough resources on the system to meet demand at a given time. With the advent of ISOs and RTOs, voluntary interruptible load programs (which are run by utilities) have given way to emergency demand response programs (which are run by the ISO/RTO system operator). These programs are organized within the context of a wholesale market: The ISO calls on both energy- and capacity-based emergency resources to reduce demand, and those resources are compensated for their reductions at the prevailing market rate for electricity.

Demand response can also provide environmental benefits. During peak demand times, the system operator must rely on the most inefficient, expensive, and pollution-intensive resources to meet demand. By reducing demand during these peak times, demand response can likewise reduce the output of some of the most environmentally harmful generating facilities, at least for a limited number of hours. As renewable resources become a larger percentage of total energy supply, demand response can also improve the reliability of these resources, which provide energy on an intermittent and variable basis. Thus when the sun isn't shining or the wind isn't blowing, output from these resources obviously decreases. When this occurs, system operators can call on demand response resources to reduce consumption, which will help maintain balance on the grid. Thus demand response is an integral component to increasing the penetration of renewables in the nation's energy mix.

An example will help illustrate how demand response and load shedding work in practice. On September 10–11, 2013, the PJM Interconnection (PJM is an RTO that serves a region stretching from Pennsylvania to parts of North Carolina and Illinois) experienced a confluence of conditions that forced it to call an unprecedented amount of demand response resources into service while also having to invoke mandatory load shedding in various regions. PJM has about 2,500 mW of economic demand response and 9,000 mW of emergency demand response that it can call upon to serve its peak load, which in July 2013 reached 157,509 mW. On Tuesday, September 10, 2013, demand soared past the previous September record. At the same time, the region was experiencing unusually high temperatures, and several major transmission and generation facilities were out of service. The transmission system was already constrained as a result of the transmission outages, which limited PJM's ability to import power into these problem areas. Thus PJM asked for and received about 700 mW of demand response from two of its energy zones in Ohio. With transmission constraints limiting the ability for outside assistance to these zones, PJM ordered manual load shedding for 150 mW of utility customer load within these zones in order to avoid a larger blackout. This was PJM's first manual load shedding since January 19, 1994. Together, the presence of demand response and system operator action prevented this incident from turning into a cascading blackout like the one that occurred in August 2003 and resulted in fifty million people losing power.[7] PJM explained that "extreme heat in the western region of PJM resulted in record demand for September at a time when many power plants and some transmission lines were off for seasonal maintenance. Our only option to prevent a potential equipment overload and failures that would cause a much bigger interruption was to call for emergency relief in the form of controlled outages."[8]

On the next day, Wednesday, peak load climbed to 144,370 mW, which exceeded PJM's highest September peak. PJM received support from 5,949 mW of demand response resources, which was the largest amount of support PJM ever received from its economic and emergency demand response programs. Of this amount, two of the nation's largest third-party demand-response aggregators—EnerNOC and Comverge—provided 2,000 mW and 426 mW, respectively, to support the PJM grid.[9] Wednesday's grid challenge resulted from a PJM-wide spike in demand, and both demand response and supply-side resources were able to meet this demand and prevent any further mandatory load shedding.

TYPES OF DEMAND RESPONSE

There are a variety of different means of implementing demand response, and thus, there are various classifications for demand response resources, including those used by the North American Electric Reliability Corporation and the Federal Energy Regulatory Commission.[10] Demand response can be voluntary or mandatory. It can also be controlled by retail price signals or through direct load control by a utility

Categories of
Demand Side Management

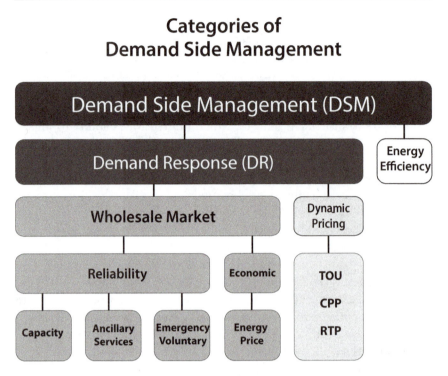

(Source: Adapted from NERC)

or other third party. NERC classifies demand response resources as those that are dispatchable or nondispatchable resources. FERC categorizes demand response resources by whether they are incentive-based programs or time-based programs. Although these classifications are useful, we will focus our discussion on two broad types of demand response programs: retail dynamic pricing programs[11] and wholesale market programs. For 2012, FERC reported that total potential peak reduction for all demand response programs was 66,351 mW, which was a 25 percent increase from 2010.[12]

DYNAMIC PRICING

Dynamic pricing generally refers to retail pricing that utilizes time-varying rates to reflect the value and costs of electricity in different time periods. Dynamic pricing is designed to persuade customers to shift their electricity use from higher priced peak periods to lower priced nonpeak periods. Dynamic pricing is a retail program, so the rate structure must be approved by state regulators and contained in a utility tariff or, in states with

Dynamic Pricing and Customer Risk

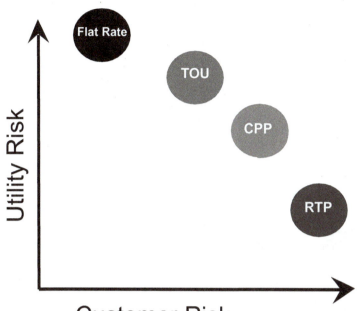

retail competition, contained in pricing plans offered by competitive electric suppliers, which are more lightly regulated. The availability of dynamic pricing options for customers is being greatly expanded with the introduction of smart meters and AMI, which allows the recording of customer energy use at a given time of day. There are three broad types of dynamic pricing programs: time-of-use (TOU) rates, critical-peak pricing (CPP), and real-time pricing (RTP). One of the defining factors of these rates is that as more customers shift from traditional flat rates to TOU, CPP, and RTP rates, price risk shifts from the utility to the individual customer.

The reason for this is relatively simple. Electric utilities and competitive third-party suppliers are subject to higher peak energy prices, and to the extent they can incentivize their customers to use less energy during higher priced peak periods and possibly shift use to lower priced off-peak periods, the costs the utility pays to serve their customers will decrease. Flat retail rates do not reflect this price variability, and thus, customers are sent a signal to use more than is cost-effective during peak periods and less than is cost-effective during off-peak periods.

Time-of-Use Rates

Time-of-use rates usually reflect at least two pricing periods: on peak and off peak. On-peak prices would be priced slightly higher than the standard flat rate, and off-peak periods would be priced slightly lower. There could be additional pricing periods, such as super-off-peak pricing, which would be prices lower than off-peak rates during the lowest demand hours. The schedule of prices for TOU rates is usually fixed well in advance by season, day of week, and time of day. One increasingly popular version of TOU rates are rates for electric vehicle charging that incentivize the EV owner to charge in the evening, when demand on the system and prices are lower.

Critical Peak Pricing

Critical peak pricing sets prices at the normal TOU rates. However during a finite number of hours—usually triggered by a system reliability problem—electricity rates are set very high. The rate for critical peak hours is generally known in advance, but the specific hours are not designated ahead of time. If CPP is to go into effect, the customer's energy service providers will typically inform customers up to twenty-four hours in advance. Critical peak prices can be three to ten times as high as standard rates.

Real-Time Pricing

Real-time pricing is a reflection of the actual hourly marginal cost of electricity, with prices generally based on hourly wholesale electricity prices. When used in a retail dynamic pricing program, the customer's electric service provider typically provides customers a schedule of hourly prices a day in advance. RTP can also be implemented on an hourly basis, with prices known an hour or less in advance. Real-time pricing places considerable risk on the customer, given the potential volatility of market prices. Retail service providers have generally shown limited interest in pure real-time pricing and when utilized have generally opted to provide prices a day in advance based on wholesale day ahead market prices.

Peak-Time Rebate

Another potential dynamic pricing option is the peak-time rebate. The peak-time rebate combines some of the security of flat or time-of-use rates with the pricing benefits of critical peak pricing. Under the peak-time rebate, customers are enrolled in either a flat rate or time-of-use rate. During critical peak events, participants in the peak-time rebate will be notified in

Time of Use Rate with Critical Peak Pricing

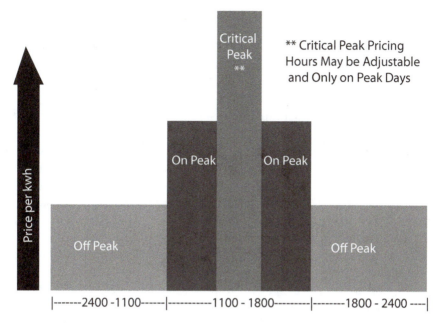

Time of Day

advance of the critical peak hours. Customers who reduce their demand during these hours will be rewarded with a rebate, but customers who do not reduce their energy will not be charged extra. Unlike other dynamic pricing programs, customers are eligible for a credit if they reduce load but face no additional penalty if their load rises during the critical peak hours.

CONSUMER PROTECTION CONCERNS

One potential problem for dynamic pricing is the concern that low-income customers may be negatively affected during high-price periods. Particularly with CPP rates, low-income people who live on a fixed income may be particularly vulnerable given the threat of balancing higher electricity bills with other living essentials such as food, health, and shelter. There is also concern for customers who have a medical or similar need for electricity. Such customers include those requiring pumped oxygen, air conditioning or filtering, refrigerated medicines, and similar electricity-powered aides. Even if the utility offers only peak-time rebates, which do not penalize a customer for failure to reduce demand at the critical peak hours, some fear that such customers may feel that they must reduce demand.[13] Analysis of utility programs demonstrates that a majority of low-income customers have actually benefitted from dynamic pricing and that low-income customers actively participate in these programs.[14] Consumer advocates have responded by raising concerns that these results may not be consistent from one jurisdiction or utility to the next, and that there has been no evidence that some portion of vulnerable customers will not be harmed.[15]

One option that has been utilized to reduce these fears is providing "bill protection" and shielding dynamic pricing customers from price risks by, for example, guaranteeing that in total they will only be charged up to the flat rate or some regulated rate such as a TOU rate. Bill protection has been used by some utilities as a means of phasing in dynamic pricing so that customers can feel comfortable before they face the full market risk. Indeed, if bill protection is offered for the first year after a customer is defaulted into a new dynamic pricing rate, bill protection may in the long term lead to greater customer participation and peak load reductions. Active customer engagement and education is critical to the success of dynamic pricing programs. Customers must in advance understand these more complex and risky rates as well as their options to respond to the price signals. However, to ensure that customers actively respond to price incentives, bill protection should be phased out over time.[16]

VOLUNTARY VERSUS DEFAULT SERVICE

Another significant policy debate is whether dynamic pricing programs should be voluntary or mandatory. Typically, three options are considered. One option, which is strongly supported by consumer advocates but not dynamic pricing proponents, is a voluntary opt-in service. Under voluntary opt-in service, a customer would participate in a dynamic pricing rate only if that customer affirmatively chooses to join that rate program. This option offers additional protection for a customer since they would not participate in this rate unless they choose to do so. If a customer makes a proactive choice to join a program, one can assume that they would be better informed of the consequences of their decision. The down side to voluntary opt-in programs is that participation rates tend to be significantly lower, which limits the overall peak reductions that can be achieved. A second voluntary option is default service with a customer opt-out provision. Under default service with opt-out, all customers are placed in some form of dynamic pricing program, but the customer has the option to leave that program and go to another rate option, including standard flat rates. Default opt-out service is seen as fostering significantly higher participation in dynamic pricing.

Finally, there is mandatory default service. Under mandatory default service, the customer is placed in a dynamic pricing program and is not allowed to move back to a standard flat rate. Consumer advocates do not favor this approach since it can place customers in a rate class in which they are not equipped to proactively participate. Mandatory default service may lead to increased enrollment in dynamic pricing programs and, combined with sufficient customer education, could lead to higher load reductions and increased environmental benefits. Both mandatory and opt-out default service places a higher burden on the utility for ensuring successful customer engagement and education to sufficiently prepare customers for these new rates.

Some utilities have demonstrated that voluntary opt-in rates can be moderately effective in attracting customers and achieving results. In 2010, the Salt River Project's TOU rate program achieved peak load reductions of 100 mW. As mentioned previously, SRP's prepay program has almost 116,000 customers, and it has achieved significant programmatic success. In the previous chapter, we also noted that Opower requires customers to be placed in its Home Energy Reports program on a default opt-out basis and has achieved very strong participation and significant results. However, placing a customer in an informational program by default does not raise the same concerns as default service for a more risky dynamic rate program. As discussed later in this chapter, SMUD's Smart Pricing Pilot has seen above average success with both its opt-in and default opt-out alternatives. California's IOUs have been experimenting with default opt-out dynamic pricing for larger commercial and industrial customers and transitioning customers with lower peak demand into the program. Retention rates for customers considering opting-out ranged from 36 to 60 percent at the three IOUs in California.[17] SMUD has proposed a new rate plan that would convert all customers to time-of-use rates by 2018 (commercial customers are already on TOU rates). According to SMUD, the "gradual multi-year transition will bring all customers in line with the true cost of electricity and will avoid some customers paying more than it costs for SMUD to serve them."[18]

SMART APPLIANCES AND PRICES TO DEVICES

In chapter 3, we discussed some means for encouraging active customer engagement through direct feedback, but there are new technological options that could supplement this approach. This alternative approach is sometimes referred to as the "prices to devices" or "set it and forget it" model. Under this approach, technology is being developed to automatically respond to prices so that customers do not have to monitor their usage on a daily basis.[19] The first adoption of this technology has been and will likely continue to be focused on smart thermostats. Given that in many parts of the country air conditioning load is the largest contributor to peak loads, there is significant opportunity for improvement.

What is a smart appliance? According to the Association of Home Appliance Manufacturers, a smart appliance "refers to a modernization of the electricity usage system of a home appliance so that it monitors, protects and automatically adjusts its operation to the needs of its owner." The trade association identifies three essential requirements for the smart grid's interaction with consumers:

1. Pricing must provide incentives to manage energy use more efficiently and enable consumers to save money.
2. Communication standards must be open, flexible, secure, and limited in number.
3. Consumer choice and privacy must be respected.[20]

Household appliance manufacturers such as General Electric and Whirlpool are making major strides in helping to define this technology. In Chicago, Whirlpool and ComEd have begun experimenting on a pilot basis with a variety of product and service offerings to both test what works in getting customers to sign up via "My Smart Appliance" apps and how to maximize energy savings.[21] The Whirlpool appliances are not just a vision for the future. Whirlpool has a refrigerator, dishwasher, and washer/dryer unit currently on sale, along with an iPhone app available for download.[22] Whirlpool is testing the waters in Chicago first, but it plans on rolling out the products across the country, even before utilities are ready to support such technology with dynamic pricing options. According to Warwick Stirling, Whirlpool's global director of energy and sustainability, "the energy piece is an interesting story, but not the most compelling one for the customer," since these new appliances are consumer goods with multiple features such as remote control, networking, and energy saving features. Whirlpool plans on connecting its appliances to the utility's AMI through residential WiFi networks, and it estimates that smart appliances could cost one hundred to two hundred dollars more than the nonnetworked equivalents. For the time being, Whirlpool is introducing its smart technology in its top-line models.[23]

General Electric is taking a slightly different approach and is introducing its smart diagnostics in all of its new models, and for now is focusing on improving the accuracy of its service calls.[24] GE has also participated in pilot programs with utilities such as Louisville Gas and Electric (LG&E) in order to test a variety of energy saving approaches to reduce power use during peak power periods, including delaying refrigerator defrost cycles, slightly powering down microwave ovens and delaying start times for dishwashers.[25] Participating households will also be equipped with smart appliances provided by Whirlpool and other manufacturers.

The Pecan Street Project is serving as a testing ground for smart appliance technology, as well as a demonstration project for consumer use and acceptance. The Pike Powers Commercialization Laboratory will provide opportunities to conduct field testing, establish interoperability among smart grid-enabled appliances, measure the impact of new equipment on the grid, and test prototype devices for standards compliance. This will give participating companies an opportunity to test their new and developing technology before it is deployed to consumer homes to ensure a positive experience for the study participants. Participating households will then be equipped with both Home Energy Management Systems and smart appliances provided by Whirlpool and other manufacturers as part of the demonstration project.

PRELIMINARY RESULTS FROM DYNAMIC PRICING

Early results indicate that customers respond to dynamic pricing by reducing electricity consumption during periods of peak demand. In Oklahoma, Oklahoma Gas & Electric (OG&E) partnered with Silver Spring Networks to distribute various home energy management devices—including programmable thermostats, in-home displays, and access to an online web portal—to nearly sixty-six hundred customers throughout OG&E's service territory.[26] The utility then allowed these consumers to opt in to one of two dynamic pricing plans—a time-of-use plan, in which prices would only change a few times per day, and a variable peak pricing plan, in which homeowners were notified of hourly changes in power prices based on wholesale market rates.[27] The devices provided customers with real-time information about their energy use and the current price of electricity, allowing those customers to manage their energy use in the most cost-effective manner possible. Upon review, Silver Spring found that customers reduced their peak energy use by anywhere between 11 percent (for those with in-home displays) and 33 percent (for those with programmable thermostats).

Interim results from SMUD's Smart Pricing Options Pilot (SPO) are equally interesting. SMUD's pilot included two recruitment strategies for customers. Some customers were allowed to voluntarily opt in to the SPO, while others were assigned on a default basis to dynamic pricing rates. The opt-in customers were allowed to choose from a TOU rate and a CPP rate. The default customers were assigned to a TOU rate, a CPP rate, or a rate that included both a TOU block as well as CPP. SMUD had opt-in rates of 16–19 percent, which exceeded their target and were high by industry standards. The default customers displayed extremely high enrollment rates (93–98%). Very few customers chose to drop out of the opt-in or default groups. The critical peak price rate for each of the groups was $0.75/kWh, the on-peak TOU rates were $0.27/kWh, and the off-peak rates ranged from $0.07/kWh to $0.18/kWh. The critical peak hours were 4:00–7:00 p.m. on up to twelve event days between June and September (approximately 1 percent of all summer hours), and the on-peak TOU hours were 4:00–7:00 p.m. on all nonholiday weekdays from June to September (approximately 10 percent of all summer hours). According to analysis of the SMUD program by Freeman, Sullivan, and Company, results for summer 2012 found that the average default customer on critical peak pricing reduced demand by approximately 12 percent, which was roughly half the reduction of opt-in customers, whose reductions exceeded 20 percent. The analysis also found that customers on the TOU/CPP rate had the same reduction on CPP event days but also produced an average 8 percent reduction on non-CPP event days. Based on the results of the SPO, if SMUD implemented new pricing options using default enrollment, aggregate impacts would be roughly twice as large on high-demand days, compared to an opt-in approach.[28]

Freeman, Sullivan, and Company also evaluated the nonresidential CPP programs in place for Pacific Gas and Electric, Southern California Edison, and San Diego Gas and Electric for 2011 and 2012. Each utility was analyzed separately, and demand reductions were in the range of 6 to 7 percent. PG&E and SCE each had critical peak periods from 2:00 to 6:00 p.m. on selected days, and SDG&E had a longer period, from 11:00 a.m. to 6:00 p.m. Event days varied by utility due to differing weather patterns across California.[29]

WHOLESALE MARKET PROGRAMS

As indicated above, local distribution utilities usually run retail demand response programs, and they do so by implementing dynamic pricing programs that encourage off-peak energy use. However, demand response can also act as a resource in wholesale electricity markets.[30] That is, demand response resources—as individuals or through aggregators like EnerNOC—can bid into wholesale markets just like a power plant could. Whereas generators supply additional electricity to meet demand, DR resources offer to reduce electric consumption to meet that demand. In this way, demand response resources not only help balance supply and demand, but they can also provide a cost-effective alternative to traditional generation resources. Demand response resources may be able to meet customer demand at a lower cost than dispatching additional generating resources. As more and more DR resources are integrated into wholesale markets, they will increase competition, which will, on the whole, put a downward pressure on wholesale electricity prices.[31] Finally, when demand response resources bid into wholesale markets, they can improve system reliability because they "can provide quick balancing of the electricity grid."[32]

Demand response has become relatively well integrated into the wholesale markets that are regulated by FERC (e.g., the ISO–New England, the New York ISO [NYISO], and the California ISO [CAISO]). A number of recent FERC decisions provide demand response resources with better access to wholesale energy and ancillary services markets and will increase the revenues that they can receive for the load reductions that they produce. For example, FERC has required that transmission planners treat all resources—including generators and demand response resources—comparably when engaging in transmission planning studies.[33] RTOs and ISOs must also consider DR resources on a comparable basis with all other resources in wholesale markets for ancillary services.[34] Finally, and perhaps most important, FERC has ordered that when demand response resources can cost effectively balance supply and demand in a wholesale market, those resources must be compensated at the prevailing market price for electricity, which is referred to as the locational marginal price (LMP).[35] In 2012, FERC reported that potential peak reduction for wholesale entities was 28,807 mW, which was a 26 percent increase over the 2010 potential reduction.[36]

DEMAND RESPONSE AGGREGATORS

Demand response aggregators have been critical to the growth of wholesale market programs. DR aggregators sign up end users to participate as a group in wholesale demand response markets. An aggregator is a business that sponsors demand response programs that recruit and contract with end users, and sell the aggregated demand response to utilities, RTOs and ISOs. In wholesale market jargon, an aggregator is also known as a "curtailment service provider." The demand response aggregation business has undergone fast growth with companies such as EnerNOC, Comverge, and Energy Curtailment Specialists managing thousands of megawatts of demand response. These businesses typically have their own centralized control centers that serve an intermediary function between the customer and the utility or system operator. Demand response aggregators have mostly been focused on larger commercial and industrial customers, given that their larger peak loads offer more opportunity for recovering implementation costs and earning a profit. One of the hurdles to providing demand response aggregation services has been the up-front cost to provide advanced metering and communications. With the ongoing rollout of smart meters and associated communications technology to residential and commercial customers, aggregators will be able to avoid incurring the up-front costs of these technologies and more cost-effectively serve these customer classes in the future. In addition, as DR aggregators seek to sign up residential customers, it is important to understand that motivating residential customers to reduce demand may take extra effort. One study noted that, to maximize benefits, "utilities [and third parties] must effectively educate, engage, and incentivize their customers to consume energy in a manner that is aligned with system and societal needs. Investments should prioritize deploying new media tools and applications that make customer feedback easy to access and understand."[37]

As the profit margins on providing retail energy services to residential customers have declined, retail service providers have looked to demand response as a service that allows them to differentiate themselves within a market. As a result, retail marketers have been acquiring demand response firms, including "Constellation Energy's purchase of CPower in 2010, Direct Energy's July [2013] purchase of Hess' energy marketing assets that includes DR offerings, and NRG Energy's August 22 [2013] purchase of Energy Curtailment Specialists."[38]

In regions where utilities remain vertically integrated, companies like EnerNOC have worked directly with the utility. In 2009, SRP selected EnerNOC to provide 50 mW of demand response under a three-year agreement. EnerNOC works with SRP to enroll a wide range of commercial, institutional, and industrial customers—such as shopping malls, data centers, schools, and other organizations—into SRP's PowerPartner. The SRP can count on EnerNOC to deliver significant reductions in just ten minutes, providing a much needed resource during peak demand.[39]

Economic Demand Response

As noted in the figure on page 68, demand response can participate in both reliability and economic product offerings in wholesale electricity markets. Simply put, economic demand response means that demand response resources can voluntarily reduce their electricity consumption in return for compensation. Economic demand response can participate in wholesale energy markets through load bids, which allows demand response to offer load reductions at the prevailing market price. FERC Order No. 745, which was issued in March 2011, requires that demand response resources be compensated at the full market price of energy when the resource is capable of balancing supply and demand in the wholesale energy market and it is cost effective. FERC reported that economic DR for 2012 represented approximately 4,066 mW.[40]

Reliability Demand Response

Reliability demand response consists of demand response resources participating in wholesale capacity, voluntary emergency energy, or ancillary services markets. Load as a capacity resource allows demand response to play an important role in ensuring resource adequacy within a region. Capacity resources are resources that count toward a region's installed reserve requirement—that is, the amount of generating capacity a regional system operator has under its control in order to meet expected peak load plus a reasonable amount of excess in reserve to account for system outages and unexpected events. ISOs model regional resource adequacy needs to evaluate how many megawatts of resources are needed in a region to meet reliability criteria. Generally, installed reserve requirements require that there are enough resources committed to a region to meet 110 to 115 percent of the region's forecast peak load. When demand response resources participate in capacity markets, they must demonstrate that they can curtail load on short notice. For providing this service, loads are eligible to receive monthly capacity payments. In 2012, load as a capacity resource provided 29 percent of all reported DR potential peak reduction.[41]

Another reliability-based DR program is emergency demand response. This voluntary demand response program provides incentive payments to customers for load reductions achieved during a system emergency. In 2010, emergency demand response was the dominant demand response program type, with 13,000 mW of capacity. In 2013, this figure dropped to 4,339 mW, with most of its capacity migrating to the capacity resource program.[42] As mentioned, there have historically been a significant number of utility run industrial interruptible load programs, but over time, those are largely being transitioned to wholesale market programs, including emergency demand response and load as a capacity resource.

The final category of wholesale DR programs is ancillary services. Ancillary services are meant to ensure the reliability of the grid and support the transmission of electricity to customer loads[43] as well as include regulation and operating reserves. Regulation provides increases and decreases in load in response to real-time signals from the system operator. Issued in October 2011, FERC Order No. 755 requires that resources providing regulation service that differed in their response rate should be compensated for the difference. Operating reserves, those resources that are essentially on "standby" to ensure that electrical service will continue in the event a contingency (i.e., loss of a generator or transmission line) occurs, require a demand resource to be available to provide demand reduction when called upon. In 2012, demand response resources provided 1,364 mW of ancillary services.

Direct Load Control

Direct load control is a form of demand response in which the demand response aggregator can turn off or cycle a participating customer's electrical equipment. According to FERC, DLC accounted for 9,777 mW of reported potential peak reduction in 2012, making it one of the largest demand response resources in the country in terms of potential peak load reductions.[44]

The driving force behind the growth in DLC is incentive payments that aggregators and their customers receive from participating in wholesale electricity market programs to provide energy, capacity, or ancillary services. The opportunities for utilizing DLC are numerous and include air conditioning, water heating, and refrigeration for residential loads; heat pumps, refrigeration, HVAC systems, and lighting for commercial loads; and induction and ladle metallurgy furnaces, agricultural irrigation, aluminum smelting, and water pumping for industrial loads.[45]

Direct load control offers significant opportunities for reducing peak load in the commercial sector and success can be amplified with participation from both the building owner and tenant. The landmark Empire State Building offers an interesting example: "During the Empire State Building Retrofit, Johnson Controls, Inc. discovered that it was able to submit 5% of a 10 mW peak load to DR programs from centrally controlled devices. When tenants were allowed to collectively bid into DR programs, facilitated by the building's management, DR capacity grew to 25% of the building peak load."[46]

MEASURING LOAD REDUCTION

The success of a DR program, including direct load control, is largely evaluated on whether the DR resource achieved its intended load reduction. Auditing this result can prove particularly difficult because the utility must measure the program's baseline load both before and after the load reduction occurred. Given data collection limitations, measuring demand reductions has historically been difficult. Monthly electric bills were the most readily available and least expensive option. Comparing electrical usage on a monthly or annual basis, adjusted for weather, would allow the utility to calculate a participating customer's pre- and post-program kWh reductions (or for customers on a demand rate, their kW reductions). Other than the customer's monthly bill, the utility would need to conduct some spot metering or more sophisticated building or end-use load research. This would involve either making special trips to the customer site to either read the meter more frequently or temporarily installing more sophisticated metering.[47]

Accordingly, accurate data is critical for calculating a DR baseline. Since the baseline determines both the level of DR delivered by the load as well as the payment the load should receive, it is important for utilities to accurately measure and audit peak load reductions. Bad data or faulty methodologies create opportunities for gaming. In fact, a number of the ISOs and RTOs have reported attempts to game these DR measures. As one example, in an August 29, 2013, order, FERC penalized a Maine paper mill and a consulting firm, requiring them to pay more than $14 million in penalties—including disgorgement of profits—for manipulating customer baseline levels for an ISO-NE demand response program.[48]

DEMAND RESPONSE AND RENEWABLE RESOURCES

There is significant literature that discusses the valuable role that DR, including direct load control, can play in integrating a large penetration of renewable resources.[49] DR's ability to provide valuable ancillary services— such as regulation and operating reserves—is being demonstrated in wholesale power markets today. Although various reports suggest that DR could play a significant role in integrating more renewable generation, analysis from PNNL and other sources suggests that both solar PV and wind resources could achieve local renewable portfolio standards of 20 percent without creating serious challenges to the existing grid infrastructure. Modeling by NREL has found the grid able to handle renewable penetrations up to 32% (10% PV, 10% CSP, and 12% wind) in 2030 and balance supply and demand.[50] It is not until renewables exceed these levels that smart grid technologies will become necessary to support renewables integration into the grid. In fact, PNNL's estimate of the ability of DR in 2030 to reduce energy use and carbon emissions for the additional ancillary service requirements was only equal to the energy equivalent of 0.02 percent of U.S. electricity consumption and associated carbon emissions.[51]

Although PNNL found that the direct benefit of the smart grid for renewables integration was modest up to 2030, the laboratory also estimated the potential indirect benefits of using DR and other smart grid technologies to support intermittent renewables with RPS of 25 percent.

According to PNNL's analysis, if the capital cost savings from not building this additional reserve generation capacity were invested in cost-effective energy efficiency or renewable generation, energy use and CO_2 emissions could fall by 5 percent.[52] For local regions that might meet or exceed a 25 percent penetration solar PV, a smart grid could help overcome future barriers by "controlling additional voltage regulators and batteries, and by providing short-circuit protection schemes that adapt to on-the-fly reverse power flow."[53]

CONCLUSION

Demand response has undergone dramatic growth, largely as a result of wholesale electric markets increasingly treating load reductions comparably to other generation resources. The introduction of smart meters and AMI will facilitate additional growth through retail dynamic pricing programs. By encouraging consumers to shift load to off-peak periods, DR achieves consumer benefits by making better use of existing generating capacity. As we discuss in depth in chapter 5, this principle is very important for achieving the true environmental promise of electric vehicles. However, analysis by the Pacific Northwest National Laboratory estimated that by 2030, load shifting on its own will contribute relatively little to reduced carbon emissions—only a 0.03 percent reduction. PNNL's analysis assumed an estimated 10 percent reduction in peak load. Given that system peak demand only happens for a very limited period of time (e.g., the hottest hours of the hottest summer days), the total number of hours that comprised this 10 percent reduction in peak demand only involved 168 hours that load was shifted downward.[54] Although demand response has important reliability and economic benefits, more work must be done to enhance its potential environmental benefits.

5

ACHIEVING THE ENVIRONMENTAL PROMISE OF THE ELECTRIC CAR

The car has transformed America perhaps more than any other machine, and its history in this country stretches back over a century. The oil boom of the 1860s coincided with a breakthrough in the design of the internal combustion engine. It was not until the early twentieth century, however, that the gas-powered car really gained traction among consumers. Early auto industrialists such as Henry Ford, William Durant, John and Horace Dodge, James Packard, and John Studebaker "developed a mechanized auto industry capable of delivering inexpensive cars to the masses."[1] At the time, however, car manufacturers were still debating key components of the automobile's construction, and it was far from certain that gasoline and the internal combustion engine would prevail as the leading model for the automobile. Indeed, a variety of viable fuels and engines, including steam-based and electric-based technologies, competed alongside the internal combustion engine for market share.[2] Notably, any one of these systems could have provided the foundation for the American transportation system.

The electric vehicle was a leading contender. The first practical storage battery, invented in 1859, allowed electric vehicle technology to advance alongside conventional vehicles.[3] In 1910, as Detroit witnessed the consolidation of the conventional automobile market (largely under the General Motors banner), twenty-seven companies were still selling electric vehicles.[4] But electric vehicles were generally slow and expensive, they took a long time to charge, and they had a very short battery range, which placed them at a competitive disadvantage.[5] These drawbacks paved the way for America to become, quite literally, an oil-driven society. By the early twentieth century, the gas-powered car had gained popular appeal. The expansion of the nation's road infrastructure in the 1920s and

1950s, alongside the relative low cost of vehicles, turned America in to a highly mobile society. By the end of that century, roughly 220 million motor vehicles were registered on American roads.[6]

Now, nearly one hundred years after electric car production stalled, people and policymakers are advocating for the (re)electrification of the American automobile. An increased awareness of the conventional automobile's downsides—such as its adverse effects on health and the environment, not to mention the foreign policy drawbacks of a transportation sector that is entirely dependent on oil—has spurred a movement to electrify the transportation sector. The question is, what will make the beginning of this century any different from the beginning of last one?

Many of the problems that plagued the electric car in the 1900s still linger today. First, although America has a more robust and developed electricity infrastructure, large portions of the electric distribution network need updating, especially if the grid is to support increased load from electric vehicles. Second, the network of public charging infrastructure for electric vehicles remains small, and is inadequate to support widespread electric vehicle deployment. Third, the limited range of electric car batteries contributes to consumer "range anxiety." Extensive road infrastructure and cheap, abundant oil have turned America into a highly mobile society. Electric vehicles, however, are ill equipped to travel long distances for extended periods of time, and consumers may be reluctant to shift to a technology that does not reflect this cultural norm.[7] Fourth, although electric batteries are generally more efficient than the internal combustion engine at converting fuel into mechanical energy, batteries have less energy density than gasoline—that is, they must use more energy to go the same distance as a conventional vehicle.[8] So far it has been too costly for manufacturers to develop a battery that has an energy capacity equivalent to a full tank of gasoline. Finally, although charging times have dropped to as low as an hour, this time span remains significantly longer than the five minutes it takes to fill up a tank of gasoline. From a consumer convenience perspective, extended charging times could be a big downside to electric vehicles.

Although smart grid technology cannot solve all of these problems, it can help automakers, utilities, and the public address some of these barriers and facilitate wider adoption of electric vehicle technology. Policies that coordinate smart grid implementation and electric vehicle deployment can help utilities ensure that consumers and society realize the full economic and environmental benefits of electric vehicles. Specifically, utilities can

- use the smart grid to provide dynamic pricing structures that encourage low-cost charging behavior (thus allowing consumers to recover the cost of their electric vehicle and charging equipment through lower fuel costs),

- design and deploy public and private charging infrastructure compatible with smart grid technologies,
- use electricity usage data from smart meters and other advanced metering infrastructure to identify areas requiring distribution network updates (thus providing consumers with access to charging infrastructure without compromising grid reliability), and
- develop and deploy vehicle-to-grid (V2G) technologies (which can turn electric vehicle batteries into back-up capacity during times of high demand).

This chapter first provides an overview of the current state of electric vehicle technology in the United States and familiarizes the reader with the progress and challenges of the industry. It will then describe the benefits of electric vehicles, focusing specifically on the economic and environmental advantages of oil independence. Finally, it will draw upon case studies to analyze how utilities can use the smart grid to facilitate the widespread, commercial-scale deployment of electric vehicles and present recommendations that policymakers, utilities, and auto manufacturers should embrace to facilitate widespread EV use and ensure that early adopters have a positive experience.

ELECTRIC VEHICLE TECHNOLOGY

According to the California Air Resources Board, "No technological barrier [exists] to building battery powered [electric vehicles]; the issue is cost and consumer acceptance."[9] Historically, although technological constraints have limited the range and increased the cost of electric vehicles,[10] using electricity to power motor vehicles is no difficult feat of engineering. Rather, developing a low-cost, long-range electric vehicle that can compete with conventional vehicles—and thus gain traction among consumers—is the real challenge. As a result, American automakers have been reluctant to make the investments necessary to deploy electric vehicles on a widespread, commercial basis.[11] Companies that manufactured electric vehicles did so in such small numbers that they were unable to obtain the necessary economies of scale that lower costs for the broader public.[12] However, recent technological advances have made deploying electric vehicles on a broader, commercial basis more feasible and more profitable. Thus a number of electric vehicles—most notably, the Chevrolet Volt and the Nissan Leaf—became commercially available at the end of 2010. Several market forecasts predict that further progress will be made to lower costs and increase electric vehicle adoption among consumers.

When discussing electric vehicles, it is important to clarify terminology. The term "electric vehicle" is broad and can refer to a variety of technologies: hybrid electric vehicles (HEVs), plug-in hybrid electric vehicles (PHEVs), and pure electric vehicles. These vehicles differ with respect to how much they rely on electric power from their batteries for propulsion. Whereas the HEV relies on the battery only at low speeds, PHEVs and EVs can operate entirely on battery power at any speed for any given distance but must be recharged (by being plugged in to the grid) periodically. Battery sizes and operating capacity therefore vary for each vehicle. But generally speaking, all electric vehicles are more efficient and emit fewer GHGs than conventional vehicles.

Hybrid electric vehicles such as the Toyota Prius, the Honda Insight, the Ford C-MAX Hybrid, and the Lexus LS600 are the most widely available and popular electric vehicle models. They generally cost between twenty-three thousand and thirty-five thousand dollars (depending on the make and model) and have quickly gained market share, growing from .05 percent of all new vehicle sales in 2000 to 2.8 percent in 2012—a fifty-six-fold increase over twelve years.[13] HEVs retain an internal combustion engine but include a battery that provides energy to an electric motor, which in turn propels the vehicle at low speeds (typically between 0 and 30 mph).[14] HEV batteries recharge through regenerative braking, a process whereby the battery recaptures "otherwise discarded kinetic energy during braking,"[15] as well as through the internal combustion engine. HEVs are also programmed to shut down the internal combustion engine when the vehicle is stopped for a certain amount of time. They have better fuel economy and emit fewer GHGs than conventional vehicles.[16] However, unlike PHEVs or EVs, HEVs still obtain most of their energy from petroleum; thus, they represent less of an "electric vehicle" and more of a highly efficient conventional vehicle.[17]

Plug-in hybrid electric vehicles are a more recent development in the electric vehicle market, even though they use much of the same technology as HEVs. General Motors released the Chevrolet Volt at the end of 2010, which was the first commercial PHEV available on the market[18] and cost about forty thousand dollars.[19] The major difference between an HEV and PHEV is that the latter has "a larger battery and a plug-in charger that allows electricity from the grid to replace a portion of the petroleum-fueled drive energy."[20] This battery stores 16 kWh of energy and can propel the vehicle solely on electric power within the vehicle's designated electric range (the Volt's battery pack has a range of about forty miles, depending on driving conditions).[21] Once the PHEV exceeds its all-electric range, it runs on the internal

Participants in Pecan Street Inc.'s Smart Grid Demonstration Project with Pecan Street Staff and some of the 100 Chevrolet Volts involved in the project. (Photo courtesy of Pecan Street, Inc.)

combustion engine and electric motor, much like a conventional hybrid. Owners can charge their battery through an external charger and regenerative braking.[22] Thus PHEVs represent a technological middle ground between HEVs and pure EVs because although they are capable of running on a pure electric charge, their internal combustion engine serves as a backup in the event that the electric charge is depleted.[23]

Pure EVs, such as the Tesla Roadster and the Nissan Leaf, are truly all-electric automobiles because they are designed without an internal combustion engine. Pure electric vehicles rely solely on their battery to store energy that powers the electric motor, which in turn propels the vehicle.[24] Like the PHEV, the electric vehicle battery is recharged by plugging the vehicle in to an external charger. EVs have a longer electric range than PHEVs (the Leaf has an 80-mile range and the Tesla Roadster has a 220-mile range, depending on driving conditions), but a shorter range than conventional vehicles.[25] The Leaf costs around thirty-two thousand dollars, but state and federal tax breaks can help reduce that cost to as low as nineteen thousand dollars.[26] Consumers purchasing an EV like the Leaf will most likely want to install a 240-volt home charging station rather than rely on the slower 120-volt charging available from a typical wall outlet. These home charging stations generally cost about two thousand dollars, but federal tax incentives can cover 30 percent.[27]

BATTERY TECHNOLOGY

Battery cost and performance is the most important factor—and has been the biggest constraint—in making electric vehicles competitive with conventional vehicles.[28] To understand why, some technical background information is useful. There are two fundamental characteristics of battery technology.[29] The first is power density, which is a rate of energy transfer that affects how quickly a vehicle can accelerate. The second is energy density, which measures a battery's capacity to store energy and affects the range that a vehicle can travel.[30] In traditional vehicles, where the battery is used for ancillary functions such as powering the stereo, air conditioning, or headlights, neither of these values need be very high. Thus standard lead-acid batteries, which have a low power density, are well suited for conventional vehicles.[31] However, they are ill suited for electric vehicles, which must travel long distances and require greater electric charge.[32]

Nickel-metal-hydride (NiMH) and lithium-ion batteries represent an improvement upon the traditional lead-acid chemistry, but even these more advanced batteries cannot match the energy density of fossil fuels like gasoline. NiMH batteries have a high power density and a lower energy density,[33] making them well suited for hybrid electric vehicles, which use their batteries primarily "to store energy captured during braking and use this energy to boost acceleration."[34] That is, HEVs do not need batteries that can store a great deal of energy, but they do need a lot of power to support rapid acceleration.[35] Lithium-ion batteries are the most advanced—and most expensive—battery technology available for electric vehicles. Lithium-ion technologies are used extensively in consumer electronics, but have only recently been applied in the electric vehicle setting. They have a high power density and high energy density, which means they can provide rapid acceleration and extended range.[36] The Nissan Leaf and the Chevrolet Volt use varieties of lithium-ion technology.[37]

Despite these advances, batteries still cannot provide electric vehicles with the same range as conventional vehicles. This is primarily because a tank of gasoline has an energy density that far and away surpasses the energy density of a fully charged battery.[38] Although electric batteries are more efficient at converting fuel into energy, it takes forty times as much of that energy to propel an electric vehicle the same distance as a conventional vehicle.[39] Accordingly, efforts to develop a battery that rivals gasoline in energy density has proven costly.

There are a number of other technological obstacles that have hindered electric battery development—and thus, electric vehicles generally. First and foremost, battery costs are high: Although data on electric vehicle batteries is proprietary (and therefore confidential), it is estimated that batteries cost anywhere from six thousand to eighteen thousand dollars per vehicle.[40] Second, batteries are not very durable.[41] Electric vehicles need batteries that will last throughout the vehicle's life span, but battery cycling—the process of depleting and recharging a battery—inevitably reduces the amount of energy that a battery can store. Therefore, the more consumers charge their batteries (which they will obviously have to do), the more they will shorten the life of that battery. Furthermore, overcycling—that is, allowing the battery to become deeply depleted or overcharged—can damage battery health. Therefore, manufacturers have built batteries to have a 20 percent "reserve margin" at either end of the charge so that only 50–60 percent of the battery's storage capacity is ever used. While this increases battery longevity, it also increases cost.[42] Finally, ambient air temperatures affect battery performance. Although batteries can be designed to operate in high or low temperatures, it's difficult to engineer them to function efficiently in all environments.[43]

Despite these historical technological constraints, innovations in the private sector and government investment have spurred promising advances in battery technology. As a result, deploying electric vehicles on a widespread, commercial basis has recently become more technologically and economically feasible.[44] Government funding for research and development into electric battery technology in motor vehicles increased from $20 million in 2002 to almost $70 million in 2009.[45] The Obama administration provided an additional $2.4 billion in the American Recovery and Reinvestment Act to establish domestic electric vehicle battery and component manufacturing plants.[46] The Department of Energy expects that this investment could reduce battery costs by as much as 90 percent and give the United States the capacity to produce 40 percent of the world's advanced vehicle batteries.[47]

Moreover, private sector research and development indicates that the electric battery market holds a promising future. Researchers at MIT have published details on a new semisolid flow cell battery design that could "boost battery storage capacity many times today's levels and could even make 'refueling' . . . as quick and easy as pumping gas into a conventional car."[48] Researchers at the University of Illinois have likewise developed an electric battery that would allow electric vehicles to recharge in a matter of minutes.[49] Toyota has partnered with a company called WiTricity to develop a system by which electric vehicles could charge wirelessly, through radio waves that emanate from a charging station—or even from copper wires that are laid beneath the surface of a road.[50] The National Energy Technology Laboratory in Pittsburgh has received a $12-million research grant from the Department of Energy for similar wireless charging research.[51]

Perhaps most important, battery costs have decreased over the last decade. Although they still remain high, costs for NiMH batteries have decreased from $1,000 per kWh in 1999 to as low as $500 per kWh today, and costs for lithium-ion batteries have fallen from $1,600 per kWh to anywhere from $750 to $1,000 per kWh in that same period.[52] Some have projected that the cost for lithium-ion batteries will further decrease to as low as $235 per kWh by 2020.[53] Ultimately, reducing battery costs and improving battery performance will be crucial to the future success of electric vehicles.

THE COSTS OF OIL DEPENDENCE

Electric vehicles hold enormous potential to produce significant environmental and economic benefits by reducing American dependence on petroleum. Petroleum, of course, is one of the most useful resources on this planet. It is a feedstock in products such as plastics, solvents, polyurethane, asphalt, and hundreds of consumer goods.[54] Most petroleum, however, is refined from light crude oil to motor fuel for the transportation sector. In fact, the transportation sector accounted for about 72 percent of daily American oil consumption in 2011.[55] Thus while petroleum has many uses, its primary and perhaps most important function is to facilitate commerce.[56] Despite its utility, the economic, political and environmental costs associated with oil are enormous. Switching to a electricity-based transportation sector can help relieve these costs, and smart grid technologies can help facilitate that transition.

Economic Costs

America consumes a disproportionate amount of oil relative to the rest of the world, imposing enormous direct costs on the overall American economy.[57] Although foreign petroleum imports have dropped since 2006, America still imports about 45 percent of the oil it consumes.[58] American oil dependence has transferred an unprecedented amount of wealth—more than $2.57 trillion between 1970 and 2008—to oil exporting nations.[59] But as one author notes, "Oil dependence is not simply a matter of how much oil we import. It is a syndrome, a combination of factors that together create economic, political and military problems. It is comprised of the concentration of the world's oil supply in a small group of oil producing states that wield monopoly power, together with the demand-side vulnerability of the U.S. economy to higher oil prices and price shocks."[60]

Indeed, oil price and/or supply shocks have preceded every recession in the last forty years.[61] When factoring in the cost of GDP losses (from the above-market oil prices that monopoly cartels like OPEC impose) and the costs of market dislocations (from sudden price and supply shocks), the total direct economic costs of American dependence on foreign oil are between $2.7 and $4.7 trillion since 1970.[62] These oil shocks have also slowed American macroeconomic growth. Sudden spikes in oil prices effectively act as an additional tax on consumption, reducing consumer discretionary spending and weakening the overall economy.[63]

Electrifying the vehicle fleet would mitigate many of these problems by reducing transportation costs and creating greater economic and environmental stability. For one thing, the electricity market is not as susceptible to price and supply shocks as is the oil market.[64] Retail electricity prices reflect a wide range of costs, most of which are fixed capital costs associated with building, maintaining, and operating power plants, transmission lines, and distribution lines.[65] As a result, the "cost of fuel represents a smaller percentage of the overall cost of delivered electricity than the cost of crude oil represents as a percentage of the cost of retail gasoline."[66] Additionally, the fuels used in electricity generation are more diverse than those used in the transportation sector, making the price of electricity less dependent on the whims of the market for one particular type of fuel.

It is partly for these reasons that electricity prices have historically been less volatile than oil prices. Since 1960, the average real price for a gallon of gasoline has fluctuated by about 8 percent on a year-to-year basis—and about 13 percent in the last decade—but has increased overall by a staggering 89 percent.[67] By contrast, during this same period, the average real price of electricity across all end-use sectors fluctuated, on average, by only 3 percent annually,[68] and real electricity prices have actually declined by about 9 percent.[69] Thus retail electricity prices are more stable than retail gasoline prices, and have in fact declined over the last forty years.

Moreover, evidence suggests that electricity is actually a cheaper vehicle fuel than gasoline on a per-mile basis. Given the average retail price of electricity (about 8 cents/kWh) and the average price of a gallon of gasoline (about $2.19/gallon) over the last ten years,[70] it would cost roughly .04 cents/mile to operate an electric vehicle with a fuel economy of only 2 miles/kWh, but more than twice as much (about .09 cents/mile) to operate a conventional vehicle with a fuel economy of 22 miles/gallon.[71] Of course, fuel economy standards for conventional vehicles are constantly improving, which would make them more competitive with electric vehicles over time in terms of fuel costs. But if the price trends for gasoline and electricity continue the course that they have maintained for the last half-century, it is unlikely that even the most fuel-efficient conventional vehicles will remain competitive, especially as electric vehicles become more efficient themselves.

Political Costs

There are also political drawbacks to American oil dependence, for "no other commodity has been so intimately intertwined with national strategies and global power as oil."[72] Much of the foreign oil on which America depends comes from nations that are politically volatile or that harbor hostilities toward America. Geographically, about two-thirds of world oil reserves are concentrated in OPEC nations,[73] and more than half of American imports come from these nations.[74] OPEC nations have—with varying degrees of success—instituted embargos to raise global oil prices and thereby influence western foreign policy.[75] Some OPEC states, notably Iran, openly harbor anti-American sentiments or have used oil revenues to fund terrorist organizations.[76] Other oil-producing states are politically volatile or unstable, and the United States government must spend an enormous amount of military time and resources to defend oil assets in these countries. One recent study put the cost defending American oil assets in the Persian Gulf in the range of $29 to $75 billion per year.[77] Since the oil embargoes of the early 1970s, American foreign policy has been primarily oriented toward maintaining control of or access to strategic oil reserves in the Middle East: In the last two decades, America has fought two wars in Iraq, both of which were motivated by a desire—at least in part—to assure American oil security in the region.[78] Not only have these wars substantially increased federal budget deficits, but they have also intensified anti-American sentiment throughout the globe—particularly in the Middle East.

Although a certain degree of geopolitics and international brinksmanship comes with any energy resource, electrifying the electric vehicle fleet would significantly reduce the foreign policy repercussions that have attended America's oil addiction. In particular, electrifying America's light-duty vehicle fleet would improve American energy security because most of the resources that fuel the electric power sector—coal, natural gas, nuclear, and renewables—come from either the United States or North America. The United States is a net exporter of coal, which generates the bulk of American electricity.[79] The United States also produces over 90 percent of the natural gas it consumes.[80] What natural gas America does import comes mostly from Canada.[81] Although the majority of uranium used in American nuclear reactors is imported,[82] nuclear power generates less than half the electricity that coal does; thus, because nuclear power is but *one component* of the electric power sector—unlike gasoline, which is virtually the sole transportation fuel—there is perhaps greater leeway for America to depend on foreign imports for uranium. Finally, renewable resources such as hydropower, wind, solar, and geothermal are all domestic resources. Although wind turbines and solar panels are often imported, domestic manufacturers are certainly capable of producing these components.

Given that most of the resources fueling the American electric power sector are domestically produced, electrifying the vehicle fleet will improve American energy security. Rather than subject automobile owners to the whims of hostile foreign states and the volatile global market for petroleum, American consumers can instead rely on domestic (and increasingly cleaner) resources to get where they're going. More important, the United States government can spend less time subsidizing wars and defending foreign oil assets, and more time developing domestic resources—especially renewable energy. Indeed, according to one study, for the ultimate price of the Iraq war (about $3.9 trillion), the United States could have installed a half million to over a million megawatts of wind and solar capacity. Put differently, had the American government devoted the public funds it spent in Iraq to subsidizing renewable energy, the nation could be generating 21–38 percent of its electricity from renewable resources.[83] In sum, electrifying the vehicle fleet will not only reduce American oil dependence, but will also reduce the geopolitical consequences of that dependence, which could spur revolutionary opportunities in America's renewables sector.

Environmental Costs

Oil dependency has a devastating effect on the natural environment. American automobiles are a significant source of GHG emissions, including NO_x and CO_2. Indeed, the transportation sector "has led all U.S. end-use sectors in emissions of carbon dioxide since 1999,"[84] and petroleum itself is "the largest fossil fuel source for energy-related CO_2 emissions" in the United States.[85] Finding a cleaner and less carbon intensive means of fueling the American transportation sector is thus a crucial component of any campaign to reduce America's contribution to global climate change. Indeed, if the United States and the rest of the world do not take drastic steps to reduce these emissions, this phenomenon could produce drastic and devastating consequences. Some of these symptoms have already been observed throughout the world and are expected to continue into the twenty-first century.[86]

The oil extraction process has devastating consequences for human health and the environment. Extraction requires companies to construct "access roads, drilling infrastructure, and [other] associated infrastructure," which often opens up remote—and in some cases, environmentally sensitive—areas to poachers, loggers, and other negative human impacts.[87] Terrestrial drilling (as opposed to offshore drilling) also produces a vast quantity of "drilling mud" and contaminated water, which is highly toxic and must be treated with chemicals before being released back into the environment.[88] Offshore oil development, which is becoming increasingly popular as terrestrial supplies of oil dry up, produces an average of 180,000 gallons of polluted water per year, "releasing toxic metals including mercury, lead, and cadmium into the local environment."[89] And of course, there is the occasional oil spill, which has devastating effects on both the immediate ecosystem and the human population that depends on that ecosystem. Larger spills—such as that of the *Exxon-Valdez* in 1989 or Deepwater Horizon drilling rig in 2010— often receive the most press because of their far-reaching effect; however, millions of gallons of oil, fracking fluid, wastewater, and other liquids" are spilled at production sites every year, sometimes creating devastating effects on the localized environment.[90]

Pollution from end-use petroleum consumption is likewise a serious environmental issue. America's light-duty vehicle fleet is a significant source of nitrous oxide, volatile organic compounds, and fine particulate matter (PM 2.5) emissions, all of which have an adverse effect on human health and the environment. NO_X, for example, is a greenhouse gas that contributes to global warming. Moreover, when it combines in the atmosphere with SO_2 pollution from other fossil-fuel combustion activities, NO_X creates acid precipitation that has damaged forest and water ecosystems across the eastern seaboard, as well as in Europe. Although the acid rain problem has received less attention in recent years, VOCs and PM 2.5 remain significant sources of air pollution. VOCs, for example, react with sunlight to create ozone, a compound that contributes to asthma, chronic bronchitis, and other cardiovascular problems in humans, and that can further contribute to a decline in crop yields.[91] Particulate matter, such as smaller—and more insidious—PM 2.5, poses a similar risk to human health, as it has been linked to heart attacks, congestive heart failure, strokes, decreased lung functions, and asthma.[92]

Finally, as yields from conventional oil supplies peak, companies will turn increasingly toward unconventional supplies (e.g., oil sands, oil shale, and deepwater offshore drilling), each of which presents unique environmental problems. For one thing, these drilling practices can scar entire landscapes. When extracting oil sands, for example,[93] producers must dig up hundreds of tons of topsoil to prepare the site for drilling.[94] Oil shale[95] production requires producers to mine large quantities of rock, crush the rock, heat it to extreme temperatures ("retorting"), and then recover the leftover oil.[96] The biggest environmental concern associated with shale extraction centers on land use, as only about one-fifth of the rock that is mined for shale production can be retorted into usable oil and gas.[97]

Exploiting shale resources thus creates "permanent topographic changes," spurs habitat and biodiversity loss, and can require oil producers to construct additional infrastructure to gain access to the drill site—which puts additional pressure on land and animals (especially where shale resources are located in remote areas).[98] Furthermore, unconventional drilling practices raise water quantity and quality concerns. For instance, the extraction and processing of oil sands not only requires a high volume of water but also creates surface and ground water contamination risks.[99]

Of course, using electricity in lieu of oil as the primary fuel for the transportation sector will not necessarily alleviate these environmental problems. This transition would simply require Americans to trade one fossil fuel, oil, for another—coal or natural gas. After all, almost two-thirds of electricity in America comes from the combustion of these two resources.[100] Like oil, coal and natural gas are the product of environmentally harmful extraction techniques—such as mountaintop removal, strip mining, and hydrofracking—and when combusted to generate electricity, they also produce GHGs and other harmful pollutants. In this way, electrifying the vehicle fleet would do little to improve environmental quality: Any reductions in environmental harms from the oil sector would effectively be offset by increases in environmental harms from the coal and natural gas sectors.

The electric power industry's dependence on fossil fuels is certainly a matter of concern, and it is something that must be addressed if society is to harness the true environmental potential of electric vehicles. Despite this shortcoming, from an environmental standpoint electric cars remain preferable to conventional vehicles. For one thing, renewables are likely to gain greater market share in the electric power sector as time goes on. Depending on what happens with natural gas prices, current projections strongly suggest that coal will remain the largest source of electricity in the United States over the next two decades.[101] However, coal's overall share of aggregate electricity production is expected to fall as more renewables and natural gas plants are built.[102] In fact, renewables' share of generating capacity is projected to grow at a faster annual rate than any other resource in the American electricity mix.[103] Renewables could grow at an even faster rate if the federal government creates additional incentives, such as permanently extending the investment tax credit or the production tax credit, or if the EPA implements broad-based policies to reduce GHGs, such as a carbon tax.[104] In this way, electrifying the vehicle fleet would not require Americans to trade one fossil fuel for another. Instead, these policies could actually shift the transportation sector away from fossil fuels and toward a greener, renewable-based future.

In any event, even if electric vehicles ran on electricity from combusted fossil fuels, they would still produce fewer GHG emissions than their conventional counterparts. This is because electric motors are far and away more efficient than the internal combustion engine. Whereas the internal combustion engine converts only 20–30 percent of gasoline's potential energy into mechanical energy, electric motors have a conversion factor of almost 90 percent.[105] For this reason, electric vehicles actually use less energy and therefore create fewer emissions than conventional vehicles. Indeed, whereas conventional vehicles typically emit 450 grams of CO_2 per mile ($g/CO_2/mile$), an electric vehicle produces about 325 $g/CO_2/mile$, even when the electricity it consumes comes from a fossil-fuel resource like coal. If that electricity were to come from a renewable resource, this figure would drop to 125 $g/CO_2/mile$.[106] Accordingly, the widespread deployment of electric vehicles could significantly reduce emissions and energy use in the transportation sector. PNNL estimates that given today's mix of power plants and vehicles, if three-quarters of the current light-duty vehicle fleet were replaced with electric vehicles, there would be a 30 percent improvement in energy consumption per vehicle mile traveled and a 27 percent reduction in transportation-related CO_2 emissions.[107]

In short, even though fossil fuels dominate the electricity sector, this is no excuse to avoid electrifying the vehicle fleet. The efficiency of the electric motor relative to the internal combustion engine is reason enough to begin the transition immediately. And as renewables continue to gain market share, an electrified vehicle fleet will replace fossil fuels' overall share of the American energy mix at an increasing rate.

THE ROLE OF THE SMART GRID

The smart grid is integral to facilitating the commercial-scale deployment of electric vehicles and to ensuring that society realizes the full economic and environmental benefits of this technology. Widespread electric vehicle integration will create an additional load that the existing bulk power system must serve. Utilities must plan to cost effectively meet this additional load, without compromising system reliability or environmental quality. The smart grid can help achieve this objective in several ways. First, advanced metering infrastructure enables utilities and customers to record and communicate price and consumption information on a timely basis. This AMI will allow utilities to establish dynamic pricing schemes that incentivize consumers to charge their vehicles during off-peak hours, when demand for electricity is lowest. PNNL estimated that this "smart charging" would allow the grid to support eighteen million more PHEVs and EVs beyond that which could be supported with unmanaged charging.[108] Second, the smart grid will enable V2G technology to turn electric vehicles into valuable distributed storage capability from which the grid can draw during peak hours. Finally, AMI can provide utilities with consumer-use data to determine when and where charging infrastructure is needed, and to assess when distribution infrastructure may need upgrades. It is also important for utilities, third-party companies, and policymakers to consider what sort of business models will be most conducive to deploying charging infrastructure. The remainder of this chapter will consider these issues in turn.

Dynamic Pricing

Consumer demand for electricity varies on a daily and seasonal basis. Although the electric power sector must be prepared to instantaneously meet this demand, it does not need to use all available capacity all of the time. On a daily basis, electricity demand typically peaks in the morning before most people go to work or school (between 6:00 and 9:00 a.m.) and after they get home (between 5:00 and 9:00 p.m.); it is the lowest during overnight periods. Seasonally, demand typically peaks in the summer but is lowest in the spring.[109] Utilities build enough generating capacity to meet peak demand, whether on a daily or seasonal basis, but because demand eventually subsides from that peak level, full capacity is not always necessary. Indeed, a majority of capacity sits idle during the nighttime, when demand is at an all-time low.

Practically speaking, the fact that a majority of capacity sits idle or runs at less than full capacity increases the cost of the electric power system. The average capacity factor[110] for all energy sources between 1998 and 2009 was about 49.8 percent.[111] This means that the United States utilized less than half of all available generation to meet consumer demand. From a reliability standpoint, that's a good thing because it shows that we have more than enough capacity to meet demand. But from an economic standpoint, it's costly because even though utilities are not using this idle generation, they must still recover the costs associated with building and maintaining it. They do this by including the fixed costs associated with idle generating units into their retail rate structure. Moreover, when utilities "cycle" these units—that is, turn them on or off in response to consumer demand—operation and maintenance costs associated with those units increases. Indeed, constantly turning electric generating units on and off is an expensive process.[112] Thus, idle generation, as well as the cycling of that generation, increases retail electricity rates for all consumers.

However, if charging habits are properly managed, integrating electric vehicles into the grid can actually *reduce* the costs of the electric system. Charging electric vehicles during off-peak hours (i.e., overnight) reduces demand growth on the system by shifting load away from peak hours. This levels out the load curve by moving load to the low-demand hours, maximizing the use of existing capacity, and ultimately lowering retail electricity rates. Off-peak charging would be an obvious benefit to individual electric vehicle owners, who would pay less during off-peak hours to charge their vehicles than they would during peak hours. In this way, off-peak charging allows everybody to win:

> Delivering more electricity with the existing infrastructure can be a boon to all electricity consumers. While the total number of customers served by a given utility will remain relatively static, adding electric vehicles will increase the total amount of electricity consumed by its customers. This means that the investments a utility has made in its existing infrastructure will be spread over a larger base, which will have a positive impact on electric rates. All customers of the utility could experience reduced electricity rates due to the fixed investments in infrastructure being spread over a greater amount of electricity delivered by the utility.[113]

Utilities could use any variety of the pricing schemes described in chapter 4—including time-of-use rates, critical peak pricing, and real-time pricing—to encourage off-peak charging. Indeed, our case study analysis finds that most, if not all, utilities have implemented some sort of time-of-use or dynamic pricing scheme for electric vehicle charging in their service territory. Some utilities apply existing time-of-use rates for electric vehicle charging, eliminating the need for creating a special "electric vehicle tariff."[114] Under this rate structure, the vehicle owner does not install a separate meter for her electric vehicle, and so these rates apply to the entire household.[115] Others establish special TOU rates for which only electric vehicle owners are eligible. These special rates usually require the customer to install two meters on his property—one to measure the vehicle's electricity consumption, and another to measure the rest of the household's electricity consumption. The utility applies different rates to each type of consumption: The electric vehicle pays the TOU rate, while the rest of the household is on a separate rate structure.[116] Although TOU rates are typically voluntary pricing programs, utilities will usually require that a consumer who signs up for the TOU rate remain on that pricing structure for a certain amount of time—typically one year. Finally, absent a special TOU rate, utilities

SDG&E Experience Suggests EV TOU Rates Are Effective

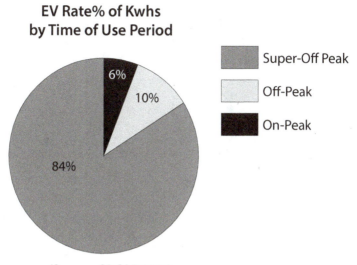

EV Rate% of Kwhs by Time of Use Period

Super-Off Peak

Off-Peak

On-Peak

6%

10%

84%

(Source: SDG&E 2011)

may charge a flat rate for electric vehicle charging, which largely removes the consumer's incentive to charge during off-peak hours. This latter approach would subsequently prove the least environmentally friendly of the options.[117]

San Diego Gas & Electric, for example, has established TOU rates for residential customers, which it hopes will encourage off-peak charging habits among electric vehicle owners.[118] The company's existing rate structure allows customers with electric vehicles to set their cars on one of two rate types. The customer can choose to set their electric vehicles on an EV-TOU rate, which is a separate rate from the usual residential rate. Thus customers who opt for this rate would have to install a second meter at their home. However, if the customer wants to meter his home and electric vehicle electricity consumption together, the "EV-TOU-2" rate provides one meter for these purposes.[119] This would spare customers the expense of paying for a separate meter. Regardless of which rate the customer chooses, the same pricing structure controls: Depending on the time of the customer's electricity use, rates range from as low as 14 cents/kWh (off-peak hours, midnight–5:00 a.m.) to 26 cents/kWh (peak hours, 12:00–6:00 p.m.), with the shoulder periods set at 16 cents/kWh.

Commonwealth Edison, which serves customers in the Chicago metropolitan area, offers three different pricing schemes for its customers.

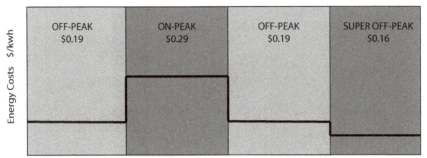

The basic electric service (BES) rate is a fixed-price rate that varies seasonally but not hourly. Thus consumers on a BES rate have no incentive to charge during nonpeak hours.[120] ComEd's second tariff option, the basic electric service hourly rate (BESH), charges consumers for electricity based on the real-time hourly wholesale price of electricity. Thus consumers would have an incentive to charge their vehicles during off-peak hours, when electricity is cheaper. Finally, consumers can opt for a retail delivery service rate (RDS), where they receive electricity not from ComEd but another retail provider instead.[121] ComEd's own studies indicate that the BESH rate is the best option for electric vehicle owners. Residential customers who opt for a BESH rate and have a level 1 charging station could cut their annual electricity costs by 27–67 percent; those using a level e charging station, which charges electric vehicles at a faster rate, could cut their annual electricity costs by anywhere between 9 and 72 percent.[122]

Finally, unlike SDG&E and ComEd, the Salt River Project, a public power entity located in Arizona, does not anticipate having to change its current pricing plans to accommodate electric vehicles. Although it offers three price plans to electric vehicle owners, these plans come from the utility's current rate structure. These customers can stay on SRP's "basic" price plan, which is a standard flat rate that may vary slightly by season and amount of power consumed. SRP warns that this pricing program would probably not be the most economical for electric vehicle owners.[123] SRP also offers its EZ-3 rate, under which customers are charged a higher rate between 3:00 and 6:00 p.m. on weekdays. Under the EZ-3 rate structure, between November and April, SRP charges customers $0.0729 for off-peak charging and $0.1238 for on-peak charging. The rest of the year, the price differential is much greater: $0.0779 for off-peak charging and \$0.2977 for on-peak charging.[124] Finally, SRP's TOU rate imposes higher energy prices for up to eight hours on weekdays but provides the lowest prices for electric vehicle owners who charge their cars at night, offering customers 6 to 7 percent savings over the basic plan.[125] Although the latter plan would expose customers to the highest peak rates, it would produce the most significant cost savings during off-peak hours.

Thus, although utilities are implementing dynamic pricing schemes for electric vehicles, they are not of one mind regarding the specifics of those rate structures. There are, however, general principles that both utilities and policymakers should keep in mind as electric vehicles gain greater market share. In particular, dynamic pricing is critical to leverage the full economic and environmental potential of electric vehicle technology. Utilities should take measures to ensure that consumers receive the appropriate price signals to incentivize vehicle charging during off-peak hours. This approach will limit on-peak charging, which in many areas of the country will increase the stress on the utility's transmission and distribution network, requiring utilities to acquire more expensive electricity from less efficient intermediate and peaking plants—generally the heaviest polluters.

For this reason, it may be beneficial for utilities to offer EV-only TOU rates that allow customers to install a separate "electric vehicle meter" at their homes. Along with washers, dryers, and refrigerators, electric vehicles consume relatively large portions of a household's overall electricity use. Indeed, for many homes EVs are likely to be the largest electric appliance. Cars are generally parked at home overnight, and in-home charging infrastructure makes it easy to charge these vehicles during that time. Indeed, it is more convenient to defer electric vehicle charging to the evening hours than almost any other type of household energy consumption.

Moreover, from an infrastructure perspective, it is critical that EV electricity consumption occur during off-peak hours. Utilities should encourage consumers to participate in voluntary dynamic pricing schemes for electric vehicle charging. Rate structures at public charging locations should also be subject to a TOU pricing system rather than a flat rate, since flat rates at public charging stations will send the wrong price signals for peak daytime charging. This is especially important if employers begin installing electric vehicle charging stations at offices and workplaces around the country. Free or flat rate charging in the workplace will incentivize employees to charge at work (perhaps during peak hours), even if charging overnight at home could meet most or all of the EV charging demand.

Encouraging dynamic pricing becomes more complicated, however, in deregulated electricity markets. In such markets, the local distribution utility provides only the infrastructure (i.e., the distribution network) for delivering electricity customers, while other private parties (often referred to as "electric service providers") produce and sell the actual electricity to those customers. The customer can choose to purchase electricity from a range of suppliers, although he will still pay the local distribution utility for delivering the electricity over the utility's distribution network. In the electric vehicle context, deregulation allows private third-party companies to develop and provide charging services to customers with less oversight and regulation from the state utility commission. These third parties can offer pricing plans for electric vehicle charging that provide varied price signals and, in some cases, give consumers unlimited charging for a flat monthly fee.[126] In Texas, for example, the privately funded subsidiary of energy giant NRG Energy, eVgo, installs charging stations in consumers' homes and offers consumers a variety of payment plans.[127] Under one of those plans, consumers pay ninety dollars per month for (1) a level 2 charging unit, (2) unlimited public charging on eVgo's network and (3) unlimited charging at home during nonpeak hours. This approach trades the economic and environmental benefits of dynamic pricing for the convenience and affordability of a flat fee.

The philosophy behind eVgo's approach is to make electric vehicle charging—whether at home or in public—simple, easy, and affordable for electric vehicle owners. The company wants its customers to have the freedom to charge their vehicles at a low cost, no matter where they are. The idea is that if these "early adopters" have a good experience, electric cars are likely to build a rapport among the public as a whole, which will increase electric vehicle market share throughout the state and the country. And in the early goings, eVgo's approach may not present much of a problem; since with so few electric vehicles out on the roads, it's not likely to make much of a difference whether those vehicles charge during on-peak or off-peak hours.

But as electric vehicles gain market share, legislatures and state utility commissions will have to consider whether allowing the flat-fee approach is a desirable policy. Unlimited charging plans make car travel virtually free. This will incentivize consumers to use electric vehicles more often, increasing the miles they travel and thereby offsetting environmental gains that smart grid technologies and electric vehicles would otherwise produce. There is a strong economic and environmental imperative to encourage TOU pricing for electric vehicles, and the flat-fee approach is simply not consistent with that imperative.

Vehicle-to-Grid Services

Closely related to the need for dynamic pricing is the issue of vehicle-to-grid services. The integration of AMI and electric vehicle technology presents an opportunity to revolutionize the way the transportation and electric power sectors interact. V2G technology creates a two-way communications stream between the vehicle and the grid, whereby the grid can draw upon—and vehicle owners can sell—power from electric vehicle batteries. To provide power to the grid, V2G-capable vehicles must be connected to the grid with a bidirectional charger (not an option available for most EVs), which is a control device that grants grid operators access to the vehicle battery.[128] With this system, grid operators can draw power from— or feed it back into—an electric vehicle battery.[129]

Surprisingly, most vehicles spend much more of their time parked in a driveway or a lot than they do on the road. The average vehicle is on the highway only 4 to 5 percent of the time, meaning that it remains parked for most of its useful life. For conventional vehicles, this is not a very big deal—the car simply remains idle in its parking space. But electric vehicles have larger batteries that can store a greater amount of electricity. Although individual vehicles cannot store enough energy to have an impact on the grid, in the aggregate, the electricity from the batteries of a group of electric vehicles could provide a significant amount of extra electricity to the grid during high-demand times. In this way, V2G technology has the potential to turn electric vehicles into "mobile, self-contained resources" that can act as additional capacity and "displace the need for additional electric utility infrastructure."[130]

Not only could V2G technology magnify some of the economic, political, and environmental benefits of electric vehicles, but it could also be a great benefit for the electric power system and electric vehicle owners alike. If every one of the passenger vehicles on American roads had a 15-kWh battery (which is similar to the size of the battery in the Chevrolet Volt), this would add about 2,865 gW of additional capacity—or about twice the nation's current nameplate generating capacity.[131] At their choice, electric vehicle owners could sell this excess capacity back to the grid when operators call for it during periods of high demand; the value of these ancillary power services could be up to $12 billion a year.[132] Another option being discussed for future V2G technology is using EV batteries for household backup power during power outages.

Of course, this technology has its drawbacks: Electric vehicle owners may be reluctant to sell power back to the grid if, when they return to their vehicles, the battery is not fully charged. That is, grid operators may withdraw so much power from the vehicle that, by the time the consumer is ready to drive it again, its battery remains at less than a full charge. Furthermore, the more that grid operators draw from and feed power back into electric vehicle batteries, the more those batteries cycle, which can decrease battery life. Finally, because the cost of electricity is measured in cents per kilowatt hour, the economic benefits to electric vehicle owners from V2G technology would likely be modest in the short run. After factoring in the wear and tear that V2G could have on electric vehicle batteries, it will likely be a while before these services are cost effective for consumers.

Most utilities in our study were familiar with the potential of V2G technology. Some had begun pilot programs to test the application of this technology in a practical setting. Widespread deployment of this technology on a commercial scale appears, however, several years away. The most promising progress in V2G is currently the ev2g project, which is a joint effort of NRG Energy and the University of Delaware. The project currently sells energy from the batteries of 15 Mini Cooper e-cars donated by BMW into PJM Interconnection's frequency regulation market. The cars earn about five dollars a day for providing the ancillary service to PJM, but it is estimated that the additional cost of the add-on technology to the cars themselves is about four hundred dollars. The Minis receive a signal from PJM that is sent every four seconds and modify their charge or discharge of energy to comply with PJM market demands. To participate in the project, PJM had to modify some parameters for its frequency regulation market to account for the relatively small size of this distributed resource—the Minis represented only 100 kW of capacity in the aggregate, compared to traditional generating plants that are measured in the hundreds of megawatts. Although these EV batteries represent a small resource, they can respond quickly to PJM's signal (in a matter of seconds, compared to most resources that take several minutes to respond) and thus are a high-quality provider of frequency regulation services.[133] The ev2g project represents an important milestone for V2G services. EV batteries now join other new technologies such as flywheels (including the 20 mW Beacon Power project in New York) in breaking new ground using distributed storage to provide wholesale power market services. Continued progress on V2G services will allow electric vehicle batteries to provide clean and reliable electricity to the power grid while helping reduce the cost of EV ownership. Furthermore, using smart V2G services to reduce the costs of ancillary services will allow for more cost-effective integration of intermittent renewables.

Upgrading the Grid's Infrastructure

Although deploying a vast number of electric vehicles will require upgrades to America's electricity infrastructure, the electric power sector already has the "infrastructural backbone" in place to support widespread electric vehicle adoption."[134] Recent reports suggest that "significant portions of the U.S. gasoline-operated vehicle fleet could be fueled with the available electric capacity."[135] Although the number of electric vehicles that the existing grid could support varies by region, from a broad, overall perspective, the existing electricity infrastructure could support anywhere between 94 million and 158 million light-duty electric vehicles—that's between 43 and 72 percent of the whole American light-duty vehicle fleet.[136] Thus while grid upgrades will certainly be required, most of the infrastructure is already in place to support an electrified transportation sector: "The U.S. electric power infrastructure is a strategic national asset that is underutilized most of the time. With the proper changes in the operational paradigm, it could generate and deliver the necessary energy to fuel the majority of the U.S. light-duty vehicle (LDV) fleet. In doing so, it would reduce greenhouse gas emissions, improve the economics of the electricity industry, and reduce the U.S. dependency on foreign oil."[137]

Of course, this estimate is premised on the understanding that policymakers and utilities properly manage charging patterns and that the majority of charging occurs during off-peak hours.[138] Moreover, although electric vehicles will not likely create problems for the distribution system in the early stages, utilities will nonetheless have to upgrade distribution infrastructure as the electric vehicle market grows. Electric vehicles may strain older transformers "that are already overloaded due to load growth or older distribution standards."[139] Furthermore, the "clustering" of electric vehicles in metropolitan and suburban areas could shorten transformer life, as those transformers would be used more often.[140]

As a result, utilities will have to prepare for the impact that electric vehicles will have on their distribution system. For generation and transmission planning purposes, many utilities have created models that forecast the pace of electric vehicle adoption in their service territory. They have also conducted studies and analysis assessing risks to their distribution system.[141] Utilities with older distribution equipment may need to perform updates or replace equipment, sooner rather than later. Moreover, utilities should work with local governments and car dealerships to develop a system where the utility is automatically notified when a consumer purchases an electric vehicle. This will aid the utility in determining where additional electric vehicle supply equipment (EVSE, commonly referred to as a "charging station") is likely to be installed and what, if anything, the utility must do to prepare for the additional load.

San Diego Gas & Electric, for example, has adopted a geographic information system (GIS) to track and monitor the installation and performance of electric vehicle charging stations. Under this system, both the vehicle manufacturer and ECOtality (a private firm that manufactures the charging stations used in SDG&E's service territory) provide SDG&E

with identification and registration information associated with the customer installing the charging unit.[142] The utility will then evaluate the
capacity of the existing distribution infrastructure, map the location of
the new load, and install sensors on transformers to monitor their performance.[143] The data that SDG&E collects can then be used to correct any
overloads or voltage problems on that specific site, and to conduct planning studies to model the impacts of future charging infrastructure.

Utilities must also determine how they will pay for upgrades to the
distribution network, in the event those upgrades are necessary. Typically,
a customer who requests an additional service or upgrade from the utility
must pay for it. Accordingly, if a customer wants to install charging infrastructure on his property, and that installation is "likely to require significant grid upgrades, [such as] replacing and or increasing the capacity of
distribution lines, transformers, and substation equipment," the customer
could be required to pay for the needed upgrades.[144] The downside to this
approach is that, by imposing additional costs on electric vehicle owners,
the utility could stunt growth in the electric vehicle market. Therefore,
instead of charging the customer, the utility might consider incorporating
the cost of electric vehicle-related distribution upgrades into its rates,
especially when distribution impacts occur "not from an individual installation, but over time from a concentration of independent charging
installations."[145]

Charging Infrastructure Development

Just as conventional vehicles need access to gas stations for refueling,
electric vehicles need access to EVSE to recharge their batteries. There
are generally three different types of EVSE, and each draws power from
the grid at different rates. Level 1 charging units take the longest
amount of time to charge vehicles but do not require owners to install
any additional equipment; consumers can simply plug their car into a
standard 120-volt wall plug.[146] These outlets are attached to a 15- or
20-amp circuit breaker, which means that level 1 EVSE can draw power
from the grid at about 2 kW per hour. This would enable a PHEV, like
the Chevrolet Volt, to fully charge in eight to ten hours.[147] A Nissan
Leaf, which has a larger battery pack, could take up to twenty-two
hours to fully charge.

Because the average American vehicle spends so much time parked
(either at home or at work), most industry experts expect level 1 EVSE to
be adequate for these charging situations: It provides an inexpensive and
convenient means of charging at a time when the car will remain idle for
several hours.[148] Electric vehicles owners can afford to wait eight or ten

A Chevrolet Volt charging at a residential Level 1 outlet with net-metered solar generating in the background. (Photo by Kevin B. Jones)

hours for their vehicle's battery to recharge because they have dedicated that period of time to something else (presumably, sleeping or working). Likewise, level 1 EVSE may also be appropriate at railroad stations, park-and-ride lots, and other public transit centers or transportation hubs where vehicles are already idling for eight or more hours. The benefit of level 1 infrastructure is its low cost and wide availability: The only thing that electric vehicles need to plug in is a standard 120-volt outlet. Furthermore, level 1 charging limits the demand on the grid to what is typical for a residential home, preventing unnecessary burdens on electric infrastructure.

Level 2 EVSE provides a faster charging solution than level 1 equipment, but it requires homeowners (or whomever is installing the charger) to install a separate electrical circuit for the charging unit. These are the same sort of circuits on which electric clothes dryers operate; they typically draw 208 to 240 volts at 30 amps (although they can range from 12 to 80 amps) and can therefore provide about 6.3 to 7.2 kW of energy in an hour. Some electric vehicles, however, cannot take advantage of all this potential energy because their battery packs have a limited charging rate—usually 3.3 or 6.6 kW per hour. At these rates, an all-electric vehicle like the Nissan Leaf could charge its battery in three to seven hours (depending on the configuration of its onboard chargers). Installation costs for level 2 EVSE range from five hundred to twenty-five hundred dollars, depending

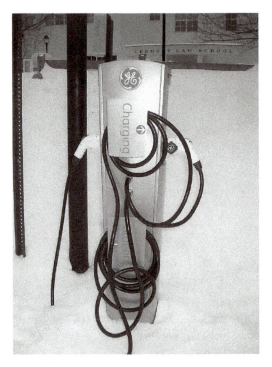

A General Electric Durastation dual Level 2 charging station on the Vermont Law School campus. (Photo by Kevin B. Jones)

on whether the homeowner needs to upgrade their electrical panel and whether more commercial quality charging stations are installed.[149] Installing a networked commercial level 2 station could potentially more than double a vehicle owner's installation costs.

Although costlier, level 2 EVSE is attractive because it can provide electric vehicles with a fuller charge in a shorter amount of time. For consumers who can absorb the cost, level 2 may be attractive for its speed and may be necessary for commuters or household members that travel long distances on a daily basis. In the public realm, level 2 may be popular in workplaces where employees do not work standard eight-hour workdays, or where their job requires a lot of driving. It would also be appropriate for retail centers, movie theaters, and other areas where cars remain idle for short periods of time.[150] Public level 2 charging stations often participate in national charging networks run by third parties such as ChargePoint or Blink.

From a utility infrastructure and energy management perspective, one downside to level 2 chargers is the increase in demand they place on the electric grid as compared to level 1. Newer models of the Leaf charging systems, which were initially designed to draw 3.3 kW off the grid (almost twice the demand from level 1 charging), will now demand 6.6 kW or greater from level 2 systems (the Tesla Roadster can charge at 16.8 kW). Level 2 charging thus has the potential for placing significantly greater peak electric demand on the grid over time. According to PNNL's analysis, if charging times are not properly managed, widespread availability of level 2 units could cut the number of electric vehicles that can be supported by unmanaged charging in half.[151]

In any event, the speed at which level 2 units can charge electric vehicles may be irrelevant for many consumers. Focusing too much on expediting charge time may prove unwise because electric vehicle owners will not require a full charge on a daily basis. Indeed, a standard level 1 outlet running overnight can provide enough electricity for a forty-mile commute on the following day.

DC Fast Chargers (sometimes referred to as level 3 EVSE) are the closest thing to a gas station for electric vehicles, in that they provide a charge quicker than any other type of unit. They draw 200 to 600 volts at varying amperages, and can provide anywhere from 25 to 60 kW (Tesla's new supercharger network will allow 120 kW charging) of electricity in a single hour. That said, some electric vehicles are not compatible with DC fast chargers. For those that are, an hour of charge time is usually not necessary: DC fast chargers can charge an electric vehicle battery to 80 percent of its capacity in under thirty minutes. Because these units require such high levels of voltage and current, it is more difficult to find acceptable locations with enough available power to support the infrastructure. Sites able to support fast charging may nonetheless require electrical system upgrades, and will likely have to go through lengthy permitting processes. Moreover, fast chargers require an enormous capital investment, costing between twenty-two thousand and sixty thousand dollars, depending on the manufacturer and the model.[152] Tesla is building out its own private national super charging network which will be free for Tesla owners that have paid for the supercharger option. Under this network, Tesla Model S owners will be able to recharge their batteries in less than half an hour. To put these figures in perspective, the demand that these chargers would place on the grid would equal the demand of about forty to fifty homes in California.[153]

Because of their expense and the strain that they put on the distribution grid, DC fast chargers are impractical for household installation. DC fast chargers also undermine the objective of "smart charging," which promotes lower voltage (level 1 and level 2) charging at off-peak hours. Given the expense of DC fast-charging infrastructure, federal funding has been necessary to spur investment in this technology.[154] Furthermore, many utilities commercial electric rates include demand charges, which impose a charge based on peak usage in addition to the kilowatt hour charge. This approach is intended to disincentivize use during peak power periods, as DC fast-charging infrastructure lends itself to high traffic during peak time periods.

Currently, electric vehicle owners are generally responsible for purchasing and installing EVSE in their homes. To help cover these costs, the federal government offers a maximum 30 percent tax credit, and some states and utilities offer tax incentives and rebates. Financial support for public charging infrastructure is less certain. That is, the market model for developing and deploying public charging infrastructure has not fully coalesced. There are several possible explanations for this uncertainty. First, the model for electric vehicle charging services differs greatly from the conventional "gas station" model. Given that most charging can occur at home rather than at something akin to a gas station, there has been less of a focus on providing public infrastructure. Second, the electric vehicle market is still in its early stages of development, so private firms and utilities may be reluctant to invest in charging infrastructure if demand is low. Indeed, given the high capital cost of installing and operating charging equipment and the relatively low retail cost of electricity, charging stations must have high utilization rates if their owners are to turn a profit.[155] Finally, the unique—and in some cases, antiquated—regulatory regime for the electricity industry is still adapting to an emerging electric vehicle market. Accordingly, regulatory reform, particularly at the state level, may become necessary to accommodate electric vehicles and their associated charging infrastructure.

The market for public charging infrastructure could take several routes.[156] At this early stage, no singular market model has predominated, which is probably a good thing, since some experimentation is usually necessary for stakeholders to determine which market structures work and which do not. Subjecting the current market of EVSE providers to the pressures of competition will ensure that the most cost-effective model for EVSE providers emerges in the future. And it may end up that several of these models exist alongside of one another, for they are not necessarily mutually exclusive: Just as government-owned utilities like the Tennessee Valley Authority exist and operate alongside investor-owned utilities like Duke Energy, government or utility-owned EVSE providers may exist along private EVSE firms, such as ECOtality or ChargePoint. We describe several potential market models for EVSE deployment below.

The Government's Role in EVSE Infrastructure Development and Ownership

Government deployment of public charging infrastructure is usually justified on economic grounds. There is not yet a large demand for public charging stations because there are very few electric vehicles currently on the roads. There are, however, significant costs associated with supplying EVSE. Providers must pay for manufacturing, permitting, installing, and maintaining the charging unit, as well as hosting it on a nationwide network where consumers can locate and reserve it.[157] Installation costs could be especially high if the provider has to pay to upgrade the electrical system or distribution network at a given EVSE location. Based on conservative estimates, EVSE providers could incur forty-two hundred to seventy-two hundred dollars in costs when installing a single level 2 charger and upward of fifty thousand dollars for installing DC fast-charging technology.[158] Because there are so few electric vehicles on the road right now, the utilization rate for many public charging stations could take time to develop.[159] Combine high up-front costs with modest utilization rates, and charging providers may be forced to impose large markups on their services, causing electric vehicles to lose a competitive edge.[160]

Because of these financial risks, private firms would have little economic incentive to deploy charging infrastructure, leaving the government to fill the void and deploy charging infrastructure or subsidize the cost of private infrastructure. Several municipalities have taken this approach. The city of San Francisco, for instance, has constructed a series of public charging stations at city-owned garages and parking areas.[161] The County of Los Angeles has received a grant to install and operate forty-eight public charging stations throughout its jurisdiction.[162] Governor Andrew Cuomo of New York has recently announced that he wants to invest $50 million over five years into public and workplace charging infrastructure. These are all examples of governments using their own resources to subsidize the deployment of electric vehicle charging infrastructure.

Rather than directly deploying charging infrastructure, governments could also subsidize private EVSE vendors, who would use public funds to defray the capital costs associated with charging infrastructure. This is the approach that the federal government has taken. Through the American Recovery and Reinvestment Act, the Department of Energy has provided over $100 million to ECOtality, which is distributing public EVSE in eighteen metropolitan areas throughout the country. It has also installed, free of charge, in-home chargers for approximately eight thousand electric vehicle owners. Accordingly, the federal government has been heavily responsible for growing one of the nation's major EVSE firms: About 72 percent of ECOtality's 2012 revenues came from the federal government.

In addition to providing a source of funding, governmental bodies have other roles they can play in facilitating investment in infrastructure. Since laws and regulations governing the electricity sector were not specifically developed with the electric vehicle industry in mind, legislatures and utility commissions in many states need to clarify the extent to which providers of public charging services will be regulated under the state's utility code. Of course, charging providers do not want to be regulated as utilities because this would create "a burdensome operating environment for the emerging EVSE industry, undermining the creation of a competitive market for EV charging services and the rapid deployment of charging infrastructure."[163] However, most state utility codes only permit regulated public utilities to resell electricity to the general public. This means that charging providers cannot sell electricity in kilowatt-hour increments to their customers. Indeed, forty-one out of fifty states prohibit private, independent charging companies from selling electricity to electric vehicle owners at public charging stations.[164] Practically speaking, forbidding charging providers from selling electricity on a per-kilowatt-hour basis also prevents those providers from implementing dynamic pricing schemes. Many charging providers circumvent this conundrum by charging for hourly access to the charger, rather than the electricity that passes through it, thereby allowing the provider to offer its services to the public.

Charging for hourly access is only a partial solution, however, as it creates unnecessary barriers to sophisticated pricing alternatives. If state utility commissions allowed charging providers to resell electricity, those providers could implement dynamic pricing schemes and time-of-use rates, which will further encourage efficient and environmentally sound charging behavior among consumers.[165] California took this approach when the general assembly codified the Public Utility Commission's decision not to regulate the "ownership or operation of a facility that sells electric vehicle charging services."[166] This action has been hailed by lawmakers, trade associations, and industry participants alike as providing market certainty and creating a regulatory atmosphere that will promote private development of charging infrastructure.[167] At least nine other states have followed suit.[168] And although such legislation provides certainty and regulatory relief for firms providing charging services, regulators should bear in mind that electric vehicle charging could impose significant costs on ratepayers and broader society if managed improperly. Accordingly, regulators should consider measures that incentivize off-peak charging, such as requiring charging providers to establish TOU rates or dynamic pricing at public charging stations.

Local governments should also play a leadership role in developing EVSE services. For instance, homeowners installing level 2 charging units in their homes may require upgrades to their electrical system. Because these upgrades often require a permit, states and localities can streamline the permitting process by updating or amending building codes, or by revising and simplifying local permitting procedures. Local governments should also coordinate with utilities and local automobile dealerships to educate customers as to how the permitting process works, such as through websites or informational pamphlets. Additional efforts may include policies that prepare for electric vehicle integration or studies that research how to integrate EVSE facilities into regional transportation plans in order to promote coordinated transportation services.

Utility Role in EVSE Ownership and Development

Given their historic role in producing and distributing electricity, local utilities can play a key role in EVSE development. This role, however, may be limited by policymaking at the state level. Some states allow utilities to supply and own EVSE. Others allow utilities to own and provide EVSE alongside private third-party companies, and still other states ban utilities from EVSE ownership altogether.

In one development model, local utilities would own and deploy EVSE and charge consumers on a per kWh basis for the energy their electric vehicles use. Utilities could then track customer consumption at public charging stations by assigning the customer (or her vehicle) a unique identification number and include the cost of each charging session to the consumer's next utility bill.[169] Utilities could recover the costs of this infrastructure in one of two ways. First, they could impose the costs of deploying public EVSE only on those who use it (i.e., electric vehicle owners). Presumably, this means that charging rates at public EVSE would be higher. Or second, utilities could spread the cost of this infrastructure across their entire customer base and increase electricity rates for all customers.

There are a number of justifications for utilities owning and deploying EVSE. First, by deploying EVSE infrastructure themselves, utilities could more closely plan for and monitor the impact that EVSE facilities have on the distribution network. As electric vehicles become more and more popular, this will minimize reliability concerns, as utilities will be able to control where charging stations are deployed so as to ensure grid stability. Second, the utility can select EVSE that is compatible with its existing smart grid infrastructure; this will make it easier to integrate electric vehicle tariffs, direct load control programs, and other customer programs into its new charging infrastructure. Moreover, by having control over EVSE deployment, the utility can ensure its charging infrastructure will not become obsolete at a later date. Third, as with other utility investments, utility ownership could help achieve economies of scale that would ensure that services are ubiquitous, reliable, and cost effective. Finally, having utilities deploy and control public charging infrastructure will ensure that charging rates will be transparent to electric vehicle owners, who will receive the same incentive to charge off peak in public as they do at home.

To date, this has not been the preferred model. By and large, the role of utilities in deploying EVSE has been piecemeal, with various degrees of utility ownership or subsidization. In many states, substantial legal questions remain as to whether utilities should be permitted to deploy and own charging infrastructure.[170] In Illinois, for example, utilities are statutorily limited in what public services they can offer, which has frustrated EVSE development.[171] At the Illinois Commerce Commission's Initiative on Plug-In Electric Vehicles, many utilities noted that existing law could be interpreted to require public utilities to offer charging services, or it could be interpreted to permit private companies to provide charging services.[172] Commonwealth Edison has argued for the latter interpretation, recommending that the state not require public utilities to provide charging services.[173] The ICC has indicated that it will consider supporting legislation to clarify the extent to which charging services will be regulated under state law, but that its support will depend on the specifics of any proposal.[174]

In California, however, the Public Utilities Commission has clearly forbidden utilities from owning or deploying charging infrastructure. Investor-owned utilities such as SDG&E argued that the CPUC should not place an outright ban on utility ownership of EVSE. It argued that the CPUC should allow utilities to make specific requests to provide EVSE in certain circumstances. In particular, under one proposal, the utility would have to show how its ownership would benefit ratepayers, how it would advance electric vehicle deployment, and how costs associated with the proposal would be recovered.[175] But the CPUC had already concluded in an earlier proceeding that utilities could not recover the costs associated with EVSE from ratepayers. In 2011, it extended this ruling by precluding utilities from owning EVSE. It did not believe that utility ownership would provide significantly greater safety advantages or cost savings than what would be achieved if EVSE were left to the private market. The CPUC did note that it would revisit this decision in the future and allow utilities to deploy EVSE in cases of market failure, or in areas where populations were underserved by electric charging infrastructure.

By contrast, the Oregon Public Utility Commission has essentially adopted the approach advanced by SDG&E before the CPUC. The Oregon PUC concluded that, given the nascent stage of electric vehicle development in the country, it would be better to "allow all market players, including electric utilities," to own and operate charging stations.[176] It also concluded that a utility can recover the cost of deploying electric vehicle infrastructure through its rates, so long as it can show that its owning and operating EVSE will be beneficial to ratepayers.[177] In particular, the Oregon PUC would permit rate recovery if (1) utility ownership of the infrastructure provides a net benefit to ratepayers, (2) the infrastructure is essential to facilitating EV adoption in the area, (3) there is no likelihood that another private company or utility affiliate could provide the charging infrastructure, and (4) the utility has a separate EV rate class.[178] Granted, utilities could own and operate charging infrastructure without meeting this criteria; they simply would not be allowed to recover the cost of that infrastructure through their rates.

Unlike California, which has placed an outright ban on utility ownership of EVSE, the Oregon PUC has essentially encouraged utilities to provide charging infrastructure only when the private sector cannot do so more efficiently or affordably. There is a historical basis for this approach. Just as electric utilities had no incentive to expand service into rural areas during the 1920s and 1930s because of high capital costs and low profit margins, private EVSE providers will have little or no incentive to deploy charging infrastructure in rural areas where it will rarely be utilized (absent a utility or governmental subsidy). In such situations, the utility could act as a "backstop," providing ratepayers with the necessary infrastructure when private companies can or will not do so and recovering the associated costs through rates. This approach would help grow the private market for EVSE firms while allowing utilities to fill in a service void when there is no profit incentive to do so.

The primary disadvantage to involving utilities in EVSE deployment is that assigning utilities primary responsibility over charging infrastructure could stifle development of the private EVSE firms and the innovation that they bring to the industry. Retail electric utilities have a monopoly over their retail service area and have statutory authority to recover costs through their rates. In the context of the EVSE market, this would give them an unfair competitive advantage over independent, third-party charging providers, who would have difficulty competing with a publicly subsidized entity.[179] Similar to the arguments against a utility providing electric service in states where there is retail competition, utility provision of EVSE could stifle competition and consumer choice in the market for EVSE, which could reduce cost-effective innovations.[180]

Third-Party EVSE Ownership and Development

A number of private companies have been key players in deploying public EVSE throughout the country with varying levels of success. ECOtality, for instance, received a $115 million grant from the Department of Energy and, with matching private funds, was deploying approximately fourteen thousand chargers in eighteen major metropolitan areas across six states.[181] These stations were to be integrated into ECOtality's Blink network, an

Internet-based platform that allows electric vehicle owners to locate and reserve charging stations.[182] Electric vehicle owners can charge their cars for one dollar to two dollars an hour, although prices may vary depending on local electricity rates. ECOtality also used some of this funding to provide free residential charging equipment to participating Volt and Leaf owners at no extra cost. In return, ECOtality could collect data on the vehicle owner's charging behavior (duration, cost, etc.). Consumers pay for home charging based on their residential utility rates, and the consumer's relationship is with the utility.[183] In September 2013 ECOtality filed for Chapter 11 bankruptcy, and in October 2013 the Blink charging stations and the Blink network were auctioned to the Car Charging Group, Inc., a nationwide provider of car charging services. The former Blink network now operates under the Car Charging brand of stations.

Another private company, ChargePoint, has also been at the forefront of deploying EVSE services. ChargePoint does not install, own, or set rates for electric vehicle charging stations. Rather, it provides a cloud-based network through which EVSE owners can manage, administer, and market their infrastructure. Much like ECOtality's Blink network, the ChargePoint network allows electric vehicle owners to locate and reserve EVSE, but the station owners establish fees for access to the infrastructure.[184] Thus the ChargePoint network offers station owners a system by which they can manage their stations, as well as exposure to electric vehicle owners looking for their services.

Some observers question whether private firms can profitably provide public charging infrastructure on a large scale basis. Deploying public charging infrastructure on a widespread basis requires a significant supply of capital investment. At the same time, hourly charging rates must remain low enough that electric vehicles remain cost competitive with conventional vehicles in terms of fuel expenses. If public charging is too expensive, electric vehicle owners will have no incentive to use public infrastructure, which will lead to low utilization rates and ultimately prevent owners of this infrastructure from recovering their investment.

This catch-22 raises questions about the business case for private firms providing public charging infrastructure. Indeed, much of the progress that private firms have made in deploying public charging infrastructure is the direct result of government intervention. ECOtality was one of the leaders in the private market for EVSE providers, but much of its revenue stream resulted from funding from the federal government. Its bankruptcy certainly raises concerns about the viability of the private sector EVSE model. And given the current state of the federal budget, it is doubtful that the federal government will put forward additional resources to grow the market for public charging infrastructure. As a result, investors and market observers are skeptical as to whether private firms can thrive without government support.

Of course, private EVSE vendors such as ChargePoint and Car Charging Group are not the only businesses that can fill the market for public charging infrastructure. Many retailers, hotels, and other businesses purchase charging stations from manufacturers and provide charging as a free or low-cost amenity to customers. Although these firms may absorb the cost of providing charging services, they attract additional business from electric vehicle owners, which helps them recoup their investments in providing EVSE. These opportunities for EVSE development are likely to complement other models for EVSE development.

Even in states such as California, where third-party provision of EVSE is the law, state governments are finding creative ways to use available opportunities to incent investment. As a result of a settlement between the state of California and the energy company NRG, resolving litigation dating back to the California energy crisis, NRG will pay to install a minimum of two hundred public fast-charging stations, with 20 percent of these stations in low-income areas. The company will also install infrastructure for plug-in units, or "make-readies," for at least ten thousand charging stations at about one thousand locations for multifamily housing, workplaces, and public interest sites. NRG will have exclusive rights for eighteen months to install charging stations and over time support the installation of level 1 and level 2 chargers from all charging companies. Further, to meet the CPUC's goal of ensuring that the electric vehicle charging infrastructure is available to Californians of all income levels, NRG will ensure that mixed-income housing locations are identified, evaluated, and pursued for the make-readies. ECOtality unsuccessfully challenged the legality of this agreement in court and before the Federal Energy Regulatory Commission claiming it unfairly benefited NRG's eVgo business.

Ultimately, charging an electric vehicle will be very different from refueling a conventional vehicle. Most charging is expected to occur at home and overnight. So instead of going to the gas station to fill up, most people will likely do so in their garages.[185] Accordingly, time will tell whether the development of public charging stations is a defining feature of an electric transportation future; EVSE could be an issue largely resolved at the workplace and the residence. Ultimately, where electric vehicle drivers decide to charge their batteries will determine how environmentally friendly electric transportation will be. If electric vehicles are primarily charged at home and then topped off at the workplace as necessary, then the existing grid could support high EV penetration. If consumers get in the habit of charging electric vehicles at fast DC chargers during the daytime, then there is a whole lot of new electric infrastructure that will need to be developed to support this habit.

CONCLUSION

Smart grid technologies can facilitate the electrification of the transportation sector, which would be a boon for both the American economy and the environment. But the mass market success of electric vehicles will certainly depend on whether manufacturers can address the range and cost challenges facing battery technology. That is, until electric vehicle range and costs are more in line with conventional vehicles, the electric vehicle will face continuing challenges competing with conventional vehicles. The continued improvement of electric vehicle technology will be critical, therefore, to facilitating electric vehicle adoption throughout the country. That said, there are a number of things that both policymakers and utilities can do to promote electric vehicle integration, independent of addressing these technological shortcomings.

First, states should move quickly to establish clear and consistent policies regarding how electric vehicle charging services will be regulated. California is a case in point. It implemented a clear state policy indicating that electric vehicle charging stations would not be regulated as utilities under state public utility law. Many states still must—and should—address this crucial public policy issue, because in most states, "companies that engage in the sale or resale of electricity are considered to be utilities and fall under the jurisdiction of the public utilities commission."[186] Although it's debatable whether such companies should or should not be subject to PUC jurisdiction, California took a clear stand on this issue, providing certainty to charging station owners. Investors and owners of charging station infrastructure now know what to expect, and can adjust their business strategy accordingly to further provide charging infrastructure throughout the state. Although private sector innovation has been and will continue to be crucial to electric vehicle deployment, state and national governments must implement policies that make that innovation easier, more affordable, and more certain.

Second, utilities should set up special TOU rates for electric vehicles to send the right price signals to consumers and to maximize the economic and environmental benefits of electric vehicles. TOU rates should be implemented to incentivize electric vehicle owners to charge during off-peak hours. Off-peak charging can increase utilization of existing capacity—thereby lowering electric rates for all consumers—and will ensure that the power system integrates electric vehicles without compromising system reliability. Although widespread on-peak charging is technologically feasible, it could end up raising electricity rates by resulting in the need for significant new electric infrastructure investment in order to meet growing peak electricity demand. This is an undesirable result.

Third, utilities should create systems to prepare for and monitor electric vehicle sales, as well as installation of charging infrastructure. SDG&E's system serves as a good example of how utilities can plan for the increased load that electric vehicles will place on the grid. It plans for increased electric vehicle adoption by collaborating with charging station companies and auto manufacturers, taking the data those partners provide and plugging it into a GIS mapping system and then making upgrades as necessary. Ultimately, this may be a matter for state public utility commissions or legislatures to address. Utilities would have a much easier time tracking electric vehicle load growth if charging station owners and auto manufacturers were required by law to report whenever they install a new station or sell a new electric vehicle. In the future, as electric vehicles become more popular, utilities will need to be in close contact with these third parties for the purposes of distribution planning.

And fourth, very few utilities have taken concrete action on deploying widespread V2G technology; however, utilities should conduct pilots and studies to determine how that technology might be used in the future. V2G technology could be an important resource in providing both demand response and as a storage resource during critical peak hours. Similarly, there also could be important EV owner revenue from providing services such as frequency regulation. Various pilots and other projects are underway, and there needs to be continued investment as this technology will become more important and useful as electric vehicle adoption increases. And while utilities must test the application of V2G technology in a practical setting, product manufacturers must likewise plan to integrate this technology into future vehicles and charging stations.

6

THE FUTURE OF DISTRIBUTED
TECHNOLOGIES

As utilities begin to integrate smart grid technologies into their generation, transmission, and distribution systems, one of the often-heard re-
frains is that the smart grid will enable the emergence of more renewable
energy generation. The story goes that through the use of better communications technologies, the availability of more information regarding
both small renewable energy generators and demand-side resources, and
the introduction of smart technologies that can help better manage voltages on the distribution system, the smart grid will help overcome the
barriers to integrating high levels of renewable resources. Despite the talk
the evidence supporting this trend seems to be quite mixed. There is no
doubt that distributed generation such as solar photovoltaic[1] is on the rise
and that there is increasing discussion and study of associated distributed
technologies such as energy storage and microgrids. On the other hand, in
practice, there are few significant examples of how smart grid technology
is currently required to facilitate a transition to a more distributed energy
future, at least in the near term. The fact that these are still emerging
technologies did not prevent the Edison Electric Institute, which is the
trade association for investor-owned utilities, from warning its members
about the future when it noted that "today, a variety of disruptive technologies are emerging that may compete with utility-provided services.
Such technologies include [PV], battery storage, fuel cells, geothermal
energy systems, wind, micro-turbines, and EV-enhanced storage. As the
cost curve on these technologies improves, they could directly threaten
the centralized utility model."[2]

This chapter will address the opportunities and challenges that distributed technologies create for smart grid deployment. We will begin by focusing on distributed generation, specifically those intermittent and variable

renewable energy resources that proponents of smart grid deployment hope to integrate by the gigawatt along with smart grid technology rollout. The chapter will then take a look at a corollary sector, energy storage, to determine what role it is currently playing, and could play, in the future of smart grid technology deployment. Finally, we will introduce the concept of the microgrid, which is increasingly entering the dialogue when we talk about both the smart grid and distributed technologies.

DISTRIBUTED GENERATION

The traditional definition of distributed generation is a catch-all label that includes any small-scale electricity or combined heat and power (CHP) generator, including back-up diesel generators, located within a utility's service territory. For purposes of this chapter, however, a more refined definition is required. For our purposes, distributed generation means renewable energy generators (solar, wind, small hydro, and bioenergy technologies) with capacities that are generally less than 20 mW and are primarily connected to a utility's distribution rather than transmission system.

Historically, utilities favored large, central station generation to take advantage of economies of scale. These generators produced electricity miles from load centers, which was then transported across high-voltage transmission lines to customers. But beginning in the late 1990s, distributed generation began to gain a foothold. This was the result of a number of factors, including increased demand for power, deregulation of the utility industry, environmental concerns related to coal and nuclear power, and improvements in generating technologies like wind turbines and solar panels.[3] More recently, the increasing number of state renewable portfolio standards (RPS) and standard offer/feed-in tariff policies, tax credits, and the declining costs of technologies such as solar PV have created increased momentum in the distributed generation market. Despite this growth, distributed generation technologies remain a minor player in regards to total U.S. capacity. Specifically, solar energy installations with installed capacities of 20 mW or less represented less than one-tenth of a percent of total installed capacity in the nation, while wind represents a slightly larger share of the mix at 3 percent.

However, solar PV is on the rise, and if the installed costs continue to decline, it could become a disruptive technology in the future. Former FERC chairman Jon Wellinghoff recently stated that "solar is growing so fast it is going to overtake everything."[4] According to the report "U.S. Solar Market Insight," cumulative installed solar PV could surpass 10 gW in 2013, with 4.4 gW of PV installed in 2013, which is a

A 9 kW commercial net-metered solar photovoltaic project with SolarWorld panels. (Photo by Kevin B. Jones)

30 percent increase from the previous year. This could be a result of declining costs, as prices for residential PV systems and utility-scale installations have fallen to $4.81/W and $2.10/W, respectively.[5] According to the Department of Energy, once solar installation costs reach $1.0/W, they will be competitive with the wholesale rate for electricity without additional subsidies.[6] GTM Research has predicted that "in the next 2 1/2 years the U.S. will double its entire cumulative capacity of distributed solar—repeating in the span of a few short years what it originally took four decades to deploy."[7] Distributed solar PV has many documented benefits, including reducing peak demands and line losses on the transmission and distribution system and reducing greenhouse gas emissions.

Challenges Posed by Distributed Generation

With the exception of bioenergy technologies, distributed generators are inherently intermittent and variable in nature,[8] which creates challenges for utilities attempting to integrate them into the existing system. Solar energy is only produced during daytime hours and can be further impacted by weather conditions; wind turbines only produce electricity when the wind blows. Grid operators, who have for decades been used to relying on large controllable power plants, are concerned by both the variability of the output of intermittent wind and solar generation as well as the uncertainty of what the output level will be at any point in time. It should be noted that variability and uncertainty, while of concern with intermittent generation, are inherent characteristics of electric power systems.

Voltage Control, Power Quality, and Islanding

Variability in the output of solar PV plants, which results from the rising and setting of the sun on a daily basis as well as seasonal changes in the sun's position, is predictable and can be planned for. Utilities are more concerned with the rapid manner in which power from a distributed resource can "ramp up" or "ramp down," such as when the sun is quickly covered by a cloud or emerges from cloud cover. This can create situations in which the voltage on a given circuit fluctuates beyond the range that is acceptable under reliability standards. Distributed solar PV systems can raise the voltage levels on a distribution line, and when there is a sudden drop in PV output from a weather event (such as rapidly increasing cloud cover), it can cause voltage levels to drop too far before the electric system can compensate. Similarly, variations in voltage and frequency from weather events could lead to power quality problems that negatively impact the performance of customer electrical devices. There is some concern that these voltage and other power quality issues over time could shorten the life of both utility and customer end-use equipment.

One simple means to reduce fluctuations in voltage is to spread the PV generation over a larger geographic region. High penetration levels of PV on the distribution system can also lead to increases in power losses. Low to moderate PV penetration levels tend to decrease power losses until they reach a minimum. At high penetration levels power losses tend to increase.[9]

Solar PV Production on a Sunny and a Cloudy Day

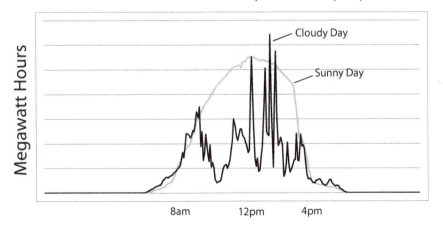

Another issue created by the intermittent nature of distributed generation technologies is the potential for what is known as "islanding." Distributed generation has the potential to keep operating during an outage on the system, which means that part of the distribution system could become a power island—a radial portion of the distribution grid temporarily supported by local distributed generation. When a utility stops the flow of power to a given circuit, power generated by distributed generators within the circuit can continue to flow in a reverse direction over the distribution line, resulting in an isolated power island. Unchecked islanding could become a real safety hazard for unsuspecting line crews and other customers on the islanded portion of the grid. Currently, IEEE Standard 1547 for PV (and other distributed generation) embedded on distribution systems requires automatic shutdown (also referred to as "tripping") in the case of abnormal grid voltages and frequencies. This requirement stems from safety concerns surrounding inadvertent islanding. An unintended consequence of these rules, however, is that widespread automatic shutdown of PV will occur for large grid disturbances, such as transmission faults that depress voltages below existing tolerances.[10]

As a result, all PV inverters for systems on the distribution system automatically shut down the PV system when they sense that voltage has fallen below a certain level and do not restart the system until power has been restored on the distribution system. While PV is subject to a low-voltage tripping mandate as a result of IEEE Standard 1547, FERC Rule 661a prohibits low-voltage tripping for utility-scale generation. At some point, low-voltage ride through (LVRT) capability, the ability to remain connected to the grid during low-voltage conditions, will be needed for larger PV systems or areas where there is large penetration of PV.[11] In a simple sense, this is because when voltage dips due to the loss of a large, distant generator, having significant solar PV resources automatically shutting off could worsen an already dangerous situation in regard to maintaining the operation of the grid.

Smart Distributed Generation Solutions

Smart grid technologies can help resolve these issues. According to PNNL, islanding is a barrier to high penetration of solar PV systems (20 percent and higher), but the smart grid could overcome this barrier. Smarter PV inverters, such as those with wireless communications and data gathering technologies embedded in them, can provide utilities with information about islanding. Armed with this information, utilities could use voltage regulators to maintain adequate voltage levels in neighborhoods where there is a significant solar PV presence. Utilities could also install batteries to manage solar production peaks and valleys. Finally, utilities could provide additional "short-circuit protection schemes that adapt to on-the-fly reverse power flow."[12] In markets like San Diego and Phoenix, where high penetration of distributed generation is taking place, these issues are magnified.

Smart inverters could be of particular help to utilities. Although IEEE 1547 regulations currently require that solar inverters disconnect if the grid becomes unstable, companies like Petra Solar are already using inverters designed to "survive [these events], ride through it for seconds at a time, and immediately resynchronize and continue wattage output as the fault clears."[13] Under current IEEE regulations, if the inverter is not on utility property, then this feature cannot be turned on. This essentially marginalizes the benefits such inverters could provide in controlling islanding from distributed generation units because those units are, by their very nature, not on utility property. Similarly, "existing distribution interconnection standards discourage active control of voltage from distributed energy resources," and thus PV inverters are set to operate at a unity power factor (a fixed voltage setting). But both the IEEE and utilities are considering revisions since it has been shown that variable voltage control (leading and lagging reactive power support) from PV inverters can be very effective in reducing voltage swings.[14] In Germany, strict inverter settings are being relaxed so that they can be used to better control grid voltages. If the states adopt new regulations that permit the use of robust inverter technologies, these devices could be an important means of stabilizing the grid when more distributed generation is present.

Although reverse power flow could be a serious barrier to deploying additional distributed generation, it should not pose too significant of a problem until the penetration of this technology approaches 20 percent of load. Similarly, the PNNL analysis finds that the problem of intermittency arising from both solar and wind generation does not pose a challenge to the grid until state RPS levels go somewhere beyond 20 percent. Moreover, according to a study by the National Renewable Energy Laboratory (NREL), even if renewables made up 32 percent of America's overall generation mix, "balancing supply and demand appears feasible on hourly and seasonal timescale."[15] This view, however, is not universal. A survey by the firm Accenture found that 72 percent of utilities are concerned that their grids will face challenges or require upgrade even before the penetration of solar PV reaches 24 percent.[16] In the meantime, cheap natural gas prices suggest that when renewable energy production drops off due to intermittency, burning natural gas is both a cost-effective and

An SMA Sunny Boy Solar PV Inverter and Elster Smart Meter on a commercial net-metered solar system. (Photo by Kevin B. Jones)

reliable solution, if not a carbon neutral one. In the near term, as renewables reach 20 percent or more of electric supply, PNNL and NREL's analysis suggests that the grid should be able to integrate these resources without major investments in smart distributed technologies.

ENERGY STORAGE TECHNOLOGIES AND POLICIES

Smart grid implementation is just as important to energy storage technologies as it is to distributed generation. This is because energy storage is complimentary to distributed generation and is capable of providing, in some cases, a hedge against the variability of distributed generation resources. As we discussed previously, one of the challenges with distributed generation sources such as wind or solar is that there is no guarantee that they will produce energy precisely when it is needed. As a result, having the ability to store clean but intermittent sources of electricity would add significantly to the value of distributed resources. Unfortunately, electricity is an inherently difficult (and thus expensive) commodity to store. Unlike solid or liquid primary fuels, electricity cannot be put into a tanker or onto the back of a truck and moved from place to place. Absent some form of storage, electricity must be produced and consumed at the same time and thus load and supply must be intricately balanced. The California Public Utilities Commission defines electric energy storage (EES) as "a set of technologies capable of storing previously generated electric energy and releasing that energy at a later time. EES technologies may store electrical energy as potential, kinetic, chemical, or thermal energy."[17] An important difference between storage and conventional generation is that storage tends to be a limited energy resource. Unlike traditional power plants, which can constantly produce electricity up to the plant's nameplate capacity (assuming a continuous fuel supply), storage technologies can only produce a limited quantity of electricity before they must be recharged.

Common Storage Technologies and Their Uses

Storage can be classified as either bulk storage or distributed storage, depending on the specific role that the technology or project will serve for the electric grid. Bulk storage technologies are measured in megawatt capability, are likely to be interconnected to the transmission system, and generally provide energy and "ancillary services" to the wholesale market. Ancillary services are used to correct temporary imbalances that occur on the electric system when (for example) a power plant goes out of service, a transmission line goes down, or load is increasing rapidly. Providers of ancillary services must be prepared to dispatch electricity within seconds or minutes to address these imbalances.[18] Distributed storage is more likely to be measured in kilowatt or perhaps single digits of a megawatt and provide support to the utility distribution system.

Electric energy storage technologies come in many forms and can be used for a variety of purposes. Most logically, energy storage can be used to store electric energy when there is excess energy or prices are low and release it when there is peak demand and prices are high. Energy storage can also be used to provide ancillary services, such as regulating supply in ISO/RTO markets and helping balance load and supply over short time frames. Electric energy can be stored when prices are low and then released quickly to regulate and balance supply and demand over short time frames. Finally, EES could be used to reduce the amount of power generating capacity necessary by offering its services as a capacity resource. By storing energy that is produced during off-peak hours for use during peak hours, EES can replace expensive peaking plants, effectively reducing the total amount of capacity that must be constructed. Some of the most common forms of EES are described below.

Batteries. Batteries range in size from small, backup batteries connected to a solar energy system in a home to those the size of city blocks. These are perhaps the most common and recognizable form of energy storage.

There are a variety of different types of batteries including lithium-ion (which, as we discussed previously, have become increasingly popular for electric vehicle storage) to sodium-sulfur, nickel-cadmium, and lead-acid batteries. Batteries are a reliable and well-understood technology, but they can be expensive and require a significant amount of land.

Flywheels. Flywheels work by accelerating a cylindrical assembly called a rotor (flywheel) around a central shaft at very high speeds and maintaining the energy in the system as rotational energy. The energy is converted back into electricity by slowing down the flywheel. Flywheels are capable of providing electric energy quickly (they respond in milliseconds) and may be used for up to an hour. Their energy densities are much greater than batteries thus they use much less space per kilowatt stored. Flywheel technologies have recently been used for providing ancillary services in wholesale electricity markets.

Pumped hydro. Using off-peak power, water is pumped uphill into a reservoir. The water is later released downhill through a turbine when power is needed during high-demand periods. This technology is proven and has been used to produce large-capacity facilities that can release their energy over a prolonged period of time. It is the largest source of installed storage capacity in the United States. The future of pumped hydro stations will depend on finding suitable sites.

Compressed air. Similar to pumped hydro, air is compressed into tanks using off-peak energy and then the pressure is released to turn turbines during high-demand periods. Compressed air units are usually combined with natural gas-fueled generation, which allows these units to use significantly less fuel when generating energy.

Molten salt. Molten salt is a more recent development. Salt is heated using excess energy (usually from a solar thermal energy plant) and kept at a temperature of more than 1,000 degrees Fahrenheit. The heat is then used to turn turbines when the sun isn't shining or at night. Molten salt provides significant thermal energy storage.

Ultracapacitors. Ultracapacitors are electrical devices that consist of two oppositely charged metal plates separated by an insulator. The device stores energy by increasing the electric charge accumulation on the metal plates and discharges energy when the electric charges are released by the metal plates. These are best at providing power during brief periods.

Distributed thermal energy. Commercial buildings and residences have made use of various thermal energy storage technologies, which use either hot or cold energy storage to supplement that building's heating or air-conditioning systems.

Of the multitude of storage options, pumped storage hydro is by far the most widely used, with 127,000 mW installed worldwide. Compressed air energy storage is the second most popular, with 440 mW installed, and sodium-sulfur batteries follow up in third, with 316 mW of installed capacity. All remaining energy storage resources total less than 100 mW.[19] Various studies and reports have identified a myriad of uses for EES technologies, including improved power quality, reliable and cleaner back-up power, reduced need for peak generation capacity, more efficient use of renewable and other off-peak generation, reduced need for transmission and distribution capacity upgrades, and lower greenhouse gas emissions.[20]

Challenges for Adoption of Storage

In the past, there have been generalized claims that EES faced regulatory and market rule barriers to further development. More recently, system operators such as the New York Independent System Operator, where Beacon Power operates a 20-mW flywheel resource, have openly welcomed storage technologies as ancillary service providers. In addition, FERC Order 755 (enacted in 2011) and Order 784 (issued in 2013) require RTO/ISO markets and other transmission providers to pay or responding resources like flywheels and batteries because they provide better performance relative to slower conventional technologies.

Although there are many uses that the EES technologies can play in today's complex electric markets, they are not a primary generation resource. Rather, EES is mostly designed to meet peak load needs by acting as a substitute for conventional dispatchable generation resources or demand response. Many EES technologies are still in an early stage of adoption and thus face both technological and economic limitations. The economic hurdle these resources face is increased by low natural gas prices, which make it both cost effective and convenient to use conventional energy supplies such as natural gas as the primary backup to intermittent generation.

THE EMERGENCE OF MICROGRIDS

It was not long ago that "living off the grid" referred to what we experienced when there was a power outage. Consumers would only forgo a wired connection to the local utility in the rare instances when a line extension to a new home was significantly more expensive than the cost of a solar array with battery backup. But more and more, there is interest on the part of both consumers and businesses in keeping their lights on while untethered to the local utility. The new buzzword for this concept is the "microgrid." One common definition for a microgrid is "a group of interconnected loads and distributed energy resources within clearly defined electrical boundaries that act as a single controllable entity with respect to the grid. A microgrid can connect and disconnect from the grid to enable it to operate in both grid-connected and island mode."[21]

In concept and practice, the microgrid is not new. In the microgrid's simplest form, any home or business with a back-up generator can be automatically or manually disconnected from the grid and reenergized as a power island. Balancing of load and generation can happen manually through practice as users understand what appliances or other electrical uses can be turned on simultaneously while not overpowering the generator's maximum rating and causing the lights to flicker. As you add more resources and loads to the microgrid, the balancing process becomes increasingly difficult and automated intelligent control becomes necessary. The arguments in favor of microgrids have included improved reliability, reduced costs, and reduced emissions. Depending on a microgrid's configuration, some or perhaps all of these benefits may hold true.

In its most elegant form, a microgrid has a great deal of consumer appeal. The ideal microgrid would feature a digital control system that could integrate solar PV, efficient combined heat-and-power generators, battery storage, thermal storage, demand response, and electric vehicle charging. This system would intelligently manage both supply and demand resources in a manner that ensures high reliability, reduces carbon emissions, and saves consumers money. The microgrid could operate disconnected from the utility system or could reconnect and sell any excess resources back to the interconnected grid for a profit. In essence, this would be the ultimate implementation of the smart grid.

Many market and technological trends suggest that the microgrid era could be on the not-too-distant horizon. Declining costs for solar PV, low natural gas prices, abundant biofuels, advances in distributed storage alternatives, and the rapid development of energy management technologies suggest that some of the microgrid buzz is justified. There are even predictions that a microgrid industry is not only on the rise, but that "just like the independent power industry did for generation, microgrids could break the seal on the utility compact, introducing competition in the energy industry's last great monopoly—the electric distribution business."[22]

Where the Microgrid Is Beginning to Thrive

The early focal points of microgrid development are rural village electrification, university campuses, military bases, and more recently critical community facilities during emergencies. In regards to village electrification, the United Nations has established the Sustainable Energy for

All program with the goal of eliminating energy poverty by 2030 for the 25 percent of the world (1.6 billion people) that has no access to electricity. A microgrid that harnesses small-scale renewable technologies for community use could create progress on this goal.[23] As one early example, EarthSpark International is developing microgrids in Haitian villages, where electricity is reaching villagers for the first time. EarthSpark's microgrid model is designed to "tap existing diesel generating capacity, and add solar PV, battery storage, SCADA, and prepaid metering systems—to provide power for nearby homes and businesses."[24] In areas where there is no grid power, a microgrid can offer a cost-effective means to increase access to electricity while potentially reducing a region's carbon footprint.

Both university campuses and military facilities have also shown that they are a natural fit for microgrid development given that their buildings are centrally arranged and usually have their own electric distribution facilities. Universities are a niche microgrid market both for their physical as well as intellectual architecture. First of all, a university campus is the ideal physical setting given the multiple building loads, favorable infrastructure for CHP, the usual presence of back-up generators, the increasingly common solar PV systems, the presence of campus sustainability

Pre-pay meter technology on a village microgrid system in Haiti. (Photo Courtesy of Earthspark International)

plans, and an island-like setting where the college or university often owns all of the electrical distribution system on their side of the utility transformer. On campus there are also diverse intellectual resources and research budgets to support microgrid development.

One such leading example can be found at the University of California at San Diego (UCSD). UCSD owns a 69-kV substation, ninety-six 12-kV underground feeder circuits, and four 12-kV distribution substations. This infrastructure provides UCSD with an ideal framework for its 42-mW microgrid. The university-distributed resources include a 30-mW co-generation system containing two gas turbines and a steam turbine, a 3.8-million-gallon thermal energy storage system that aids in campus cooling, 3.0 mW of solar PV covering close to 100 percent of usable rooftop space, and a 2.8-mW fuel cell powered by biogas from the city sewage treatment plant. UCSD is also becoming a leader in energy storage and electric vehicle charging technology. The university is in the process of installing a diverse portfolio of energy storage that will be integrated with its PV generation and will soon have installed twenty-five ECOtality level 2 electric vehicle charging stations, and twenty-six level 2 and DC smart chargers from the German utility RWE. UCSD's diverse distributed resources are optimized by a master controller that monitors and controls the real-time operation of the microgrid, which allows the university to self-generate 92 percent of its own annual electricity and 95 percent of its heating and cooling load. UCSD has worked closely with San Diego Gas & Electric, its local utility, to pioneer numerous demonstration projects. As a result, San Diego has one of the most advanced implementations of smart grid technology.[25]

The final microgrid focal point, critical community facilities during an emergency, has emerged as a public policy focus following recent emergency situations created by devastating storms such as hurricanes Katrina, Irene, and Sandy. In addition to the human suffering caused by these storms, they have clearly demonstrated that critical infrastructure, including the electric grid, is vulnerable to severe weather. Hurricane Irene left over seven hundred thousand electric customers in Connecticut without power, causing Governor Malloy and state legislators to support a grant program to fund the creation of microgrids that keep critical facilities powered during electrical outages. The Connecticut microgrid grant program, which passed in 2012, was the first of its kind in the country. Since the passage of this legislation, Connecticut has approved nine projects that will receive $18 million in funding to be implemented within two years. Hurricane Sandy later wreaked havoc on the Northeast, knocking out power for 8.5 million people (including much of New York City) and spurring further public debate in New York state over the need for public microgrids.[26] Although there has been significant discussion in New York concerning microgrids, the state has proceeded more cautiously due to the legal and regulatory hurdles that exist in regard to providing electric services.

Two big picture legal issues that any state will face in promoting microgrids include utility franchise rules and the definition of an electric utility. Given that electric distribution service has for decades been a monopoly function of electric utilities, states have through various means granted exclusive franchises to the local utility, which may present significant barriers to allowing non-utility microgrids. In addition, since electric distribution service has been implemented through these monopoly franchises, a microgrid could be subject to rate of return regulation by the state regulatory commission if the microgrid meets the definition of an electric utility under state law. Another emerging legal concern is the issue of who would be liable for problems with microgrid service reliability. If a third party, independent of the local utility, is responsible for balancing supply and demand on a microgrid, then close consideration must be given to the question of who would be responsible for any damages or loss of revenue resulting from poor power quality or service disruptions. Although it is unlikely that concern over extreme weather or the debate over microgrids for critical public facilities will fade soon, any desire for immediate state action will be tempered by the existence of technical, legal, and budgetary hurdles that microgrid development will present.

Are Microgrids Coming Soon to Your Neighborhood?

One home and one backup generator obviously do not make a microgrid, but what would be necessary to expand a microgrid to the neighborhood level? If a group of neighbors were to decide to pool resources by sharing their various neighborhood electric resources, such as home generators and solar PV, they would first need to add some automated controls and batteries for storage to assist in balancing the system. Next, they would likely be confronted by the reality that most electric distribution systems are designed as a radial system. That is, each home is effectively a "spur" off the utility transformer; the distribution network is not designed as a networked system in which distribution feeders run from one home to another and enable homeowners to share distributed energy resources. Accordingly, a neighborhood microgrid would require some costly rewiring. Unfortunately, reconfiguring the neighborhood distribution system would not be easy since those poles and wires connecting the neighborhood are owned by the local electric utility and everything associated with them is controlled by a utility tariff, and governed by state laws and regulations protecting the utility franchise. At the end of this hypothetical exercise, the increased costs of additional technology, the physical limitations of the distribution system, and legal and regulatory hurdles suggest that the utility distribution business should not be placed on the endangered species list quite yet. Although rapidly changing technology and declining costs of distributed resources deservingly has generated some buzz for the microgrid, it is rather uncertain whether one will be coming soon to a neighborhood near you.

EARLY UTILITY IMPLEMENTATIONS OF DISTRIBUTED ENERGY TECHNOLOGIES

Our case study research revealed two clear examples of utilities, San Diego Gas & Electric (an investor-owned utility) and the Sacramento Municipal Utility District (a publicly-owned utility), that include distributed energy technology projects as part of their smart grid implementation plans.

The San Diego Gas & Electric Experience

San Diego Gas & Electric is located in an area of the nation rich in renewable resources, and it has been an active player in developing distributed generation. SDG&E stands out for linking distributed generation with the smart grid. This synergy has occurred in San Diego for a number of reasons, including having a strong state RPS target to meet, being in an area rich in renewable resources, and the fact that the CPUC has supported distributed generation needs through smart grid rollout. Many customers in SDG&E's service territory have distributed rooftop solar units. In fact, SDG&E customers have already installed more megawatts of rooftop solar in San Diego—approximately 163 mW and twenty-two thousand customer interconnections as of 2013—than utility customers in any other American city.

The utility has also said that the smart grid's ability to automate services and information flow will allow it to "mitigate the problems caused by the intermittency of distributed renewable resources like wind and solar." To this end, SDG&E is building out a network designed to acquire information about electricity generation from distributed generators and other intermittent generators. According to SDG&E, the utility plans to use "energy storage . . . advanced control and management . . . and solid state voltage regulation as part of their smart grid developments."[27] The utility has also indicated that new technology developments in the storage and voltage control areas should "help mitigate some of the problems that come with distributed generation," like intermittency.[28] SDG&E

plans to install enough smart transformers, inverters, synchrophasors, and capacitors to control voltage fluctuations by 2020, which will better integrate all of the distributed resources on its system.

Borrego Springs Microgrid Demonstration Project

Perhaps one the most far-reaching utility smart grid demonstration projects exploring the potential of the microgrid is located in the San Diego County California community of Borrego Springs, which is located about ninety miles outside of San Diego. The goal is to showcase and test various aspects of microgrid technology, including smart meters, distributed renewable energy generation, and energy storage. While not completely cut off from the main grid, the Borrego Springs microgrid acts as a self-contained grid that can maintain power on its own should the California grid experience a power shortage. Given that Borrego Springs is in a less concentrated region of SDG&E's service territory, service reliability is generally lower than the more urban region.

Borrego Springs is a small community with residents who have aggressively adopted rooftop solar, with 600 to 700 kW of distributed generation that is already deployed. Rooftop solar was chosen to enhance overall reliability, to capitalize on the opportunity to balance supply and demand, and to be more self-sufficient as a locality. Aside from the installation of solar, energy storage is a key technology in the Borrego Spring demonstration project. SDG&E plans to install a 0.5-mW (instantaneous capacity) by 1.5-mWh (total energy production) battery at the substation and three 25-kW by 50-kWh batteries for community energy storage. Three residences will also receive utility-supplied batteries that are capable of delivering 4.5 kW by 12 kWh of electricity.

There are two important microgrid applications for batteries that are being evaluated. They can be used for operating as an island delivering electricity when generation sources are offline. The storage systems can also be used to smooth variability of intermittent sources of power so that drops and surges in voltage do not create problems on the distribution grid. SDG&E will test both applications. The objective of the project is to conduct a pilot scale "proof of concept" demonstration to determine how advanced information-based technologies and distributed energy resources may increase utilization and reliability of the grid. In order to execute this project, SDG&E has developed specific project strategies to design and demonstrate a smart electrical grid that incorporates sophisticated sensors, communications, and controls. Specifically, SDG&E is incorporating solar power generators on homes and businesses into the electrical delivery system, enabling coordinated demand response programs, and integrating reliable electrical storage devices to operate the microgrid in a more cost-effective manner.

The Sacramento Municipal Utility District

The Sacramento Municipal Utility District has been active in the distributed generation space for a number of years, primarily with larger projects located at water treatment facilities. SMUD has set a goal to obtain 33 percent renewable power by 2020 and surpassed the 20 percent mark in 2010, including 35 mW of solar PV. The utility has said that smart grid will be a key to reaching this level of renewable energy. SMUD, like other utilities, is concerned about the technical challenges distributed generation poses.

Anatolia SolarSmart Community Storage

The Sacramento Municipal Utility District is also examining storage as a way of supporting its renewable energy plans, primarily in the area of solar energy. The utility has plans to adopt large-scale storage rollout by 2050. To that end, SMUD has undertaken a series of demonstration projects including the Anatolia SolarSmart Community in conjunction with Lennar Homes. The Anatolia project is designed to quantify the costs and benefits of deploying EES and distributed generation so that SMUD can deploy these technologies throughout its broader service territory. Anatolia is planned as a 795-home community in Rancho Cordova, California, just southeast of Sacramento, and will have over 600 Solar-Smart Homes, each with 2.0 kW to 5.0 kW of solar PV. In addition, as part of the SMUD smart grid pilot, fifteen residential energy storage systems with 5 kW (instantaneous capacity) by 8.8 kWh (total energy production) of battery storage have been installed along with three community energy storage systems, which are linked to five to ten homes, providing 30 kW by 34 kWh of battery storage capacity. The residential energy storage units are essentially a refrigerator-sized battery that can be located in the garage. The homes with solar PV systems and battery storage are being studied to see if, when deployed together, renewables and storage can reduce peak load, regulate voltage, and improve reliability. The ultimate goal is to gain experimental data on how storage can help overcome the variable output of PV systems. The total project cost is expected to cost approximately $5.9 million, with funding support from the Department of Energy, SMUD, and industry partners.[29]

CONCLUSION

Over time, distributed energy technologies have the potential to mag-nify the environmental benefits of the smart grid. In particular, linking distributed generation and energy storage rollout with smart grid tech-nologies will likely be necessary when the amount of renewable genera-tion available exceeds current state RPS levels. Taking advantage of the synergies inherent in these projects would give utilities valuable field experience with smart grid technologies that could improve their inter-nal operations, allay public concerns about the smart grid, and assuage regulators' fears about these technologies' cost-benefit ratio. Moreover, integrating the distributed generation, energy storage, and smart grid planning processes would allow utilities to better understand their own systems and operate them more efficiently. Pilot projects are incredibly important as well. Utilities must study the impact that high penetra-tions of distributed generation resources will have on their systems. In addition, they must also work to implement smart grid and energy stor-age technologies designed to mitigate these impacts while maximizing the power output that these resources are capable of generating. Regulators should support these types of pilot projects and allow utilities opportunities for fair cost recovery. Finally, public funding will be key to moving forward. Through the American Recovery and Reinvestment Act and other Department of Energy programs, the federal government has put a large amount of money into developing and deploying distrib-uted generation and smart grid technologies. This funding has been largely responsible for the pilot programs discussed above. This is not to say that all federal funding in the distributed generation space has been a success. The recent bankruptcy of solar panel manufacturer Solyndra, which received a sizable federal loan guarantee, is a clear example of the perils of subsidizing emerging energy technologies. However, the failure of one firm, which was on the losing end of a growth trend in the solar energy market, should not lead to a reduction of governmental support for emerging technologies, especially those technologies that can reduce the carbon footprint of the United States and lead to a more robust grid.

7

CONSERVING ENERGY THROUGH DISTRIBUTION AUTOMATION

Historically, the utility industry has been plagued by operational ineffi-ciencies. The average fossil-fuel power plant is only 33 percent efficient, using three units of fuel to produce a single unit of electricity.[1] Energy losses also occur in the transmission and distribution sector: Some re-ports estimate that as much as 13 percent of the electricity transmitted across these networks is lost as waste heat.[2] In addition to these energy losses, utilities must contend with other inefficiencies. When an outage occurs, utilities have to send out crews to locate the problem and then fix it, which can take anywhere from several hours to several days, depend-ing on the magnitude of the outage. More important, many utilities lack the equipment and communications infrastructure to detect and reroute equipment failures or outages without timely manual intervention. Thus they are constantly reacting to crises rather than automatically resolving them.

By automating the distribution system, utilities can correct many of these inefficiencies, as well as institute processes to decrease the electricity sector's environmental footprint. "Distribution automation" is a concept that has been around for several decades,[3] and it can refer to a plethora of technologies, systems, and processes that improve the operational ef-ficiency of distribution systems. It is therefore a vague term that means different things to different people. But generally speaking, distribution automation is primarily a means to improve both the reliability and effi-ciency of the grid. By installing a more sophisticated communications infrastructure and deploying more advanced technologies at substations and along power lines, utilities will be able to remotely monitor and con-trol the distribution network, in near real time. Distribution automation gives utilities access to a greater volume of detailed information about the grid, allowing them to improve reliability and manage the grid in a more cost-effective manner. This information will also allow utilities to more efficiently transmit power across distribution lines, thus reducing energy losses and overall energy consumption.

This chapter will begin by providing an overview of the current distribution system so that the reader can more clearly understand how distribution automation technologies improve upon that system. It will then describe the reliability benefits of distribution automation and how various technologies can be used to prevent outages, reduce outage duration, extend the equipment lifetimes, and generally improve a utility's ability to monitor the grid. Finally, it will describe how, using advanced metering infrastructure, utilities can employ a technique known as conservation voltage reduction (CVR) to monitor—and meaningfully reduce—energy consumption.

THE CURRENT DISTRIBUTION SYSTEM

To understand the current distribution system, it is important to understand how electricity travels through the previous portions of electricity infrastructure—the generation and transmission sectors. Generators produce electricity at the power plant and run it through a transformer to "step up" (increase) the voltage to anywhere between 110,000 and 765,000 volts.[4] Generators increase the voltage to these levels because too much energy is lost when electricity is transmitted across long distances at low voltages. To understand why, it's important to have a handle on some basic physical properties of electricity.

Three fundamental concepts govern the behavior of electricity as it travels through a circuit: current, voltage, and resistance.[5] Referring back to our example in chapter 1, if you compare a transmission line to a water pipe, current would be analogous to the flow of the water, voltage would be analogous to the water pressure, and resistance would be analogous to a force that impedes the flow of water (i.e., friction, gravity, or corroded pipes). Just as you get water to flow through a pipe by creating a pressure difference at either end, utilities get electrical current to flow through transmission wires by applying voltage. Thus, the amount of electric power that is transmitted across a wire is a product of current and voltage. The current is opposed, however, by resistance in the wire, which dissipates some of the energy and generates waste heat. Some materials, such as copper, have very little resistance and are classified as conductors; others, such as glass or porcelain, have a lot of resistance and are referred to as insulators. More conductive materials will produce less resistance and are therefore better for transmitting electricity because they minimize energy losses.

But even with the best conductors, it is virtually impossible to transmit large amounts of electrical current across long distances without encountering significant energy losses. This is because energy loss is not only a function of the conductivity of the wire, but also the length of that wire and the amount of current traveling on it. This first point seems obvious: The longer the wire, the more resistance the electrical current will encounter, which increases energy losses. The second point is not as obvious, but is rooted in a well-established principle of physics, namely, that energy losses along a transmission line are proportional to the square of the current. Thus, increasing current along a wire will likewise increase energy losses.

Despite these constraints, utilities are able to transmit large amounts of electricity over vast distances, primarily by increasing the voltage of the electricity. Recall that electric power is a product of voltage (measured in volts) and current (measured in amps). When the utility transmits power across long distances, it wants the quantity for current to be low, because the more current there is on the line, the greater the energy losses. But if everything else remains equal, reducing the amount of current will likewise reduce the overall amount of power delivered. The utility can compensate for this loss in current by increasing voltage, thereby delivering the same amount of power that it originally intended to deliver.

An example will help illustrate these abstract concepts. Say a utility serves a town that demands 300 mW of power at a given moment in time. The town is one hundred miles away, so the utility must transmit the power over long-distance transmission lines. To supply this 300 mW, it could choose to transmit approximately 7,692 amps of current at 39 kV, but the line losses would be substantial. So instead, the utility can reduce the current (to around, say, 392 amps), crank up the voltage (to around 765 kV), and still deliver the same amount of power, but with significantly less line losses.

After being sent across high-voltage transmission lines, the electricity goes to a substation, where the voltage is stepped down, usually below 35 kV. The line between the transmission and distribution networks is usually drawn at the substation. Substations can be configured in an almost infinite number of ways, depending on the load the substation is serving, expected load growth, land availability, reliability requirements, and the voltage levels.[6] Generally speaking, however, all substations have several basic components. On the "high-voltage" side of the substation, transmission lines feed electricity through a transformer, which lowers the voltage and feeds it into a busbar. The busbar is a large aluminum or copper bar that, for safety reasons, is usually mounted several feet off of the ground. It distributes electricity to the outgoing distribution feeders. These feeders emanate out from the substation and deliver electricity to customers. The primary feeders are the utility poles that you see on the side of a road. They have four wires: three on top, which transmit power to consumers, and one "neutral" wire beneath the transformer, which sends power back to the substation to balance the amount of energy on the line.[7] Secondary feeders are usually attached to these poles, and they run directly to residences and businesses. These secondary feeders connect to distribution transformers near a home, which further steps down the electricity to 240 volts. This allows the utility to provide both 120-volt service (for things like a television, phone charger, or hair dryer) and 240-volt service (for larger appliances, like a clothes dryer).

The substation and distribution lines also contain a number of other components, such as switching devices and voltage regulators. The former can close or open an electrical circuit to permit or impede the flow of electricity.[8] Switches, for example, can disconnect the substation from the transmission grid or disconnect certain distribution lines from the substation in the event that a fault occurs.[9] Other types of devices, including circuit breakers, fuses, disconnectors, and reclosers, are present at both substations and on distribution feeders. Generally speaking, these devices interrupt or redirect current when a fault occurs or when a certain piece of equipment needs to be repaired.[10] Voltage regulators, such as load-tap changing transformers and capacitors, regulate and maintain the voltage levels within the substation and on the distribution feeders.

RELIABILITY BENEFITS OF DISTRIBUTION AUTOMATION

To some extent, current distribution automation technologies allow grid operators to remotely measure—and even control—power flows across the grid. Eventually, utilities hope to deploy technologies that would make the distribution system "so automated that it virtually corrects itself without human intervention."[11] At this point, however, distribution automation is focused on providing utilities with faster access to a greater volume of information about the status of the distribution network.[12] This will allow utilities to manage the distribution network in a more efficient manner, to identify problems before they lead to outages, and to more quickly restore power to customers if an outage does occur.

There are three fundamental components of any distribution automation system.[13] The first is a control system, which provides utilities with an interface through which they can monitor and control the distribution network. The second is the data communications infrastructure through which information is collected and transmitted back to the utility control center. The third is an amalgamation of field equipment—installed at substations, on the distribution lines, or at a customer's premises—which utilities can manipulate to monitor and control power flows.[14] At one level or another, many utilities have already installed some version of these three components to manage their distribution network. As utilities continue to deploy smart grid technologies, they will likewise upgrade and optimize these components.

Control Systems

A centralized control system is necessary to allow utilities to efficiently monitor and control the distribution system. These systems are variously referred to as supervisory control and data acquisition systems, outage management systems (OMS), and distribution management systems. In fact, SCADA is a broader term than the latter two. A SCADA system is essentially an information technology architecture that is used by companies to monitor and control plant equipment in various industries, such as oil and gas pipelines, municipal waste and water systems (SCADA), and transportation infrastructure, just to name a few.[15] OMS and DMS are applications of SCADA systems in the context of electric distribution networks, although all three terms are often thrown around interchangeably.

To some degree or another, SCADA systems have existed in the electricity sector for at least the last half-century,[16] although they have primarily been used to monitor and control the transmission network, rather than the distribution system.[17] As time has passed, more utilities have deployed SCADA systems, initially in the form of OMS. As its name suggests, OMS is chiefly designed to collect data on outages in an efficient and organized manner so that crews can respond more quickly. Often, these systems are integrated with geographic information systems and other project management systems, such that they can log trouble calls from customers, analyze and identify the location of the outage, and track crews who are being sent to work on the problem.[18]

Distribution management systems are a relatively new evolution of the traditional OMS. A DMS is designed to improve the efficiency of the distribution network by allowing utilities to remotely monitor and control field devices.[19] These systems also help grid operators control power flows and monitor the system and its equipment for potential faults or failures. In the event that a fault does occur, the DMS can find the most optimal way to restore power to the largest number of customers. In this way, a DMS helps utilities proactively address potential problems with or inefficiencies in the distribution network.

Communications Infrastructure

Communications systems allow utilities to acquire data from sensors and other equipment on the distribution network and to relay control signals to operate and control that equipment.[20] As described in chapter 3, there are a variety of communications solutions that utilities could employ to transmit data back and forth between field devices and the utility control system. Utilities may use a wired infrastructure, such as fiber optics or broadband over power lines, or a wireless infrastructure, such as mesh radio frequency networks or existing 3G or 4G LTE cell phone networks, to transmit data back and forth. In all likelihood, utilities will likely use a mix of these networks.[21] They may choose to use wireless technologies to transmit data from AMI and field devices back to the substation and use wired technologies to transmit data from the substation back to the control center. Any communications infrastructure that is installed will have to have sufficient bandwidth to transmit data from both AMI and field devices in the utility's distribution automation system.

Field Devices

Utilities can improve the reliability of their distribution network by remotely monitoring and manipulating field devices that are installed at substations and along the distribution network. Utilities can install remote fault indicators and AMI, which notify grid operators and field crews when and where faults or outages occur. An outage is when customers lose electricity service completely, whereas a fault is "an abnormal circuit condition which results in energy being dissipated in a manner other than serving the intended load."[22] Of course, in many cases, the latter can lead to the former. Fault detection devices are capable of alerting a utility as to when fault signatures are present or when the voltage on a particular feeder is above or below normal levels. This allows the utility to detect, locate, and quickly respond to faults.[23] Similarly, smart meters and AMI can instantaneously report outages to utilities rather than forcing utilities to rely on customer phone calls to locate these incidents. This is because most smart meters can "transmit a 'last gasp' alert when power to the meter is lost," providing the utility with the location and time of the outage.[24] Some utilities even have meters that they can ping, which allows the utility to assess the boundaries of the outage and determine when power has been restored to a customer.[25]

Newer sensors and relays are even capable of helping utilities identify and correct high-impedance faults. In contrast to high-impedance fault, a low-impedance fault is one that instantaneously redirects a very large amount of current toward the ground. These are often colloquially referred to as "short circuits," and utilities have historically had no problem detecting and correcting them.[26] High-impedance faults, however, are another story. A high-impedance fault occurs when an object surrounding a feeder causes a small amount of current to "leak" out of its intended path.[27] An example would be when a tree or a piece of vegetation unexpectedly contacts a power line. This foreign object is not a good conductor of electricity (i.e., it has a high impedance), so it only diverts a small amount of current away from the intended load. The amount of diverted current is so low that existing sensors cannot detect that a fault has occurred. Indeed, these faults "result only slight increases in load current[, and] thus can be confused with a normal increase in load."[28] Newer sensors and relay technologies, however, are capable of detecting these faults, and improve the operational efficiency of the distribution network by reducing overall energy consumption.

When these sensors do detect faults, the utility can use a technique known as "feeder automation" to correct the faults and minimize the number of customers who experience power outages. The utility can install switches on the distribution feeders, which will then open or close in response to automated commands from the sensors or to manual commands from grid operators.[29] By opening or closing the circuit on a given feeder, these switches can isolate faults and ensure that fewer customers experience outages or losses in power quality. This also saves time for the crews sent out to address the fault; they can begin immediately working on correcting the problem, rather than having to manually locate and flip the switch that isolates the feeder (which can sometimes be a time-consuming process if the switch is located far away from the fault).

Feeder automation functions differently depending on the configuration of the feeder. Radial feeders, for example, run from a substation to a group of customers, and they are not connected to any other feeders. These are typically used in rural areas. On these feeders, automated switches can isolate the fault and simply minimize the amount of customers affected by the fault.[30] Other feeder configurations, however, are better at keeping the lights on for all customers, even when a fault or outage does occur. Looped feeders, for example, have two feeders that are interconnected, but the circuit is open at the interconnection point—that is, in normal circumstances no electricity flows through the interconnection point from one feeder to the other. If a fault occurs on one of these feeders, the utility can activate a switch that closes the circuit at the interconnection point, thereby redirecting electricity from the active feeder to the faulty one and restoring power to customers. Networked feeders are most often used in urban areas. These feeders "involve multiple power flows from multiple sources to all customers that are served by the network," such that, if a fault occurs on one feeder, the utility can redirect power through another, redundant pathway.[31]

Distribution automation technologies not only help utilities respond to outages and faults, but also to proactively prevent those problems from occurring in the first place. Utilities can install monitors and sensors in various pieces of equipment, such as transformers, to ensure that this equipment is operating efficiently. If a problem is detected, the sensor would notify the utility, and the utility could send out a crew to repair or replace the equipment.[32] Utilities can also place feeder monitors on distribution lines, which can monitor the amount of electricity flowing over the line in near real time. The sensor can notify utilities if customer demand reaches a level that could create an outage. The utility could also use this information to proactively plan for the future. If it knows that there will be a great deal of demand along a particular feeder at a particular time, it can take measures to ensure that the feeder stays online.

All of these technologies are expected to produce significant benefits for utilities. In particular, they can reduce the frequency and duration of outages, which will increase the productivity of commercial and industrial customers. Moreover, utilities spend a great deal of time and resources responding to outages, faults, and equipment failures. Automated controls that report incidents to the utility in near real time will improve utility efficiency and thereby reduce operational expenses. Usually, when utility crews go out to maintain lines or correct outages, they had to travel to multiple locations to perform switching operations that deenergized a certain section of a feeder. Likewise, crews often have to visually inspect a given piece of equipment to ensure that it is in good health. And of course, when outages occur, the utility must rely on a patchwork of customer phone calls to identify and correct an outage. Distribution automation, however, promises to cut back on the amount of time and resources that utilities must expend in performing these basic functions. In this way, distribution automation will be critical to improving the reliability of the distribution network in the coming century.[33]

ENVIRONMENTAL BENEFITS OF DISTRIBUTION AUTOMATION: CONSERVATION VOLTAGE REDUCTION

There is an aspect of distribution automation that can produce significant energy savings and likewise reduce the amount of carbon dioxide emissions from the electric power sector. It is referred to as reactive power compensation and conservation voltage reduction (CVR). CVR is a fairly simple concept. Remember that the amount of power delivered to a customer is a product of current and voltage. The American National Standards Institute (ANSI) has set a standard for voltage levels at a residential customer's meter: Generally speaking, residential voltage should be somewhere between 114 and 126 volts.[34] However, longer feeders and larger loads tend to produce correspondingly larger drops in voltage. Accordingly, utilities will increase the voltage level of electricity at the substation right below the maximum (126 volts), knowing that it will drop as the load or length of the feeder increases. The utility installs load-tap changers (LTCs) at the substation, which increase or decrease the voltage of electricity depending on the load and length of the feeder that the substation is serving. Likewise, utilities may install voltage regulators along the length of a distribution feeder for this same purpose.[35]

The existence of LTCs and voltage regulators indicates that (like many of the ideas and technologies presented in this book) maintaining customer voltage at the appropriate levels is not a new idea. Utilities have long used these devices to regulate voltage levels at substations and distribution feeders. The problem is that many utilities cannot measure or monitor voltage levels at individual customer premises. In fact, some utilities don't even bother to measure voltage levels beyond the substation. Instead, they install and program LTCs and voltage regulators along the distribution feeders based on computer models, which estimate what load will be (and thus, what the voltage should be) during high- and low-demand periods.[36] This leads many utilities to act conservatively, establishing voltage levels that are higher than necessary, which increases line losses and overall energy consumption.[37] That is, the utility does not take any steps to optimally regulate or control the voltage based on changing load conditions, largely because it does not have the information or automation technologies to do so.[38]

Example of How CVR Reduces Voltage on a Distribution Feeder

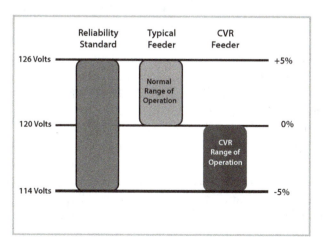

Utilities have also historically been unable to monitor reactive power or compensate for reactive power losses, which occur when inductive loads (such as motors, transformers, or any device that stores electricity in a magnetic field) draw power from the grid. Reactive power is a complicated concept, but we will endeavor to explain it in easily understandable terms. To do so, we'll again need to go over some basic principles of physics.

There are essentially three types of electrical loads: resistive, inductive, and capacitive. Resistive loads impede the flow of electricity and, in so doing, usually convert it into another form of energy (e.g., light or heat). Inductive loads store energy in a magnetic field, and capacitors store energy in a magnetic charge.[39] There are also three types of electrical power: real power (measured in kilowatts), reactive power (measured in kilovolt-amperes-reactive, or kVAR), and apparent power (measured in kilovolt-amperes).[40] Real power is electrical energy that actually does work, whereas reactive power is electrical energy that is needed to sustain a magnetic field in motors and transformers, but that does no real work. Reactive power flows back and forth between the inductive load and the grid. Apparent power is the sum of the two. Finally, power factor is the ratio of real power to apparent power: the power factor ratio essentially explains how much of the apparent power in a given system is real power (i.e., used for actual work).[41] The closer this ratio is to 1, the greater amount of real power there is in a system.

Whereas resistive loads use only real power, inductive loads use both real power (to do physical work) and reactive power (to energize their magnetic field). This means that some of the power drawn by inductive loads essentially does no work at all. Industrial customers who use large induction motors in their manufacturing processes will have low power factors, because they need to consume a lot of reactive power to sustain a magnetic field in those motors. Even though reactive power does no real "work," utilities must nonetheless supply it to their customers, which increases line losses on the distribution network. And as mentioned above, reactive power tends to flow back and forth between the inductive load and the grid. This additional traffic in electricity on the distribution lines further increases line losses.

The smart grid can correct both of these problems. With respect to CVR, utilities can deploy voltage sensors along the distribution grid and on customer premises to measure voltage levels in near real time. Utilities can deploy dedicated voltage sensors along distribution poles, or they can install smart meters that contain voltage sensors. The latter is more common. The smart meter can relay information regarding a customer's voltage level through the smart grid communications system and back to the utility. The utility can then analyze this data and remotely manipulate the LTCs and voltage regulators so that the customer's voltage is reduced to an optimal level.[42] So long as the voltage remains between prescribed levels, the customer will not see any degradation in the quality of electric service.

Of course, the effectiveness of CVR is dependent on the mix of loads on a particular distribution feeder. For example, if CVR is used on loads that are controlled by a thermostat, the amount of electricity consumed at that particular point in time may go down, but it will take longer for the customer's premises to reach the desired temperature. The customer would then leave the air conditioner on for longer, meaning that there may be no decrease in energy usage.[43]

The utility may decide to employ CVR during peak demand times, which would allow it to defer building additional generation capacity or updates to its distribution system. Or the utility may decide to continuously employ CVR to conserve its overall customer energy consumption. In either case, the utility cuts back on the amount of fuel it needs to consume to provide energy to customers, which likewise reduces emissions.[44]

With respect to reactive power compensation, utilities can use smart meters and AMI to determine which customers consume large amounts of reactive power. They can then construct—or encourage those customers to construct—capacitor banks, which reduce overall reactive power consumption. Capacitors and inductors complement each other; the former absorbs current when the latter discharges it, and vice versa. Thus when an inductive load is discharging reactive power, a capacitor can absorb that power, and then conduct it back toward the inductor. By installing capacitors, the inductive load is essentially "supplying [its] own reactive current so the utility system doesn't need to."[45] And reducing the amount of reactive power that inductive loads consume will likewise reduce the overall amount of energy that the utility must supply to the grid.

CONSERVATION VOLTAGE REDUCTION IN PRACTICE

There have been a number of pilot projects and studies of CVR in practice. In 2007, Idaho Power participated in the Northwest Energy Efficiency Alliance Distribution Efficiency Initiative Pilot Study (DEI) and found that in lowering voltage at its Boise substation it was able to achieve a 1.5–2.55 percent energy reduction (kWh) and a 1.8–2.6 percent demand reduction (kW). According to their analysis, 80–90 percent of the energy reduction was reflected in reduced customer use, while 10–20 percent of it resulted from power system efficiency gains.[46] Greentech Media has reported that CVR costs are less than $550 per kilowatt saved and approximately $20 per megawatt-hour saved, much less than the cost of conventional resources.[47] Similar studies with Snohomish PUD, a public power utility in the Pacific Northwest, found that the typical feeder had 1.6 percent energy savings and the average customer saved about 156 kWh/year. The costs to Snohomish were less than twelve dollars a megawatt-hour. Importantly, there were no low-voltage complaints experienced.[48]

Although much research on CVR continues to be under way through initiatives like the Electric Power Research Institute's Green Circuits Research Program, the acceptance of CVR as an energy efficiency resource has gained significant support. The National Association of Regulatory Utility Commissioners in 2013 passed a resolution supporting treating CVR as a resource.[49] A number of the utilities in our case studies have been evaluating CVR technology and SMUD reports that 18 percent of its circuits are CVR capable.[50] According to the SDG&E *Electric Distribution Handbook*, 95 percent of the SDG&E substations are compliant with the CPUC CVR standards.[51] The CPUC standard has been in place since 1977 and encourages maintaining voltages at the lower end of the acceptable range.

CONCLUSION

Distribution automation can deliver significant reliability and environmental benefits for both utilities and their customers. Increasing the intelligence of the distribution network will help utilities proactively prevent faults and outages and quickly and efficiently respond to problems when they do arise. Moreover, CVR and reactive power compensation can save a substantial amount of energy. If implemented on a national scale, these techniques could reduce energy consumption and carbon emissions by 2 percent of projected 2030 levels.[52] Of course, this reduction in energy use is perhaps the very reason that utilities have not implemented CVR on a widespread basis: Less energy consumption means that sales and revenues will take a hit. Regulators and government officials will need to develop policies that encourage CVR so that utilities can leverage the reliability and environmental benefits that it can provide.

8

CONCLUSION: LEADING THE DIGITAL ENERGY REVOLUTION FORWARD

In 2013, *WIRED* celebrated its twentieth anniversary as a magazine and reminded us that the publication is not about "technology" but the "Digital Generation," who, the editors say, are "the most powerful people on the planet."[1] Similarly, the digital energy revolution is not just about technology. Digital technology has existed for years, and hence in 2013 *WIRED* celebrated its twentieth anniversary, not its first or fifth. For various reasons the digital energy revolution did not begin in 1993, but it is fully under way today. As we bring digital technology to the most important aspect of our energy system, the electric grid, this powerful generation will help put our country on a path toward a smarter, greener grid—a grid that is integral to promoting a sustainable future for the planet.

Indeed, in *Reinventing Fire*, Amory Lovins describes the emergence of this new electricity infrastructure. He envisions that "electricity—along with the digital information and computer systems it enable and requires—provides the vital root system that sustains our economy. Electricity has become the connective tissue of the information age."[2] In visualizing the possibilities, Lovins notes that "electricity is poised for a profound leap in importance as the key enabler of the transitions in transportation, buildings, and industry."[3] Of course, the path to a smarter and greener electric grid is long and particularly arduous when it comes to implementing smarter technologies and policies. The challenge is not unique to the United States. Even across the Atlantic, it was noted recently that "the electrical cables in London are Victorian," the conventional coal power stations were "first deployed in the late 19th century," gas turbines are "from the Second World War," and nuclear reactors are "largely based on 1950's designs."[4]

Unsurprisingly, the smart grid has presented new legal, policy, and regulatory challenges. To overcome these challenges and realize the full potential of the digital energy revolution, electric utilities, technology companies, the government, academic researchers, and other stakeholders must collaborate to implement a smart grid that empowers customers, harnesses available technology, and promotes environmental improvement. Initially, the Obama administration fueled progress by making a smart electric grid a central component of the American clean energy agenda, including providing $3.4 billion in grants to utilities. There has also been leadership from states such as California, Vermont, and Texas, which demonstrates that states and communities can take the lead in finding a well-balanced approach to implementing the smart grid.

But there is much more to do. These early efforts are just a beginning: The costs of a fully functioning U.S. smart electric grid could require investing up to half a trillion dollars in the grid, although the benefits that result could be anywhere from three to six times that figure. In these final pages, we provide some broad recommendations as to what must be done to lead the digital energy revolution forward.

CLEAR PUBLIC POLICIES WILL SPEED SMART GRID RESULTS

While the concept is simple, the divergent results in our case studies and other national experience suggest that it bears repeating: Clear public policies will speed smart grid results. California and other states that have set clear policies are moving steadily toward their goals rather than getting bogged down in debates over what the goals should be. California has demonstrated that the development of clear state policy goals will foster successful projects. Once the state defines the policy goals, utilities, regulators, and other stakeholders can then debate the best means for achieving those smart grid goals rather than debating what the goals should be. California has not been without its own bumps in the road, but it is indisputably a national leader in smart grid implementation, for both investor-owned utilities and the public power community. Its well aligned legislative and regulatory policy is a key enabler. Similarly, Vermont's early regulatory support for its statewide initiative, as well as clear cost recovery policy, has advanced AMI adoption across the state. Likewise, Texas—a state with a vibrant competitive electric retail sector—has clearly delineated the roles between electric distribution companies and competitive retailers, which has fostered innovative technologies and services.

Setting clear state policy goals is essential, especially for an industry implementing such a capital intensive technology that presents risks such as device interoperability and early technological obsolescence. ComEd's experience in Illinois could not provide a clearer demonstration of the gridlock and inefficiency embodied in not getting this policy issue right. In addition to cost recovery policy, effective customer data privacy policy is also essential. Not only is customer acceptance important, but their active engagement is necessary to achieve the full environmental promise of the smart electric grid. Customers are not going to give utilities and state regulators a second chance; a transparent and effective privacy policy is essential to success.

State policies are critically important because utility investments in smart grid technology are governed by state regulatory regimes, but continued strong federal policies are also important. There is no doubt that the Obama administration's embracing of the smart grid as part of the nation's clean energy strategy has had significant benefits, especially through the critical ARRA funding. Unfortunately, the conflict between Congress and the administration on clean energy incentives, research and development, and climate legislation has stunted progress. Finally, continuing the work of the NIST, SGIP, and FERC on developing clear standards for interoperability of smart grid technologies is vitally important for an effective smart electric grid.

COLLABORATION WILL SPUR PROGRESS AND INNOVATION

In the Northeast, unprecedented collaboration among utilities, government, industry, and academia in Vermont has led to the rollout of a statewide smart grid. The telecomm and electric industries partnered with the state government to create a broadband infrastructure—a move that will not only enable the state's smart grid to work but also provide a big benefit to rural customers who are often without Internet access. Perhaps there is no better example of the benefits of collaboration than observing the innovation of the Pecan Street Project in Austin, Texas. This public-private partnership has brought all of the key players together and demonstrated that utilities, governments, academics, the technology industry, and NGOs can come together to create a truly robust smart grid. Other regions should take note of these collaborative examples in Vermont and Texas.

ENGAGING CUSTOMERS THROUGH SMARTER
RATES AND SERVICES

This book has been as much about smart policy as it has been about smart technology. The true energy savings potential of this technology will not be fully achieved without finding the right opportunities for exciting the human element and truly igniting the digital energy revolution. There are some encouraging examples of early and sustained success. The Salt River Project's prepay program experience—giving customers timely information about their electric usage and letting them control their consumption—has resulted in satisfied customers and a 12 percent drop in power use. As a result of its early leadership on time of use rates and its innovate M-Power (prepay electric service) program, the Salt River Project has demonstrated the opportunities that lie ahead for dynamic pricing combined with the use of technology. M-Power has demonstrated that both information and technology can empower customers to save energy. Furthermore, SRP's long and successful experience with time-of-use rates demonstrates the smart grid's promise for voluntary dynamic pricing. In the non-utility space, firms like Opower have helped the smart grid supercharge energy efficiency through their innovative behavior-based efficiency programs. As Opower expands into the demand response arena, their innovation will help take DR to the next level.

While there are promising signs for the future, significant challenges also remain. Fortunately, the Department of Energy has included a consumer behavior study component to its SGIP funding that is piloting the use of smart devices and smart rates and studying how these features can be best utilized together to save energy. The early results of these studies from utilities such as OG&E and SMUD are encouraging. These studies help to remind us that we need to invest in developing our smart policies just like we would invest in developing new technologies.

RESEARCH, DEVELOPMENT, AND DEMONSTRATION PROJECTS ARE ESSENTIAL

While utilities across the nation are largely focusing on rolling out smart meters to consumers and building the associated AMI communications networks, there are also smart grid demonstration projects that are exploring how those meter networks can provide new end-use services and facilitate the integration of clean distributed generation. The Pecan Street Project, a public-private partnership, is not focused on a utility-wide rollout of smart meters and the associated communications infrastructure but on how a smart electric grid can provide value to customers and the environment. Cutting-edge demonstration projects such as Pecan Street can both demonstrate the ultimate potential of the smart grid and at the same time help ensure that the technology operates on an integrated basis prior to rollout to the broader market. Pecan Street also features a high penetration of solar PV and electric vehicles. Studying the advanced adoption of these clean energy technologies on a focused basis will better prepare the utilities, technology companies, and other stakeholders for broader future national adoption of the technology.

For now, PNNL's analysis suggests that the smart grid will not need to play a major role prior to 2030 in supporting the integration of renewable energy, and our case studies seem to support this finding. This is not because smart technologies (such as smart inverters, demand response, and distributed storage) do not have a significant future role to play in renewable energy integration; instead, it reflects the fact that until we reach levels of renewable energy beyond current state RPS requirements (e.g., 20–30%), grid support for these variable resources can largely be provided by existing electric infrastructure. Once we begin to exceed this 20 percent threshold, particularly in leading clean energy states, smart grid technologies will need to play a larger role. Furthermore, other regions that lead in renewable energy development, such as Europe, will likely find earlier market support for these technologies.

One example our case study research highlights is SMUD, which is examining how electric storage technologies can support its plan to increase renewable energy supplies by 2050. Its Anatolia SolarSmart community demonstration project looks to quantify the cost and benefits of storage deployment and distributed solar generation. SMUD has received federal stimulus funding to support some of its demonstration projects. In order to have experience and comfort with these technologies, especially in an industry that places a premium on reliability, continued investment in research, development, and demonstration projects will be critically important. Federal funding of these demonstration projects has been an important component.

WELL-DEFINED AND INDEPENDENTLY VERIFIED METRICS FOR SUCCESS

In support of additional transparency on smart grid implementation, the CPUC has required that the California IOUs file annual reports on a variety of smart grid implementation metrics, which are to be further developed in a series of technical working groups. The California IOUs have benefited by having third parties, such as the Environmental Defense Fund (EDF), evaluate their smart grid implementation plans. Having a credible, independent third party evaluate utility smart grid implementation plans is something that other regions should consider in order to both improve on implementation and increase customer acceptance of the plan. Building upon the work of EDF in California, third parties can utilize a framework that assesses smart grid deployment plans and that can be modified to incorporate the state or regional goals for things like renewable energy portfolio standards, electric vehicle integra-tion, reliability, and privacy. Independent third parties can provide the utility with useful feedback and at the same time educate and inform the public about the project's goals and utility's implementation plan.

UNCERTAINTY WILL IMPEDE THE SMART GRID

When it comes to public policy, the flip side to clarity is uncertainty. Given the importance of policies such as cost recovery, it is clear that uncertainty has and will continue to impede smart grid development. In order to achieve the smart grid's promised operational and environmental benefits, federal and state policymakers must incent good behavior that is consistent with the nation's clean energy goals. Research has demon-strated that continued smart grid investment will be good for the economy and the environment. Both industry and government must remain focused on these issues if we are to achieve the full promise of a smarter, greener grid.

APPENDIX I: THE SMART GRID CASE STUDIES

CASE STUDY I. CVPS SMARTPOWER: A SMART GRID COLLABORATION IN VERMONT

Introduction

The Institute for Energy and the Environment's smart grid case studies focus on utilities representing a variety of sizes and approaches to implementing smart grid technology in their service territories. For two reasons, Vermont's smart grid partnership, focusing on Central Vermont Public Service, presented a relevant case to study. First, CVPS's project is part of a statewide effort to install smart grid technology across as much of the state as possible. Second, CVPS is the largest electric utility in Vermont[1] and the first, under the Vermont smart grid partnership with U.S. Smart Grid Investment Grant funding, to begin installing smart meters.[2] Thus the Vermont experience should be informative for other utilities and policymakers across the country.

Central Vermont Public Service is an investor-owned electric utility. Serving more than 160,000 customers, it is the largest electric utility in Vermont and is responsible for approximately 40 percent of Vermont's electricity sales. Not surprisingly, CVPS is also a key partner in the state's smart grid partnership, eEnergy Vermont.

In 2008, CVPS began working to implement smart grid infrastructure. At that time, CVPS proposed its Alternative Regulation Plan, which committed it to implementing advanced metering infrastructure as fast as reason and cost would permit.[3] At the same time, CVPS joined a collaboration of utilities, state agencies, and public interest organizations to develop a regulatory framework that Vermont utilities could follow as individual utilities developed their smart grid plans. CVPS used this collaboration to develop its CVPS SmartPower program implementing AMI and other technologies to improve electric service.[4] In 2009, the partners agreed to a memorandum of understanding (MOU) defining specific details related to Vermont utilities' AMI plans.[5] The MOU included an agreement on "functional requirements, telecommunications, cost recovery, and other elements."[6]

CVPS and other utilities jointly applied for a Smart Grid Investment Grant offered by the Department of Energy with funds from the American Recovery and Reinvestment Act of 2009.[7] The application sought reimbursement of 50 percent of the total estimated cost of statewide smart grid investments[8] and proposed a statewide program, eEnergy Vermont, to coordinate smart grid investment efforts. In October 2009, the DOE awarded eEnergy Vermont a Smart Grid Investment Grant for $69 million.[9] The grant will allow the installation of approximately three hundred thousand smart meters covering nearly 85 percent of all Vermont electric customers. CVPS's share of the Smart Grid Investment Grant exceeded $31 million.[10] In total, CVPS expects to spend more than $63 million to implement CVPS SmartPower.

In 2010, the Vermont Public Service Board approved CVPS's implementation plan.[11] With regulatory approval and support from a network of utilities and Vermont policymakers, CVPS began implementing CVPS SmartPower. CVPS expects to have installed nearly 180,000 meters by the end of 2012. Meanwhile, CVPS is testing rate designs, in-home displays, and customer communication methods and is collaborating with eEnergy Vermont to develop new time-of-use and dynamic rate designs to offer to all customers.

As CVPS implements SmartPower, three important factors contribute to its success. First, CVPS has collaborated with other Vermont utilities and interested parties at every step of the process. The eEnergy Vermont project involved the collaboration of twenty publicly owned and investor-owned utilities, as well as the statewide energy efficiency utility, Efficiency Vermont. "The level of coordination from the utilities was frankly inspiring," Chuck Ross stated.[12] Ross was the state director for Senator Patrick Leahy's office at the time, and he worked with the group of utilities applying for the Smart Grid Investment Grant. This collaboration has helped reduce potential regulatory hurdles and enabled shared analysis to reduce the need for duplication in reviewing and selecting particular equipment, rate designs, and policies. Furthermore, this collaboration will help to ensure that utilities manage customers' expectations collectively. Once advanced meters are installed, CVPS plans to continue collaborating with Vermont's energy efficiency utility, Efficiency Vermont, and other entities to expand demand-side management opportunities. Without this coordination, CVPS Smart-Power, and other smart grid investments across Vermont might cost more, deliver fewer benefits to customers, and take longer to implement.

Yet this collaboration has also come at some expense. While the end result of statewide collaboration might have been beneficial, CVPS has described the collaboration as "very time-consuming." For example, CVPS had already developed a positive business case and plan for AMI investments when the opportunity to apply for federal funding arose. Later, the Vermont Public Service Board ruled that the utility consider alternatives with increased social benefit. The resulting collaboration with other utilities in Vermont slowed the decision-making and implementation process. In the end, however, the collaboration led to a successful application for a Smart Grid Investment Grant.

Second, Vermont's energy policy and regulatory agencies have developed a clear record of supporting cost-effective smart grid investments. In 2007, well before the grant opportunity from the Department of Energy, the Vermont Public Service Board initiated Docket 7307, Investigation into Vermont Electric Utilities Use of Smart Metering and Time-Based Rates. Meanwhile, the Vermont legislature passed the Vermont Energy Efficiency and Affordability Act, which asked the Vermont Public Service Board to investigate smart meters and time-of-use rates. Importantly, regulatory policy in Vermont has balanced flexibility for investments in fast-developing smart grid technology with measures to ensure that decisions about major investments are prudent.

Third, CVPS has developed a detailed employee and customer outreach program. This early and ongoing education will help accelerate customer acceptance, reduce confusion and skepticism, and ensure that customers are able to benefit from smart grid technology as soon as possible. These outreach programs will also enable the utility to collect feedback from customers and adapt processes and services as necessary.

CVPS SmartPower will be the "largest non-capital investment [CVPS] has ever made."[13] Collaboration, effective state policies, and customer education and research are three integral components to ensuring that this investment occurs without significant delay or expense while maximizing customer benefits.

Smart Meter Initiatives

Installing advanced metering infrastructure is the central pillar of the CVPS SmartPower program. CVPS plans to upgrade roughly 180,000 meters.[14] It expected to begin exchanging 2,200 meters per week in early 2012 and complete the project by the end of 2012.[15] Due to some delay in selecting a network provider to transmit meter data, CVPS amended the program schedule in late 2010 in order to explore an opportunity to collaborate with the development of Vermont's 4G broadband system. As a result, CVPS delayed its first meter installation and accelerated the pace of meter installations to complete the installation sooner than originally expected.[16] Altogether, purchasing and installing AMI equipment throughout its service territory will cost CVPS more than $35 million. Perhaps in part for that reason, the Vermont Department of Public Service (DPS) acknowledged that choosing the best metering equipment poses "a formidable undertaking."[17]

Vermont's 2011 Comprehensive Energy Plan reports that a "statewide smart grid initiative is well underway" to deploying advanced meters in over 85 percent of the state within the next few years.[18] The state's policy is that all eEnergy Vermont investments must involve coordination and collaboration among utilities.[19] In order to ensure that CVPS makes the best long-term investment in AMI and can take advantage of cost efficiencies, CVPS collaborated with Green Mountain Power to procure an AMI system. CVPS and GMP released a joint request for proposals and began reviewing AMI proposals in 2010. Their goal was to take advantage of cost efficiencies from sharing network equipment and vendor services.[20]

This collaboration should help ensure that CVPS and other utilities select equipment that can provide common benefits to all Vermont ratepayers and support interoperability among systems used by different utilities, including Efficiency Vermont, and other third parties. Early on, CVPS hosted a meeting to discuss interoperability and system design among the different partners in eEnergy Vermont.[21] The DPS acknowledged CVPS's leadership in working with partners across the state to promote a system of open architecture.[22] According to CVPS, interoperability enabled by equipment that uses open communication standards, whenever possible, will encourage creativity in the development of applications that may benefit consumers.[23]

CVPS indicated that the AMI system it selected must include several features that will enable the utility to expand services for customers. The list of factors includes

- two-way communications,
- hourly interval data,
- meter data management system integration,
- power outage notification,
- tamper detection alerts,
- remote upgrades,
- direct load control,
- web presentment integration,
- whole house service switch,
- home area network communication chip in meter, and
- end of line voltage recording.[24]

CVPS also sought a system that could support load control and outage management as well as be accessible to third parties.[25] The utility recognized that these features will help maximize the benefits enabled by AMI equipment for individual consumers and the electric grid as a whole.

Some of these features will enable new services as part of the initial AMI implementation, while other features will unlock opportunities for future services. For example, CVPS will present customers' hourly use information online via a secure customer Web portal to all residential and small commercial customers. This portal will display customer electricity-use data online so that customers can access their own data. With this feature, customers who do not purchase in-home displays will still be able to take advantage of the data the meters collect. The Web portal will provide analytic tools that allow customers to see their consumption patterns over time and to perform "what-if" scenarios to determine if there are utility rate options that might be more cost effective for them based on these patterns. Initially, as a dynamic pricing option for all customers, CVPS will promote its newly refined, existing time-of-use rate,[26] which seventy-six customers use as of May 2010.[27] The new time-of-use rate (Rate 17) is an optional rate where all service is taken through one meter. The time-of-use rate is divided into three pricing periods that are designated as peak, intermediate, and off-peak hours. Efficiency Vermont may also provide programs to help customers acquire and use in-home displays.[28] Moreover, customers will have flexibility to choose devices from third-party suppliers that enable them to understand their real-time electric use.

As part of the eEnergy Vermont project funded by the Department of Energy, CVPS and Vermont Electric Cooperative are both conducting consumer behavior studies of a targeted subset of customers. The CVPS study, in Rutland, Vermont, focuses on testing the effectiveness of dynamic pricing and rebates supported by information feedback. This study tests a variety of means of communicating with customers, through the AMI-enabled features, to signal them to reduce their load to lower the peak total demand and total electricity usage. These alerts include but are not limited to blinking lights on an in-home display, text messages, and email messages.[29] As one example of a new feature, customers can use in-home displays that show, in near real time, electricity use, prices, and other signals to help allow customers to reduce load.[30] In-home displays are one particular technological application that will compliment advanced meters and help consumers manage electricity use. As part of its consumer behavior study, CVPS will provide free in-home displays to roughly 600 Rutland customers who have agreed to participate in the research project. In addition, CVPS will offer an in-home display at no charge to an additional 250 customers who sign up for its refined "beta" time-of-use rate (previously Rate 9).[31]

The CVPS consumer behavior study will explore dynamic pricing alternatives, including a study of fifteen hundred customers using peak-time rebate and critical peak pricing. Under the PTR, customers will continue to pay the standard flat rate for electric service, but will be eligible for a rebate for reducing electric service during declared peak events. Under the CPP program, CVPS will offer customers a slightly discounted flat rate with substantially higher prices during a limited number of declared peak events. CVPS and its partners are offering financial and technical support for in-home displays as part of these initial research pilots to determine if it is cost effective to offer ongoing financial assistance to customers for in-home displays. The consumer behavior study, which will continue into 2014, will provide CVPS and other eEnergy Vermont participants with valuable information about how best to design and implement future dynamic pricing alternatives and how best to combine these rates with appropriate means for customer feedback, including home technology alternatives. CVPS has been working with the Vermont Department of Public Service and other utilities to discuss new rate designs that are enabled by advanced meters.[32] CVPS has also developed an initial draft rates roadmap identifying the new rate offerings that may be introduced in the next several years.

Legal, Regulatory, Structural, or Other Institutional Barriers

Vermont Policymakers and Regulators Encourage Smart Grid Investments

In general, CVPS does not appear to have faced many significant legal or regulatory barriers in implementing CVPS SmartPower. Although CVPS has faced some hurdles, Vermont's policymakers and regulators have encouraged utility investments in smart grid infrastructure.[33]

In 2007, the DPS petitioned for, and the Vermont Public Service Board opened, an investigation into the potential use of advanced meters and time-of-use pricing.[34] In 2008, the Vermont legislature also signaled an interest in developing smart grid infrastructure,[35] enacting the Vermont Energy Efficiency and Affordability Act, which required the board to continue investigating opportunities for utilities to install advanced meters capable of sending two-way signals and enabling time-of-use pricing.[36] This legislation required the board to compel utilities, in areas where the board determined that it would be cost effective, to file plans for deploying advanced metering equipment and advanced pricing programs.[37] The board had to report its findings by December 31, 2008.[38] In 2009, the legislature authorized public investments in integrating electric vehicles into the smart grid[39] and time-of-use rate schedules.[40] Finally, PSB chairman James Volz has served on the Smart Grid Collaborative, chaired by the National Association of Regulatory Utility Commissioners and the Federal Energy Regulatory Commission. This collaborative is facilitating state and federal cooperation on smart grid implementation.

The nature of statewide collaboration to date also reflects policymakers' general support for smart grid investments in Vermont. For example, as a condition of receiving the Smart Grid Investment Grant funds, several utilities had to commit to supplementing the grant with their own investments. CVPS and several other utilities petitioned the Vermont Public Service Board for permission to pledge corporate assets as required in the grant agreement.[41] A few days later the DPS recommended to the board that it approve the petition without further study.[42] The board promptly approved the petition, enabling the grantees to receive the funds from the Department of Energy without significant delay.[43]

Smart grid investments also fit nicely into the state's energy policy.[44] The legislature has made clear that reliability, affordability, and efficiency are among the state's top energy priorities.[45] The utilities' collaborative approach is expected to deploy advanced metering infrastructure across 85 percent of the state,[46] giving utilities the tools to respond to outages faster. Together, these initiatives suggest that, rather than impeding investments in smart grid equipment, Vermont's energy policy encourages and supports smart grid investments.

Effects of Regulatory Cost Recovery

Despite regulators' general encouragement of smart grid investments, the issue of cost recovery has posed some concerns for Vermont utilities, including CVPS. The utility's obligation to implement advanced metering infrastructure "as fast as reasonably possible,"[47] along with the rapid development of advanced metering technology, has raised concerns that some costs might be disallowed if cheaper prices or better technology emerged after the utility had already made its investment.[48] CVPS and other utilities attempted to address this concern in their MOU with regard to smart grid investments.[49] Specifically, they proposed a ruling that would have required interested parties to object to investments only at the time those investments are made. The board, however, declined to issue that ruling.[50]

Nevertheless, the board acknowledged that investments in advanced metering infrastructure present special concerns with regard to whether they will be found to have been "used-and-useful" upon subsequent review.[51] Specifically, it noted that smart meters are an "evolving field" and "any early adoption has some risk" that the investment will soon be obsolete.[52] Understanding that smart grid infrastructure poses unique circumstances, the board announced that advanced metering infrastructure made as part of an approved implementation plan "should be treated *as if* they are economically used-and-useful."[53] This declaration that advanced meter investments are, per se, used and useful demonstrates the board's willingness to provide some accommodation to encourage investments in smart grid technology.

Nevertheless, the board admonished utilities that its "determination that a Plan is acceptable will not shield a utility from a subsequent investigation and potential disallowance based upon the economic used-and-useful principle if events following approval should have led to an alteration of the AMI deployment."[54] The board's determination, however, did not alleviate the utilities' concerns. In fact, the utilities requested clarification of the meaning of the board's final caveat.[55] They argued that rapid changes in technology and the developing market for smart grid technology put important factors for satisfying the used-and-useful test outside of their control.[56] As a result, utilities feared that they could be penalized and denied cost recovery due to factors outside of their control.[57] The board agreed, confirming that investments that are prudent at the time they are made and comply with an approved implementation plan will not be disallowed for not being used and useful due to circumstances beyond the utilities' control.[58]

Despite the Vermont Public Service Board's special concession regarding used-and-useful analysis for smart grid equipment, CVPS must undergo advanced review for specific investments in order to "have some greater guarantee of cost recovery."[59] CVPS's implementation plan describes that the utility will seek the DPS's review prior to each "major milestone financial commitment."[60] This review adds another layer of protection to guarantee that investments are prudent. However, it also adds to the cost of implementation and might slow implementation of major projects.

CVPS does not appear to face significant regulatory barriers to cost recovery. The Vermont Public Service Board has balanced flexibility for investments in fast-developing technology with measures to ensure that decisions about major investments are prudent.

Enhancing Customer Value from the Smart Grid

One rarely reads an article or hears a story about smart grid investments that does not immediately refer to the potential benefits the smart grid may generate for electric utility customers. CVPS also advertises that a smart grid will be good for customers insofar as they can take advantage of additional information regarding their energy use and the price they are paying.[61]

Total smart grid investments in Vermont are expected to exceed $133 million in 2013.[62] CVPS alone expects to spend $60–65 million to implement CVPS SmartPower.[63] In its CVPS SmartPower Implementation Plan, the utility makes clear its intention that "all benefits of the Plan accrue to customers."[64] Furthermore, CVPS believes that customer benefits from SmartPower will be "compelling"[65] and that these benefits could not be achieved without the smart grid.[66] Although CVPS warns that not all benefits will be quantifiable, or immediately perceptible, it plans to monitor several factors to assess whether expected benefits are realized until new metering equipment is in place and the costs are recovered.[67] For this reason, CVPS is extremely cautious about overselling the potential cost-saving benefits for consumers, and the utility rarely, if ever, publicly predicts that customers will reap any financial benefits. Rather, CVPS markets additional control over electricity use as the primary benefit to consumers.

As evidence that some of the benefits may not be easily quantifiable, CVPS's proposal revealed a discrepancy regarding the timing of expected benefits from SmartPower.[68] This discrepancy reduced the net present value of expected benefits by $280,000 to $500,000.[69] Nevertheless, CVPS expected the plan to yield a positive benefit and later clarified that the value of the benefit should be $1.41 million or $1.63 million, depending on the use of certain assumptions.[70] The DPS responded to this discovery by asking that CVPS use a more detailed process to measure and verify that benefits had accrued.[71] Later, in 2011, CVPS updated its business case for the CVPS SmartPower project. In this update, the utility incorporated the cost and benefits associated with distribution automation into the plan and identified additional cost savings. These changes increased the net present value of the project to roughly $7 million.[72]

Central Vermont Public Service is confident that deploying new meter technology, along with new services and customer education, will enhance customers' experience and give them opportunities to save money. The next section reviews some of the challenges CVPS faces in ensuring that SmartPower enhances value, the new and improved services CVPS plans to offer, and how the utility is addressing the issue of privacy.

Challenges

Several factors make it difficult for CVPS to ensure that the smart grid enhances value for customers. As previously mentioned, the fast pace of technological development for smart grid equipment means that better or less expensive technology could emerge after investments have already been made. As a result, CVPS had to predict which investment would provide the greatest long-term value.

In addition, the scale of the investments needed to realize new benefits requires careful planning and deliberation. In order to realize the full benefits of the advanced metering infrastructure, a backend network and meter data management (MDM) system must be installed.[73] These investments will be costly. CVPS has selected Siemens Energy, Inc. to install the company's meter data management system, which it expects to cost more than $5 million.[74] This expense is also identified as a major milestone financial commitment, demonstrating its cost and importance. As a major milestone, the selection of the management system was subject to the review process described in the SmartPower Implementation Plan.[75]

In late 2010, CVPS filed a modified plan and business case that explained the company's difficulty in finding a suitable intermediate network vendor. In order to fill this need, CVPS proposed to investigate whether it was feasible to take advantage of the Vermont Telephone Company's investments in a 4G LTE broadband network.[76] Using VTEL's broadband network to satisfy the communication needs that SmartPower presented would help reduce the cost of the SmartPower program by maximizing the use of existing or developing infrastructure. Using VTEL's existing frequency, this collaboration will involve expanding the broadband network to unanticipated areas in order to accommodate the needs of CVPS's SmartPower plans.

In July 2011, CVPS, Green Mountain Power, and VTEL entered into an agreement to share the Company's 4G network to relay meter data.[77] Funding from the Department of Agriculture's Rural Utilities Service has enabled the development of the broadband system.[78] Funding from the utilities' smart grid investments will also allow VTEL to expand the network into areas where it might not have otherwise. VTEL expected the network to be complete in 2013, only shortly after CVPS expects to complete installing the smart meters.[79] The leadership of Vermont governor Peter Shumlin was instrumental in facilitating agreement among the parties.

As a result of the agreement, CVPS proposed a two-phase network implementation. To begin, CVPS will use a backhaul network composed of existing fiber, cellular, and land-line telecommunications infrastructure to serve CVPS SmartPower's digital communication needs until CVPS is satisfied that VTEL has developed a "Vermont-electric-utility-appropriate" network.[80] In part due to this concern, CVPS "stated that its decision to [use] a two-phased backhaul network approach involves 'significant risks' associated with the technological advances needed for deployment."[81] CVPS has described its position as being "on the bleeding edge of technology."[82] Indeed, relying on VTEL's 4G network will make

CVPS and its partners the only utilities in the country to rely on a commercial 4G LTE network to convey smart grid data. While this collaboration could ultimately result in project cost savings and additional functionality for CVPS SmartPower, CVPS notes that some contemplated benefits could not materialize until the network, and equipment to interface with it, is ready and usable.

Another factor that could pose a challenge for ensuring customer value is the extent to which the benefits from CVPS SmartPower depend on how customers interact with the new technology and respond to price signals. For example, in May 2010, CVPS reported that only a quarter of its customers were familiar with the term "smart meter."[83] Representatives from the CVPS SmartPower team describe the majority of their customers as "cautiously optimistic" with regard to smart grid technology.[84] In addition to this majority, some customers are eager to experience the new smart meters, while others are skeptical about the changes. The effort required to educate more than 160,000 customers, and train them to manage their energy consumption for maximum benefit, poses a substantial challenge. However, early and ongoing customer education will help CVPS to integrate new smart grid equipment as seamlessly as possible by creating a foundation for customer acceptance.

Educational Efforts

Recognizing the important role that customers' actions will play in the success of the smart grid, CVPS has committed to provide early and ongoing education.[85] In early 2011, the utility began to provide customer education as part of a detailed communication plan.[86] It began educating customers about all new products and services released in conjunction with CVPS SmartPower.[87] This education and outreach campaign included surveys, focus groups, and a well-developed print, radio, television, and social media campaign. CVPS has coordinated its surveys and focus groups with utilities across the country in order to learn from the responses and feedback other utilities have received. Marking a major increase in commercial advertising, CVPS's marketing campaign is intended to educate consumers and minimize potential concerns over new smart meters. Educational and outreach programs include presentations in communities and communication with customers through a variety of traditional and digital media. CVPS continues to conduct market research to gauge customers' awareness and expectations.

CVPS's education and outreach campaigns began with educating its own employees. For example, the utility has deputized specific CVPS SmartPower representatives, which the utility sends out into the community to give presentations, field questions, and serve as ambassadors for the utility in their own neighborhoods, religious groups, and other community associations.[88] CVPS also designated specific call-center employees to field questions related to CVPS SmartPower. In order to enable these call-center representatives to answer questions from experience, rather than just from a set of canned responses, CVPS is equipping the representatives with their own in-home displays to test, use, and experience. In addition, CVPS recognizes that customer education must be a collaborative process so that customers throughout the eEnergy Vermont partners' service territory will not have differing expectations.

Improved Services

Through SmartPower, CVPS will offer new and improved services, making the company's operations more efficient and providing customers new opportunities to manage their energy consumption.[89] As noted previously, CVPS tends to be cautious in describing the potential benefits of SmartPower, preferring to "under-promise and over-deliver."[90] According to the SmartPower plan, improved and expanded services will include new customer billing and rate options; direct and active load control; integration with in-home meter displays, distributed generation, and plug-in electric vehicles; automated meter reading; remote rate changes; web presentment; and tamper detection.[91] Additionally, CVPS's outreach materials cite benefits including improved power quality and better outage management.

Distributed automation offers one of the key benefits that CVPS expects to provide. Distributed automation will allow the utility to segment the grid remotely, which could aid in managing and minimizing the extent of power outages. Additionally, this functional control will enable the utility to maintain a consistently reliable quality of power. While customers might not necessarily see the benefits that distributed automation could provide, CVPS expects that customers will experience the benefits through better reliability and improved power quality.

With new billing and rate options, customers will have expanded opportunities to control energy consumption in a way that reduces expenses. Specifically, customers may choose to participate in direct load control programs. Load control often involves the utility remotely shutting down or cycling down a customer's electrical equipment, such as a water heater.[92] In exchange for voluntary participation in a load control program, a customer typically receives a reduction in their bill. CVPS already operates a direct load control program through which it controls 18,600 water heaters.[93] Roughly six thousand are already dynamically controlled.[94] Customers on CVPS's direct load control program are enrolled in Rate 3. This rate is for off-peak water heating and is available roughly fifteen hours each day. Rate 3 charges consumers roughly $0.08/kWh.[95] Those already enrolled will eventually undergo dynamic load control. Eventually, CVPS intends to introduce active load control. Through active load control, a customer would agree to allow CVPS to turn predetermined appliances on or off based on real-time prices.[96]

Although CVPS already provides online bill viewing and payment, advanced metering infrastructure will enable CVPS to provide electricity-use data at more frequent intervals in its online presentment. Specifically, the web presentment will include actual electricity-use data "as near to real time as is practical."[97] At the very least, all CVPS customers will be able to access their electricity-use data online the next day.[98] This increased access to information is the cornerstone of potential customer benefit, giving customers the information to manage their electricity use. The additional data will also help inform energy efficiency service providers like Efficiency Vermont and give them additional information to provide more useful efficiency measures for Vermont ratepayers.

Furthermore, the new equipment will streamline CVPS's operating procedures, allowing CVPS to detect outages sooner and respond to customer needs more quickly. For example, advanced meters will give CVPS the capability to use automated meter reading, remote meter voltage detection, and remote meter rate changing. The ability to read and communicate with meters remotely may also help reduce the three hundred thousand service calls CVPS makes per year.[99] These changes will reduce operating expenses as automated technology makes some staff positions obsolete. In fact, CVPS has already started reducing meter reading staff positions "in anticipation of CVPS SmartPower operational efficiencies."[100]

Privacy

The more frequent and granular data that advanced metering infrastructure will provide creates a double-edged sword. As noted previously, this information will enable customers, CVPS, and Efficiency Vermont to understand how best to reduce electricity use and manage load. However, this same information could also risk exposing customers' information to unintended recipients. In other parts of the country, privacy concerns are generating opposition to some smart grid project rollouts and causing regulators to approach smart grid investments somewhat cautiously. Recently, those expressing such concerns in Vermont have become more vocal.[101]

The eEnergy Vermont partnership incorporates privacy among its guiding principles. Specifically, the guiding principles state that "customer billing and usage data will not be shared with any third party without the consumer's consent except as required by law."[102] Still, the CVPS Smart-Power implementation plan includes efforts to share customer electricity usage data with Efficiency Vermont.[103] CVPS has made clear, however, that as it shares information with Efficiency Vermont, it will protect the confidentiality of customer information.[104]

Central Vermont Public Service, which has historically followed practices to protect consumer data, is aware of the new privacy concerns that smart grid technology raises, although it has not yet published additional privacy policies specific to the smart grid. As a result, the utility is moving forward with the continued protection of its customers' data, while considering how best to meet the new challenges of the smart grid. The DPS has proposed the "Statement of Principles Relative to Privacy," which is being discussed with the Vermont utilities and other parties as a possible supplemental memorandum of understanding.[105] One of the principles would require each utility to adopt a privacy policy consistent with the DPS's statement that would be readily available to customers.

Opt-Out Policy

Controversy has arisen in states from California to Maine over various concerns with smart meter installation, such as health concerns associated with radio frequency radiation from meter communication devices. Recognizing this concern, CVPS has proactively implemented a smart meter opt-out policy for customers who choose to have the company provide a meter that does not use wireless communications.[106] The customer simply has to notify CVPS by telephone of their desire to opt-out.[107] If a customer opts-out from a meter at their premises, all meters associated with that premise must opt-out. Additionally, that customer would no longer be able to use time-of-use rates with the wireless meters that serve as the time-of-use communication device. Customers who choose to opt-out must pay an additional service charge of ten dollars per month for each meter.[108]

Improving Reliability

Central Vermont Public Service has suggested that its SmartPower program should improve reliability. For example, Bruce Bentley, leader of CVPS's Transmission Tariff, Integrated Planning, and Regulatory Team, has written that using smart meter technology to help integrate distributed generation, monitor electric loads, and assess and implement demand-side management options can help improve reliability.[109] In addition, automatic distribution switches could enable CVPS to repair problems sooner and avoid loss of power.[110]

Meeting Clean Energy Goals

Both the state of Vermont and CVPS have viewed clean energy as an important component of meeting the state's electricity needs. For example, in 1999 the Vermont legislature created an energy efficiency utility, Efficiency Vermont, which achieves enough electricity savings to make it "Vermont's second largest power plant."[111] In addition, Vermont offers a net metering program and a feed-in tariff to support distributed renewable energy generation. CVPS has also been active in renewable energy through its CowPower program, which generates energy from methane digesters on several dairy farms, and through solar and wind investments. Although Vermont's 2011 Comprehensive Energy Plan calls for a smart grid that will help expand renewable energy projects, the CVPS SmartPower program was not developed in pursuit of a particular clean energy goal.[112]

Nevertheless, CVPS expects that advanced metering infrastructure might play a role in expanding the deployment of renewable resources. In particular, this benefit would likely take the form of distributed automation facilitating group net-metering projects. SmartPower could also benefit renewable energy deployment by providing more intricate data to inform load forecasting and, therefore, stabilize intermittent resources and improve reliability. In addition, Bentley has described other means by which advanced metering infrastructure could expand renewable energy generation.

Specifically, Bentley notes that the cost of connecting and metering new distributed resources have barred some smaller projects. However, advanced meters with heightened communication capability will reduce the cost of measuring and reporting data for electricity generation. Additional data regarding generation from distributed resources may also inform interconnection studies and help utilities avoid "burdensome analyses and expensive interconnection system changes."[113] Moreover, integrating distributed generation output data with other information, such as weather data, can improve forecasting generation from intermittent resources like wind and solar.

In addition, Bentley notes that time-of-use rates, which CVPS already employs and which will be easier to implement after advanced meters are installed, could make some renewable energy options more attractive. For example, rate designs with higher peak costs could spark increased interest in solar photovoltaic systems by increasing net metering rates during the day. Solar thermal systems could also see increased interest if electric rates made the investment a more cost-effective option for offsetting hot water during the day.

The data and hardware necessary to reap these benefits, however, will not come overnight. Bentley and his colleagues are careful not to oversell how smart grid technology might benefit renewable energy. They acknowledge its possibility but note that it will take time to install the necessary equipment and acquire the data to help integrate additional renewable energy generation. In fact, CVPS does not plan to incorporate distributed generation until 2014.[114]

Integrating Electric Vehicles

Similarly, CVPS expects that smart grid technology will eventually help integrate electric vehicles and help schedule charging cycles appropriately.[115] It is important to note, however, that integrating electric vehicles through smart grid applications will not occur until customers become familiar with advanced meters and associated rate designs. As a result, although CVPS recognizes both that the smart grid can enable broader use of electric vehicles and that electric vehicles might be used to help stabilize intermittent resources down the road, it is not focusing on vehicle to grid applications at this stage. Nevertheless, the utility intends to use its newly refined existing time-of-use rate as a separate rate for electric vehicles.

Conclusion

Vermont has long been known for innovation and forward thinking in the field of energy efficiency. The statewide smart grid investments taking place will help keep Vermont in the front of the pack in this and related areas. What follows are several notable lessons learned from Central Vermont Public Service's smart grid implementation planning.

Statewide Collaboration Is Spurring Progress and Innovation

Collaboration is arguably the most important lesson that the CVPS study provides. Collaboration has made developing and implementing CVPS SmartPower, as well as other utilities' smart grid investments, more efficient, cost effective, and technically sound. As part of the statewide smart grid effort, CVPS has been able to share analysis with other utilities, such as Green Mountain Power, which reduced costs in selecting AMI equipment. This collaboration also likely made eEnergy Vermont's Smart Grid Investment Grant application more attractive to the Department of Energy. As one of the only statewide grant applications, the Vermont collaborative model provided a unique feature for the DOE to nurture. As previously noted, the former state director for U.S. Senator Patrick Leahy called the level of coordination from the utilities "frankly inspiring."[116] In particular, leadership, innovation, and collaboration evidenced by partners in Vermont were key factors in moving toward the dual goals of universal broadband coverage and a smart electric grid. This effort is likely worth studying and replicating elsewhere. To date, this collaboration makes CVPS and Green Mountain Power the only utilities in the country to rely on a commercial 4G LTE network to communicate smart grid data. This coordination is expected to result in both increased coverage for VTEL's network and cost savings for the utility customers.

Clear Policies Speed Smart Grid Results

Vermont's energy policy and regulatory agencies have developed a clear record of supporting cost-effective smart grid investments. Since 2007, Vermont's legislature and Public Service Board have been inquiring into the development of smart grid infrastructure and dynamic rate options. This effort has effectively balanced flexibility for investments in a rapidly developing field of technology with measures to ensure those investments are prudent.

Consumer Outreach and Research Leads to More Effective Implementation

With their efforts at consumer outreach and consumer behavior research, CVPS is laying the groundwork for a smooth transition in its smart grid implementation. These efforts include training call-center technicians to answer and properly route smart grid questions, deputizing staff members as smart grid ambassadors in their community, and developing print and Internet-based educational materials. CVPS has moved forward quickly with efforts to educate customers. Building awareness, encouraging customers to accept the new technology, and demonstrating the advanced meters' benefits should help CVPS ease the transition and acclimate customers to advanced meters and the additional services they enable. In case some customers are concerned about issues such as radio frequency radiation from wireless meters, CVPS is prepared with a smart meter opt-out policy. The CVPS consumer behavior study should provide CVPS with valuable information on how to both structure dynamic pricing tariffs and encourage the utilization of technology that will unleash the capabilities of the smart meters, which will lead to more efficient utilization of energy.

One area where more work needs to be done is formalizing a customer data privacy policy. Both Vermont's utilities and regulators have expressed a strong interest in protecting the privacy of the more granular customer data that the smart meters collect. The Vermont Public Service Board, through recent workshops and filings, is reviewing the establishment of privacy principles. These principles would include the development of a clear utility smart grid privacy policy that would be available to customers. The imminent rollout of new meters makes it important for CVPS and Vermont regulators to complete the development of a transparent smart grid privacy policy to clearly inform customers about their privacy rights and responsibilities.

Finally, these efforts mark a starting point, rather than an ending point, for CVPS and Vermont in establishing a truly smart grid. To be sure, the implementation of smart meters and related AMI investments represent an important step in smart grid implementation. Yet in many ways it is only the first phase. The Electric Power Research Institute has estimated that fully implementing a smart electric grid will cost between $1.3 and $2.0 trillion nationwide, with benefits likely exceeding costs by a factor of three or more.[117] This represents a significant amount of additional investment compared to the $3.4 billion of Smart Grid Investment Grants from the Department of Energy. The additional investments will need to be made in future years and will involve ongoing negotiation with regulators and other parties.

Research from Pacific Northwest National Laboratory has estimated that with full implementation of a smart electric grid by 2030, U.S. energy consumption and carbon emissions could be reduced by 12 percent.[118] A smart electric grid allows utilities to expand energy efficiency and demand response services to all customers, and the results of the CVPS consumer behavior study will assist in expanding these services. Yet as noted previously, it will take time to develop and offer additional technologies and rates to customers. In some areas, however, the smart grid will likely spur greater electricity use, such as smart charging of electric vehicles, in order to achieve efficiencies in total energy use across the economy.

Continued investment in automation of the utility distribution system will offer future opportunities for improving reliability and optimizing energy use. In order for electric vehicles to reach the levels of consumer adoption included in PNNL's analysis, there will need to be significant new policies at all levels of government and the build-out of new infrastructure. Furthermore, as renewable energy reaches higher levels of development across the utility service territory, greater investment in smart grid technologies will be needed in order to reliably and cost-effectively manage these resources.

At CVPS and across Vermont, smart grid implementation is off to a productive start. Ongoing policy refinements, project development, and infrastructure investment will be needed in order to achieve the smart grid's full, long-term potential.

CASE STUDY II. SALT RIVER PROJECT: DELIVERING LEADERSHIP ON SMARTER TECHNOLOGY AND RATES

Introduction

As utilities across the country are deploying smart meters, rolling out miles of fiber, and grappling with cyber-security and data-management challenges, "smart grid" is the ultimate buzz word in the industry. Yet providing an exact explanation of what the smart grid is made of, what it can do, and what benefits it will bring is illusive.[119] For the Salt River Project in the greater Phoenix area, the smart grid is nothing new. Noted by Smartgridnews.com, SRP has been investing in smart grid technologies before the term "smart grid" became an industry buzz word.[120]

This is a case study of SRP's smart grid programs. The impetus for this study was SRP's award of a $56.9 million investment grant to expand its smart meter network awarded by the Department of Energy through the American Recovery and Reinvestment Act. However, SRP's smart grid investments reach far beyond customer-centered smart meter applications. SRP's unique governance and regulatory structure has allowed it to focus on essential smart grid backbone infrastructure supporting the full spectrum of its power system.

Background of Salt River Project

The Salt River Project is the third largest public power entity in the United States, serving approximately 940,000 customers in Arizona.[121] SRP's unique history and governance structure plays an important role in its investment and strategic operations. Originally founded in 1903 through the National Reclamation Act of 1902,[122] SRP is comprised of two entities, the Salt River Valley Water User's Association, a private corporation that supplies water and manages water rights, and the Salt River Project Agricultural Improvement and Power District, which is a political subdivision of the state. The Salt River Project Improvement and Power District, now simply referred to as the Salt River Project, was formed in 1937 to operate power generation and distribution systems and meet the expanding power needs of the area.[123]

As a political subdivision of the state of Arizona, SRP is not subject to regulation by the Arizona Corporation Commission (ACC) in the same manner that investor-owned utilities are.[124] Rates, investments, and day-to-day activities of SRP do not require ACC approval. SRP is only subject to ACC regulation for approval of generation projects over 100 mW or transmission projects over 115 kV.

Instead, SRP is governed by landowners within its service territory through elections of board and council members.[125] The board sets specific policy objectives and works with officers and executive management members to operate SRP,[126] while the council is responsible for broader policies and communication with constituents.[127] In many ways, being free from ACC regulation allows SRP to operate with more flexibility. As discussed below, this structure has proved advantageous in SRP's smart grid investments.

SRP is an integrated utility with ownership interests in generation as well as being responsible for transmission and distribution services.[128] SRP has 8,094 mW available to serve peak demand and reported annual total sales of 33,064 gWh in 2009.[129] The utility has full or partial ownership interest in natural gas and coal fired plants, one nuclear facility, and 493 mW of renewable power.[130] Hydro facilities compose 57 percent of SRP's renewable resources, or 383 mW.[131] SRP also owns over fifteen hundred miles of transmission lines and fourteen hundred miles of fiber optic lines.[132] SRP recognizes that improving efficiencies in its systems through smart grid technologies can help lower costs and improve reliability while continuing to meet the modern energy challenges of a rapidly growing metropolitan area.

Overview of the Salt River Project's Smart Grid Program

Broad Perspectives

The Energy Independence and Security Act of 2007 established new standards under Section 111(d) of the Public Utilities Regulatory Policy Act (PURPA). One of those new PURPA standards required utilities to consider investments in smart grid systems based on cost effectiveness, improved reliability, security, system performance, and societal benefits.[133] SRP's board adopted the new PURPA standard in full, with the exception of Section 16B, Rate Recovery, and 16C, Obsolete Equipment. These two sections were not applicable to SRP because they refer to each state making a policy determination about these topics. These standards relate largely to investments in "non-advanced" technologies.

The company had been working in the smart grid arena for several years prior to the new standards developed in the EISA. It began installing fiber optics in the late 1990s and has now connected over 98 percent of substations with fiber optics, began deploying smart meters as early as 2003, and has been offering time-of-use rates for decades.[134] SRP is currently investing in smart grid technologies for all aspects of its power system. In doing so, it is focused on building out the backbone of a smart grid system to support all components of the smart grid and ensure interoperability with future technologies.

For SRP, investing in the smart grid at this stage requires expanding infrastructure in three key areas. First, communications systems at the transmission level must be enhanced. Enhanced systems begin with SRP's fiber network but extend to mobile communications, system automation, and network controls. Second, SRP is investing in IT infrastructure. According to Joe Nowaczyk, manager of electronic systems at SRP, much of the smart grid requires linking information technology with operations technology. A successful smart grid IT infrastructure requires unified communications to efficiently manage and utilize data across multiple smart grid components and corporate departments. Finally, SRP is working to develop an enterprise strategy for smart grid cyber security. As the grid becomes intertwined with more data and communications technology, it is essential that information is managed securely.

The ability of SRP to focus on these fundamental pieces of smart grid infrastructure is in part due to its unique self-regulated structure. As a political subdivision of the state, SRP is not subject to ACC approval for its investments nor required to submit regulatory filings or demonstrate immediate benefits from smart grid infrastructure. Therefore, SRP only needed internal approval to begin investing in backbone communications infrastructure. While immediate reliability benefits of backbone infrastructure investments are often difficult to quantify, they are fundamental investments that will help ready SRP for future smart grid technologies. Other utilities across the country remain focused on consumer-centered technologies such as smart meters and advanced meter infrastructure because they are commonly thought to provide the most immediate benefits. Yet some utilities are still encountering regulatory hurdles. Anecdotally, Baltimore Gas and Electric's original proposal to install 1.2 million smart meters was denied by the Maryland Public Service Commission in June 2010, threatening the company's eligibility for DOE funding.[135] While the Baltimore utility's plan was conditionally approved on resubmission,[136] this exemplifies the type of regulatory hurdles that SRP does not have to face. Certainly SRP is subject to internal review from its board and council, but this process is easily contrasted with the review of a public service commission.

Just because SRP has been focusing on the smart grid backbone does not mean it is unconcerned with consumer benefits or measuring system improvements. In fact, SRP began installing advanced meters in 2003, and with the help of a DOE grant SRP plans to reach 100 percent installation of smart meters in its service territory by 2013. The key point is that

SRP's core smart grid investments reach far beyond smart meters. Before realizing the full potential of end-user benefits, utilities must start with the backbone of a smart grid system and gain benefits on the utility side.[137] To that end, SRP developed seven key initiatives in 2009:[138]

- Improve existing cyber security strategies.
- Implement automated tools for WAN monitoring.
- Create and deploy an integrated substation LAN strategy.
- Utilize a single unified communications infrastructure for field devices.
- Expand the deployment of distribution feeder automation.
- Deploy an electrical system data acquisition and management project for automation and analysis.
- Implement an integration bus for secure enterprise application integration between applications and databases.

Each of these areas fit within the three key elements discussed above of communications systems, IT infrastructure, and cyber security. There are also synergies across these seven areas that, to the extent possible, SRP is attempting to take advantage of. A brief synopsis of these seven initiatives is provided below.

Program Management and Development

SRP has been integrally involved in the Electric Power Research Institute's smart grid initiatives. It is a participating utility and original funder of EPRI's Intelligrid program,[139] a collaborating utility in the Smart Grid Demonstration Initiative,[140] and a participant in the Green Circuits Initiative.[141] SRP retained EPRI in 2008 for the development of case studies about the use of smart grid technology and assistance developing a smart grid roadmap.[142]

The company obtained executive staff approval of its Smart Grid Roadmap in July 2008.[143] The roadmap identifies the seven key areas discussed above. It also adopted four guiding principles: leveraging investments, integrating technology, developing open standards and protocols, and engaging industry efforts.[144] Management teams were created at two levels. The Smart Grid Leadership Team was appointed to promote the guiding principles,[145] and seven cross-functional teams were created in September 2008 to evaluate each of the seven initiatives.[146] The leadership team has representatives and participation from ten different SRP departments.[147]

The company's "Smart Grid Vision" is to develop "a power delivery infrastructure that enables practical integration of advances in communications, computing, and electronics to optimize system reliability, contain costs, and accommodate the delivery of services to meet the future needs of [SRP] customers."[148] SRP's mission statement is to "plan and deploy a well coordinated, interoperable, cost-effective corporate infrastructure that will enable the development, integration and application of new technologies throughout SRP that provide secure, high-quality, cost effective, reliable services both internally and externally."[149]

SRP's Smart Grid Roadmap: Seven Key Initiatives

Cyber Security

The goal of SRP's cyber security initiative is to develop a secure infrastructure spanning from technology platforms to policies, procedures, and employee culture to meet information requirements in a secure manner.[150] SRP identifies cyber security as a high-impact but relatively easy initiative to begin to implement. Though the initiative was one of the first to begin, SRP understands that a comprehensive enterprise-wide cyber security implementation will be difficult and take years to fully develop. To date, SRP has completed development of an enterprise strategy for cyber security and goals for fiscal year 2011 were centered on implementation of that strategy.[151]

The company's security model includes both preventive and reactive measures, covering risk management, standards compliance, incident management, and security operations.[152] In addition to compliance with NERC Critical Infrastructure Protection standards, SRP's enterprise cyber security plan is modeled after two National Institute of Standards and Technology standards. NIST publication 800–37, *Guide for Applying the Risk Management Framework to Federal Information Systems*, assisted the development of preventative security protocols. NIST publication 800–53, *Recommended Security Controls for Federal Information Systems and Organizations*, guided SRP in developing its enterprise security control framework.[153]

While SRP is moving forward with cyber security standards, challenges persist. SRP notes that NIST standards should be developed before NERC CIP standards to ensure consistency between industry standards and regulatory requirements that could produce significant penalties.[154] SRP also notes that like much of the industry, it is still struggling with the issue of consumer privacy.[155] One key may be to physically separate networks for certain types of data in order to control a secure perimeter for that data.[156]

Wide Area Network Monitoring

Wide area network monitoring refers to managing the growing network of data associated with smart grid developments. SRP is looking for ways to integrate advances in communications and IT technology with the physical electric system. SRP visited network operations centers at two utilities, Arizona Public Service and Southern California Edison, and one telecom utility, Calence, to assess the tools others were using to manage their communication networks.

Recognizing there was an immediate need for additional monitoring tools, SRP worked with existing vendors to expand monitoring capability.[157] SRP has recently developed a communication network operating center to allow for more robust monitoring of SRP's extensive communication network.[158]

Integrated Substation Local Area Networks

Advanced communications inside the fence of a substation can help to provide system operators with fast and reliable event data.[159] When SRP first evaluated this topic in 2009, EPRI assessments stated several benefits from fully integrated substation LANs. However, surveys of other utility experiences showed almost no U.S. participation with the most current International Electrotechnical Commission (IEC) 61850 standard[160] and mixed results from other automation experiences.[161] SRP recommended pursuing an implementation strategy including further research and expanded funds to accelerate a lab pilot study.[162] Some utilities are adopting IEC 61850 as the standard design for substation automation in newly constructed substations. However, SRP is currently monitoring the maturity of this technology for consideration of use in future substations, but has no plans at this time to deploy it.[163] SRP currently uses DNP3/IP IEEE-approved protocol.

Unified Communications

The unified communications initiative essentially refers to creating and managing the telecommunications infrastructure that will support and integrate SRP's smart grid activities.[164] SRP considered this initiative to have the highest impact but to be moderately challenging to achieve. Main challenges include connecting various applications already using field communications with new systems, anticipating future automation needs, and determining what physical technology has the best business case in each application. The SRP communications functional team divided its challenges into three areas: communications infrastructure, AMI and the smart grid, and enterprise planning and collaboration.[165]

The purpose of building out communications infrastructure is to eventually unify the various systems so that multiple smart grid functions can work seamlessly together. For instance, one potential long-term goal is connecting the AMI infrastructure with distribution feeder automation (DFA) infrastructure. This would improve outage management by allowing individual customer data from smart meters to alert system operators about faults or voltage problems on the distribution system. Next the automated system will reroute power and pinpoint outage locations for more efficient crew utilization and reduced restoration time. However, achieving this link is not realistic in the short term because of bandwidth issues, SCADA requirements, intelligent distribution devices, and AMI/DFA architecture.[166] In short, smart meter data is downloaded once every twenty-four hours through the AMI infrastructure, while SCADA operates by pinging substations once every four cycles (referring to the AC voltage cycle, for which there are sixty every second), and intelligent devices such as Intelliruptors, digital fault recorders, and automated capacitor controllers all currently use varying methods of communications. Since every smart meter collects data on fifty different types of information and there will eventually be over nine hundred thousand smart meters on SRP's system, there is simply not enough capacity with the existing communication systems in place to run both AMI and DFA together. Essentially, this is a problem of latency and bandwidth limitations due to the amount of data and existing communication infrastructure of the two systems. SRP is currently reviewing multiple communication options to determine the best solutions to address these issues.[167]

Establishing the proper AMI is essential to SRP's, or any utility's, success with the smart grid. AMI supports meter to bill information management and it is the precursor to many benefits including outage management, system automation, and residential demand response. SRP has undertaken significant research to anticipate future needs as AMI is expanded. More detail regarding the AMI infrastructure is provided below.

In sum, creating solutions for unified communications systems will support almost all aspects of the smart grid. While challenges still exist, SRP recognizes that "successful implementation of AMI and integration via Meter Data Management system is fundamental to enabling the Smart Grid of the future."[168] Furthermore, collaboration between departments and effective planning will be critical to maximize returns on investments.[169]

Distribution Feeder Automation

The Salt River Project already has fifteen years of experience with automation and has over 179 automated switches throughout its system.[170] As

SRP expands DFA and creates guidelines and policies, it plans to take advantage of existing designs that already allow flexibility.[171]

When EPRI made recommendations for increasing efficiencies, improving reliability, and incorporating green practices during its Green Circuits initiative, SRP had already implemented much of what EPRI recommended.[172] SRP was already purchasing the most efficient transformers and had shorter feeders in the range of three to ten miles, which helps reduce inefficiencies.[173] EPRI's modeling of four SRP circuits indicated a potential 2 percent energy savings across the system. SRP then ran a field study in the summer of 2010 to test whether these modeled results could be achieved. The company's field study is currently being evaluated to determine if EPRI's 2 percent energy savings across the system is achievable. If field results verify the modeled results, then a full cost/benefit analysis will be run. However, to realize the full potential benefits of energy reduction, communication, and automation between meters, capacitor controllers, load tap changes, and possibly inverters would need to be developed along with the applications to analyze and make the automated system decisions.[174] Large-scale penetration of distributed renewable energy may require the same type of communication, automation, and applications to ensure reliability of the distribution system.

With reference to future DFA initiatives, SRP is considering several implementation plans. These include expanding on existing concepts, linking fiber hot spots with DFA, remotely controlling future distributed generation projects, integrating PHEVs, automating capacitor controls and fault location, and controlling demand response.[175] SRP has broken these segments out as near-term opportunities and long-term opportunities as well as estimating build-out costs for each segment.[176] SRP continues to study new opportunities in these areas.

At this stage, SRP is deploying feeder automation technology strategically. Upgrades are focused in specific areas with reliability issues; SRP is taking a geo-targeted approach.[177] SRP also offers optional enhanced service agreements for some commercial and industrial customers to achieve a higher level of reliability. These are customers that demand continuous power service for their operations, such as data processing centers, chip manufacturers, and hospitals. Automated switches are placed on their feeders to decrease the probability of any potential outages to near zero.[178]

Electric System Data Acquisition and Management

The immense increase in automated processes and data gathering associated with smart grid activities creates a significant data management problem. The data acquisition and management initiative seeks to support the smart grid by developing a system to collect, manage, and utilize information across various systems.[179] Data management will help to improve operational efficiency, mainly in more technical system operations areas. Data acquisition plans are aimed at all intelligent devices located within SRP's electric and water system.[180] Ultimately, these systems will help to enhance grid efficiencies, operations, maintenance, and diagnostics.

Implementing these systems within the IT department presents an enormous challenge. SRP is in the early stages of implementation, and the full process will require a high degree of personnel development to familiarize IT staff with the intelligent devices. IT staff must be familiar with the types of data each device sends, where it sends the data, how the data is formatted, how the data is currently used, and who else within the company might be able to utilize this data. SRP must also overcome challenges related to storing this data for enterprise access, securing it, and determining who will have ownership of the information.

Enterprise Application Integration

Integrating applications will allow smart grid data to benefit the full range of SRP's system. It requires linking the masses of data with the back-office functions that need, or could benefit from, accessing that information. SRP ranks this initiative as the *most difficult* and *highest impact* out of all seven initiatives.[181] Currently, SRP describes the system of data sharing as "spaghetti," because of the many different corporate divisions that need to use this data. Corporate IT, transmission and generation, distribution, operations, power generation, and customer services departments all need access to smart grid systems information.

SRP is using the common information model (CIM) to make data transferrable between departments.[182] A CIM standardizes data interfaces and allows multiple parties to access and exchange information. SRP is working internally with its IT department to develop a robust multidisciplinary CIM.

Smart Meters and Advanced Metering Infrastructure

Smart Grid Investment Grants

In late 2009, SRP was awarded $56.9 million by the Department of Energy from American Reinvestment and Recovery Act funds to continuing expanding its smart meter infrastructure.[183] The funds are part of the Obama administration's larger commitment of $3.4 billion in grants for investments in smart grid technologies to help improve efficiency and reliability in the nation's electric grid.[184] Prior to this award, SRP was well advanced in smart meter installations. SRP installed its first smart meter in 2003[185] and reached 54,822 installations by the close of 2006[186] and 374,457 by 2009, when the ARRA funds were awarded.[187]

The DOE selected SRP for its Smart Grid Investment Grant as one of one hundred companies to receive funding for smart grid projects, and one of thirty-one approved AMI projects.[188] SRP is matching the ARRA funds with $57.1 million in its own funding. SRP will use the bulk of the funds to install 540,000 additional smart meters while a portion will cover software updates for data management.[189] SRP's smart meters are manufactured by the Elster Group, a global manufacturer and leader in AMI technology.

The project, referred to at SRP as Advanced Data Acquisition and Management (ADAM), puts SRP on track for 100 percent deployment of smart meters by 2013—three years ahead of its prior schedule.[190] As of April 1, 2011, SRP's website reported 642,631 meters installed. As reported by Michael Lowe, manager of customer services at SRP, this pace requires approximately 14,000 meter installations every month by a crew of about twenty-five employees.[191] The ADAM work plan calls for 163,000 meters installed in 2011, 170,000 in 2012, and 145,000 in 2013. Customers cannot request installation, and customers on SRP's prepay program, M-Power, will not receive the Elster smart meters.[192] Only customers who opt into SRP's new EZ-3 rate structure can obtain installation outside of SRP's installation schedule.[193]

The investment grant with DOE is a three-year program with two years of subsequent metrics and benefits reporting.[194] SRP negotiated a look back period of 8–9 months to obtain DOE cost sharing for prior investments in AMI network and smart meter installation.[195]

Advanced Metering Infrastructure Communications Network

Successfully utilizing these 980,000 smart meters will require a strong communications system connecting the meter to the back office. Each Elster meter collects over fifty data points every fifteen minutes, which are downloaded nightly by SRP. To collect this massive amount of data, SRP relies on GPRS wireless communications between the radio frequency mesh endpoints and other field-deployed smart grid devices.

Salt River Project deployed its backhaul wireless communication network and infrastructure well in advance of receiving the DOE grant, and before beginning wide-scale installation of smart meters.[196] The RF mesh network transmits smart meter data from the home over a 900-MHz unlicensed network to collector meters.[197] SRP then transmits the meter data from the collector meters over the GPRS wireless and Public Switched Telephone Network (PSTN) to SRP's office.[198] SRP is considering transitioning the PSTN communication network to a more advanced wireless (CDMA) communication network, which will also provide redundancy. SRP is currently reviewing multiple communication options to identify the best solutions to meet the needs of SRP and its customers.[199]

Once data reaches SRP offices, it enters SRP's meter data management system. SRP has recognized that developing a successful MDM system is critical to fulfilling the potential of smart meters to provide services such as outage management, demand response, voltage verification, load profiling, and customer services.[200] SRP is working with EnergyICT, a division of Elster, to help develop an MDM system.[201] One major challenge facing SRP's MDM system is the ability to share data across different corporate departments. When SRP's IT department conducted an initial survey and study, thirty-two different organizations within SRP expressed interest in utilizing varying data elements attainable from smart meters for various analysis and services.[202] SRP developed a prioritization matrix based on these results. Yet for the time being, the key priority is "meter to bill data," giving the customer service and billing departments first access to the advanced MDM system. Along with its early experience with smart meters, SRP has been dealing with back-office meter data for years.[203] Originally the IT department internally developed an application to link smart meter data with SRP's billing system.[204] As the MDM system advances, SRP will use meter data in operations to aid outage management, and then it will begin linking with other management systems according to the prioritization matrix.[205] This phase of the project will begin after the DOE grant closes in 2013.

For now, the AMI and MDM systems are linking smart meters in the home with SRP's back office, enhancing billing practices, and empowering customers with information. After data is received in SRP's MDM system, customers can access data about their daily usage through the "My Account" application on SRP's website. SRP expects to support hourly usage information in the near future, but it does not currently support in-home displays or PC applications.[206]

Cost Savings

Salt River Project's smart meters have no net cost to the customer. The benefits of automated meter reading are more than covering the costs of upgraded service. As of March 2011, SRP has remotely addressed over 1.2 million service orders, saved over 401,000 labor hours, avoided 2.0 million driving miles, and conserved 198,000 gallons of fuel.

Dynamic Pricing

Salt River Project offers customers four price plans to choose from. They include a basic plan with seasonal rates, a time-of-use plan, an EZ-3 plan offering time-of-use rates with a shorter peak period, and M-Power—SRP's unique prepay plan. SRP's basic plan uses seasonal rates with an inclining block rate (IBR) above high usage levels.[207] The E-26 TOU rate has been offered for over twenty years but has been selected by more customers as smart meters become available. EZ-3 is a newly introduced time-of-use rate which requires installation of a smart meter to enroll. SRP's M-Power program is the nation's largest prepay electricity program with over one hundred thousand customers enrolled, leaving many utilities looking to SRP as a prepay success story. SRP's dynamic pricing programs are all voluntary, opt-in programs.

Time-of-Use Rates

Salt River Project's standard time of use rate, E-26, charges higher peak prices from 1:00 to 8:00 p.m. May through October, and from 5:00 to 9:00 a.m. and 5:00 to 9:00 p.m. November through April.[208] On-peak pricing varies throughout the seasons. Pricing information available through smart meters along with more accurate metering offers consumers the opportunity to save more with TOU pricing. Since the advanced rollout of smart meters, SRP has seen a 20 percent increase in voluntary TOU program participation. As of early 2011, SRP had 219,703 customers in the TOU program. The TOU program had verified peak load reduction rates of 95.7 MW in 2010.[209]

EZ-3 Rates

The EZ-3 rate is a new rate design that SRP introduced with its smart meter deployment. In 2010, 6,127 customers were enrolled, but SRP planned to enroll 36,000 customers in 2011. It is a voluntary rate program, but it requires participating customers to install a smart meter.[210] The EZ-3 rate employs a smaller peak price period from 3:00 to 6:00 p.m. Monday through Friday. It also has seasonal prices from May through October and November to April. The rates in the EZ-3 plan are higher than the TOU plan, significantly so for summer months.[211]

The EZ-3 plan was designed to encourage greater amounts of peak shaving with the deployment of smart meters. According to Scott Trout, manager of the ADAM program, the EZ-3 program has produced measurable savings in peak demand. SRP reports for 2010 show 9.2 mW in load reduction as a result of the plan and project 54 mW reduced in 2011 if enrollment increases to the projected level of thirty-six thousand customers. For the program to work well for customers, a programmable thermostat is essential. Arizona is a summer-peaking state with large air-conditioning loads. To account for and take advantage of the small peak period in this rate, customers need to pre-cool their home before 3:00 p.m. then raise their thermostats during the 3:00 to 6:00 p.m. time block.[212] On average, customers on this plan use only 10 percent of their energy during on-peak hours. The success of SRP's TOU rates offers evidence that voluntary dynamic pricing programs can attract participants and reduce peak demand.

M-Power

Salt River Project has the largest prepay electric service program in the nation serving over one hundred thousand customers.[213] The program started in 1993 with one hundred residential customers and has grown at a rapid rate since then.[214] Other utilities from across the country have expressed great interest in the M-Power program. While the prepaid program is not necessarily a full blown smart grid technology, M-Power does use advanced data and is an excellent customer behavioral pricing program. By accessing information from an in-home display unit and monitoring spending with smaller transactions, customers on M-Power have more control of their electric consumption and have reduced their usage by an average of 12 percent.

M-Power customers use user display terminals (UDTs) in their homes, corresponding "Smart Cards," and 95 "PayCenters" across the SRP service territory.[215] When a customer initiates service under the M-Power program, a technician installs a new AMPY Landis+Gyr meter, which is linked to the UDT and two Smart Cards. The Smart Card is unique to the customer's UDT and account; they will not work in another customer's system.[216] To add more money to the account, a customer takes her Smart Card to any SRP PayCenter, inserts the card, and deposits the desired amount of cash (as low as one dollar) onto the account. The customer then returns home and inserts the Smart Card into the UDT. The full credit is immediately transferred through the UDT to the meter and drawn down as the customer continues to use electricity.

The key to the M-Power system on the customer side of the meter is the UDT. The UDT displays valuable information, including the following:[217]

- The current rate per hour displayed as dollars/hour, based on the amount of electricity used the previous hour
- The rate charged, displaying as a kWh rate

- Today's cost (estimated)
- Yesterday's cost
- The cost this month
- The cost last month
- An estimated number of days of service remaining with the current credit
- The remaining credit

The customer can toggle through this array of information on the UDT display. Usage information helps the customer budget usage and makes the customer very aware of consumption patterns. A customer can plainly see how running the air conditioner or doing laundry impacts electric usage, and more importantly, the customer's wallet. Of course, the UDT information is critical to notifying customers when their account balances are low. The UDT gives a beeping signal when the customer's account balance falls to ten dollars.

On the utility end of the meter, SRP receives usage information through the Smart Card and PayCenters. While the M-Power meter is similar to a smart meter, it does not provide two-way communication to SRP. Instead, customer information is transferred from the Smart Card to SRP each time the customer purchases credits at a PayCenter.[218] SRP did not develop this unique M-Power back-office system until 2007.[219] Prior to that, the company merged M-Power customers with their existing system, generating a monthly "bill" for record-keeping purposes.

Most M-Power customers save money under the prepay program. The most immediate benefit is reduced service initiation fees. An M-Power system requires a $99 deposit, compared to the $275 deposit required for traditional service.[220] Additionally, M-Power customers spread their electric payments out throughout the month. Average M-Power customers deposit credits in the $20 range four times a month in the winter and seven times a month in the summer.[221] If a customer account is drawn to zero, service will be disconnected unless the account reaches zero during the "friendly credit" hours of 6:00 p.m. to 6:00 a.m. Because M-Power customers are not charged a disconnect or reconnect fee, they save additional money under the program. Traditional programs would charge between sixty and one hundred dollars for reconnection of service.[222]

Despite the instant UDT rate and consumption information, M-Power service has a flat electric rate. M-Power customers cannot receive TOU rates. The M-Power kWh rate varies seasonally, similar to the basic rate plan. However, M-Power rates are slightly lower than the basic plan in summer months and slightly higher in the winter. M-Power also has a monthly service fee of fifteen dollars as opposed to the twelve-dollar service fee in the basic plan. The M-Power service fee is drawn down periodically throughout the month. Most M-Power customers experience lower overall electric costs because they tend to conserve electricity. However, a 2010 EPRI analysis shows that under equal consumption, M-Power customers could pay as much as thirty-eight dollars more per year than basic service customers.[223]

One major criticism of the M-Power program is that it is aimed at low-income customers. Indeed, SRP launched prepay with a one-hundred-home pilot program when the Arizona legislature encouraged new developments to assist low-income residents.[224] However, in subsequent years, M-Power has grown to over one hundred thousand residents, making it difficult to say that SRP is targeting low-income residents. Nevertheless, a 2010 EPRI report shows that 82 percent of M-Power customers earned less than thirty thousand dollars in 2010, compared to 64 percent earning below thirty-five thousand in 1999.[225] Especially during the current economic recession, M-Power is well suited for customers with poor credit, living paycheck to paycheck, or who are in arrears. Customers in arrears can switch to M-Power, and SRP will apply 40 percent of their credit purchases toward their debt. As recently recognized by Mike Lowe, manager of customer services, SRP's bad debt write-off would likely be higher without M-Power.[226] The same EPRI analysis suggests that the arrears payment could skew price responses since a twenty-dollar purchase will only buy twelve dollars in energy, sending a distorted price signal to the customer, equivalent to a 67 percent increase in prices.[227]

Despite the criticisms, the M-Power program is extremely successful. Between 83 and 96 percent of M-Power customers report being satisfied or very satisfied with their prepay service.[228] Most customers enjoy the ability to budget their energy costs, gain information from the UDT, and generally report a feeling of greater control over their energy use. SRP has also enjoyed the results of M-Power. The program won the National Energy Resources Organization award for energy efficiency,[229] and other utilities continually look to SRP as a successful model for prepay systems.[230]

In sum, the M-Power prepay program is a unique system with high customer satisfaction, significant conservation effects, and cost savings for both the customer and utility. The M-Power example, with its 12 percent average reduction in consumption, suggests that using today's technology to provide increased customer feedback and control can result in substantial improvements in energy conservation. While the M-Power program is not fully leveraging smart grid technology as much as other TOU and smart meter programs do, it takes advantage of behavioral changes through increased access to rate and usage information—as smart meters are expected to do. The program is a valuable example of how increased access to usage information can affect customer demand. The degree to which prepaid service can further leverage smart grid technologies is currently unclear. SRP's neighboring service provider, Arizona Public Service, recently filed a prepaid service plan with the ACC which plans to leverage its expanding AMI.[231] Without a doubt, SRP's M-Power program is a national leader in prepaid service and is deserving of the attention it has received.

Demand Response

One of the many promised benefits of the smart grid is increased demand response services. SRP offers a demand response program called the SRP PowerPartner. Under this program, SRP can call on participating facilities to voluntarily curtail their usage based on financial triggers or reliability constraints in exchange for annual payments. SRP can call up to fifteen curtailment events per year for a total of sixty hours of actual load curtailment from the participant. Only two events were called in 2010. In 2010, the program had forty-two participants, annual rebates of $742,493, and a load reduction of 21.1 mW.[232]

As part of its smart grid initiatives, SRP contracted with EnerNOC, an energy services company based in Boston, Massachusetts, to provide demand response services. Under the three-year contract with SRP, EnerNOC will provide 50 mW of verified demand response capacity, dispatchable within 10 minutes of an event. EnerNOC works with industrial and commercial facilities, installs automated demand response technology free of charge, and dispatches load curtailment events from its network operating centers. SRP expects this partnership to help manage peak load in a reliable, clean, and cost-effective way. SRP has not needed to fully utilize this program because of low load growth resulting from the economic downturn.

Electric Vehicle Integration

As infrastructure investments are made in the T&D system, utilities must account for the projected increase in plug-in hybrid electric vehicle and electric vehicle ownership. SRP is planning for PHEV deployment as a part of its DFA initiative. SRP is monitoring locations within its service territory where customers are purchasing PHEV or EV cars. The reliability impact of fast charging is the largest concern for SRP and most utilities, but for now, SRP is not taking any immediate action.

SRP is confident that its distribution system can handle an increase in PHEV or EV charging without a threat to reliability because the transformers on SRP's system are rated to handle significant air conditioning load at the residential level. Therefore, near to medium term, SRP can support charging at 120 volts and 240 volts at the home with little to no system impact.[233] However, SRP does not currently encourage fast charging (one hour or less and greater than 6–7 kW) at the residential level and anticipates near-term industry practice will be to limit fast charging to commercial sites. Fast charging, 20 kW or more, would exceed the capacity of many service entrance sections.

Nor does SRP foresee changing pricing plans or incurring any additional costs from the integration of PHEVs in the near term. SRP will encourage customers to use current TOU pricing plans for vehicle charging, and the company and will not offer any special nighttime rates at this time. Furthermore, if customers want or need increased capacity to accommodate PHEVs, the customer will bear the cost of adding additional capacity out of the main panel to a subpanel, and a dedicated circuit (240 V) for the electric vehicle supply equipment. For the most part, SRP anticipates that challenges integrating PHEVs or EVs with the grid will not be an issue in the short term and the auto manufacturer will address many of the issues currently being discussed in the utility industry. SRP will evaluate the system impacts of the vehicles to determine in the longer term if changes in pricing policy, design standards, or other adjustments are necessary.

Implementation Issues

Building out the smart grid is a tremendously complex process with an array of challenges. Utilities must work to integrate many different operational systems, manage a flood of new data, ensure security of the system and information, and plan for new technologies. While SRP is a leader in many of its smart grid initiatives, barriers to full implementation still exist.

As previously mentioned, SRP does not face any of the regulatory approval or cost recovery barriers that other utilities have experienced. As a political subdivision of the state of Arizona, SRP is not subject to regulation by the ACC. The board approves investments internally; therefore, SRP has a greater degree of flexibility to make investments—allowing SRP to build out the backbone of a smart grid system first to efficiently support future applications.

Although SRP's unique regulatory situation has prevented some barriers to smart grid implementation, the company faces several challenges in structure, technology, and standards. Back-office issues present a challenge to fully utilizing and integrating smart grid technologies. SRP is also working to overcome technological struggles to connect communications with the "last mile" of its distribution system and to link the AMI system with the DFA system. Lastly, SRP notes several barriers created by a lack of, or slowly developing, federal standards.

The growing smart grid will allow utilities to gather more system information than ever before. Managing this wealth of data and connecting corporate departments with the information they need is a daunting challenge. SRP ranks the Enterprise Application Integration initiative as the most difficult, but highest impact section of its smart grid plan. This is an IT challenge that requires SRP to create systems for data exchange across departments to link all of its assets. SRP is planning and assessing its needs and designing an integration system. The system will utilize a common information model specific to SRP's needs and IEC standards.

Salt River Project faces the challenge of automating and connecting the "last mile" of its distribution system from the residential meter to the substation. SRP is not alone in this challenge. Many utilities are struggling to find the right communications technology to create a secure, reliable connection at an efficient cost. SRP is considering whether to develop this technology itself or to use a third-party provider.

As a related issue, SRP notes that there are barriers to integrating the AMI system with the DFA system. The two systems use disparate communication technology with varying latencies and capacities. Adding fifty data points from each of one million smart meters along with the data flow requirements of increasingly intelligent devices throughout the electric and water system is not currently feasible with the existing communication systems in place today. The current system cannot handle the latency and increased bandwidth requirements of linking these processes. Should SRP determine linking the AMI and DFA systems is in the best interest of SRP and its customers, SRP estimates that even the first stages of linking the AMI and DFA systems are at a minimum of five years out.

The company has also noted two key standards issues. The first is related to the "last-mile" communications infrastructure. Smart grid technologies require two-way wireless communications between customers and the utility. Currently, the FCC controls dedicated spectrums for wireless, and utilities do not have a secure dedicated spectrum. SRP currently uses both licensed and unlicensed spectrum; however, unlicensed spectrums are subject to interference or interruption and are not secure enough for all applications. SRP notes that a common spectrum for utilities will allow for interoperability between vendors and raise competition in services.[234] In addition, it notes that NIST cyber security standards should coincide more effectively with NERC CIP standards.

The recent economic recession has impacted SRP's smart grid initiatives. Many of the smart grid initiatives described in this report are becoming standards for new construction, but the demand for more energy and new projects has recently declined in Arizona. As a result, the development of the smart grid has slowed in SRPs service territory. Constrained capital budgets also make some projects difficult for SRP to execute. The ARRA grant for smart meter deployment helped to offset these new constraints on capital investment.

Observations and Conclusion

SRP has enjoyed considerable success with its smart grid initiatives, and much of its work represents best practices in the field. SRP views the current priority of smart grid investments as building out the backbone of the system. Yet while SRP's smart grid investments are arguably more "utility centric" rather than customer focused, SRP remains committed to customer service. In fact, SRP has been awarded the highest score in customer satisfaction for residential and business electric services by J. D. Power and Associates for eleven of the past twelve years.

With programs such as M-Power, TOU rates, energy efficiency services, and smart meter deployment, SRP is enhancing value to its customers. M-Power has an enormous satisfaction rate of 89 percent or more, and most customers believe they are using energy more wisely which has been confirmed by internal and external analyses. Other programs at SRP give customers more access to real-time energy information or simply more education about their electricity usage. SRP offers Internet-based tools about efficiency improvements, Kill A Watt meters, and an Internet account to monitor and control consumption. In sum, smart grid improvements ultimately give the customers greater control of their electric services.

There are a number of valuable lessons from the SRP experience, including the following:

1. SRP has been successful in a wide range of smart grid application and its success has come through advanced planning and policy support, a successful partnership with EPRI, and a full system approach to smart grid technologies. SRP has emphasized the necessity to develop the technological backbone for the smart grid and has demonstrated its technological competency through its implementation.
2. SRP's longtime experience and leadership on voluntary time-of-use rates, which it has further leveraged with smart meter technology, offers promise that voluntary, opt-in approaches to dynamic pricing can be successful with good program design and strong credibility with customers.
3. SRP's M-Power prepay program demonstrates that giving customers both current feedback on their electrical usage and the ability to control that usage through appropriate technology can lead to significant reductions in electrical usage and highly satisfied customers.

Salt River Project is a unique utility with a deep history, but it is taking aggressive steps to modernize its electric system. Like other leaders in smart grid implementation, these efforts mark a starting point, rather than an ending point, in establishing a truly smart grid. To be sure, investment in smart meters and AMI represents an important step in smart grid implementation. Yet in many ways it is only the first phase in a complex process. The Electric Power Research Institute has estimated that fully implementing a smart electric grid nationally will cost between $1.3 and $2.0 trillion, with benefits likely exceeding costs by a factor of three or more.[235] The $3.4 billion in Smart Grid Investment Grants from the Department of Energy represents only a fraction of the total cost for a national-level smart grid build-out.

Research from Pacific Northwest National Laboratory estimated that with full implementation of a smart electric grid by 2030, U.S. energy consumption and carbon emissions could be reduced by 12 percent.[236] A smart electric grid allows utilities to expand energy efficiency and demand response services to all customers, and SRP's leadership in TOU rates and M-Power place it a step ahead of most other utilities. Yet as noted previously, it will take time to develop and offer additional technologies and rates to customers. In some areas, the smart grid will allow customers to use electricity more conscientiously, for example, by charging electric vehicles during off-peak hours in order to achieve efficiency in total energy use across the economy.

Continued investment in automation of the utility distribution system will offer future opportunities for improving reliability and optimizing energy use. In order for electric vehicles to reach the levels of consumer adoption predicted in PNNL's analysis, all levels of government must implement significant new policies and utilities must build new infrastructure. Furthermore, as renewable energy grows to constitute a larger percentage of generation, utilities will need to invest in smart grid technologies in order to reliably and cost-effectively manage these intermittent resources.

At SRP, smart grid implementation is not only off to a productive start, but because of SRP's long-established leadership with TOU rates and prepay electric service its experience should be used as a model for other utilities' planning and implementation. However, ongoing policy refinements, project development, and infrastructure investment will be needed in order to achieve the smart grid's full, long-term potential.

CASE STUDY III. SMUD'S SMARTSACRAMENTO: A CLEAN TECHNOLOGY PIONEER

Introduction

The federal government allocated $4.5 billion in federal economic stimulus funds for smart grid development through the American Recovery and

Reinvestment Act. The smart grid is an electrical grid in which information about behavior and use of electricity on the consumer and supplier level is organized to promote more reliable and efficient services. The Energy Independence and Security Act defines the smart grid as the "modernization of the nation's electricity transmission and distribution system to maintain a reliable and secure electricity infrastructure that can meet future demand growth."[237] In addition, the smart grid has been adopted as a way to protect the environment by increasing energy efficiency and limiting climate change. The smart grid's technological improvements are expected to reduce energy consumption, avert the need to build more power plants, and create a more reliable and secure electricity infrastructure to meet future energy growth.

The Sacramento Municipal Utility District is one of a number of utilities developing a smart grid program. In 2009, SMUD received $127.5 million from the Department of Energy to support its smart grid efforts. SMUD has been applying this grant to its $308 million smart grid investment SmartSacramento, which includes a joint venture with community partners who are the California State University at Sacramento, the state Department of General Services, the County of Sacramento, the Sacramento City Unified School District, the Elk Grove Unified School District, and the Los Rios Community College District. This paper presents a case study of SMUD's smart grid programs, namely, SmartSacramento, a project that encourages customers to be part of the energy solution. It involves enhanced technology infrastructure, AMI, distribution automation, demand response, customer applications such as Internet access to energy usage and analysis, a consumer behavior (pricing) study, cyber security, and partner projects. These various projects started in 2009 and are projected to be completed by 2014. However, the SmartSacramento project is just one of SMUD's initiatives that leverages smart grid, energy efficiency, and clean technology efforts.[238]

Background on the Sacramento Municipal Utility District

The Sacramento Municipal Utility District is a community-owned, not-for-profit electric utility that has provided public power throughout Sacramento since 1946.[239] It has an elected board of directors that does not report to a city council and is owned by its customers. The board has exclusive legal authority to establish the rates and rules for electricity customers within its service territory.[240]

SMUD is the sixth largest community-owned electric utility in the United States and the second largest in California, employing 2,036 people.[241] SMUD currently serves 529,695 residential customers and 68,510 business customers in a service area with a total population of about

1.4 million. SMUD encompasses a nine-hundred-square-mile service territory in Sacramento, Placer, and Yolo counties.

SMUD generates electricity using a diverse array of sources. SMUD owns a 500-mW natural gas combined cycle power plant and three natural gas-fired co-generation facilities that make up approximately 50 percent (2010) of its total production. SMUD runs its hydroelectric plants for providing peak demand, which make up about 14 percent (2010) of its generation. In addition, SMUD has actively supported renewable energy and distributed generation development to serve its customers as part of its goal to reduce its greenhouse gas emissions to 10 percent of its 1990 level by 2050.[242]

SMUD promotes renewable energy and energy efficiency.[243] It has pioneered green technology and its energy efficiency and renewable energy programs are recognized nationally for their leadership and innovation. In 2008, SMUD adopted a goal to procure 33 percent renewable power by 2020 before it was mandatory for all California electric utilities.[244] SMUD was also the only large utility that met the previous 20 percent renewable goal by 2010 using eligible resources under the current California Energy Commission Renewable Portfolio Standards Eligibility Guidebook. It has 102 mW of wind-powered facilities and 35 mW of photovoltaic generating facilities. These renewable energy sources generate almost 3 percent (2010) of SMUD's energy output with the remaining renewable energy supplied by Power Purchase Agreements. Thus SMUD's total energy from renewable energy sources in 2010 was approximately 24 percent.[245]

SMUD's policies focus on serving the community. For example, its vision is to "empower its customers with solutions and options that increase energy efficiency, protect the environment, reduce global warming and lower the cost to serve its region."[246] SMUD provides its customers with information and other useful tools to keep down their electricity bills. It also sets competitive rates, which are typically below neighboring utility rates.

Overview of SMUD's Smart Grid Programs

SMUD is transitioning to a smart grid in order to give customers more flexibility and choice in their electricity use while also meeting the organization's environmental goals. SMUD received a $127.5 million Smart Grid Investment Grant from the Department of Energy through ARRA to advance smart grid implementation. The award is one of the ten largest in the nation. The contract was signed on April 23, 2010, and has a total budget of $307,697,792. Hence, SMUD is charged with implementing almost $308 million worth of projects. This amount was 63 percent of the SGIG money allotted to all California electric utilities. SMUD's initial phase of the smart grid program, focused on installing a functional AMI (e.g., smart meters), is expected to be fully deployed by the end of the first quarter of 2012. The rest of the projects are projected to be completed by 2014.

Consumer-Owned Perspective

SMUD is considered one of the most progressive of the mid-sized utilities in the United States[247] because of its focus on promoting renewable energy and energy efficiency and on developing the smart grid. "Energy efficiency is the most cost-effective way for SMUD and Sacramento to move beyond carbon."[248] SMUD expects to be the first utility to meet the state's clean power mandate, while also exceeding California's energy efficiency mandate. SMUD expects that its smart grid program will improve the grid and help meet the clean power and energy efficiency goals.

The utility plans to use multiple strategies simultaneously to achieve these goals. It is installing smart meters; focusing on consumer behavior through pricing programs, surveys, focus groups, and communication with customers; and automating portions of its distribution system. In addition, it is improving technological infrastructure by installing a state-of-the-art demand response management system, implementing innovative demand response programs which leverage the new smart grid infrastructure, conducting research and development through several pilot programs, and addressing cyber security issues. SMUD is focused on supporting its smart grid initiatives through implementing a comprehensive customer relationship management system that integrates directly with its billing system.

The utility developed its smart grid programs based on a vision of a regional solution that will integrate smart meters and home area networks with upstream, automated distribution operations. To improve system reliability and efficiency SMUD plans to optimize distribution system operations. Further, it will enable its customers to fully participate in the electricity marketplace through dynamic pricing and demand response programs.[249]

Organization of Programs

Through its smart grid program, SMUD plans to reduce greenhouse gas emissions to 10 percent of 1990 levels by 2050.[250] It will achieve this objective by assuring a reliable, diverse power supply through its smart grid programs. SMUD's funded smart grid projects include

- AMI and smart meters,
- a consumer behavior study and dynamic pricing,
- a DRM system and programs,
- distribution system improvements and automation,
- technology infrastructure,
- customer applications (partner projects), and
- cyber security.

The Sacramento Municipal Utility District received other grants promoting the smart grid through ARRA, including the Smart Grid Demonstrations–Storage for Grid Support initiative, which awards a subgrant to Premium Power for two battery systems to demonstrate the integration of photovoltaics and energy storage into smart grid applications.[251] In addition, SMUD plans to develop infrastructure standards for plug-in hybrid electric vehicles that charge off-peak and feed electricity back to the grid during peak periods. SMUD will also test the effectiveness of battery storage and power management products. Another project, PV and Energy Storage for Smart Grids, develops tools modeling a distribution system into smart grid applications. SMUD is developing its smart grid through various approaches and has received funding and other support to plan and implement related initiatives.

The smart grid research and development budget is $42.9 million, bringing the total smart grid budget to over $350 million. Additional R&D projects include a microgrid demonstration, residential information and controls pilot, smart controls in multifamily projects, and dairy digesters. The R&D demonstrations will test the capabilities, costs, and benefits of emerging technologies and will lay the foundation for future smart grid deployments.

Program Management and Development

In 2008, the SMUD Board of Directors resolved to adopt a smart grid policy. The staff needed the approval of the board prior to investing in new technology. SMUD recognized the importance of working with its customers and partnering with local organizations.[252]

The utility has partnered with six public agencies in its service territory to implement a portion of the smart grid grant as subrecipients. These partners include Los Rios Community College District (LRCCD), the California Department of General Services (DGS), the Sacramento City Unified School District, the County of Sacramento, the Elk Grove Unified School District, and California State University at Sacramento (CSUS). Energy management systems will be installed or updated with advanced controls, the capability to monitor electricity use, the ability to identify buildings that use excessive energy, and the ability to reduce peak loads. These partners will enable energy management systems to respond to automated demand response (Auto DR) events to reduce peak loads. In addition to its formal subrecipients, SMUD met with equipment and software vendors to assess the available technology and to test equipment in order to determine which equipment to deploy.

The utility's smart grid program and its partnerships are managed by a smart grid manager who implements SMUD's plan with the focus on ARRA projects through 2014. The manager will develop a strategic plan to guide the program beyond 2014. A major focus of the plan is customer communications and customer experience before, during, and after the implementation of smart grid. SMUD will use brochures, media, an on-line presence, and presentations; it will assign staff specifically to address customer concerns about smart meters.

Moreover, SMUD has also collaborated with the Electric Power Research Institute on its SmartSacramento demonstration project. The two have worked together on demonstrations and a host-site project integrating distributed generation and smart grid development.[253] Finally, California and SMUD's pioneering leadership in clean technology positioned SMUD particularly well to be a successful leader in smart grid technology.

Estimated Costs

The Sacramento Municipal Utility District estimates that it will cost $307.7 million to implement all of the projects involved in its SmartSacramento program.[254] This figure includes not only investment in technology, but also accompanying behavioral and consumer studies.[255] In addition to the ARRA funding allotted to SMUD by the Department of Energy to develop various smart grid solutions in Sacramento, the utility received $19.2 million in ARRA and California Energy Commission grants to partially fund $42.9 million in smart grid-related research and develop demonstration projects.[256]

Sacramento Municipal Utility District's Smart Grid Roadmap: Seven Key Projects

Smart Meters and Advanced Metering Infrastructure

Initially, SMUD focused on installing advanced metering infrastructure, primarily smart meters. SMUD identified smart meters as the first step toward a smart grid, connecting SMUD to its customers by integrating the delivery and consumption of electricity using two-way wireless communications.[257] Smart meters collect and store a customer's electricity usage data at regular intervals. The customer's data is then securely transmitted to a local collection point. The collection point securely transmits the data to SMUD. The utility then uses the information to bill the customer and provide energy usage data online. The two-way communication between a customer's home and the utility enables SMUD to explore pricing that varies by season and time of day.[258]

Installing AMI will significantly improve SMUD's knowledge of circuit-specific conditions. The smart meters will reduce SMUD's operating costs and improve reliability. Because customers will be able to see their usage by hour online, customers will be easily informed and capable of making decisions based on the costs of their energy consumption. SMUD focuses on the potential of customer data and information to empower customers to make choices about consumption. This smart grid project coincides well with SMUD's community-based structure and mission.

SMUD makes a compelling business case for AMI because more than $9 million annually prior to AMI was spent on meter reading. By installing meters that can communicate wirelessly, SMUD anticipates significant financial savings. In addition, SMUD predicts other benefits from AMI. AMI enables time-differentiated rates and critical peak pricing opportunities and makes demand response possible through automatic or remote control of appliances and equipment. AMI facilitates loading information and automation along the entire supply chain.

SMUD's implementation of AMI calls for the installation of approximately 615,000 new smart meters for all customers by the first quarter of 2012.[259] To date, SMUD has installed 610,000.[260] SMUD completed a seventy-eight-thousand-meter pilot project in 2010, installing selected Silver Spring Networks, Inc. and Landis+Gyr meters.

As of January 2012, approximately 98 percent of the customer meters had been replaced with smart meters. The remaining 2 percent were expected to be replaced by March 2012. SMUD's communication network is 100 percent complete. SMUD's rollout of its wireless smart meter technology received little criticism, generating very few customer complaints, all of which SMUD responded to quickly. Importantly, more than 95 percent of customers were satisfied with the installation as of December 2011.[261]

As SMUD develops its system, customers will be able to go online and see detailed information about their energy use, manage demand response events, and make adjustments as desired using their cell phone or computer. SMUD sends each customer a letter and brochure before the smart meter is installed so that the customer understands the change. To avoid adding burdensome responsibility to the customer, SMUD does not require customers to do anything, except remove barriers to access, so customers need not be home for the meter installation. The meter programming and back-office features can be used remotely through wireless communication technologies.

SMUD is training its employees and board members to be available to customers for smart meter presentations. Since October 2009, SMUD has given 116 customer presentations and 71 internal employee presentations.[262] SMUD presents to city councils and county boards of supervisors, individual elected officials and their staff, community planning councils, social civic clubs, chambers of commerce, and neighborhood associations. SMUD is making a big effort to ensure that customer service, transparency, and understanding are priorities in its smart grid program.

SMUD's board adopted a policy to allow those few customers (less than 0.4%) who have expressed concern about the possible privacy and health issues associated with installing wireless AMI devices on their homes to opt-out. SMUD charges a fee to customers who opt out so it can recover the incremental costs related to opting out, such as meter reading. SMUD does not want its customers to subsidize the alternative metering solution for the opt-out customers. Customers who opt-out may not realize the many benefits of smart meters, such as time-of-use rate options and customer programs that are available only to customers who have wireless smart meters.[263]

Consumer Behavior Study and Dynamic Pricing

Sacramento Municipal Utility District is a customer-owned public utility. Its policies focus on serving the community, setting competitive rates below published rates, and educating its customers about how to keep down their electricity bills: "Maintaining competitive rates is a core value of SMUD."[264] In responding to customer needs, SMUD is providing customer education and new tools to manage energy usage information while making usage more transparent and giving customers more control. Along these lines, SMUD is partnering with customers to make them part of the energy solution by helping them to reduce peak load and improve energy efficiency.

SMUD has budgeted about $13 million for a Consumer Behavior Study; the final cost will depend on the ultimate scope of the study. This study will evaluate the impacts of time-based rates, enable technologies, and recruit treatments on energy consumption and peak demand.[265] The study will take place from June 2012 through September 2013, with interim evaluation reporting in April 2013 and final evaluation reporting in January 2014. It uses the same methodology as the 2009 Residential Summer Solutions Study, which tested the use of dynamic pricing and communicating thermostats in the small commercial sector. The 2009 study showed 20 percent energy savings and bill savings of 25 percent.[266] This customer behavior study will be used to "develop strategies for rate design, provide information on real-time use display, measure satisfaction by demographics, and measure value for the consumer and SMUD."[267] Seven randomly chosen groups of residential customers were offered one of seven equipment and rate configuration treatments. SMUD will use the results of this study, consisting of a sample frame of approximately fifty-seven thousand residential customers,[268] to statistically measure the capability of the equipment and rate configurations to reduce electricity use, reduce peak demand, and determine the likelihood of participation by demographic.

SMUD currently uses a two-tier residential rate structure designed to encourage conservation based on its inclining block rates,[269] which increase as usage increases. The more kilowatt-hours used, the higher the rate. The rates vary by seasons as well. Layered on top of these rates, SMUD adds a Rate Stabilization Fund surcharge of about one-quarter cent per kilowatt-hour that is applied during low hydro years. SMUD's rates are designed to achieve goals ranging from linking the marginal cost of when energy is used to rates, reducing use during peak times, and encouraging energy efficiency and conservation. SMUD's rates are designed to "offer flexibility and options to customers, be simple and easy to understand, meet needs of customers with fixed low incomes and severe medical conditions, and equitably allocate costs across customer classes."[270]

Demand Response/Energy Efficiency

Sacramento Municipal Utility District is developing demand response resources to meet its integrated resource planning goals and to fulfill resource procurement and operational requirements. SMUD has allotted $15 million to demand response over a three-year period and approximately $35 million per year to energy efficiency. It will install a Demand Response Management System to serve as the common platform for all demand response activities. The new system will support both price-based and incentive-based demand response programs. It will integrate with many of SMUD's other business systems such as AMI, CIS, MDM system, GIS, and energy operations center. As part of the DOE grant, SMUD will install up to 1,800 home area network devices and encourage homes and businesses to participate in direct load management programs. The Customer Applications component of SmartSacramento will equip approximately nine hundred homes with HAN.[271]

The utility will expand its current demand response portfolio, which consists of programs that have provided as much as 8 percent peak load reduction capability.[272] It will also integrate new renewable resources and help manage larger percentages of distributed generation. SMUD believes that offering customers a variety of demand response programs and automating demand response will provide customers with tools to manage their bills, reduce system peak, and respond to dynamic pricing.

The utility will design and deliver programs for medium and large commercial customers to automatically respond using Open ADR communication protocols tied to their energy management systems. These programs would include both price-based and incentive-based offerings. SMUD would provide medium and large commercial customers with technical assistance to modify their technology so it can automatically respond to signals from SMUD to reduce load. SMUD is also integrating demand response and energy efficiency by connecting automated demand response technology and Open ADR to energy efficiency programs for commercial customer energy management systems and advanced lighting technologies.

Distribution System Improvements and Automation

Sacramento Municipal Utility District will install automated controls throughout the distribution system to improve system efficiency, reduce operations and maintenance costs, and improve reliability by reducing the duration of outages by 20–25 percent.[273] In SMUD's comments to the California Energy Commission, Timothy Tutt, SMUD's government affairs representative, stated, "The primary mission for our distribution system is keeping the lights on for our customers in a manner that leads the industry in safety, reliability and customer service."[274]

The utility plans to spend $58.2 million on distribution automation. It will upgrade aging infrastructure by replacing electro-mechanical relays with digital relays at many medium voltage substations. SMUD plans to use smart grid technology in its distribution system to enable advanced operations management for volt optimization, conservation voltage reduction, and automated sectionalization and restoration. SMUD will be able to restore power much more quickly in the event of an outage because automated switching will allow it to optimize its distribution network and enhance operating capability.[275] Automating distribution will also expand SMUD's supervisory control and data acquisition system.[276]

The utility plans to install SCADA at forty substations and install automated line devices with two-way communication on 18 percent, or 109, distribution circuits. SMUD will automate 44 percent, or twenty-four, of SMUD's subtransmission circuits.[277] SMUD will install intelligent switching and monitoring equipment and a wireless communication system.

In the near term, SMUD expects to implement an advanced operating system in 18 percent of its service territory that will sectionalize and restore power to customers after an outage, optimize distribution circuit voltage to enable energy savings, and reduce losses. The desired results include increased system efficiency, improved power factor, reduction of system losses, reduction of energy consumption, and decreased frequency and duration of outages.[278]

The utility's conservation voltage reduction and volt/var optimization (VVO) strategies will be deployed in order to make the grid more energy efficient. SMUD completed testing of their CVR and VVO strategies in the summer of 2011. Although energy savings will differ by circuit based on various types of loads, the testing results were very promising. SMUD's initial testing included two substations in different geographical areas and the three circuits connected to each of the two substations. Testing of CVR and VVO on the feeders associated with the first substation yielded an average of 2.5 percent demand reduction, an average demand reduction of 315 kW at peak (between 4:30 and 6:30 p.m.) and minimized line losses by maintaining power factor at approximately .95 leading. The second substation and associated feeders yielded an average of 1 percent demand reduction, an average demand reduction of 150 kW at peak (between 4:30 and 6:30 p.m.) and minimized line losses by maintaining power factor at approximately .95 leading. SMUD is currently undergoing vigorous lab testing of their automated sectionalization and restoration control logic prior to "turning on" the automated control logic on their distribution system.

The Sacramento Municipal Utility District has invested in its software infrastructure as well. It installed the Enterprise Service Bus software platform to reduce the cost of communications between systems by reducing the number, size, and complexity of interfaces between systems. The new platform will ultimately improve the speed of service to the customer. SMUD is currently upgrading its existing Outage Management System to include Web Methods functionality, ease the integration with other systems, and enable SCADA integration through an ICCP gateway. SMUD will tie together the upgraded outage management system with their AMI system for outage reporting from smart meters. Once smart meters are used to report system outages to distribution system operators, SMUD will introduce automated, proactive outage communication with their customers. SMUD will notify customers of outages that are affecting their service, provide estimated restoration times, and confirm restoration of service.

The utility also installed Customer Relationship Management System software to provide customer representatives a real-time view of energy usage. This software integrates a customer service call center with SMUD's back-office billing system.

Plug-in Hybrid Electric Vehicle/Battery Electric Vehicle Infrastructure and Integration

The Sacramento Municipal Utility District is committed to examining customer applications for an electric vehicle infrastructure. It is dedicating a portion of its smart grid resources to plug in hybrid electric vehicles and battery electric vehicles (BEVs), together known as plug-in electric vehicles (PEVs). The purpose of SMUD's Smart Grid Smart Charging Pilot Program is to offer time-based rates to PEV drivers in order to learn how best to encourage off-peak charging. During the first year of the pilot project, two or more time-of-use experimental rates will be offered to 180 residential PEV drivers. Up to 60 of the drivers will be offered two-way communicating EVSE that will be used to give them a "managed charging" option. As part of the partner programs, up to twenty-five two-way communicating smart charging stations will be installed on the CSUS and Cosumnes River College campuses. SMUD will incentivize customers to charge their batteries during off-peak periods by using price signals. SMUD is conducting applied research that in the future may allow for V2G electricity sales and home energy storage demonstration projects. It is also working on a project with the California Energy Commission to test the effects of electric vehicles on the grid. In the future, SMUD may be able to pay customers to feed power from their EVs into the grid to support reliability, while ensuring that the battery charge will not fall below a pre-specified level.

Because electric vehicle owners tend to cluster in certain areas, SMUD plans to test the impacts of multiple electric vehicles on a single distribution transformer. It will model this scenario using multiple EV battery systems on a transformer in a test bed setting. SMUD is also using a load simulator to simulate reactive and resistive variable loads. It will apply to the most common transformers (25 kVA, 50 kVA, and 75 kVA) in the system. SMUD will mount transformers at the Hedge Substation, where its training facility is located.[279]

The utility has also tested and used alternative fuel vehicles. It has explored the practical uses of electric vehicles and is purchasing and testing EVs in daily operations to advance the technology, such as the Chevrolet Volt.[280] To further encourage off-peak charging that will improve overall system efficiency, SMUD offers an EV time-of-use rate that provides power at a much lower rate during the night.[281]

Finally, SMUD has developed tools to help customers with plug-in EVs. SMUD has an EV Web page with a cost calculator to assist potential EV buyers in their decision process, a section on its website with FAQs about EVs and charging the vehicle, and an in-house staff ready to answer customer questions.

Customer Applications

The Sacramento Municipal Utility District is partnering with six public agencies to implement part of its smart grid grant from DOE. Of the estimated $308 million for SMUD's SmartSacramento, SMUD's subrecipients are contributing approximately $18.3 million for $36.6 million worth of projects. The ARRA grant covers 50 percent of the cost for subrecipient projects.

Each subrecipient will install or update energy management systems on its campus to monitor electricity use, identify buildings that use excessive energy, save energy, and reduce peak loads. For example, advanced controls and submetering will be installed on all 57 buildings on the CSUS campus. Smart electric vehicle charging stations will be installed on some subrecipient campuses. Linda Hafar, director of Utilities and Facility Services at CSUS announced that 16 electric car charging stations would be constructed; and, the grant would also support a new energy management system to better control building heating and cooling systems.[282]

The utility's partnership with CSUS has included developing a shared vision and investing resources for CSUS's new California Smart Grid Interpretive Center, a living laboratory to showcase the use of smart grid technologies. SMUD and CSUS will develop course work to educate students about energy efficiency. They will also upgrade the CSUS distribution system to increase campus grid reliability.

The utility has developed other "customer applications," including services for residential and commercial customers that educate, inform, and enable them to access and use the information available through the smart grid to better manage their energy use.[283] Initiatives include pilot projects to enable customers to manage their bills, reduce peak demand, and increase energy efficiency. Pilot offerings combine technology and dynamic pricing at varying levels of customer commitment, equipment cost, and SMUD involvement in energy management. Technologies include smart thermostats, in-home displays, smart appliances, online interval usage graphs, and energy management systems.[284] Commercial applications include rebates for installing advanced, controllable lighting systems; updating the commercial energy information and tools software package; and installing energy management systems for buildings.

In addition, SMUD is partnering with a local developer on a forty-two-home subdivision to create a smart grid-enabled, net-zero energy development in the heart of downtown Sacramento which includes photovoltaic systems, energy storage, controllable appliances, home energy management systems, and energy efficiency.

Cyber Security

In addition to the goal of improving reliability, incorporating information technology into the electric industry through the smart grid may make the electric grid more vulnerable to attacks and loss of service. SMUD has allotted $3.3 million[285] in total project costs to cyber security. Although the smart grid has many purported benefits, the federal government and general public have high-level security concerns about an increasingly complex and vulnerable grid.

An often noted additional risk is the potential to compromise data confidentiality, such as breach of customer privacy. SMUD has assured its customers that their energy use information will remain confidential and safe. SMUD is using DOE's approved cyber security plan.[286] It will perform ongoing cyber security assessments. SMUD will also install tools that will detect intrusions, and it will install vulnerability management tools to maintain a secure computer system. The smart meters will transmit customer energy use information to SMUD's secure servers, run by the same wireless network and same types of security as the Department of Defense and the online banking industry.[287]

The goal of SMUD's cyber security initiative is to enact security programs and procedures that conform to and exceed government-mandated standards. It will continue its current best practices with and increase the level of funding for those programs to support smart grid initiatives. SMUD has implemented a "holistic and robust cyber security program"[288] to protect confidentiality, integrity, and information related to customer data. Also, SMUD plans on implementing the cyber-security protocols needed for system security. SMUD will focus on the technical and communications infrastructure necessary to optimize its system and cyber security protocols over the next few years.

Implementation Challenges

Despite SMUD's success in receiving funding for its smart grid programs[289] and even with its strong reputation supporting energy efficiency, renewable energy programs, and local generation, transforming the old electric grid to a smart one is an intensive, complex process. SMUD has invested significant time and resources into developing short, medium, and long-term plans for building the smart grid, however actually implementing the necessary changes will be challenging. In an "I 4 Energy" seminar, Jim Parks, the SMUD program manager for energy efficiency and customer R&D, talked about SMUD's current success in putting together the prescriptive pieces of a smart grid, but he noted that parts of the system do not currently communicate with each other and may not for a few years. He suggested that the ultimate goal is to manage and link the entire system. He also offered that the funding SMUD has received is not enough to fully implement smart grid throughout its entire service territory, so it is focusing on a few areas for now.[290]

The utility is still in the nascent stages of its smart grid build-out. As of March 2012, the SmartSacramento project was still in the process of being implemented, with approximately 55 percent of the project completed. Although SMUD does not have to prove that proposed benefits are real to regulators, as a customer-owned electric utility, SMUD's Board of Directors and customers should understand the value of the system. Additionally, SMUD is affected by California state policy decisions generally.[291] Moreover, although SMUD has always been closely allied with its consumers, some SMUD customers may find the adjustment to a new system difficult or may feel wary about privacy and security concerns. Only a few customers have expressed concern about keeping their personal information confidential.

In its communication plan for AMI, SMUD anticipated customer concerns over high bills. Therefore, when questions arose, SMUD simply followed the processes set forth in the plan.[292] Even from the beginning, SMUD has received very few customer comments on this concern.[293] In fact, since the early stages, SMUD's customers have generally provided positive feedback about the smart grid; however some have expressed concerns about different rate structures, especially time-of-use rates.

The utility recognizes that it faces challenges to their smart grid program that present implementation issues. SMUD suggests that the most pressing challenges will be based on the amount, size, location, and voltage levels of the interconnected resources; the capabilities of those resources for dispatch and communication (and similar smart grid capabilities); and the ability of the grid to accept generation at multiple distributed sites and flow power as needed in the opposite direction as initially designed.[294] Although they have not fully implemented their program, SMUD has concluded in its first few years that more research and development is needed and that it will take ten to twenty years to build out its smart grid.[295]

Intermittent resources play a significant challenge in SMUD's management of the grid. For example, SMUD anticipates that its current 35 mW of solar capacity and 102 mW of wind will increase to 160 mW of solar and 250 mW of wind in the next three years.[296] For example, one of SMUD's largest capital investments is the Solano Wind project, which consists of fifty-five 260-foot-high turbines that will generate approximately 128 mW to power enough electricity to light 38,000 homes.[297]

Some PV resources cannot be fully integrated into the smart grid until there is sufficient two-way communication and control capability between the utility and PV inverters.[298] Erik Krause, product development manager for SMUD, suggests that utilities can gather information by installing separate meters to measure production at the PV systems.[299] Integration between the inverters and smart meters could eliminate the need for a second meter, but are not required to gather data. As the percentage of total generation that is renewable rises, SMUD's ability to provide infrastructure, capacity (V2G, storage plants), and effective "smart" demand-response management will be critical. SMUD is identifying key research and development questions related to issues like the integration of intermittent resources, and noting how the smart grid can play a role. Intermittent resources require extensive planning to coordinate effectively. However, SMUD does not currently have the means to manage this increasing resource.

The utility is also examining storage to support its plan to increase renewable energy supplies by 2050. It is performing demonstration projects, such as the Anatolia SolarSmart community with Lennar Homes, to quantify the cost and benefits of storage deployment and distributed solar generation. In that project, SMUD equipped more than 270 homes with battery storage tied to the solar grid to see if firm renewables would reduce peak load and improve reliability. This demonstration monitored inverters using AMI communication from smart meter to inverter. In addition, SMUD has received federal stimulus funding for PV and energy storage. It has already installed fourteen of the planned seventeen PV systems; and it is developing tools to model a distribution system while demonstrating PV integration and energy storage into smart grid applications.[300]

The utility also notes that many of the software and technology packages are very new so it is difficult to determine overall product reliability, accuracy and whether the products will be supported in the long term. The delayed release of the ZigBee SEP 2.0 interoperability standard is another technology issue facing all utilities with demand response implementations using ZigBee HAN devices. This delay is also impacting SMUD's ability to support EVSE and PV inverter communication and control over AMI networks.[301] Further demonstration projects and pilots are needed to assess the viability of new products. SMUD is currently taking advantage of Itron technology for meter data management. SMUD may eventually implement distribution management software, but anticipates that implementation is three to five years out because the software is premature, lacks standardization, and cyber-security concerns persist.

It is aware of the technical challenges that come with the addition of significant percentages of distributed generation. For example, meeting the requisite standards for solar power on a partially cloudy day may be challenging. However, SMUD suggests that balancing authority performance requirements should be further evaluated to avoid this problem. It will take time and experience with the new grid infrastructure before operators understand how best to integrate distributed generation on a circuit-by-circuit basis and address the potential for two-way power flow.

Importantly, SMUD plans to implement the smart grid only after necessary research has been done on the cumulative impacts to the grid. For example, it has no plans to acquire widespread adoption of communication technology for monitoring and control of all systems before receiving the results of its research projects. Although SMUD is installing technology, it is in the exploratory phase of smart grid. Based on the results obtained from the SmartSacramento project pilots and other research and development projects and pilots, SMUD will evaluate the results and make decisions about how to best proceed for highest benefits for its customers.[302] Moreover, SMUD's smart meter deployment plan called for initially installing seventy-eight thousand smart meters and then paused temporarily to perform a series of performance tests on the meters and communication system to ensure full system functionality and to help minimize public concerns.[303] Only when SMUD was satisfied with the results did the deployment continue, with up to sixty-five thousand installations per month, until being completed in the first quarter of 2012. As programs are implemented and lessons are learned, plans must be reevaluated.

Conclusions and Lessons Learned

The Sacramento Municipal Utility District has the basic resources and infrastructure to implement a successful smart grid program for its customers. It has invested a lot of time, money, and expertise to plan for a thriving and functional smart grid that will completely modernize and transform the electric grid as it is currently known.

Focusing on Strategic Planning and Strong Communication with Customers

Early on in the process, SMUD has focused intensively on its plan and its communication with customers. After all, SMUD is a customer-owned and customer-based utility. As Michael Gianunzio, SMUD's chief legislative and regulatory affairs officer, expressed, "We have been very careful and deliberative in our communications with customers. We have some time to go before studies will be underway that evaluate the behavioral aspects of this kind of thing; lots of groundwork and contracts and strategies need to be developed well in advance. It will be years, I am sure, before we have a complete picture of how successful this can be."[304] SMUD's smart grid program is in the full implementation stage right now. SMUD will start to evaluate the projects in late 2012 and will develop a smart grid roadmap that identifies the next steps. Demonstration projects that show strong potential will be considered for broader scale deployment in the future. Additional demonstration projects will also be identified.

Despite a few concerns, customers responded positively to SMUD's smart grid program, understanding the perceived benefits, such as SMUD's ability to provide future outage information and create new programs for energy efficiency. Given its customers' acceptance of the changes so far, when SMUD moves deeper into the implementation phases of its program, it is likely to be successful.

In its early stages of implementation, SMUD has made the transition to a smart grid relatively easy for its customers. SMUD does not require customers to be home for the smart meter to be installed. They also provide customers with adequate information about the technology, the justification for the shift, and the expected benefits. SMUD invites and encourages volunteers to participate as early adopters. SMUD demonstrates how a smart grid provides the customer with greater understanding and control of their electric services.

While it is too early to analyze lessons learned or to suggest that SMUD has been successful in making an impact on its clean energy goals and improving system reliability, it appears that it has enhanced customer value. At the very least, its customers were informed as they received their smart meters and invited to take advantage of the increased accessibility of their electric information.

Expertise and Leadership in Clean Energy Technology Leads to Success in Smart Grid Implementation

Its pioneering leadership in clean technologies, including energy efficiency, renewable energy, and storage, position SMUD to be a successful leader in smart grid technology. Moreover, SMUD's plan is at least designed to enable more renewable energy, higher levels of energy efficiency and better integration of distributed resources. Hence, SMUD's strategic and advanced planning offers a great opportunity for SMUD to be a leader in the smart grid movement, as it is in renewable energy and customer services. SMUD's pioneering leadership and expertise in clean technology, including energy efficiency, renewables, and storage, has positioned it well to be a successful leader in implementing the smart grid.

California's Clean Energy Leadership and Clear Policies Have Been Supportive

The state of California has been recognized for its innovative and forward-thinking energy policies supporting clean technology. California's investment in renewable energy, energy efficiency, and enhanced storage capacity helps not only to support its public utilities and independent service operators, but also the consumer-owned utilities, such as SMUD. Consequently, California and SMUD's pioneering leadership in clean technology has positioned SMUD particularly well to be a successful leader in smart grid technology.

Although the California Public Utilities Commission does not regulate SMUD—SMUD reports to a board of directors—it benefits from operating within a state that supports investing in clean technology and recognizes the need for infrastructure investment. California's legislation directly and indirectly drives some of SMUD's priorities, as SMUD strives to be an industry leader and a good neighbor to the customers who own it and the environment that surround it by empowering its customers with solutions and options that increase energy efficiency, protect the environment, reduce global warming, and lower the cost of service within its region.

CASE STUDY IV. COMED'S SMART GRID INNOVATION CORRIDOR: PILOTING THE REGULATORY ENVIRONMENT IN ILLINOIS

History and Background

For over a hundred years Commonwealth Edison has provided electrical service to Chicago and northern Illinois, operating as the state's largest electric utility. Established in 1881 by George H. Bliss, ComEd first operated as a subsidiary of Thomas Edison's company and sold Edison's generators and lighting systems to Chicago's burgeoning downtown commercial district. In 1907, Chicago Edison (one of nearly thirty electric companies operating in Chicago by that time) merged with Commonwealth Electric to form the Commonwealth Edison Company. Six years later the company acquired the Cosmopolitan Electric Company, effectively giving it a monopoly on electrical service in Chicago.[305]

In 1997 the Illinois legislature passed the Electric Service Customer Choice and Rate Relief Act requiring a transition to retail choice for electric service beginning first with industrial customers and later residential customers. While participation rates have been high for industrial customers, residential customer participation has been low resulting in ComEd remaining not only the distribution company but also the electric supplier for many residential customers. In 2000, ComEd's parent company Unicom merged with PECO Energy (formerly Philadelphia Electric

Company) to form Exelon, one of the largest utilities in the United States, serving over 5.4 million electricity customers and nearly 500,000 natural gas customers. As a subsidiary of Exelon, ComEd today delivers power to more than 3.8 million customers in Illinois. The utility works under regional operator PJM Interconnection and owns more than seventy thousand circuit miles of transmission and distribution lines and thirteen hundred substations.[306] In 2010, the company employed over fifty-eight hundred people and enjoyed pre-tax income of almost $700 million.[307] On March 12, 2012, Exelon merged with Constellation, the parent company of Baltimore Gas and Electric, and became the largest competitive integrated energy company in the United States.

Overview of ComEd's Smart Grid Program

ComEd has adopted a "Smart Grid Vision" that seeks to "enhance customer value with cost-effective technological advancements that empower customers and leads to more efficient utilization of electricity, reductions in future demand growth, improvements in the environment and a more reliable and secure system."[308] Its near-term strategy for achieving this vision includes expanding existing smart grid technology deployments and conducting limited pilot programs of smart grid technologies at the distribution and substation levels.

In 2009, ComEd launched its Smart Grid Innovation Corridor, one of the broadest collections of smart grid pilot projects in the nation. The corridor encompasses more than ten Chicago-area communities and five pilot projects divided into three major areas: expansion of AMI, intelligent substations, and integration of PHEV and all-electric vehicles.

Advanced Metering Infrastructure

In 2008, the Illinois Commerce Commission issued Order No. 07-0566, establishing the Illinois Statewide Smart Grid Collaborative for the purpose of developing a strategic plan to guide the development of smart grid in Illinois and recommending smart grid policies that the ICC should consider.[309] The order also authorized a series of stakeholder workshops to aid ComEd in a test deployment of an AMI pilot program. The order charged ComEd with engaging statewide stakeholders through a series of workshops beginning in late 2008 and with filing a formal plan, including requests for cost recovery, after receiving feedback from the community.[310]

In late 2009, after stakeholder feedback, the ICC issued Order No. 09-0263, which approved a two-part AMI pilot program: an AMI meter and support technology program, including installation of 131,000 smart meters to evaluate operational benefits and costs and the Customer Applications Pilot (CAP) program, designed to test how eight thousand ComEd customers would respond to smart grid consumer applications.[311]

ComEd began implementation of its meter program in October 2009. The utility deployed approximately 128,000 meters with nearly 100,000 meters in nine communities within the I-290 Corridor, and nearly 30,000 meters in Chicago. ComEd formally kicked off its Customer Applications Pilot, a subset of the AMI pilot footprint, in May 2010. ComEd notified customers by mail in March about new rate structures and how to access ComEd management tools via the Internet. In April, CAP customers received in-home devices designed to work with their home area networks. CAP customers received monthly bills explaining the new rate structure and inserts from ComEd suggesting how to adjust usage during peak hours to save money. By June 2010, ComEd began providing CAP customers with next-day price notifications and gathering customer feedback. Throughout the pilot, customers were compensated for completing surveys, the results of which ComEd has added to the large amount of data it is using to evaluate the project's effectiveness in meeting the utility's smart grid vision.

Infrastructure

For both projects of the AMI pilot, ComEd chose General Electric and Landis+Gyr solid state electric meters designed to communicate with HAN devices. The meters allow two-way communications with time-of-use measurement and thirty-minute interval data collection. They also support outage management, tamper detection, and bidirectional metering.

Under the larger AMI pilot, advanced meters communicate with each other and, ultimately, to ComEd access points in pilot neighborhoods using a mesh radio frequency network. Access points collect information and communicate directly with ComEd IT systems linked to ComEd's billing, customer information, and outage management departments. Billing and HAN activities are accessible by customers through the Internet. Data acquisition and communication is handled by Silver Spring Network's two-way communications solution, a robust smart meter communications platform also in use at Florida Power and Light, Pacific Gas and Electric, and PEPCO.[312]

ComEd also deployed a number of IT tools, including a metering headend telecommunications system, customer web presentment, a meter data management system, and a business process management suite designed to integrate customer applications with ComEd's existing Asset Management System, Customer Information Management System, Outage Management System, and Customer Data Warehouse.

Additionally, ComEd mailed two different types of in-home displays to two separate, randomly chosen CAP study groups. One group received a basic in-home display, capable of providing basic cost information as well as real-time consumption information pulled directly from the customer's meter. Another group received a more advanced display, enabling customers to program multiple data formats as well as utilize "enhanced" in-home devices capable of being controlled remotely or preprogrammed to respond to information from ComEd's AMI infrastructure.

Rate Structure

ComEd's CAP pilot employed an opt-out recruitment design whereby customers chosen randomly to participate were automatically enrolled in the program, informed of their new electrical service rate and the technology they would be using. Enrolled customers remained in the program unless they took actions to opt-out. ComEd adopted this pilot design despite its own focus group data that found that customers dislike opt-out approaches.[313] ComEd's pilot design, however, provided for the possibility that a large number of customers could elect to opt-out of a particular application, but would ensure that a statistically sufficient number remained to validate its testing.[314]

For its CAP pilot, ComEd informed customers that it would be changing their electricity rates from flat-rate pricing to one of two pricing schemes: "Shift-and-Save" or "Reduce-and-Save." Reduce-and-Save uses an inclining block rate to provide incentives for customers to reduce their net electricity consumption. Under Shift-and-Save, the price customers are charged for their electricity use varies from hour to hour. ComEd sent "peak day alerts" the day before it expected to experience substantially high demand from 1:00 to 5:00 p.m. (The utility did, however, guarantee customers that it would declare no more than ten peak days during the summer.)[315] The CAP pilot then tested customer response under various combinations of six different rate treatments:

1. Real-time pricing: hourly and daily prices conveyed through an hourly price schedule issued each day
2. Critical peak pricing: in addition to real-time pricing schedules, customers are subject to event-specific prices that increase the price of electricity to $1.74 per kWh over the real-time price during peak periods (1:00–5:00 p.m. weekdays)
3. Peak-time rebate: customers are paid $1.74 per kWh of reduced load during critical peak periods

4. Time-of-use pricing: customers pay according to fixed time-of-use schedules issued diurnally

5. Inclining block rate: customers are charged different rates according to inclining levels of monthly consumption

6. Flat rate: a control group of AMI-metered flat rate customers served as the basis for comparison[316]

One unique provision of ComEd's AMI pilot program was its "hold harmless variable," which prevented customers from paying more than they would have had they not participated in the pilot program. The variable compared, on an individual customer basis, the costs to the customer as billed according to the new rate application to what the customer would have paid if billed according to the standard flat rate. For customers for whom the amount billed exceeded what they would have paid, ComEd credited the difference to the customer.[317]

In early 2011, the Electric Power Research Institute performed an initial assessment of the effect of CAP rates on electricity consumption. EPRI's hypothesis was that consumers with in-home displays would be more likely to pay attention to usage information and respond to price signals.[318] EPRI found that customers under real-time pricing (alone or in combination with the real-time rebate or critical peak pricing) exhibited statistically significant responses. EPRI's preliminary analysis, for example, found that 5 to 7 percent of CCP and RTR customers reduced event-period load by 32 to 37 percent. However, while these customers shifted load significantly, EPRI did not find evidence that they reduced total energy consumption.[319]

When EPRI compared the impact of in-home displays on customer loads across pricing structures, it found no statistically significant effect attributable to technology or pricing applications. However, researchers caution that any effect may be hard to detect because of low technology adoption rates. For example, EPRI found approximately 15 percent customer adoption of basic in-home displays and less than 10 percent customer adoption of advanced in-home displays, far less than is required to detect scientifically robust causation.[320]

By late 2011, EPRI had concluded its evaluation of the CAP program's likely effect on electricity consumption.[321] In the final analysis researchers found statistically significant responses by customers to dynamic pricing applications, but warned that responding customers represented only about 10 percent of all CAP participants enrolled in a dynamic rate program.[322] EPRI noted, however, that researchers were unable to detect measurable event-day load reductions on aggregate load and speculated that ComEd's use of an opt-out enrollment method for CAP may explain why ComEd's results appear inconsistent with the results of other pilot programs. Indeed, pilot programs that utilize an opt-in enrollment scheme experience both low participation rates and, as one would expect, are populated largely by those predisposed to respond to inducements to reduce or shift load.[323]

EPRI itself acknowledged that the utility of its analysis is severely limited due to a number of problems with the available data set:

1. There is bias inherent in the composition of the control groups intended to represent customers who did not receive AMI metering that precluded accurately testing whether AMI had any influence on customer usage.[324]

2. Some dynamic rate groups were comprised of samples that tended to overrepresent high-usage customers.[325]

3. The selection of customers for the inclining block rate sample was restricted to those with at least five years of billing history, which also tended to under-represent low-use customers living in multi-family units and smaller homes who tend to move more frequently than the average ComEd customer.[326]

4. Because the in-home display technology did not always operate properly for customers residing above the first floor, the customer sample also under-represented low-usage customers who tend to live in multistory apartment buildings.[327]

5. Less than 10 percent of customers offered programmable controllable thermostats actually installed the devices, and very few customers offered in-home displays for purchase chose to install them. This small sample size precluded EPRI from testing either the effects of customers' response to time-based rate or the effects of partial payment applications of in-home displays.[328]

Stakeholder Engagement

In its order approving a limited AMI pilot program, the ICC required that ComEd include a workshop process to educate stakeholders about AMI technology; develop project goals, timelines, and evaluation methods; and develop criteria for determining which technologies would be selected for pilot implementation. The ICC also selected R. W. Beck and Plexus Research (an industry-leading consulting firm acquired by SAIC in 2009) to facilitate the workshops. Over 125 individual stakeholder representatives participated in a series of workshops from December 2008 to May 2009. ComEd also held separate meetings at which nonvendor stakeholders reviewed confidential materials relating to the technologies, capabilities, costs, and technical scoring of the competing vendor solutions.[329]

The ComEd stakeholder workshops resulted in a set of defined criteria for determining AMI technology vendors whose bids met minimum requirements. The criteria, ranked highest to lowest priority, included (1) security, (2) capability, (3) flexibility and scalability, (4) network performance, (5) interoperability, (6) maturity, (7) obsolescence risk, (8) economic stimulus, (9) demonstrated programs to protect the environment, and (10) support for minority- and women-owned businesses. ComEd issued an RFP in February 2009 to ten vendors with prior experience deploying AMI systems. By March, ComEd had received responses from eight. Applying the selection criteria, ComEd and participating stakeholders found that only three responding vendors met the minimum requirements. In the end, ComEd went with GE and Landis+Gyr.

Cost Recovery

Arguably, ComEd's greatest hurdle in implementing its Smart Grid Innovation Corridor has been recovering the costs of its AMI pilot program in the context of Illinois' controversial experience with electricity deregulation and the energy price spikes that resulted. While cost recovery issues have a long history in Illinois, ever since Illinois began experimenting with deregulation, ComEd has faced greater regulatory and political hurdles when attempting to recover costs. In the late 1990s, Illinois initiated the transition to a deregulated electricity generation market designed to encourage competition, expand customer choice and reduce energy costs. The Illinois General Assembly passed the Electric Service Customer Choice and Rate Relief Law of 1997, ordering most Illinois utilities (including ComEd) to divest their generation assets and give their customers the option of purchasing generation from other suppliers. The law also reduced residential electricity prices by 20 percent by the year 2001 and froze that rate for ten years while the state's utilities developed a competitive market for obtaining their electricity.

As the end of the rate freeze approached in 2006, a fully competitive electricity market threatened residential customers with rate increases of nearly 33 percent, sparking a public outcry against deregulation and a spirited debate among state legislators about whether to extend the rate freeze for several more years while they decided whether to suspend the deregulation experiment altogether. Faced with an extension of the rate freeze, ComEd responded that it likely would bankrupt the company.[330] As part of a compromise, in 2007 ComEd devised a new rate plan that allowed customers to defer payment of any increases in the delivery portion of their electricity bills, subject to about 3 percent interest on any unpaid portion. The experience, however, left many Illinois ratepayers wary of price hikes and suspicious of ComEd's intentions.[331]

On June 1, 2009, ComEd filed a petition with the Illinois Commerce Commission seeking approval to recover from ratepayers certain costs associated with its AMI pilot program.[332] Cost recovery for smart grid deployment has been highly controversial in Illinois. Stakeholders disagree about whether ComEd's smart grid costs should be restricted to a traditional rate base method or whether the ICC should approve nontraditional riders (designed to recover the costs associated with specific smart grid deployments) to the base case. Some stakeholders worry that nontraditional cost recovery methods would shift the risk of smart grid investments from utilities to ratepayers and lead to substantially higher monthly energy bills.[333] Others, including ComEd, believe that the rider method of cost recovery is essential to accelerate deployment of smart grid technologies and leverage federal funding of smart grid demonstration projects.[334]

In its 2007 rate case, ComEd had proposed a rider to act as a mechanism for recovering the costs of system modernization projects likely to occur between its general rate cases. However, the ICC approved only a subset of the proposed rider—renamed Rider AMP (for Advanced Metering Pilot)—which covered only limited deployment of the pilot program while ComEd further defined the project through stakeholder workshops. The ICC required ComEd to file an additional request seeking approval to recover costs associated with the final AMI project as defined through the workshops. Ultimately ComEd proposed an amendment to Rider AMP to permit the utility to recover incremental operating expenses of the CAP study and also to attempt to procure matching funds from the Department of Energy smart grid development funds provided under the American Recovery and Reinvestment Act. In 2009, the ICC issued its final order approving ComEd's AMI pilot program and a rider designed to recover most of the associated costs.[335]

Several stakeholders, including the state's attorney general and the Citizens Utility Board (a consumer advocate), appealed the ICC's approval of AMI costs through a rider to the Appellate Court of Illinois. On September 30, 2010, a unanimous three-judge panel of the Second District rejected the ICC's approval of the AMI rider on the grounds that it violated the state's prohibition on single-issue rate making.[336] The court held that the ICC had discretion to approve a rider mechanism to recover costs if (1) they were imposed on the utility by external circumstances over which the utility had no control and (2) the cost does not affect the utility's rate of return. The court found that the AMI rider did not meet these criteria since the expenses related to AMI and the adoption of smart grid technologies generally were not unexpected and that ComEd was pursuing the program precisely because the increased costs would be more than offset by corresponding savings. Since ComEd historically recouped the costs of distribution improvement through traditional rate making, the Court found no reason that ComEd's smart grid expenses should be treated differently.[337]

Ultimately, the ICC allowed ComEd to include many of the AMI pilot costs in its traditional rate case in an order issued May 24, 2011.[338] The experience, however, motivated the utility to lobby hard in favor of House Bill 14/Senate Bill 1652, bills in the state legislature that would change the nature of smart grid cost recovery in Illinois. The legislation lays a groundwork for rolling out smart grid in Illinois, while capping customer rate increases at 2.5 percent per year. Under the proposal, ComEd's profit margin is limited to 10.25 percent and the current ICC review process of eleven and a half months would be replaced with a quicker rate review process defined in the legislation.[339] Though the bill passed both houses of the Illinois legislature, Governor Quinn vetoed the legislation. Intense lobbying on behalf of affected utilities, however, convinced the legislature to overturn the veto, and the new cost recovery procedure became law in October 2011.[340]

Benefits

ComEd justifies its Smart Grid Vision by referencing the economic and environmental benefits that might accrue from the smarter provision of electrical service. It is ComEd's hope that its various smart grid pilot projects might validate the business, customer, and environmental cases for adopting smart grid technologies throughout the service area.

The 2008 Business Case

ComEd's AMI pilot was designed, in part, to enable it to quantify the degree to which AMI can help moderate future electricity prices by quantifying operational cost savings, consumer load shifting, and avoided energy purchases. In its 2008 case to the ICC, ComEd estimated that one-time capital costs to deploy AMI throughout its service territory would be $800 million ($720 million for AMI meters, communication network infrastructure, installation, and vendor costs; $74 million for IT software and hardware integration; $6 million in additional operation and management; and $2 million for miscellaneous project costs).[341]

ComEd's estimation of the cost savings resulting from system-wide AMI deployment (the business case) postulated seven potential ways smart grid would reduce utility costs:

1. *Automated meter reading.* ComEd estimates that automated meter reading would reduce the number of meter reading positions, clerical labor, supervision and management, and related benefits, pensions,

and incentives. Additionally, automated readings may reduce vehicle and fuel purchases, capital expenditures for fleet replacement, office and reimbursed expenses, recruitment and training costs, worker compensation claims, and overtime costs.[342]

2. *Remote disconnect/reconnect.* ComEd estimates that remote disconnect abilities would allow the utility to better manage past due receivables, increase the timeliness of collections, and reduce its bad debt expenses.[343] Additionally, remote disconnect/reconnect abilities may avoid labor costs associated with field meter tests and investigations of high bills.[344]

3. *Reduced calls.* ComEd estimates that its customer call center may experience reduced call volumes because AMI would increase the accuracy of usage data, reduce the number of estimated bills, and provide customers with access to usage and billing information on a self-service basis.[345]

4. *Digital meters.* ComEd estimates that the increased accuracy provided by smart meters will reduce the number of corrected bills that its accounts receivable department must issue, resulting in marginal clerical cost savings.[346]

5. *Reduced outage calls.* ComEd estimates potential cost savings associated with unnecessary trips to investigate nonstorm outage calls that turn out to be false.[347]

6. *Operational efficiency.* ComEd estimates cost savings through real-time customer information in two ways. First, AMI meters will provide real-time power outage and restoration information, allowing better area-wide outage analysis and more effective crew deployment. Second, since AMI meters provide time-stamped, thirty-minute-interval data from each customer, ComEd can employ actual usage data rather than statistical samples to estimate the relationship between cumulative usage and coincident demand. ComEd's current load factor method program uses biweekly readings from a statistical sample of metered transformers to compute monthly loads on distribution transformers. ComEd runs the calculations twice a year, in May and October. As a result, summer peaking transformer overloads in June are not identified until November. ComEd believes that AMI would facilitate daily load factor calculations and help to more quickly identify and replace overloaded transformers with optimal replacement sizes for the identified loads.[348]

7. *Avoided energy purchases.* ComEd estimates that AMI would reduce its purchases of energy required to supply unbilled, unaccounted-for, stolen, and unmetered electricity. Unbilled energy is supplied where a customer has terminated service but electricity is still

flowing to the residence or business. Currently, it is not economical for ComEd to manually disconnect service to every customer who cancels service, resulting in significant amounts of unbilled usage. Unaccounted-for energy is associated with slow, stopped or tampered meters. The automated communication features of AMI meters will allow ComEd to detect meter tampering and remedy it more quickly. In addition, the improved accuracy of solid-state digital meters should allow ComEd to reduce unmetered energy costs and increase cost recovery.[349]

The Customer Case

Most ComEd customers pay an average flat rate for a system of electrical service whose primary costs are driven by peak demand, which occurs only a few hours of each year. Since base-load electricity cannot effectively be stored using current technology, generators have built peaking plants designed to meet these few hours of demand. These plants, however, impose substantial costs that are reflected in higher average prices for all customers. ComEd's business case for a proposed AMI build-out suggests that if customers were provided with financial incentives to reduce their electricity use during periods of peak demand, these marginal reductions would result in significant decreases in every customer's electricity costs.[350]

The Environmental Case

ComEd believes that its smart grid build-out could have a substantial effect on the utility's carbon emissions in two ways. First, since AMI should reduce its purchase of energy to supply unbilled, unaccounted-for, unmetered and stolen electricity, ComEd believes AMI should also result in avoided energy generation and, therefore, reduce CO_2 emissions.[351] Additionally, it believes that AMI would reduce the need for meter readers and thus decrease the number of required field visits. The resulting reduction in vehicle miles driven should, therefore, decrease the utility's net CO_2 emissions.

The 2011 Business Case: Black and Veatch's Evaluation

In 2011, at the request of ComEd, Black and Veatch, a consultancy, performed an evaluation designed to validate ComEd's business case to determine whether future full-scale AMI deployment within ComEd's service territory would be justified from a cost-benefit perspective. From January 2011 through April 2011, Black and Veatch worked with the ComEd AMI project team and ComEd customer operations, distribution operations, regulatory, and finance managers to refine the scope of potential AMI investments, identify and resolve some key questions about ComEd's formulation of its business case, and to gather pertinent information from AMI's pilot project that would help the consulting firm construct an independent view of the business case. Black and Veatch issued its final report in July 2011.[352]

Black and Veatch's evaluation found that ComEd would expect to invest $996 million in new capital and incur $665 million of operation costs to run the new AMI system-wide. However, the company concluded that cumulative benefits over the twenty-year evaluation period would significantly exceed cumulative costs. In fact, according to Black and Veatch, ComEd should expect benefits to result from improved operational efficiencies ($1,625 million), reduced power purchase costs ($707 million), reduced bad debt expenses ($791 million), new energy revenues ($1,051 million), and new delivery service revenues ($564 million). Admittedly, a large majority of the benefits Black and Veatch expect to result from a system-wide AMI deployment are driven by reductions in theft and tamper conditions and reduction in consumption on inactive accounts.[353] Using these assumptions, however, and taking into account all costs and benefits and assuming adjustments to customer rates, Black and Veatch estimated that the net present value of the AMI program to ComEd customers would be $1,296 million over twenty years.[354]

While the Black and Veatch evaluation finds that the cumulative benefits of AMI deployment exceed costs by almost a factor of three, its evaluation makes a number of significant assumptions that may substantially alter the actual costs and benefits of a system-wide AMI rollout. For example, Black and Veatch assumed that system-wide AMI could recover 100 percent of ComEd's losses due to consumption on inactive meters and otherwise unaccounted-for energy consumption.[355] Given this assumption, the company calculated that ComEd could recover nearly $2 billion in revenue over a twenty-year period.[356] However, Illinois Administrative Code (Part 280) currently requires an in-person notification before ComEd (or any Illinois provider) may disconnect service. While Part 280 disconnection rules are being rewritten, it remains uncertain whether they will be clarified to allow remote disconnection. Black and Veatch also assumed that Illinois regulators will allow the company accelerated depreciation on investments it has already sunk into old analog meters.[357] But the ICC has yet to approve a rate recovery plan consistent with these assumptions. Adding to this uncertainty is whether the results from ComEd's AMI pilot program—representing less than 3 percent of ComEd's total meter population—can even be extrapolated to a system-wide customer base of almost four million.[358]

Challenges

Illinois stakeholders have articulated major concerns with the cost of replacing older meters, the effect of time-of-use pricing on low-income customers, the security of private customer data, and the elimination of manual meter reading.[359]

Meter Replacement Costs

Some stakeholders view smart grid merely as an acceleration of routine investments ComEd must take as part of its ongoing grid modernization.[360] Since some perceive that the potential benefit of smart meters accrue to the utility (or society), it may be difficult for many ratepayers to understand how the utility justifies passing on to ratepayers the costs for meter replacement. The Black and Veatch evaluation is, therefore, instrumental in demonstrating that the sum total of consumption on inactive meters and other unaccounted-for consumption currently is passed onto the consumer. In theory, therefore, an effective AMI system will reduce these losses, leading to reductions in the rates customers would have paid otherwise. In fact, under the ratemaking process included in the approved legislation, changes in the utility cost structure will result in benefits passed back to consumers on an annual basis.

Time-of-Use Pricing

Illinois stakeholders have raised significant concerns that customers may put their health or safety at risk by overreacting to time-variant rates.[361] Opponents of time-variant rate structures worry that they could reduce or eliminate the intraclass cross-subsidization inherent in flat rates. Under a flat retail rate, customers who use more energy during off-peak periods subsidize the cost of customers that tend to use energy during peak periods. While load shifting from peak to nonpeak periods is one of the major driving forces behind time-variant rates, some stakeholders worry that customers who must use electricity for health- or safety-related purposes during peak periods could be penalized by their inability to shift their energy usage to nonpeak times.[362] One potential area of concern involves ComEd's marketing of competitive retail rate structures that may become available after system-wide deployment of AMI. ComEd has elected to become an Independent Distribution Company (IDC) under Illinois' quasi-regulated market. According to Illinois Administrative Code 452.240(a), however, qualifying IDCs may not "promote, advertise or market with regard to the offering or provision of any retail electric supply service."[363] While this provision does not preclude ComEd from "advertising or marketing permissible IDC services other than retail electric supply services," it seems clear it would limit

ComEd's marketing of various rate structures it could offer with widespread deployment of AMI.

Data Privacy

A key feature of the smart grid is the ability to capture and transmit data about how customers are using electricity in near real time. ComEd's AMI meters, for example, record customer usage data and transmit it to the utility in thirty-minute intervals. Some stakeholders have been concerned that unsecured customer data could be used by unauthorized individuals in ways not known or approved by customers.[364] By one estimate, the average AMI-connected home generates from 750 to 3,000 points of data a month.[365] Some stakeholders worry that utilities, not accustomed to handling large amounts of customer data, will now know a great deal about people's lives. An AMI system that records when customers turn down their thermostats might create a theft risk by determining when people are out of town or a system that records when and where a wayward spouse recharges his or her plug-in electric vehicle could prove tempting fodder for an enterprising divorce lawyer.[366]

Many issues associated with customer data security are being addressed at the national level. In 2007, for example, Congress directed the National Institute of Standards and Technology to develop interoperability standards for smart grid technologies, many of which will help in the development of privacy protocols.[367] But loopholes in statewide privacy standards raise serious concerns. Illinois state law prohibits utilities from disclosing customer-specific data to electricity retailers. But it is silent on whether utilities may provide customer data to third parties. As a result, some customers are concerned that ComEd will mine the AMI data, package it, and sell it for millions of dollars to everyone from appliance vendors to home security companies.[368] For its part, ComEd insists it is strongly committed to customer privacy and does not disclose personal information about customers without prior approval, except as required by law and regulation.[369] However, its official privacy policy leaves some room for interpretation: "We do not disclose or sell any personal information about you to third parties without your prior approval, except as required by law, requested by regulatory agencies and governmental authorities, arises from the sale of all or a portion of any of its businesses, or is used for legitimate business purposes."[370]

Elimination of Manual Meter Reading

Some stakeholders have been concerned that, by eliminating manual meter reading, hazardous conditions at customer sites could go undetected. Automatic service disconnection also raises some concerns that ComEd could curtail electrical services to low-income or prepaid service customers most burdened by any increases in electricity prices. Currently, ComEd must prioritize disconnections, taking into account the costs associated with visiting the premises to disconnect service at the meter. Some stakeholders worry that automated disconnection could risk the health and safety of some customers if the utility no longer makes visits to premises or interacts with residents present during meter disconnections.[371] A site visit, for example, might reveal medical or mental health situations or other mitigating circumstances that might render a delay in disconnection appropriate.

Additional concern is that Section 280 of the Public Utilities Act requires that, "a utility shall attempt to advise the customer that service is being discontinued by directing its employee making the disconnection to contact the customer at the time service is being discontinued." It is unclear how ComEd will comply with this provision when employing remote disconnection of service. However, the ICC has held that the regulation clearly contemplates a site visit by a utility upon disconnection and has prohibited ComEd from remotely disconnecting customers unless the disconnection is made in accordance with PUA provisions.[372] As noted, efforts are underway to rewrite section 280. Their outcome will have a substantial impact on whether a system-wide AMI rollout is likely net beneficial.

The Advanced Metering Infrastructure Deployment Plan

On April 23, 2012, ComEd filed with the Illinois Commerce Commission for approval of its Smart Grid Advanced Metering Infrastructure Deployment Plan, pursuant to the Illinois Public Utilities Act (PUA), as amended by the Energy Infrastructure Modernization Act (EIMA). EIMA required ComEd to file with the commission a smart grid AMI deployment plan "within 180 days after the effective date of this amendatory Act of the 97th General Assembly or by November 1, 2011, whichever is later." According to ComEd's AMI plan, the "EIMA provides the blueprint for Illinois electric utilities, working with the Illinois Commerce Commission and stakeholders, to accomplish this decade-long transformation. The EIMA establishes policies and goals, calls for utilities to make the investments necessary to achieve them, defines investment timetables and performance metrics to measure that achievement, and provides the means to fund those investments."[373] While this case study focuses on the implementation of ComEd's smart grid pilot projects, the subsequent regulatory issues related to ComEd's AMI plan, pursuant to the requirements of the EIMA, are relevant to the lessons learned for this case study. ComEd's AMI plan provides for investment over a ten-year period that is sufficient to implement the plan across its entire service territory in a manner that is consistent with subsection (b) of Section 16-108.5 of this PUA. As required by the statute, ComEd's AMI plan contains the following:

- A smart grid AMI vision statement that is consistent with the goal of developing a cost-beneficial smart grid
- A statement of ComEd's smart grid AMI strategy that includes a description of how ComEd evaluates and prioritizes technology choices to create customer value, including a plan to enhance and enable customers' ability to take advantage of smart grid functions beginning at the time an account has billed successfully on the AMI network
- A deployment schedule and plan that includes deployment of AMI to all customers of ComEd
- Annual milestones and metrics for the purposes of measuring the success of the AMI plan in enabling smart grid functions and enhancing consumer benefits from smart grid AMI
- A plan for the consumer education to be implemented by ComEd

According to ComEd, the present value of the total benefits of the AMI plan exceeds the present value of the total costs of the plan. Therefore, implementation of the plan will be cost beneficial, as that term is defined in the PUA, consistent with the principles established through the Illinois Smart Grid Collaborative, giving weight to the results of the commission-approved ComEd AMI pilot designed to examine the benefits and costs of AMI deployment. Important to ComEd, it anticipated that the plan as filed would allow ComEd to recover the reasonable costs it incurs in implementing the AMI plan, including the costs of retired meters through its tariffs, pursuant to the performance-based formula rate tariff within the PUA.

On June 22, 2012, the ICC approved, with minor modifications, ComEd's AMI plan. The ICC found that the ComEd plan met the conditions of the EIMA and was cost beneficial. The ICC's modifications to the plan included adopting additional tracking measures and a requirement that ComEd work with the Smart Grid Advisory Council and other stakeholders to explore how to maximize adoption of dynamic pricing rates, including a possible ComEd TOU rate. The ICC order also reiterated what it considers current commission rules requiring a site visit prior to service disconnection for nonpayment. Issues related to remote service disconnection, which are a significant anticipated cost savings of the AMI plan, are subject to a separate ICC proceeding. While the ICC largely approved the plan, the ICC approval does not address the ongoing controversy of ComEd cost recovery, which is addressed in a separate proceeding on ComEd's formula rate. The formula rate is meant to allow distribution utilities such as ComEd to recover prudently incurred costs. On May 29, 2012, the ICC issued an order on the ComEd formula rate that cut customer rates by approximately $179 million, which was over four times what ComEd had proposed for a rate decrease. While the ICC's changes to the formula rate plan addressed issues such as the recovery of pension assets and did not directly involve the recovery of costs from the AMI plan, ComEd has asked for a rehearing of the formula rate order and these actions continue the controversy in Illinois over AMI cost recovery.

On July 6, 2012, ComEd filed with the ICC for rehearing of their AMI order. In its filing, ComEd sought rehearing on three aspects of the order arguing first and foremost that "the plan approved by the Commission in the AMI Order for ComEd's AMI deployment schedule is no longer sustainable in light of the Commission's Order in Docket No. 11-0721 ('the Formula Rate Order')."[374] According to the ComEd Application for Rehearing, "ComEd simply cannot make $2.6 billion of new investments —including nearly $1 billion in AMI—while being denied the total revenues that are needed to fund them."[375] In its filing, ComEd noted that it "has been forced to delay the AMI deployment originally scheduled for 2012 and to reevaluate its participation in the scheme enacted by the EIMA." ComEd also stated that "even if the Commission grants relief in the formula rate proceeding, however, the AMI deployment schedule will need to be revised to account for the delays that have occurred as a result of the uncertainty." If the formula rate order is not revised, according to ComEd, the schedule will require "more sweeping changes" including the possibility of "withdrawing from EIMA altogether." The two other issues addressed in ComEd's Application for Rehearing to the ICC related to concerns regarding statements in the AMI order about remote disconnection issues and whether onsite contact ("door knock") should be required and concerns with the order's various proposals regarding "at-risk" and "vulnerable" populations.

On October 3, 2012, the ICC issued its Order on Rehearing in ComEd's formula rate tariff, which determines the specific level of cost recovery for smart grid infrastructure investments. The order sets rates through the end of 2012 and represents a $133 million reduction in ComEd revenue, but is approximately $35 million in additional revenue compared to the ICC's previous order.[376] Following the ICC order, ComEd announced in a news release that "because the ICC is not fully funding the grid deployment program, ComEd is forced to make modifications to its program to align the deployment of key infrastructure with the ICC decision. ComEd must delay installation of additional smart meters until 2015."[377] In its news release, ComEd stated that the ICC's decision will result in the under-recovery of revenues by nearly $100 million per year starting in 2014. The loss of these revenues will cause the delay of more than $2.3 billion in customer savings and the creation of two thousand jobs. ComEd will appeal the rate order in court.

Interestingly, the dispute between the ICC and ComEd is not about the merits of the costs of the smart grid infrastructure build-out (which were determined by the EIMA and approved by the ICC order on ComEd's implementation plan) but mostly about how ComEd is allowed to calculate its return on the investments in the formula rate. Of specific dispute are how infrastructure investment balances are calculated, to which a rate of return is applied, and additionally, the interest rate applied to annual adjustments to those investment balances.

Part of the controversy as acknowledged by the ICC decision is that

> the rate setting process put in place by the [EIMA] . . . is quite different from the traditional rate setting process known by the Commission. Although some aspects of traditional ratemaking . . . are still applicable, the input data, the formula rate itself, and the reconciliation practice specified in the Act do not fit neatly into the traditional ratemaking paradigm. Each of the parties argues that the new provisions support their position. . . . While some claim to know what was intended when [the EIMA was] . . . enacted, the Commission is not bound by the views of a few as to what the statute requires. The record in this case warrants the finding that the language used in the statute leaves room for interpretation by the Commission.[378]

Underlying the controversy is the fact that in the EIMA the Illinois legislature laid out in significant detail how the ICC is to treat these smart grid infrastructure costs, and it did so in a manner that was not consistent with previous ICC policy. In doing so, the ICC and various parties believe that the legislature left some discretion with the ICC. The fact that there is significant tension on intended cost recovery of smart grid investments is highlighted in the comments of Jonathan Feipel, the ICC's executive director. According to the *Chicago Tribune*, Feipel stated that the legislature's "resolution was hyper-specific" and amounted to the legislature taking over the ICC's role as regulator.[379] These are unusually critical words by a regulator toward a legislature, since the ICC's statutory authority is determined by that legislative body.

Electric Vehicle Integration

By the end of 2012, most major domestic and foreign car manufacturers intend to bring plug-in electric vehicles to market. Projections from the Electric Power Research Institute found that the potential U.S. market share could range anywhere from 3 to 11 percent of new vehicle sales by 2020.[380] However, using Prius adoption patterns as a leading indicator of potential PEV adoption, ComEd has concluded that PEVs are not likely to be distributed evenly across the United States during early years of market development. Further information from EPRI suggests that total cumulative PEVs on the road in ComEd's service territory by 2020 will be between 75,000 and 280,000.[381]

In anticipation of the emerging PEV market, ComEd has adopted the Electric Vehicle Strategy, which is designed to achieve four key objectives:

1. Gain firsthand experience with PEV technology and charging infrastructure.
2. Study vehicle impacts on the system and utilize advanced methods to mitigate them.
3. Prepare the Chicago region by collaborating with stakeholders to address factors that will affect consumer adoption.
4. Assess the impacts of electric vehicles on the electricity grid and their interaction with smart grid technologies.[382]

ComEd has pursued these objectives, in part, through several initiatives, including demonstration of PEVs in its own vehicle fleet and participation in and support of the Illinois Commerce Commission's Initiative on Plug-In Electric Vehicles.

ComEd Electric Vehicle Demonstration Projects

The "Green Fleet"
ComEd has been supporting the development and deployment of alternative fuel vehicles since 2002, when the utility first began using soy-based diesel for its on-site fueling of its diesel-fueled fleet. It was also one of the first utilities in the country to deploy electric hybrid bucket trucks in 2006.[383] Since then, the company's hybrid fleet has grown to the seventh largest green fleet in the country, including 20 hybrid bucket trucks, 40 hybrid sedans, 142 hybrid SUVs, 10 converted Toyota Prius plug-in hybrid electric vehicles, and 10 Chevrolet Volt extended-range electric vehicles.

In 2009, ComEd converted ten Prius hybrids into PHEVs. This conversion involved adding a second battery pack capable of being charged with a 120-volt outlet. These ten PHEVs plus two Prius PHEVs in the I-Go car sharing fleet were then equipped with smart charging technology consisting of a vehicle control module that communicates directly with the vehicle's on-board computer, wireless communications and back-end software that allows remote acquisition of vehicle performance data as well as the ability to manage vehicle charging using a variety of advanced methods. Two of these methods were (1) using real-time price signals to manage charging times and (2) dynamically controlling the charging of a group of vehicles so that the aggregate load remained below a predetermined threshold.[384]

ComEd is participating in a project under a Transportation Electrification Grant from the DOE with EPRI and over forty other utilities across the United States to demonstrate PHEV utility vehicles in fleet applications. ComEd expects to deploy its PHEV vehicles in 2012 and to evaluate the costs and benefits of PHEV work trucks, in particular the benefits of using vehicle mounted aerial equipment powered by the PHEV's battery.[385]

General Motors' Volt Demonstration
ComEd partnered with EPRI, General Motors, and several other utilities to demonstrate Chevrolet's Volt in two separate studies running over three years, beginning in 2010. First, ComEd deployed ten GM Volts in its fleet to validate PEV performance in a commercial fleet application and to help educate consumers on PEVs and charging. Second, ComEd deployed one additional Volt to demonstrate the ability to manage vehicle charging using on-board original equipment manufacturer (OEM) smart charging technology.

The Illinois Commerce Commission Initiative on Plug-In Electric Vehicles
In 2010, the ICC launched its Initiative on Plug-In Electric Vehicles to create a statewide forum to determine the impact on the state's electric grid of the initial deployment of PEVs, determine potential regulatory considerations, establish consistent statewide policies for managing PEV infrastructure, generate accelerated interest by auto manufacturers for introduction of PEVs into the Illinois market, and craft consumer education and outreach programs. ComEd and the other Illinois electric utilities submitted initial assessments of these issues to the Initiative in December 2010. Since then, the ICC has held public meetings and stakeholder working groups to further understand and address policy issues related to consumer adoption of PEVs.

Grid Impacts of Plug-in Electric Vehicle Charging
The majority of PEV charging is expected to take place at home. Currently, ComEd provides two options for charging EVs at home:

1. Level 1 charging requires access to a standard, grounded three-prong 120-volt outlet with a ground fault circuit interrupter. It has an electrical load of 15–20 amps, or about the same as a large microwave oven. Most PHEVs can be fully charged using a level 1 charging station in eight to ten hours. Because of their larger battery size, fully battery-powered EVs can take twelve to twenty-four hours to charge at level 1.

2. Level 2 charging requires installation by a licensed electrician of a 240-volt charging station. A level 2 charging load is similar to what is needed to operate an electrical stove or central air conditioning system. Level 2 charging typically will charge an EV in about half the time of level 1 charging. However, level 2 charging may require upgrading a home's electrical service. ComEd's analysis shows that the use of level 2 charging can pose a potential risk to local distribution equipment if even a small number of charging stations are located in close proximity. The company anticipates that early PEV adoption is likely to be geographically clustered in certain areas, similar to the patterns seen in early adoption of hybrid vehicles. In such a situation, multiple PEVs charging concurrently at level 2 can quickly overload local distribution equipment (such as service transformers) if not managed properly.

Since the PEV owner is the cause of any additional service upgrades, he or she would also incur the costs, including installation of any additional meters. However, planned smart grid technology, with its two-way communication coupled with time-variable rates, may help provide ComEd with real-time information about loading on the distribution system and notify ComEd when the load on individual system components reaches levels that require attention. This automatic notification facilitates load balancing and ensures reliability on a system-wide level. Thus the costs of identified upgrades would be socialized across the entire rate base.[386]

Electric Vehicle Tariff

Section 1305 of the Energy Independence and Security Act of 2007 directs the National Institute of Standards and Technology to establish protocols and standards to increase the flexibility and use of the smart grid. Among several priority action plans NIST has defined is development of data standards to enable charging of PEVs. NIST standards will cover charging at home or away from home under special rate schedules, discharging of PEV energy storage for demand response purposes, and administration and monitoring.[387]

In considering whether ComEd, which operates as an integrated distribution company, may choose or be required to offer electric service for PEV charging, Illinois' Public Utilities Act (PUA) states that "the Commission shall not require an electric utility to offer any tariffed service other than the services required by [the act], and shall not require an electric utility to offer any competitive service."[388] Nevertheless, certain provisions of the PUA and ComEd's own rules suggest that the utility may amend its current offerings to include a tariff for PEV charging. For instance, the PUA expressly provides that, "nothing in this subsection shall be construed as limiting an electric utility's right to propose, or the Commission's power to approve, allow or order modifications in the rates, terms and conditions for such services pursuant to [the act]."

However, should ComEd choose to offer a PEV charging tariff, one hurdle it faces is that Illinois' rules for integrated distribution companies do not permit electric utilities to "promote, advertise or market with regard to the offering or provision of any retail electric supply service."[389] Thus ComEd's ability to promote, advertise, or market a pricing structure for PEV charging services may be limited unless the ICC grants it a waiver under the PUA. This concern is hardly academic. While PEV charging stations will be outfitted with technology that uses real-time pricing to automatically detect the cheapest times to charge, the technology is useless unless consumers sign up for it. But preliminary data suggests that marketing pricing options may be critical. Most ComEd residential customers, for example, continue to pay flat rates for electricity and may not know that real-time pricing even exists.[390]

Stakeholder Engagement

ComEd has leveraged its relationships with several key stakeholders and business partners, including the Chicago Area Clean Cities nonprofit coalition, to educate consumers about its electric vehicle strategy. In fact, ComEd's manager of EV and technology serves on the coalition's board, which holds seminars every year to encourage companies to use clean fuels and vehicle technology, including hybrid and plug-in electric vehicles. The company also launched a Green Vehicle Web page to further educate the public on ComEd's efforts related to PHEVs. In 2009, ComEd joined Chicago's Climate Task Force, which aims to decrease transportation-related greenhouse gas emissions through improved transportation options, public transit, green fleets, fuels, and freight.[391]

Challenges

In order for many PEV drivers to charge their vehicles more quickly, they will need to use level 2 or DC fast-charging stations. However, who may provide and install these charging stations raises a legal issue concerning whether or not providing PEV charging services is one of ComEd's service obligations under Illinois's Public Utilities Act. Under PUA, ComEd must continue to offer each tariffed service that it offered on the effective date of the Electric Service Customer Choice and Rate Relief Act of 1997, which restructured the state's electricity market. The law also requires ComEd to offer electricity delivery services and real-time pricing as a tariffed service. The ICC cannot, however, require ComEd to offer any other service.[392]

Because distribution and installment of PEV charging stations is not part of any existing ComEd tariffed service, the issue becomes whether or not deployment of PEV charging infrastructure is considered part of delivery services. The PUA defines delivery services generally as those "necessary for the transmission and distribution systems to function so that retail customers . . . can receive electric power and energy." Because customers will be capable of charging their PEVs through the standard 120-volt electrical outlet, it seems clear that additional PEV charging stations are not a "necessary" delivery service obligation required of ComEd.

Instead, the sale and installation of PEV charging stations appear to fall within the PUA's definition of a competitive service, "related to, but not necessary for, the provision of electric power and energy or delivery service." In that case, it is unclear if the ICC would have regulatory authority over the deployment of PEV charging stations in ComEd's service territory.

Should the ICC choose to regulate PEV charging stations, therefore, it must address whether ComEd is required to offer the service, and if so, what rates the utility may charge for it. Resolution of these regulatory decisions has the potential to delay deployment of faster PEV charging infrastructure in the greater Chicago area. Ultimately, ComEd believes that the competitive model is "the most effective and efficient method to promote the development of the necessary charging infrastructure to support the deployment of electric vehicles. Attempts to regulate either the charging infrastructure or the pricing for charging services will likely cause market uncertainty, which could delay the development of this market."[393]

Distribution Automation

Intelligent distribution automation constitutes a substantial part of the future of the smart grid. ComEd, along with many utilities, is exploring

technology designed to monitor, measure and track key substation equipment performance and to move toward a more condition-based maintenance program that calls for equipment to be worked on only when
needed and triggered by information provided by monitoring devices.[394]
As part of its Smart Grid Innovation Corridor, ComEd embarked on three
interconnected demonstration projects. First, the utility constructed its
first truly intelligent substation to pilot a suite of advanced substation
devices and software designed to significantly automate substation monitoring and analysis. ComEd chose a substation that encompasses Chicago's near western suburbs and some neighborhoods within the city.

This intelligent substation was equipped with digital asset monitoring
devices linked to microprocessor relays serving as substation data collection gateways. These relays then report to operations control rooms via
digital SCADA control systems. Operations and maintenance personnel
utilize online analysis tools to monitor substation assets and deploy maintenance resources when conditions warrant.[395]

Second, ComEd installed a system of smart electricity delivery
automation, sensors, and controls to test their ability to provide real-time
reporting of distribution status and outages. The demonstration also
included automated control of relays and reclosers as well as field
force management.[396] Not only was this project intended to demonstrate
the viability of these smart grid components, but it will also help validate
the expansion of system-wide voltage regulation and selective conservation voltage reduction.

Observations and Conclusions

ComEd has made remarkable efforts to achieve its Smart Grid Vision.
The sheer scale of the Smart Grid Innovation Corridor project and
ComEd's attempt to expand its AMI system-wide provides valuable insight into the challenges and opportunities presented when implementing
smart grid innovations.

Lessons in Smart Grid Pilot Study Methodology

ComEd's experience with its pilot projects raises several issues likely faced
by other utilities seeking to experiment with smart grid technologies.

Voluntary Participation
ComEd's experience raises the possibility that voluntary participation in
smart grid pilot projects may encourage self-selection by those customers
most interested in responding to smart grid price signals and potential

environmental benefits. EPRI's evaluation of ComEd's CAP program, for example, found that a small number of self-selected project participants accounted for a large proportion of observed load reductions. This self-selection not only skews pilot studies but also complicates efforts to extrapolate the results of pilot projects to widespread adoption of smart grid technologies. Since those customers whose behavior is most dramatically affected by smart grid technologies may self-select for voluntary participation in pilot programs, they represent "low-hanging fruit" whose load shifting behavior may not be representative of larger, random samples of utility customers.

Opt-Out versus Opt-In
ComEd's experience allowing randomly selected customers to opt-out rather than opt-in to smart grid pilot programs highlights an important problem utilities may face when attempting to avoid the self-selection problem. ComEd's own focus group data revealed that customers resented opt-out procedures that required program participants to affirmatively act to avoid inclusion in the program. The customer backlash that may result from imposition of an opt-out scheme risks stakeholder support for expanding smart grid programs after the initial pilot and may outweigh the value of an opt-out provision in expanding the sample of pilot participants. EPRI, for example, concluded that even with its opt-out provision, the sample size of ComEd's CAP pilot did not provide sufficient data upon which it could accurately project how system-wide adoption of AMI and dynamic pricing schemes might affect customer behavior. However, as the program progressed, ComEd found opt-out rates to be quite low and is not considering an opt-out provision when pursuing full system-wide AMI deployment.

Hold Harmless Variable
Similarly, ComEd's "hold harmless variable" may induce greater program participation while sacrificing accurate examinations of customer reactions to more immediate price signals. It is unclear, for example, how program participants respond to price signals given the foreknowledge that they may never have to pay higher prices. It is equally unclear that participant behavior under a 'hold harmless variable' can be extrapolated to valid conclusions about customer behavior without one.[397]

Load Shifting versus Reduced Consumption
After EPRI issued its initial assessment on the effects on electricity consumption of ComEd's CAP pilot, some media outlets and stakeholders pounced on the information to report that the AMI program largely failed

to achieve its objectives. This conclusion may be attributed to a fundamental confusion about load shifting versus reduced net consumption. While it is true that EPRI's initial assessment found little evidence that in-home displays had a statistically significant effect on consumer usage, it did find that customers served under the most dynamic pricing options exhibited statistically significant responses. EPRI found, for example, that pilot participants substantially decreased energy consumption during peak periods, if largely by shifting consumption to off-peak periods.

ComEd's business, customer, and environmental cases for smart grid implementation rest largely on benefits achieved without substantial changes in net energy consumption. Ideally, service area-wide AMI will reduce ComEd's net electricity purchases as a result of increased operational efficiency and a reduction in unbilled, unaccounted for, and stolen electricity. What efficiency benefits ComEd does intend accrue mostly through customers shifting their load to off-peak periods rather than reducing their net energy consumption. Unfortunately, a simplistic understanding of electricity markets and utility operating procedures may obscure public perception of this important distinction.

ComEd's experience highlights the delicate balance between marketing smart grid programs as utility efficiencies that will eventually be passed through as cost savings to consumers and the direct benefits of decreased customer consumption. Broad public engagement with messages that raise unrealistic expectations will backfire. Marketing the true benefits of smart grid requires a direct, intensive, and sustained public conversation that involves individuals and organizations with credibility that the utility may lack with certain constituencies.

Inequitable Burden of Time-Variant Rates

Several stakeholders were concerned that ComEd's time-variant rates risked an overreaction by consumers responding to peak period rate increases. These stakeholders worried that increased peak period rates might disproportionately be borne by low-income customers who, for reasons of health or safety, may be unable to shift consumption to off-peak periods. Should involuntary dynamic pricing schemes be adopted system-wide, the most vulnerable customers may end up facing the highest prices. But voluntary programs might risk diminishing the business case for AMI by reducing the cross-subsidization of peak period usage.

ComEd's experience with its AMI pilot program, however, suggests that this concern may be unfounded. Internal data from ComEd's AMI pilot demonstrates that a higher percentage of low-income customers saved money under dynamic rates than any other income group. In fact, ComEd's data suggests that low energy users (often lower income customers) generally subsidize higher energy users under a flat pricing system. Because the number of customers that actually responded to AMI price signals was so low, however, ComEd's experience suggests that there is a case to be made that lower income customers might be relative winners under an AMI program with a properly designed dynamic rate.

Lessons in System-Wide Smart Grid Implementation

ComEd's experience demonstrates that clearly articulated state smart grid policies are essential to achieving the full benefits of smart grid investments. When regulated utilities initiatives are ahead of legislative and regulatory policy, their efforts are likely to get tangled in a morass of unclear laws and regulatory goals that delay progress, limit benefits, and ultimately cost ratepayers. After working to integrate smart grid technologies for well over three years, ComEd continues to face several hurdles involving how to maneuver around existing state laws and regulations that were adopted long before a smarter grid became a technological reality. These hurdles include policies that prevent remote disconnection of electrical service, provide for the competitive provision of electric service, and limit rate recovery mechanisms that ensure that smart grid investments reap their full economic and environmental benefits.

Regulations Preventing Remote Disconnection

ComEd's business and environmental cases for smart grid deployment rest substantially on its ability to capitalize on remote connection and disconnection of electrical service. ComEd's projection of reduced electricity purchases, for example, assumes its ability to recover unbilled and unaccounted for electricity through remote disconnection. Additionally, ComEd's projection of reduced carbon emissions rests largely on reduced vehicle miles from suspension of site visits.

However, pending a rewrite, the ICC has clearly interpreted Illinois Administrative Code Part 280 to require a site visit, at least before disconnection of residential service. Presumably, this interpretation originally was motivated to avoid potential inequitable impacts of suspended service on those who, for economic, health, or safety reasons, may be incapable of shifting or reducing load. Indeed, in 2012 the Health Impact Assessment, written by the National Center for Medical Legal Partnership, the Citizens Utility Board, and leading energy consultants, recommended that the ICC disallow remote disconnection because Illinois' most vulnerable populations—the sick, the poor, and the elderly—may be unlikely to receive the benefits of the smart grid reforms they are paying for.[398]

In part to address this issue, the final smart grid legislation passed over Governor Quinn's veto included a provision that would require peak-time rebates be offered to all customers with meters. Since the value of the rebate would be based on the market value of capacity, it should provide lower-income customers with the ability to shift load under a dynamic pricing scheme. It does little, however, to address the problem of those whose load shifting is restricted by health and safety concerns. However, this problem may be one more of perceiving an opportunity lost than the reality of a cost incurred. While some customers, for health or safety reasons may be incapable of taking advantage of time-based pricing, for example, they would remain under their current rate structure and, presumably, be no worse off than before AMI deployment. Additionally, the Citizens Utility Board has recommended ComEd survey vulnerable populations in its service territory and design the smart grid to automatically notify a family member when their elderly or ill relative has lost power.[399]

Retail Choice and Restrictions in Advertising New Rate Structures

Since the introduction of retail choice for electric service, Illinois' regulated utilities have operated with restrictions on advertising rate structures and specific services. Arguably, the PUA prohibits ComEd from advertising voluntary smart grid electricity supply rate programs. Nevertheless, ComEd sought and achieved a special waiver allowing it to market its CAP pilot program and may need either an additional waiver or an amendment to the PUA in order to market any optional electricity supply rates as it seeks full AMI deployment. As AMI is more fully deployed there is uncertainty in how successful dynamic pricing programs will be achieved with both low levels of customers selecting competitive retail suppliers and restrictions on ComEd's ability to develop and market such pricing alternatives. Perhaps the new dynamic pricing options available when smart meters are deployed will be the catalyst that ultimately fuels retail choice in Illinois.

Requirements to Provide EV Charging Services

ComEd, like all regulated utilities in Illinois, are subject to provisions of the Public Utilities Act that require it to supply all necessary electrical services. There is some uncertainty whether the ICC should determine that PEV charging stations are a "necessary" provision of electrical service and whether ComEd would be required to supply these services under the PUA. ComEd argues that deploying charging infrastructure is not a utility obligation, and would instead be considered a "competitive service" under the act. Uncertainty surrounding who should provide this service could slow adoption of electric vehicles.

Limitations on Cost Recovery

ComEd's struggle to clarify cost recovery policy for its smart grid pilot programs have been dramatic and public, significantly impacting the perception of both the company and the benefits of smart grid investments with both the Illinois news media and the public it serves. The utility has faced significant challenges in reaching a balanced cost recovery approach that ComEd, state regulators, the legislature, and the courts could all accept. This public controversy has clearly reduced the momentum of ComEd's smart grid technology leadership. Following the passage of the EIMA it was anticipated that the controversy regarding the investment in and recovery of AMI costs would be lessened, unfortunately the experience to date appears to be the opposite. ComEd's experience suggests that something as far ranging in impact as smart grid deployment requires a solid policy foundation based on clear policy leadership from state legislators and regulators. Legislation that establishes a basic policy for recovery of smart grid investments may avoid sparking substantial public opposition and protracted litigation. When cost recovery is uncertain and subject to expensive regulatory lag, utilities may observe ComEd's experience and decide against making the types of investments required to achieve the full benefits of the smart grid. In the case of the state of Illinois, there are meaningful impacts to customers, the local economy, and the business and physical environment to continued dispute and litigation over the recovery of investments that parties seem to agree are publicly beneficial. In ComEd's view, the result has been the delay in more than $2.3 billion in customer savings and two thousand new jobs.

The Electric Power Research Institute has estimated that, nationally, fully implementing a smart electric grid will cost between $1.3 and $2.0 trillion, with benefits likely exceeding costs by a factor of three or more.[400] This represents a significant amount of additional investment to be made in future years and will involve ongoing negotiation with regulators and other parties.

Research from Pacific Northwest National Laboratory has estimated that with full implementation of a smart electric grid by 2030 U.S. energy consumption and carbon emissions could be reduced by 12 percent.[401] Yet as noted previously, it will take time to develop and offer additional technologies and rates to customers. In some areas, however, the smart grid will likely spur greater electricity use, such as smart charging of electric vehicles, in order to achieve efficiencies in total energy use across the economy.

Continued investment in automation of the utility distribution system will offer future opportunities for improving reliability and optimizing energy use. In order for electric vehicles to reach the levels of consumer adoption included in PNNL's analysis, there will need to be significant new policies at all levels of government and the build-out of new infrastructure. Furthermore, as renewable energy reaches higher levels of development across the utility service territory, greater investment in smart grid technologies will be needed in order to reliably and cost-effectively manage these resources. In Illinois these longer-term benefits will be delayed while controversy continues at the state policy level on how ComEd should recover the costs of the installation of the customer meters and related investments.

CASE STUDY V. THE CUSTOMERS' SMART GRID: PECAN STREET'S ENERGY INTERNET DEMONSTRATION PROJECT

Introduction

Our current electric grid has gone through several changes for over a century to become the system we use today. Beginning with the first central power system built by Thomas Edison in 1882, the development of power pools and utilities, the emergence of federal power, and the creation of three major interconnections, the grid has experienced many changes. In today's society, electric utilities prepare to put the grid through another change; turning the electric grid into a *smart* electric grid.

The purpose of this case study is to examine Pecan Street, Inc., a leading organization in the digital energy revolution, and its efforts to demonstrate the operability and functionality of a smart grid community. The case study explores how Pecan Street developed its Energy Internet Demonstration project and the smart grid technologies it plans to deploy, how those technologies will be integrated, and the policy and regulatory implications of the project. In addition, we will identify lessons learned from Pecan Street, Inc. and policy solutions that can be adopted by decision makers across the country. The Department of Energy awarded Pecan Street, Inc. $10.4 million from the American Recovery and Reinvestment Act, which spurred interest in the project and this case study of its progress. Pecan Street, Inc. is highly unique due to its public-private partnership, which demonstrates how the public and private electricity sectors can work together to achieve smart grid innovation. This structure has allowed greater efficiency in working with regulatory organizations and resolving customer issues in order to develop an advanced smart grid test project.

Pecan Street's Energy Internet Demonstration, located in and around the Mueller development in Austin, Texas, will demonstrate the capabilities of a fully functioning smart grid community. The project focuses on four key program areas: (1) the utility side of the meter systems, (2) the customer-premises systems, (3) pricing and commercialization, and (4) data collection and management. After introducing the key members of the implementation team, the demonstration project is discussed in greater detail.

Pecan Street, Inc.

Pecan Street, Inc. is a 501(c)(3) nonprofit research organization head-quartered at the University of Texas and the lead team member for the Energy Internet Demonstration project. The organization was formed in 2009 by representatives of the City of Austin, Austin Energy, the University of Texas, the Austin Technology Incubator, the Greater Austin Chamber of Commerce, and the Environmental Defense Fund. These founding partners each have representatives on the board of directors of Pecan Street, Inc., while many are also members of the demonstration project implementation team.

The City of Austin relies on Austin Energy, the municipal utility provider, to supply a portion of its operating budget.[402] As Roger Duncan, former general manager of Austin Energy, states, "Our city budget is closely tied to a utility whose revenue is a direct result of how much energy it sells."[403] Acknowledging that existing efforts by Austin Energy to promote energy efficiency and encourage development of distributed, renewable energy will harm this business model and risk Austin's financial stability, Pecan Street's founders recognized an opportunity to proactively address this issue. In developing Pecan Street, they sought to "preserve Austin's quality of life and chart a path toward new economic opportunity."[404] Environmental benefits were also recognized as a core benefit of the project. Over the course of a year, founding members crafted a deliberate strategy to accelerate the energy system evolution in Austin and to position the community as a clean energy and smart grid leader. This effort, conducted prior to the Department of Energy's solicitation for smart grid demonstration projects, and with a wider community development lens, sets the Energy Internet Demonstration project apart from other demonstration projects. It reflects an active community engagement in defining and realizing a sustainable economic and energy future for Austin. The Energy Internet Demonstration project is one component of a larger plan to transform Austin's energy and economic future.

As it developed this plan, Pecan Street sought to answer the following questions:

1. How can the Austin community accelerate the evolution of its energy delivery system?
2. Can we accelerate the evolution in a way that creates new economic opportunities for central Texas?[405]

In developing answers to these questions, Pecan Street, Inc.'s founders adhered to several unique guiding principles, which differentiate it from other smart grid projects. First, environmental protection is a core objective. The Environmental Defense Fund was invited into the process to ensure that this objective was realized. Second, as a result of wanting other communities to be able to learn from Austin's experience, the project uses an "open source" approach, and intends to make its findings and lessons learned available to the public and the energy industry at large. Creation of new companies and jobs in Austin remains the third core focus of the project. As a result, Pecan Street will measure success in terms of utilizing Austin talent, installing equipment, and using services provided by Austin companies, not simply in terms of renewable energy capacity, environmental benefits, or energy savings. The fourth objective is to preserve the economic stability of Austin and Austin Energy, which means ensuring that the plan does not threaten the revenue stream of Austin Energy. Recognizing and capitalizing on the ability of smart grid technologies to empower consumers to use energy more efficiently or to install renewable energy systems is the fifth objective. The sixth objective integrates the community into the project in many different facets. The project envisions "tomorrow's energy system as integrating all the systems and community assets that will consume or generate electricity,"[406] including electric vehicles, homes and buildings, the city's water utility, distributed generation facilities, and the policies and programs that impact those assets. The final objective focuses on the collaborative process used to develop Pecan Street and its mission. More than two hundred people from a wide spectrum of government, utility, academic, advocacy, and corporate backgrounds were involved in crafting the organization's vision and the recommendations. Community members, civic leaders, and Austin Energy customers were also consulted throughout the process.

The resulting March 2010 Working Group Recommendations create a roadmap for transforming Austin Energy from its current role as an energy provider, into a utility of the future as an energy manager. It also sets out a plan for harmonizing the water utility's resources, the City of Austin's policies, and the job training and economic development components needed to accelerate the shift to a sustainable energy and economic future for Austin. The recommendations for evolving Austin Energy fall within four broad areas: (1) renewable distributed energy deployment and testing,

(2) smart grid testing and pilots, (3) a new rate structure, and (4) a new business model. The main focus of the remainder of this analysis is the Energy Internet Demonstration project, an outgrowth of one portion of these recommendations. The results of this project will feed into Austin Energy's and Pecan Street's ongoing efforts to implement the remaining recommendations. Pecan Street implements the Energy Internet Demonstration project as well as contributes to efforts to realize the broader vision for Austin, Texas, as described in the Working Group Recommendations. Its main partners in both efforts are Austin Energy and the City of Austin.

Austin Energy and the City of Austin

Austin Energy is the nation's ninth largest community-owned electric utility, serving more than four hundred thousand customers within the City of Austin, Travis County, and Williamson County. Austin Energy functions as a department of the City of Austin, with dividends returned to the community each year. With a service territory encompassing 437 square miles, Austin Energy owns more than five thousand miles of overhead power lines, four thousand miles of underground power lines, and forty-eight substations. It also owns 2,600 mW of generation, including three natural gas plants, one coal plant, partial ownership of the South Texas Project nuclear facility, a 13-mW landfill methane plant, and numerous wind farms with a total wind capacity of 439 mW. In early 2012, Austin Energy began operation of a 30-mW photovoltaic solar facility, the largest in Texas and the largest solar installation commissioned by a municipal utility.[407]

In October 2009, Austin Energy completed implementation of its Smart Grid 1.0 program, the first fully operational smart grid deployment in the United States. It installed 86,000 smart thermostats and 410,000 smart meters (from Elster, GE, and AMI partner Landis+Gyr), covering its entire service territory.[408] The deployment also includes twenty-five hundred sensors and three thousand computers, servers, and network gear, which gather "100 terabytes of data and service a million consumers and 43,000 businesses throughout the Austin metro area."[409] As a result, Austin Energy's outage duration and frequency ratings rank among the best in the nation. At a cost of $150 million, Austin Energy expects the benefits of this first generation of smart grid technology to come primarily in the form of more efficient and less costly data acquisition, and faster, more accurate information about how its customers consume electricity. Austin Energy also has extensive plans for a Smart Grid 2.0 program, within which the Energy Internet Demonstration project will operate.

Austin Energy operates the nation's longest running and most subscribed green power program in the country.[410] The GreenChoice program offers Austin Energy customers the option of subscribing to a batch of clean electricity resources. GreenChoice subscribers pay a fuel charge of 5.7 cents/kWh instead of the standard fuel charge of 3.105 cents/kWh. Customers purchase 875 million kilowatt-hours of renewable energy annually.[411] The program is supplied by renewable resources such as wind and methane gas from landfills.

Austin Energy also operates a solar rebate program for its commercial and residential customers. As of April 2011, the program supports more than twelve hundred customer-owned solar energy systems, one hundred commercial projects, thirty-seven municipal projects, thirty-two school installations, and six libraries. Together, these produce more than 4.7 megawatts of generation capacity.[412]

The City of Austin operates the country's oldest and largest green building program, which continues to lead the industry on sustainable building practices. The Austin Energy Green Building (AEGB) program was created in 1990 and aims to lead the transformation of the building industry to a sustainable future. AEGB developed and maintains its own Austin-specific energy rating system, which it uses to pave the way for baseline building energy code changes.

As a result of Austin Energy's early smart grid efforts and Austin's green building program, Pecan Street is uniquely situated to demonstrate the potential of a fully integrated smart utility grid. With a focus on the consumer experience and benefits of smart grid applications, instead of the benefits accrued to the utility, Pecan Street is poised to deliver tangible benefits to Mueller and demonstrate the breadth of smart grid capabilities for consumers across the country.

Smart Grid 2.0 at Austin Energy

Austin Energy's Smart Grid 2.0 is a comprehensive plan to build on and expand the utility's Smart Grid 1.0 efforts.[413] Under the Smart Grid 2.0 plan, 100 percent of Austin Energy's customers will be equipped with advanced two-way meters. This will allow the utility's entire service territory to be served with real-time data management, visualization systems, and an automated transmission system. Austin Energy has already deployed the Landis+Gyr UtiliNet Mesh Network to provide two-way communications with customer meters. Smart Grid 2.0 includes plans for substation and distribution automation, smart electric vehicle chargers, energy control gateways, and customer-controlled energy management. In particular, Austin Energy is installing a new automated substation at the distribution feeder for the Mueller development, and has already upgraded its customer billing system to allow integration of innovative rate and incentive structures, both of which will support many of the Energy Internet Demonstration project's research endeavors. The customer billing system will also provide real-time access to usage data, empowering customers to monitor and adapt their usage behavior. The Pecan Street project will play a key role in determining the most effective ways of communicating with customers, in order to maximize the benefits of Austin Energy's smart grid investments.

The Pecan Street Energy Internet Demonstration Project: Overview

The Pecan Street Energy Internet Demonstration project is a unique public-private partnership, with team members from different sectors of the energy industry. Team members include Pecan Street, Inc., the University of Texas, Austin Energy, the Environmental Defense Fund, the National Renewable Energy Laboratory, the City of Austin, and the Technology Review and Advisory Committee.[414] Pecan Street is leading the demonstration project.[415]

Technology Review and Advisory Committee

The Technology Review and Advisory Committee is a regional committee organized to provide a forum for knowledge and technology sharing in the central Texas region. Members include the Electric Reliability Council of Texas (ERCOT), Bluebonnet Electric Cooperative, CPS Energy of San Antonio, Oncor, and Pedernales Electric Cooperative.[416] Like the City of Austin, which relies on Austin Energy for a portion of its operating revenues, several other central Texas municipalities, including San Antonio, rely on their municipally-owned utility for revenue. The Technology Review and Advisory Committee will help inform Pecan Street, Inc.'s development of a new utility business model and disseminate lessons learned throughout the region.

Project Goals

The main goal of Pecan Street, Inc. is to transform Austin Energy into the urban power system of the future, while making the City of Austin and its local partners a model clean energy laboratory and hub for the world's emerging clean technology sector.[417] More specifically, the demonstration project aims to "give consumers more control over their electricity usage and bills, preserve utility finances, reduce water usage, greenhouse gases, criteria pollutants and other environmental impacts, and promote clean energy job opportunities."[418] As a demonstration project, Pecan Street will implement and operate smart grid technologies in the Mueller community on a level that is capable of being reproduced nationally, without the need for major technological redevelopments.

The Mueller Community

The Mueller community, currently under development, sits approximately three miles away from downtown Austin and comprises a 711-acre LEED new development, mixed use, urban infill redevelopment community. Located on the site of the former Robert Mueller Municipal Airport, Mueller will provide an advanced platform for testing the impacts of a concentrated smart grid system. When fully developed, Mueller will have approximately three million square feet of commercial and institutional space and forty-nine hundred single-family and multifamily dwelling units housing more than ten thousand residents. At completion, at least 25 percent of the residential units will be affordable for households earning less than the median family income in Austin. Mueller is already home to Austin Energy's Mueller Energy Center, the Dell Children's Hospital, the University of Texas Academic Research Center, as well as more than two thousand people who live or work in the community.

Energy and environmental considerations are incorporated into all aspects of Mueller. All commercial buildings over twenty-five thousand square feet must achieve at least LEED or the AEGB program two-star rating, while all single-family homes must meet the AEGB three-star rating. Additional building specifications require the installation of programmable thermostats that can be managed through an online interface and advanced wiring that enables a homeowner to easily add home energy, irrigation, and lighting management upgrades. Water is also a concern, so native or water-wise plants must account for at least 90 percent of the landscaping in all public open spaces, commercial, and residential lots. Mueller will also utilize reclaimed water and a water-efficient irrigation system to irrigate public landscapes.

The Mueller Energy Center, adjacent to the Dell Children's Medical Center, is a combined heat, cooling, and power plant installed by Austin Energy. The advanced energy system uses waste heat from natural gas turbines to create steam, which is used for building systems, hot water in the hospital, and to run a 930-ton absorption chiller. The water from this and two additional electric chillers are used to cool office buildings more efficiently. A third electric chiller is planned, and the entire energy system is expected to generate half as much carbon as the national average for grid-supplied electricity.

More than six hundred households are already complete and occupied; while an additional one thousand housing units are expected to be completed within the next five years. As the Mueller community is developed, the Pecan Street project will recruit families and businesses to voluntarily participate in the smart grid demonstration project.

Project Details

Because Austin Energy had already deployed smart meter technology throughout its service territory and developed a plan for implementing Smart Grid 2.0, Pecan Street is uniquely situated to focus on smart energy use and integration of innovative renewable and efficient technologies at the consumer level. The Pecan Street project will recruit up to one thousand residential meters and seventy-five commercial meters for the demonstration project.[419] An additional two hundred homes will further incorporate smart water and smart irrigation systems into the demonstration.[420] Pecan Street will deploy smart appliances, electric vehicles, rooftop solar, home energy storage, and home energy gateways/networks in the participating homes and businesses. Project participants will allow Pecan Street to record their energy use down to the device level, as well as monitor the impact that new energy technologies, price signals, and educational messaging have on participants' energy use.

The project will use Internet and cable modems in the homes and businesses to act as the two-way gateway for information flow and to create an "energy Internet." This technology allows the project to receive energy-use data four times a minute. Using the Internet technology, Pecan Street will demonstrate (1) energy Internet capabilities on the utility side of the meter, (2) energy Internet capabilities on the customer side of the meter, and 3) plug-in electric vehicle integration onto the local grid.[421] By mimicking the Internet's ability to connect several different aspects of society, Pecan Street expects to use the same technology to integrate the several different energy systems within a community, such as electricity use, transportation systems (electric vehicles), and water systems (transport and treatment).

In addition to using volunteers in the Mueller community to test home energy management systems and new technologies, Pecan Street is building a demonstration house and research facility located in Mueller. Pecan Street also intends to create a medium where new technology can be developed and tested. The project seeks to deploy a minimum of 300 mW of clean distributed energy within Austin Energy's service territory by 2020 and introduce Austin Energy's grid as a "'test lab'" for companies developing and testing clean technology in the future.

Pecan Street aims to achieve five objectives through its demonstration project:

1. Create an interoperable, standards-based technical approach that can be integrated into other systems with minimal additional engineering and design.
2. Establish a cyber security protocol that can be integrated into other systems without risking the security and privacy of participants.
3. Demonstrate and optimize integration of customer-side smart grid systems along with deployment of utility-scale distributed solar and storage on the distribution feeders serving the Mueller community.
4. Deploy and compare different pricing models and features, including dynamic pricing, decoupled pricing, and net metering, to identify a menu of pricing options that incentivize investments in smart grid systems without jeopardizing utilities' revenue stream.
5. Construct and operate a demonstration house located in Mueller that will serve as a testing laboratory and public education facility.

Project Partners

In addition to Pecan Street and Austin Energy, the regional demonstration project includes the University of Texas, Environmental Defense Fund, and City of Austin. The University of Texas will lead the data collection and analysis aspect of the project, and support commercialization of new technologies through its Austin Technology Incubator. The Environmental Defense Fund will serve as an independent third party ensuring that environmental benefits are maximized and actually realized. EDF will also share best practices and lessons learned with other utilities and stakeholders across the country. The City of Austin will manage the Mueller redevelopment as it relates to the demonstration project.

Project Costs and Metrics

Pecan Street estimates the demonstration project will cost $25 million and has received funding from three main sources. The Department of Energy awarded Pecan Street a $10.5 million Smart Grid Demonstration Project Grant to conduct research in the newly developed Mueller neighborhood, the Doris Duke Foundation provided a matching $350,000 grant to extend this research to include one hundred existing homes in surrounding neighborhoods, and the remaining funding came collectively from Pecan Street's partners, which contributed about $14 million. This includes contributions of $5.6. million from Austin Energy, $0.3 million from the Austin Technology Incubator, $0.25 million from the Environmental Defense Fund, $0.7 million from the University of Texas, and $7.3 million from the City of Austin.

Because the goal of this project is to demonstrate the capability of smart grid technologies in a modern community, the demonstration project does not include a utility business case. Rather, the experimental technologies demonstrated in the community will be evaluated to determine whether smart grid technology in the home and business will create value for the customer. In particular, the project metrics will analyze how the deployed smart grid technologies

- influence the customer's environmental impact;
- affect the customer's electric bill;
- promote private sector interest in offering innovative new products and services;
- provide financial incentive for customers, utilities, and the private sector to invest in energy efficiency;
- impact load curve of customers; and
- impact utility revenues.

These metrics reflect Pecan Street's guiding principles, which focus on environmental improvement, creating value for the utility customer, and creating a sustainable business model for Austin Energy. This focus sets the demonstration apart from other more traditional approaches to smart grid implementation, which focus more exclusively on a utility's bottom line.

Demonstration Project Details

Objective 1: Create an Interoperable, Standards-based Technical Approach

Implementing Pecan Street's demonstration project requires integrating a wide variety of technologies and functions from both the customer premise and the utility system. This means figuring out how to get all the "pieces of the puzzle," including smart appliances, smart meters, solar panels, customers, home area networks, the utility distribution system, and utility dispatchers to communicate with each other in a way that is meaningful to each component. Although the National Institute of Standards and Technology is actively engaged in developing such interoperability standards, absent national standards defining this communications protocol, the plethora of companies working in this field developed different communications platforms for their smart grid components. Thus Pecan Street will create an interoperable system, which facilitates effective communication among these components. Pecan Street is also striving to develop a smart grid system in which new technologies can be integrated with minimal additional engineering or tweaking.

The Home Energy Management System
The key component to creating Pecan Street's interoperable system is the Home Energy Management System (HEMS). Installed on the customer premise, the HEMS is a communications gateway that enables different smart grid components to communicate with each other and provide meaningful information to the consumer. The HEMS will use the customer's home area network, or Internet hub, to communicate with the different devices and potentially manage energy usage, based on customer preferences and price signals from Austin Energy. The system does not allow the utility itself to directly control usage inside the home. Instead, the customer or a third-party service provider will manage systems in the home through the HEMS. Using an open RFI process, Pecan Street identified four HEMS service providers to test their services. Best Buy along with Check-it, Intel, Sony, and Whirlpool, will each deploy their proprietary HEMS systems in a discrete group of test homes.

Interoperability and Standards
Pecan Street is following open platform principles in this endeavor. Much like open source software allows anyone to access the computer coding that drives the software in order to add new features or change the software to suit their needs, the technical specifications of Pecan Street's open platform approach will be open to the public and industry at large. This will allow others to build on Pecan Street's expertise and refine the system to suit an individual utility's system, or for technology developers to design their products to integrate easily with the Pecan Street system. Similar to the Internet, the neighborhood electric grid of the project will be an open platform that allows third parties to deploy their applications on the system. Pecan Street anticipates that this open source, plug and play approach will foster innovation and development of third-party "applications" that complement the values of the project, such as reducing carbon emissions and water usage associated with electricity consumption.

The Standards Committee will evaluate and test the interoperability standards developed for the Pecan Street system. Reflecting the importance of interoperability, the committee is co-led by Bert Haskell, Pecan

Street's technology director and a former executive with the Microelectronics and Computer Technology Corporation, and Dr. Robert Hebner, the director of the University of Texas' Center for Electromechanics and the former acting director of NIST.[422] Committee members will also actively engage in the NIST process, as well as the Institute of Electrical and Electronics Engineers' Standards Association, to share lessons learned from the Pecan Street demonstration project and advance the interoperability of smart grid systems nationwide.

Standards and Best Practices for Managing Environmental Impact
In keeping with its focus on the environmental impact of smart grid technology, Pecan Street also intends to develop standards and best practices for managing household environmental impact. These standards will eventually allow consumers to manage their energy use, not just to reduce costs or overall usage but also to minimize the environmental impact of their electricity consumption. Pecan Street is supporting the Galvin Electricity Initiative's Perfect Power Seal of Approval (PPSoA). The Galvin Electricity Initiative, a nonprofit organization, created the PPSoA as a comprehensive, consumer-centric, data-driven system for evaluating power system performance. Launched in October 2011, PPSoA evaluates a microgrid's performance in four key areas: reliability, cost, efficiency and environment, and consumer empowerment. Pecan Street is the first institution to adopt the PPSoA metrics and will use its experience with the demonstration project to help refine the PPSoA for future users.[423] As such, each HEMS provider will be evaluated and must meet the PPSoA metrics.

Objective 2: Establish a Cyber Security Protocol

In recognition of the importance of preserving participants' privacy and ensuring a reliable, secure electricity grid, the Pecan Street project will devote significant resources to ensuring this objective is realized. Austin Energy's Interoperability and Cyber Security Plan, already being implemented as part of its Smart Grid 2.0 efforts, will also be used for the project. The comprehensive approach ensures that "cybersecurity will be addressed in every phase of the engineering lifecycle . . . including design and procurement, installation and commissioning, and the provision of ongoing maintenance and support."[424] Austin Energy anticipates developing a methodology and guidelines consistent with international standards ISO 9001 and ITIL certification. In addition, a third party will audit Austin Energy's equipment and system architecture before it is deployed to its customers and the demonstration project participants.

Objective 3: Demonstrate and Optimize Integration of Customer-Side Smart Grid Systems

The bulk of Pecan Street, Inc.'s efforts will be dedicated to creating and optimizing a customer-focused smart grid system, which includes both utility scale distributed solar and storage along the distribution feeders serving Mueller. Participating households will have the opportunity to test new smart grid technologies, such as smart appliances, HEMS services, electric vehicles, and distributed solar, within the context of their everyday lives. Pecan Street will evaluate how these technologies impact utility operations and determine what combination of pricing models, features, and incentives maximize the benefits of the technology. Pricing will be discussed in the next section.

Open Innovation Strategy

In May 2011, Pecan Street issued an RFI seeking like-minded companies to participate in the demonstration project. The RFI included a summary of the challenges facing Austin Energy, Pecan Street's mission and core principles, and a description of the unique opportunity to participate in this demonstration project. Pecan Street sought companies to participate in three areas:

- HEMS providers (up to five)
- Core project assets, such as rooftop PV, electric vehicles and charging stations, home energy storage, and fuel cells
- Open innovation, such as LED lighting, vehicles powered by alternative fuels, Internet and smart-phone applications, smart appliances, and other distributed generation

As a result of this RFI, Pecan Street is partnering with the following companies:

- HEMS providers: Best Buy with Check-It, Intel, Sony, and Whirlpool
- Core Project Assets:
  - Electric vehicles: Chevrolet to provide one hundred Volts for lease or purchase to participating residents
  - Smart appliances: Whirlpool and Best Buy's Geek Squad
  - Rooftop solar PV: SunEdison
- Open Innovation:
  - Home solar charging of EVs: SunEdison

Pecan Street's open innovation strategy benefits the private partners and the demonstration project in several ways. First, the partnering companies will benefit by using the project participants as a real-world test market for rapidly developing technology before it reaches the marketplace. Second, Pecan Street is stretching its federal research funding by partnering with private companies to supply a significant amount of the technology it will deploy. In many cases, Pecan Street is providing an incentive or matching an existing Austin Energy incentive, instead of purchasing the technology outright. This also benefits the project by ensuring that participants are interested in and will use the technology, because they've had to invest their own resources in procuring it. Third, in selecting HEMS providers, Pecan Street Inc. identified several different companies with different HEMS platforms and services. Because this is still a developing technology, Pecan Street is providing an opportunity for the different service providers to refine and enhance their products, which will ultimately benefit the larger smart grid marketplace. This approach also avoids picking a "winner" before the market is fully developed.

The Participant Experience

Pecan Street, Inc. conducted a baseline survey of one hundred homes for one year before deploying any technology. These homes were monitored without receiving any feedback about their usage and without the use of any energy management devices. This data will serve as the baseline against which the demonstration project results will be measured.

Pecan Street is recruiting households from the Mueller community and surrounding neighborhoods to participate in the demonstration project. The organization has developed relationships with the developer of the community, a neighborhood council, as well as early participants to market the project and recruit participants. Most recruitment has taken place via community events and neighbor-to-neighbor outreach. As such, there is concern that the study group comprises early adopters and those who are eager to demonstrate their "green" credentials. Pecan Street is cognizant of these issues and conducted a demographic survey of the study participants to determine how the study group differs from the general population. University of Texas researchers and Pecan Street will use this data to inform the demonstration project results and determine how replicable the results are.

Each participating household will be equipped with a HEMS provided by one of the selected companies. The HEMS will be the enabling platform to allow integration of other smart grid technologies. HEMS will also be capable of providing services such as home security, energy management, health-care monitoring, home improvement, entertainment, and labor-saving services. Participating households will also be equipped with smart appliances provided by Whirlpool and other manufacturers.

Although participating households must make some commitments to Pecan Street, they are free to use the technology as they wish. In order to participate in the demonstration project, households must commit to participate in the project for at least one year, purchase continuous broadband Internet service during their participation, and provide Pecan Street and its service providers with access to their home in order to install the smart grid technology. In return, Pecan Street will provide households with the necessary technology to participate in the project, including the HEMS system and smart appliances. Pecan Street will divide its participating households into four discrete groups, with each group receiving a different HEMS technology. Select homes will also receive rooftop solar devices, and others can choose to purchase a Chevrolet Volt at a reduced price through the project. Once the technology is installed, Pecan Street will monitor how the households interact with and utilize the new technology.

Rooftop Solar

The Austin Energy PowerSaver program offers its residential customers a financial incentive for installing rooftop solar PV. In order to qualify for the rebate, homes must meet established energy efficiency criteria, the solar panels must face south (with some exceptions for east or west orientation), and the system must be installed by an approved contractor. The standard rebate for qualifying equipment is $2.50/watt, with an additional incentive up to a total of $3.125/watt for qualifying equipment at least sixty percent manufactured or assembled within the Austin Energy service area.

Rather than invest its limited budget in purchasing and installing PV equipment for a small number of study participants, Pecan Street is capitalizing on Austin Energy's existing incentive by providing an additional $0.50/watt for south-facing panels and $0.75/watt for west-facing panels to its demonstration project participants. As a result, more than 165 participating homes have installed PV systems. An additional 40 nonparticipating homes in the same neighborhood have installed PV through the Austin Energy program alone, resulting in more than 1 mW of installed PV in the Mueller neighborhood and surrounding community. Pecan Street believes this is the densest deployment of retrofit (installed on existing homes, not as part of new construction) solar PV in the country.

Photovoltaic systems are usually installed with the panels facing south, to maximize electricity generation. However, Pecan Street believes that although west-facing panels produce slightly less electricity overall, the production matches the demand curve more closely than output from south-facing panels. As a result, it hypothesizes that west-facing panels will have a greater impact on mitigating peak demand than will south-facing panels. Over the course of the demonstration project, Pecan Street will monitor and analyze the impact of both south- and west-facing PV installations to determine whether its hypothesis is correct.

Customers with a solar system may enroll in Austin Energy's net-billing program. Each kilowatt hour generated, up to the amount consumed in a given month, is credited the full retail rate (8.065 cents/kWh up to 500 kWh and 12.875 cents/kWh for more than 500 kWh), which includes the base energy rate plus a fuel adjustment charge and transmission service adjustment rider. Each additional kilowatt hour above the amount consumed is credited to the customer at the adjustable fuel charge rate (3.615 cents/kWh in 2012), not the full retail rate.[425] Thus these customers receive only a modest incentive to make additional energy efficiency improvements in their homes or to install a larger PV system because they do not receive the full benefit of the costs avoided by the utility. Pecan Street will explore how different pricing schemes, including paying the full retail rate for net generation each month impacts both the utility's bottom line and the customer.

Austin Energy is in the process of revising its entire rate structure, including the way its solar-generating customers are compensated. In its December 2011 rate proposal, Austin Energy staff recommend crediting all residential solar PV generation at an annually calculated "value of solar rate" (12.8 cents/kWh in 2011).[426] At the same time, these residential customers would pay the applicable retail rate for all electricity consumed.[427] Austin Energy expects the proposed changes to provide these customers, "a more fair and equitable rate" while maintaining the incentive to conserve through continuing to pay an inclining rate for electricity consumed.[428] Pecan Street is waiting for Austin Energy to complete its rate case before the Austin City Council to determine what rates its participants will pay. It may simulate this proposed rate to demonstrate its effect to customers; however, the existing rates will be used to determine actual utility bills.

Electric Vehicles

Participating households will have the option of purchasing or leasing a Chevrolet Volt at a reduced price. Chevrolet agreed to make one hundred Volts available to participating households, and Pecan Street is providing a financial incentive of seventy-five hundred dollars toward the purchase of the vehicle.[429] When combined with the federal tax incentive currently available, the purchase price for a new Volt will be reduced to approximately twenty-five thousand dollars for demonstration project participants. These participants may also choose to install a level 2 home-charging station (220/240 V) free of charge. Austin Energy's pilot Plug-In Partner's program provides a 50 percent rebate (up to fifteen hundred dollars) on the installation of a level 2 in-home charging station, and Pecan Street is covering the remaining 50 percent of the cost for these project participants.

SunEdison will provide 150 rooftop solar installations, which will provide solar-charging services to most of the Volt owners. Some Volt owners will also receive in-home battery storage technology. All of the solar installations will integrate with the HEMS services provided by the participating companies. Pecan Street will monitor and evaluate the participants' home-charging and public-charging (via OnStar) patterns.

Austin Energy provides public charging through its Plug-In EVery-where network. It currently has 116 level 2 charging stations at fifty-seven locations throughout its service territory.[430] Access to the stations is gained by joining the network for a six-month fee of twenty-five dollars, which provides unlimited charging at the public stations. Austin Energy supplies the electricity to these charging stations with its GreenChoice renewable energy. Pecan Street Inc. project participants may also sign up for this program and share their charging habits with project researchers via OnStar.

Pecan Street will study a number of factors related to electric vehicles. Researchers will document how participants charge and use their electric vehicles, as well as how they respond to different price signals. This will help inform future rates for electric vehicle charging both at home and at public charging stations. Level 2 home charging stations are expected to strain existing transformers in some areas. Pecan Street's high concentration of electric vehicle owners, utilizing level 2 home-charging stations, will give researchers the opportunity to see if these problems materialize. The researchers will also experiment with different price signals to encourage charging behavior that avoids overloading the local transformers. Pecan Street's research will also document the environmental benefits of switching to electric vehicles in the Austin Energy service territory, as well as test the ability to charge the Volt using solar PV technology.

Home Energy Storage

Pecan Street will provide up to fifty participating homes with energy storage technology. The details of this aspect of the project are still in development. However, the storage technology will be installed in combination with other project technology. For example, some homes with a Volt will receive the storage technology, as will homes with solar PV, as will homes with a combination of Volt and PV technology. Other homes without any additional technology will also receive the storage technology.

Commercial-Scale Solar Installations

Pecan Street plans to support a community solar installation in the Mueller neighborhood. However, the details of this aspect of the project are not finalized. Pecan Street expects to partner with Austin Energy to leverage existing resources.

Objective 4: Deploy and Compare Different Pricing Models

While installing smart grid technology is key to realizing Pecan Street's goal of demonstrating tomorrow's energy system, designing and deploying effective pricing models is crucial to its success. Pecan Street will develop several different pricing models, including dynamic pricing, decoupled pricing, and net metering to test how participants respond to different pricing structures and signals. These pricing models will be evaluated based on their ability to incentivize additional investment in smart grid technology without jeopardizing a utility's revenue stream.

Pecan Street anticipates developing additional pricing features that can be applied across the pricing models. Pricing features will be layered on top of the various pricing models to further incent desired energy consumption patterns. The pricing features will be compatible with all pricing models, and will include information such as real-time usage data, carbon impact information, and peer-to-peer comparisons of energy consumption or patterns. Participants will receive this information from the HEMS systems as well as an Internet information portal. Pecan Street is developing different Internet portals, which will be tested for their efficacy in shifting participant behavior. Participants will also be able to program their HEMS system to respond automatically to price or other signals from Austin Energy and Pecan Street. Pecan Street will use the data collected from the demonstration project participants to determine the most effective combination of pricing models and features.

Pricing Models

Traditional utility rates tie the recovery of the cost of providing electricity service to a flat cost per kilowatt-hour consumed. This is calculated based on the expected sales of electricity. Pricing models will range from traditional volumetric pricing, in which a customer pays an established price per kilowatt-hour, to nonvolumetric pricing, in which the customer pays a flat fee for electricity service.

Objective 5: Construct and Operate a Demonstration House and Laboratory

Originally conceived as a demonstration home and laboratory, Pecan Street is now constructing the Pike Powers Commercialization Laboratory. Pecan Street partnered with the National Renewable Energy Laboratory to develop the technical specifications for the laboratory, which will provide a neutral, third-party facility in which multiple utilities and vendors can work collaboratively alongside University of Texas and NREL researchers to conduct real-world smart grid research.

Pike Powers Commercialization Laboratory

The Pike Powers Commercialization Laboratory, which opened in June 2013, is the nation's first nonprofit smart grid research lab. Located within the Mueller community, the laboratory will promote research, commercialization, and educational opportunities for University of Texas students and faculty and start-up companies from the Austin Technology Incubator. The mission of the Pike Powers Commercialization Lab is to serve as an elite, industry-caliber facility where Pecan Street and University of Texas students and researchers can collaborate with the private sector on cutting-edge applied research in consumer-focused smart grid, wireless, IT, clean energy, and health-care applications. The laboratory will provide commercialization opportunities, including the ability to test, refine, and demonstrate products to commercialize new technologies, and bring advanced products to market, such as electric vehicle chargers with integrated demand management and energy monitoring. The laboratory will also provide opportunities to conduct field testing, establish interoperability among smart grid-enabled appliances, measure the impact of new equipment on the grid, and test prototype devices for standards compliance.

In 2012, Pecan Street hosted its first weeklong Commercialization Bootcamp, at which selected UT students and aspiring entrepreneurs spent a week working with the laboratory's team and advanced testing equipment to develop the skills necessary to create successful companies. Pecan Street also anticipates developing educational materials to teach policymakers about smart grid technology and energy conservation, as well as materials on commercialization and testing for smart grid entrepreneurs.

The three-story laboratory will serve as both a research and outreach facility. The first floor will be open to the public, including education space and opportunities for general outreach to the community. The second and third floors will contain the research lab, including a "home" on the third floor. This third floor home will be capable of simulating multiple home environments. Before deploying HEMS and smart appliance technology into participants' homes, the technology will first be installed and tested in the home laboratory. This will give participating companies an opportunity to test their new and developing technology before it is deployed to consumer homes to ensure a positive experience for the study participants.

Observations and Conclusion

Since its inception, Pecan Street, Inc.'s Energy Internet Demonstration project has received positive coverage from both the popular and industry media outlets. Much of this praise is well deserved, and the results of Pecan Street's research will likely play a positive role in shaping the future of the smart grid experience across the country. With its focus on the customer's experience, maximizing environmental impact, and minimizing the impact on utility revenue streams, Pecan Street is addressing the challenges facing every utility in the United States. Although the full results of the study are several years away, Pecan Street's project offers several early lessons.

Demonstration Projects Are Critical to Advancing Customer Acceptance of Smart Grid

In some parts of the country, customer opposition to smart grid technology and smart meters in particular, is delaying the rollout and full implementation of the utility side of the technology. In others, customers lack a full appreciation of the opportunities presented by smart grid, and adoption of customer-side technology is slow. The Pecan Street Energy Internet Demonstration project and other such projects funded by DOE will play a critical role in documenting real customer experiences with smart grid technology, as well as proving the technology effective. Demonstration projects are important to identify challenges, develop workable solutions, and document the benefits of the technology. The lessons learned and best practices identified by Pecan Street over the next several years will provide a solid foundation for other utilities to implement smart grid on a larger scale. In addition to the technical solutions identified by Pecan Street, the participant experiences will also need to be shared and disseminated.

In order to justify the costs of smart grid technology, most utilities have focused on the business case for smart grid and used long-term operational savings to justify investments. This focus on saving money has left many customers wondering what's in it for them. Pecan Street's focus on the customer experience and its attempts to open the historically closed utility system to innovation and new market actors will help develop answers to that question. Utilities across the country would be wise to examine the project's results and apply the answers in their own service territories.

Public-Private Partnerships Spur Innovation

The Department of Energy's American Recovery and Reinvestment Act funds support sixteen smart grid regional demonstration projects in nine states. The government's $433,216,568 investment was matched with $442,927,439 in direct private-sector funding, although indirect private investment is likely to bring this total even higher.[431] For example, Pecan Street Inc. leveraged its initial project funding to attract additional private investment in the form of HEMS systems for deployment and testing, and successfully encouraged project participants to invest in smart grid technology by matching existing incentives for solar PV and electric vehicles. The DOE's grant funding also supported the development of the Pike Powers Commercialization Laboratory, which will conduct smart grid research and support commercialization of new technologies long after the initial grant funding is spent. This kind of public-private partnership is needed to drive innovation and advancement of smart grid technologies. More funding for demonstration projects, particularly those aimed at maximizing the customer experience and demonstrating a fully integrated smart grid system, are needed to ensure that the benefits of smart grid are fully realized.

Community Approach to Energy Planning Is a Model for Other Communities

Pecan Street grew out of an effort to transform the energy system in Austin as well as revitalize the community. With its focus on capturing environmental benefits, ensuring a positive customer experience, sustaining utility revenues, and committed community engagement, Pecan Street is a model for other municipal utilities facing similar challenges. Pecan Street's community engagement in the planning process, as well as the implementation of the demonstration project, can also serve as models for utilities engaged in smart grid implementation. Neighbor-to-neighbor education and involvement, as well as efforts by community groups, have driven much of the participation in the project. Although the Mueller community likely comprises some early adopters inclined to embrace smart grid technology, the project's use of community engagement has reached others who wouldn't necessarily seek out the opportunity to participate in the project. The engagement process has built community interest and support for the technology that will be tested and demonstrated through the project, and will likely lead to greater support for the changes in rate structure and incentives Austin Energy will make in the future.

The Pacific Northwest National Laboratory estimates that smart grid technology can lead to a 12 percent reduction in carbon emissions in 2030. However, this estimate assumes aggressive adoption of the technology across the country. Pecan Street Energy Internet Demonstration project is embracing this possibility and attempting to design and implement an electricity system capable of capturing and maximizing these environmental benefits. More study and development will be needed; however, the results of Pecan Street's work will provide an excellent starting point on which to build future smart grid implementation across the country.

CASE STUDY VI. SAN DIEGO GAS & ELECTRIC: THE SMART GRID'S LEADING EDGE

Introduction

History and Background

San Diego Gas & Electric has been providing electricity services since 1881, when five San Diegans met in the parlor of the Consolidated Bank to incorporate the first San Diego Gas Company. At its beginning it served 89 gas customers. Today SDG&E is a regulated public utility that serves 3.5 million customers. Its service area covers 4,100 square miles in San Diego County and southern Orange County in the state of California. It is a subsidiary of Sempra Energy, a San Diego-based Fortune 500 Company.[432] Sempra was founded to take advantage of opportunities in the open competitive energy markets. Sempra's 17,500 employees provide services for 31 million customers not just in San Diego, but all over the world.[433]

As of December 31, 2010, 1,160 mW of combined cycle plants, 960 mW of steam plants, 688 mW of simple cycle peaking plants, 157 mW of co-generation plants, and 75 mW of renewable generation were interconnected to the SDG&E transmission system.[434] The SDG&E transmission network includes 500-kV, 230-kV, 138-kV, and 69-kV lines that are overhead and underground. In terms of SDG&E's own procurement resources, in 2011 they were 40 percent carbon free and 20 percent renewable. SDG&E's transmission infrastructure is commonly described as an "electrical cul-de-sac" because it is located in the southwestern corner of California near the ocean and the Mexican border.[435] SDG&E's distribution grid is a radial, open-loop system. SDG&E already uses SCADA for its distribution circuits, which allows some self-healing and resilience in the grid.[436] In fact, SDG&E was ranked by an independent utility consulting firm as having the "best" reliability in the western United States for five years in a row and earned the honor of "Best Reliability in the Nation" for 2009.[437]

San Diego Gas & Electric's SunRise Powerlink was recently completed, adding 115 miles of 500-kV and 230-kV transmission lines.[438, 439] The 1,000-mW line will bring solar and wind power from the Imperial Valley to San Diego and power roughly 650,000 homes. The new transmission line has the potential to reduce greenhouse gas emissions by one million tons a year by carrying cleaner electricity to San Diegans.[440] In order to obtain approvals to construct this line, they addressed siting and endangered species habitat concerns among other issues.[441] Construction of the Sunrise Powerlink could prove extremely beneficial to the San Diego region given the outage of the San Onofre Nuclear Power facility, currently out of service indefinitely. In September 2011, six million people lost power in California, Arizona, and a part of Mexico as the result of human error of an employee of Arizona Public Service, an Arizona company that owns a transmission line feeding San Diego.

State and Federal Policy Goals

In 2007 Congress passed the Energy Independence and Security Act, which authorized the Smart Grid Investment Program and the Smart Grid Demonstration Program. In 2009 Congress passed the American Resource and Recovery Act, which appropriated $4.5 billion to fund the federal smart grid programs. San Diego Gas & Electric was awarded $5 million in funding under a Smart Grid Investment Grant through the ARRA.[442] Also in 2009, the California state legislature demonstrated policy leadership and required its investor-owned utilities—Pacific Gas and Electric, Southern California Edison, and San Diego Gas & Electric—to submit plans to the California Public Utilities Commission to implement smart grid technologies throughout their service territories.[443] Through California Senate Bill 17, the California legislature directed its IOUs "to modernize the state's electrical transmission and distribution system to maintain safe, reliable, efficient, and secure electrical service" making the deployment of smart grid technology the policy of the state.[444] Former Governor Arnold Schwarzenegger signed the bill into law on October 11, 2009.

Following up on the legislature's policy leadership the CPUC instituted a rule-making proceeding that then "determine[d] the requirements for a Smart Grid Deployment Plan (SGDP) consistent with the policies set forth in [Senate Bill 17] and federal law."[445] The CPUC set guidelines for the major IOUs in California to file smart grid deployment plans by July 1, 2011. Their directive outlined the content required in the plans, each of which was to include the following:

1. Smart grid vision statement
2. Deployment baseline
3. Smart grid strategy
4. Grid security and cyber-security strategy
5. Cost and benefit estimates and metrics

The CPUC decision further reiterated the policy goals outlined in Senate Bill 17 that were to be the focus for the major utilities in California.[446] Those policy goals include that the smart grid

1. creates a self-healing and resilient grid;
2. empowers consumers to actively participate in operations of the grid;
3. resists attack;
4. provides a higher quality of power and avoids outages, thus saving money;
5. accommodates all generation and storage options;
6. enables electricity markets to flourish;
7. runs the grid more efficiently;
8. enables penetration of intermittent power generation sources;
9. creates a platform for deployment of a wide range of energy technologies and management services;
10. enables and supports the sale of demand response, energy efficiency, distributed generation, and storage into wholesale energy markets as a resource, on equal footing with traditional generation resources; and
11. significantly reduces the total environmental footprint of the current electric generation and delivery system in California.[447]

San Diego Gas & Electric's vision as outlined in their deployment plan is that "San Diego Gas & Electric, in collaboration with key stakeholders, will create the foundation for an innovative, connected and sustainable energy future."[448] SDG&E worked with a number of its key stakeholders, including other organizations and its customers, to develop a plan that would best meet SDG&E's obligations to the CPUC and the California legislature, its customers, other interest groups, grid reliability, and the environment. SDG&E set a vision and goals for attainment for 2015 and 2020 completion in its deployment plan filing with the CPUC. SDG&E president and COO Michael R. Niggli pointed out in a letter accompanying the SDG&E deployment plan that unlike in other areas of the country, San Diego's customers are "driving" the plan. Niggli noted that even prior to the filing of the plan, over thirteen thousand customers had installed over 100 mW of photovoltaics and customers were adopting plug-in electric vehicles at one of the highest rates in the country. Customers were already taking advantage of real-time information about their energy use to make more informed decisions, and there was broad support for California's environment friendly policies.[449]

Overview of San Diego Gas & Electric's Smart Grid Program

Collaboration among Stakeholders

In an effort to gain the approval for its smart grid deployment plan from its customer base and other local constituencies, SDG&E partnered with

- academia,
- business organizations,
- municipal utilities and governmental organizations,
- a ratepayer advocacy organization (UCAN),
- energy NGOs,
- environmental NGOs,
- a corporate customer, and
- labor interests.

These groups helped SDG&E form some parts of its smart grid deployment plan regarding work-force vocational education, security and privacy, environmental impact, and community input. The Environmental Defense Fund has stayed involved and recently evaluated the three SGDPs from IOUs in California (more on that in the "Environmental Defense Fund Evaluation" section below). Additionally, SDG&E has said it would like to continue to work with unions and vocational schools to enable its work-force transition.

Advanced Metering Infrastructure and Home Area Network

San Diego Gas & Electric has already integrated significant smart grid technology into its operations over the past ten years. By the end of 2012,

SDG&E had replaced about 1.4 million electric meters and retrofit 900,000 gas modules.[450] As of June 30, 2012, SDG&E's deployment was 98.7 percent complete.[451] Additionally, thirty-six thousand programmable communicating thermostats and remote turn-on, turn-off devices for all residential meters are a part of SDG&E's efforts to upgrade its residential and commercial meter infrastructure.[452]

Since SDG&E has already installed most smart meters, the next goal is to facilitate two-way communication between the customer and the utility. Once SDG&E and its customers can communicate with each other about real-time electricity use, the utility will deploy tools to incentivize different habits on both ends of the distribution line to increase efficiency, decrease costs, and decrease emissions. Tools deployed based on the new data will range from smart transformers, to EV charging stations, to new dynamic rates.

San Diego Gas & Electric is currently using Itron Open Way smart meters to collect usage data. The wireless HAN signal has not yet been activated. At this time, SDG&E is installing Zigbee Smart Energy Profile (SEP) 1.0 in its pilot applications, which, the utility says, "has limitations and does not allow for upgrades to SEP 2.0 (the desired specification for mass rollout of HAN devices), for our pilots this year."[453] The upgrade to SEP 2.0 requires a standard be ratified, golden units be built and successfully tested, and finally for SDG&E testing and Firmware (FW) updates to be successful. SDG&E hopes to have their Itron smart meters to support SEP 2.0 in their AMI products by the beginning of 2014.[454] Because the HAN technology comes after the implementation of smart meters, the utility has not begun to talk to its customers about these capabilities specifically, "but rather the benefits of the HAN technology" generally.[455]

One benefit of smart meters is that they allow for meters to be read remotely. Additionally, electric service may be connected, disconnected, and reconnected without a person needing to physically go out and fix the problem. In 2012, SDG&E was able to avoid "approximately 3.2 million miles of vehicle travel." Not only does this save money, but it is better for the environment. Reductions in vehicle miles traveled resulted in a "savings of approximately 275,000 gallons of gasoline which equates into more than 2,400 tons of reduced CO2e emissions."[456]

Demand Response/ Efficiency

San Diego Gas & Electric has included automation technology that would allow demand response and energy efficiency as an element of smart grid deployment. With SDG&E's existing time-of-use rates the utility is well positioned to integrate technology that would empower its customers with information to make better electricity consumption decisions. Plug-in electric vehicles can be a part of a grid storage solution—called vehicle-to-grid—by taking in electricity at night and storing it during the day when it has the potential to help balance the needs of the smart grid load at different times of the day. The idea is to automate the technology connected to the grid to enable real-time pricing and thus create true market forces which could trigger positive reactions in customer behavior.[457] By 2020, SDG&E hopes to achieve price-driven demand response, energy efficiency, distributed generation, and storage.[458]

The utility's customers may already choose from various dynamic rate structures that offer lower costs at off-peak times to incentivize more environmentally friendly electric usage. EV owners can receive rebates and incentives from the state and federal governments[459] and may, in addition, elect to integrate their home and vehicle electric usage on the same TOU rate structure. Existing AMI created a two-way communications infrastructure between utilities and customers. It measures energy use data in fifteen-minute increments for commercial applications and hourly increments for residential applications. This has enabled electric demand response and load control that helps customers reduce peak energy use.[460]

San Diego Gas & Electric's existing dynamic rate structure allows customers with EVs to choose to charge their cars separately from their normal residential rate. Those customers also have the choice to put their residential consumption on TOU pricing as well. The first of two EV rates is the "EV-TOU" rate, which requires a separate smart meter for the vehicle. Customers who opt for this are required to have a second meter socket installed in their home. "EV-TOU-2" provides one smart meter to communicate the data of home and the vehicle electricity use together.[461]

The utility separates its time-of-use rates into "Super Off Peak," "Off Peak," and "Peak." The significant rate differential provides meaningful economic incentive to charge electric vehicles in the late evening and night. A Nissan Leaf's full charge takes about 24 kWh, while a Chevy Volt requires 13 kWh (based on manufacturers' data).

In addition to separating out pricing regimes based on the time of day, SDG&E also separates its customers into different "Baseline" groups based on their average electricity consumption. For the general "Domestic Rate" used by a majority of its customers without rooftop solar or EV, the "Baseline" level costs 13.8 cents per kWh. Those who consume 101 to 130 percent of the "baseline" pay 16 cents per kWh. At 131 to 200 percent of baseline, customers will pay 29 cents per kWh, and 31 cents a kWh for anything above 200 percent of baseline.

There are a few other rate options for SDG&E customers. Customers with solar photovoltaic electric systems are eligible for a net metered rate based off the domestic rate as a foundation (DR-SES). Net metering (NEM) allows customers who produce 1,000 kW or less of wind or solar power at their homes to get a rebate. Those customers with NEM do not have to pay some of the fixed costs as a part of their rate that non-NEM customers do. Customers who use more than 1,500 kWh per month are encouraged to use the domestic time-of-use rate (DR-TOU). The utility suggests customers to choose this rate if no one is in the home from noon to 6:00 p.m. on weekdays. Additionally, SDG&E encourages DR-TOU customers to put timers on large appliances to help decrease peak electricity consumption. Additionally, a few TOU rates are available for "Industrial" or "Non-Residential" customers.[462] SDG&E also continues to offer its Low-Income Home Energy Assistance Program (LIHEAP).[463] In order to qualify for low-income assistance, customers must either "spend a high percentage of income on energy, or have elderly or disabled members, or children under three years of age."[464]

The most recent demand response program is SDG&E's Reduce Your Use program, a demand response service, launched in July 2012. While participation in the program is optional, SDG&E automatically enrolled all residential and small business customers with smart meters in the program.[465] Under the program, SDG&E notifies customers of event days when they can earn a credit for each kWh below their previous average usage during the hours of 11:00 a.m. to 6:00 p.m. Customers can earn a credit of $.75/kWh saved or $1.25/kWh if the customer has qualifying enabling technology installed. Enabling technologies include devices that are set up to receive signals or alerts directly from SDG&E.

Plug-in Electric Vehicles

Plug-in electric vehicles are growing in popularity in the country as the Nissan Leaf, Chevrolet Volt, BMW ActiveE, Ford Focus Electric, and Mitsubishi I are supplementing the Toyota Prius as the newest, greenest vehicles on the market. San Diego has the highest penetration of EVs in the country, with about sixteen hundred vehicles on the road as of June 2012.[466] SDG&E has collaborated with the Smart City San Diego effort to launch "car2go," which is "the world's first deployment of an all-electric car sharing pilot. In the first one hundred days of operation more than 6,000 people registered as members and more than 25,000 trips were taken in the smart electric car2go vehicles."[467] This may be why manufacturers like Ford, Mitsubishi, and BMW have targeted the San Diego region for their upcoming EV releases in the next year or two. The state of California and the federal government both provide monetary rebates and incentives for customers to purchase EVs.[468] Carpool lane access is available for

EVs in California, and plug-in hybrid EV access is pending. The federal government offers a tax credit for EVs of twenty-five hundred to seventy-five hundred dollars, depending on the size of the battery in the car (4 kWh to 16 kWh), for electric-drive vehicles (both EVs and HEVs) sold after December 31, 2008. PlugInAmerica.org calls it "the best and biggest new incentive brought on by the American Recovery and Reinvestment Act of 2009." This tax credit will "[apply] to at least 200,000 units per auto manufacturer before it phases out."

EVs have proven their environmental benefit. The California Air Resources Board produced a study estimating that battery electric vehicles could emit at least 67 percent lower greenhouse gases than cars run solely on gasoline.[469] Additionally, as car batteries get lighter and more efficient, and the grid is run with more renewable sources, the environmental benefits are going to increase.

Infrastructure upgrades may be necessary to meet the increased electric load required to charge the vehicles. SDG&E's plan for EV growth in its service territory takes into account that existing residential transformers may not be able to handle the increased load of charging electric vehicles, especially if customers want to charge during peak hours. In order to make sure that appropriate infrastructure upgrades are made, SDG&E is monitoring installations of EV charging stations. The utility is working with automakers and others to track where the EV are being sold to predict where charging stations will go and, thus, where infrastructure updates are needed.

San Diego Gas & Electric is preparing for these increased challenges by supporting customer and utility charging stations. One of the biggest challenges to EV integration is the regulation of the charging infrastructure. Some states have struggled with whether the sale of electricity at the charging station is retail or wholesale. This distinction is important because the Federal Power Act gives the Federal Energy Regulatory Commission the obligation to regulate wholesale power, which is sale for resale.[470] States have jurisdiction over retail sale, which is sale for end use.[471] No matter the regulatory jurisdiction, rates should be just and reasonable.[472] CPUC had previously addressed the status of electricity sale at EV charging stations. The commission held it had sole jurisdiction over the sale of electricity from charging stations in California, clarifying its view regarding state versus federal jurisdiction.[473] In exerting its jurisdiction, it chose *not* to regulate the "ownership or operation of a facility that sells electric vehicle charging services."[474] The legislature directed the CPUC to incentivize growth in the EV market.[475] The CPUC opted to minimize regulation because, "neither the letter of the law nor the spirit of the law require commission regulation of electric vehicle charging stations."[476] The commission retained control over only setting the rate for the electricity sold by an IOU to an electric vehicle charging service as long as it is a bundled customer of the utility.[477] In September 2011, the California legislature further clarified the state regulatory role when it passed an assembly bill stating that "the ownership, control, operation, or management of a facility that supplies electricity to the public only for use to charge light duty plug-in electric vehicles, as defined, does not make the corporation or person a public utility for purposes of the act."[478] This policy supports charging stations becoming a competitive service with third parties competing to install infrastructure. This clear policy leadership has allowed third-party vendors to start the initial infrastructure investment for public EV charging with reduced uncertainty. The state's clear leadership also clarified that it would be the third parties not the utilities that would provide for this investment, which further reduced uncertainty for competitive provision of this service.

San Diego Gas & Electric, as a distribution service provider, will need to consider potential infrastructure upgrades as charging station locations are determined. SDG&E intends to install 129 utility-owned level 2 charging stations and 13 level 3 fast-charging stations next year. Storage will also be an element of the infrastructure upgrades. The utility is working on a pilot to integrate stationary batteries with fast-charging stations, which will also collect data on consumption habits for future design plans.[479]

In regard to storage technology, the California State Assembly passed a bill in June 2011 that requires the CPUC to establish cost-effective energy storage systems procurement targets for each utility by March, 1, 2012. By October 1, 2013, SDG&E will have three years to adopt the storage target. To be cost effective, there must be significant advances in this technology. A provision for a second target of December 31, 2021, exists to provide some time for better technology, if needed.[480]

One of the primary benefits to EVs is the decreased greenhouse gas emissions. But if significant numbers of EVs are being charged during the height of daily electric use, that benefit may be partly lost because the California Independent System Operator, which operates the California grid, may be forced to make up for the increased demand by dispatching additional peaking power plants. The utility plans to continue developing its TOU rates. Currently, SDG&E is studying the habits of EV owners to formulate the best rate design to incentivize off-peak charging. Their findings should be useful to other utilities to integrate EV. SDG&E hopes to support the growth of the whole EV market by supporting the services that support EV charging. The utility also supports education and outreach for residential and commercial charging through third-party contractors, municipalities, dealerships, and the media, to name a few.

Distribution Automation and Reliability

One of the things SDG&E values highly is reliable electric service. The utility complies with CPUC guidelines[481] for collecting data based on certain reliability indices during momentary and sustained outages using SAIDI (system average interruption duration index), SAIFI (system average interruption frequency index), and MAIFI (momentary average interruption frequency index). The utility then submits an annual report containing this data.[482] The CPUC also enforces standards for operation, reliability, and safety during emergencies.[483]

Reliability remains one of SDG&E's most important goals while implementing smart grid technologies. Reliability is important because electricity is so necessary for the functioning of the economy, vital health services, public transportation, and safety, just to name a few. Loss of service due to technology failure during smart grid deployment could cause noticeable power outages, and would increase the cost of smart grid implementation. According to a study by the National University System Institute for Policy Research, the most recent blackout in August 2011 in SDG&E's territory cost the greater San Diego region $97–118 million. This included costs in spoiled food, government overtime, and lost productivity. These figures are just for the San Diego region. They do not include the other parts of Arizona and Mexico that were without power. Americans lose about $150 billion a year due to small blackouts and brownouts.[484]

Fortunately, the technology updates being made to implement the smart grid should help improve reliability. The data utilities receive about voltages on their distributions system will allow SDG&E to plan for appropriate adjustments in the voltage on the grid in order to better optimize the system. The presence of smart meters on the distribution system, acting as smart sensors, will also assist the utility in knowing which residences and businesses are without power and can choose to deploy work crews based on the greatest need or on updated emergency contingency plans. Reliability will also increase as the grid will be able to heal itself without manual intervention. Automatic reclosers and other kinds of technology will trigger processes that will reconnect the power if it is interrupted. This greatly enhances the performance and reliability in the grid by decreasing the danger to line workers and creating less need for people to go out and reconnect the electricity when there is an outage.

Common Interoperability Standards are another piece of the smart grid puzzle that helps with reliability. Interoperability ensures "two [or more] different systems or components [are able] to communicate, share, and use information that has been exchanged without need for custom integrations or end user intervention."[485] Practically, electric utilities, home appliance manufacturers, grid component technology manufacturers, and consumers all need a uniform system. This idea is just like electric sockets. Everywhere you go within the United States you can be sure to find electric outlets that will be able to serve your various electric appliances because there are interoperability standards. You don't have to have a different adapter for everything. The smart grid needs this kind of compatibility too.

San Diego Gas & Electric has opted to take advice from the National Institute of Standards and Technology. NIST sets standards for things like exactly how much weight a pound is. It has also made suggestions for certain standards for the operation of the smart grid. SDG&E plans to follow NIST's interoperability standards in the areas of: operations, markets, service provider, bulk generation, distribution, transmission, customer, general, and security.[486] Matching the federal standards for these particular facets of grid operation will help decrease cost and increase practicable usage of smart grid technologies well into the future. It's important that these technologies can also increase incentives for customer adoption of demand response programs as well by ensuring that accurate electricity use information is being exchanged between the customers and the utility. SDG&E hopes that instituting standards for reliability and interoperability will also help control stranded costs.[487] These efforts in interoperability should also help "'prosumers (those that both produce and consume energy)"[488] connect to the grid more easily so that distributed generation is enhanced in SDG&E's service territory and beyond.

Distributed Generation

California's renewable portfolio standard calls for 33 percent renewable generation by 2020.[489] In 2006 the California senate passed the Million Solar Roofs Program.[490] Its goal is to install 3,000 mW of distributed electric solar photovoltaic systems by 2016. SDG&E hopes to install 180.3 mW of the state total. The California legislature further passed Feed-In Tariffs in 2006 and 2008 to help make solar more cost effective and feasible. In 2012, SDG&E connected "4,426 new systems (primarily solar) . . . for a total of 17,969 residential and commercial systems connected (over 1% of SDG&E's customer base)."[491]

The CPUC enacted Renewable Auction Feed-In Tariffs.[492] CPUC approved an additional 100 mWs of PV through SDG&E's Solar Energy Project. Additionally, combined heat and power projects, planned for completion by 2020, will displace about 30,000 gigawatt hours (gWh) of demand from elsewhere in the fuel mix.[493] That's roughly equivalent to the electricity needed to power 257,939 homes for a year or roughly half the annual CO_2 emissions of the average coal-fired power plant.[494]

San Diego Gas & Electric customers strongly support distributed rooftop solar. SDG&E customers have already installed more megawatts of rooftop solar in San Diego than utility customers in any other U.S. city. According to SDG&E estimates, by June 2012 SDG&E customers owned more than 137 mW of rooftop solar capacity. SDG&E's high penetration of PV is likely to require SDG&E to be a leader in using smart grid technology to address both the quantity of distributed generation on its distribution system as well as the intermittency of this growing source of generation.

Increased technology in storage and voltage control should help mitigate some of the problems that come with distributed generation. By 2020 SDG&E will likely have installed sufficient smart transformers, inverters, synchrophasors, and capacitors to control voltage and VAR fluctuations to make it an industry leader in this area. SDG&E plans to use "energy storage . . . advanced control and management . . . and solid state voltage regulation."[495] This will increase distributed generation penetration and increase efficiency.

One of the regulatory questions often raised with implementing smart grid is cost allocation. Clearly, the initial costs of deployment will be large. Initially, SDG&E filed with the CPUC to have a network usage charge (NUC) that would individualize, rather than socialize, the system costs of distributed solar generation. The charge would in essence base customers' costs on how much they use the grid. So "prosumers,"[496] customers pulling electricity from the grid *and* putting electricity back on it, would be utilizing the distribution system in a fundamentally different manner than customers that just draw from it. In January 2012, the CPUC rejected the NUC stating, "NUC would base the [distributed solar] generator customer's charges on network usage that is unrelated to net kWh consumption."[497] Basically, the commission would rather the costs for network updates to facilitate increased distributed solar generation be recovered from all the SDG&E customers, not just those who install photovoltaic solar panels. It argued that allocating costs discriminatorily to people with PV was not justified.

The NUC's filing included two other proposals: (1) a basic service fee and (2) a voluntary prepay program. First, in a PG&E rate case, the CPUC said in May, 2011, "We find no statutory restrictions categorically prohibiting a fixed residential customer charge."[498] The CPUC said they will extend that decision in deciding whether SDG&E's basic service fee is legal. In regards to the prepay program, the CPUC, in part, accepted the consumer advocates' arguments in opposition to the SDG&E proposals and asked SDG&E to remove the NUC and to provide input on the legality of the basic service fee and the voluntary prepay program. SDG&E filed a new request for approval of charged rates on February 17, 2012.[499]

According to a July 2, 2012, report in *Smart Grid Today*, SDG&E is undertaking a microgrid project that will jointly evaluate solar generation capabilities, energy storage, and customer behavior. The project, located in Borrego Springs, about ninety miles outside of San Diego, will evaluate the benefits of storage on a system that generates too much solar power for the transmission system to take out of the community. In order to smooth solar output, SDG&E will install a 0.5–1.5 mW storage system at a substation, three 25-kW by 50-kWh community energy storage sites, and three 4.5-kW by 12-kWh sites at individual customer residences. While Borrego Springs will remain grid connected, a goal of the project is to improve system reliability for the local customers. SDG&E is also testing customer behavior by installing smart appliances at 125 residential and small commercial customer sites in the area. This SDG&E initiative is jointly funded by $7.5 million from the Department of Energy and $3 million from the California Energy Commission.[500]

Estimated Costs

The full costs of SDG&E's deployment plan implementation are calculated for the 2006–20 period at $3.5–3.6 billion. They include "capital expenditures and operating and maintenance (O&M) expenses."[501] Other costs are already billed to customers in the electric rates. Included in the total is $1.042 billion for previously authorized investments, $1.424 billion for the 2012 Test Year General Rate Case, $237 million for active applications like demand response and dynamic pricing, $299–364 million for CPUC estimated incremental investments, and $466–555 million in FERC estimated incremental investments.[502] Provisional ranges for 2016–20 show that costs could be 25 percent higher or lower than the base case. This is due to external factors such as how some technologies implemented in this range may not have been developed yet, the health of the economy could get better or worsen, and that cost projections are inherently indeterminate. Cost estimates come from a number of investments like customer empowerment, renewable growth, electric vehicle (EV) growth, reliability, safety, security, operational efficiency, research and development, integrated and cross-cutting systems, and work-force development. Between July 1, 2011, and June 30, 2012, SDG&E had smart grid deployment costs that totaled $156,188,000.[503]

Estimated Benefits

San Diego Gas & Electric projects the benefits of smart grid technology deployment will significantly exceed projected costs. Between 2011 and 2020, the utility expects about $3.8–7.1 billion in overall benefits, which includes $760 million to $1.9 billion in societal and environmental benefits like a healthier environment and better quality of life.[504]

The 2012 *Smart Grid Deployment Annual Report* shows that in 2012 there were demonstrated benefits of $39,870,000.[505] SDG&E's "Benefits Framework" consists of four categories of issues:[506] The benefits include avoided emissions from energy reductions and peak load shifting, integrating centralized renewable energy, integrating distributed generation, and integrating more electric vehicles. These comprise $391 million to $1.324 billion of the total monetary benefits and about 7.7 million tons of carbon dioxide equivalent (CO2e) avoided. EVs specifically will save about $369–615 million and about 207 million gallons of gasoline. Between 2006 and 2020, SDG&E has estimated benefits for Economic and Reliability Benefits and Terminal Value. There is approximately $1.378 billion in benefits from previously authorized funding. The expected projects like the TY 2012 general rate case, active applications like demand response, and incremental investment benefits total an estimated $1.682 billion to $3.799 billion.[507]

Other benefits pertaining to reliability, security, and the environment were qualitatively counted. These benefits remain qualitative and not quantitative because they meet policy goals, they rely on technology that does not yet exist, or because they just have no widely recognized monetary value.[508] Benefits like customer empowerment have the chance to save money and prevent emissions because ideally customers will use less electricity, but customer empowerment has intrinsic value as well. The monetary values associated with customer empowerment come from installation of smart meters at the residential and commercial level, increased penetration of distributed generation like rooftop solar, and greater adoption of plug-in electric vehicles. Increased reliability through increased supervisory control and data acquisition and grid self-healing will enhance the benefits derived from customer empowerment. Customers should gain faith in the reliability of the smart grid and remain satisfied with their service with these improved monitoring technologies. Smart transformers manage electricity flow to and from residences and enable reliability. Rooftop solar and EVs are among the specific technology advancements that increase the efficiency of the grid itself but will also create other indirect benefits.[509]

Privacy

Currently, SDG&E protects its customer data via contractual agreements with its customers and third parties.[510] It also complies with local, state, and federal privacy protections. In the future, SDG&E will need to consider the heightened necessity for privacy protections with the increased amount of behavioral electricity usage data collected by smart meters. California Senate Bill 1476 enabled the CPUC to take their own initiative to require the major California IOUs (PG&E, SCE, and SDG&E) to establish their own Smart grid customer privacy policies.[511]

In addition to adopting NIST interoperability standards, SDG&E supports the "four dimensions of privacy" suggested by NIST as key components of its security and privacy programs:[512]

1. Personal information: any information relating to an individual who can be identified, directly or indirectly, by that information and in particular by reference to an identification number or to one or more factors specific to his or her physical, physiological, mental, economic, cultural, locational, or social identity
2. Personal privacy: the right to control the integrity of one's own body
3. Behavioral privacy: the right of individuals to make their own choices about what they do and to keep certain personal behaviors from being shared with others
4. Personal communications privacy: the right to communicate without undue surveillance, monitoring, or censorship[513]

San Diego Gas & Electric has become an industry leader by ensuring customer data privacy in the smart grid, including introducing privacy into its design. In a joint white paper issued with the information and privacy commissioner of Ontario, Canada, titled "Applying Privacy by Design, Best Practices to SDG&E's Smart Pricing Program," SDG&E announced its collaboration with the commissioner and acknowledged the "importance of proactively building privacy into its design." SDG&E created a position for a chief customer privacy officer and assigned a director responsible for customer privacy.[514] The utility will decide if data is absolutely necessary to collect in the first place before they collect it. If it does collect information, it will protect it with security controls that will be tested for weaknesses to prevent loss or theft of the information. Third parties will only be able to access information absolutely necessary to perform work promised for the utility under contractual obligations. SDG&E will only share customers' information with affected customers' consent. Lastly, SDG&E will continue to be held to applicable laws, regulations, and industry best practices.[515]

In the near future SDG&E intends to address the following sub-areas of customer data protection:

- Customer data collection
- Sharing and retention
- Data accuracy and reliability
- Protection against data loss or misuse
- Sharing customer information and energy data
- Third-party data usage purpose
- Information security and privacy for shared data
- Limitations and restrictions on third-party data
- Enforcement of limitations and restrictions
- Individuals' access to their data
- Audit, oversight, and enforcement mechanisms[516]

San Diego Gas & Electric continues to contract with third-party vendors like software companies. Some personally identifiable information will be used by these third party vendors to perform necessary services. SDG&E contractors will be under contractual obligation to maintain privacy. The utility must furnish third parties with "appropriate non-disclosure agreements regarding customer-related data."[517]

Specifically, to maintain privacy for customers' information, SDG&E has developed several measures to ensure security via the contracts with its vendors. SDG&E will cast a wide net over information within the term "Confidential Information." Vendors will be restricted from using confidential customer data for their own commercial benefit. The vendors themselves also must practice reasonable safety measures with onsite security evaluations. The third-party information privacy contract provisions for smart grid utility customers will remain in effect for perpetuity.[518] SDG&E will also protect customer data in its own normal operation procedures. Like all other California utilities, SDG&E has an existing procedure for auditing of SDG&E internal protocol and procedure. Safety, privacy, and security will continue to be at the forefront of planning for the smart grid. Customers' data and property must be secure in order for the smart grid to be considered a success.[519] To this end, SDG&E must be sure to enforce the third-party contract provisions that protect customer data. Consistent with CPUC policy, SDG&E is also a leader in offering its customers timely access to their data and has been a leading utility in participating with the federal government's Green Button Initiative. The CPUC has also required that California IOUs file annual privacy reports. The CPUC has also extended similar customer privacy protection requirements to electric service providers and community choice aggregators which provide competitive energy services to California IOUs customers.

San Diego Gas & Electric was the first utility in the nation to respond to the White House's challenge and commit to implementing the Green Button, which provides a standardized platform for the secure and private transfer of customer energy usage information to the customer.[520] In late 2012, SDG&E launched the service "Green Button—Connect My Data," which enables customers to choose a third-party information services provider to whom SDG&E will then securely transfer usage data. These third-party information service providers have already created over 60 Green Button applications that enable customers to access, engage with, and better understand their personalized energy use data via their computers, smart phones, and tablets.[521]

Opt-Out Policy

In March 2012, the California Public Utility Commission passed an order requiring SDG&E to have an opt-out policy for its customers who refuse installation of a smart meter.[522] The utility is allowed to charge an extra fee of up to seventy-five dollars per customer, plus ten dollars per month[523] for customers that opt-out of the installation. Opt-out fees were set by the CPUC for the initial order and "will be subject to adjustment upon conclusion of the second phase of this proceeding."[524] The decision came out of a Utility Consumers' Action Network filing to request SDG&E's AMI project be amended to include an opt-out provision for customers who are concerned about the impact of radio frequency radiation from the wireless smart meters.[525]

The utility has received far less opposition from its customer base than some other utilities have experienced.[526] Where opposition does exist in the SDG&E service territory, the concerns are because a small segment of customers fear that "the computerized meters [are] a potential privacy invasion liability, and a health risk."[527] The Utility Consumer Action Network was instrumental in getting the opt-out provision for SDG&E customers.[528] These concerns have not been widespread in SDG&E territory compared to other utilities' experiences and the CPUC has allowed SDG&E to proceed with installation but with an opt-out policy in place to address individual concerns.[529] While SDG&E had argued that customers who opt out should receive a meter that is capable of recording interval data, with any wireless communication disabled, the CPUC ultimately disagreed and required that customers that opt-out be offered more traditional analog meters. SDG&E has estimated the total number of customers who ultimately opt-out to be approximately three thousand residential customers.

Work-force Development

San Diego Gas & Electric emphasized employee reeducation and training to prepare for smart grid deployment and maintenance. It plans to continue to include local organizations and schools in creating vocational training to empower its work force with skills to support the future needs of the grid. SDG&E includes community colleges, trade schools, and universities to encourage smart grid-based curricula and training for smart grid implementation skills. Additionally, it plans to work with the San Diego Workforce Partnership and other union organizations in order to "develop agreements that are forward-thinking and collaborative."[530] Current employees will be expected to develop new skills to adapt to the new technological and business processes. Human Resources will adapt to create a flexible work force capable of providing the needs of a smart grid.[531]

There are a number of specific programs SDG&E will implement to do this. First, the Smart Grid Organizational Change Management will institute job training and employee management to develop new job skills for some employees, create some new jobs, and adopt business procedures to ensure reliability and safety while the deployment plan is instituted. Second, employees will be polled to gauge their attitudes and understanding of the various components of the new smart grid plan. Third, employees will be equipped with the new tools they need to meet the requirements of the new smart grid plan. Fourth, SDG&E is integrating hiring and training of employees with skills in electrical engineering and computer engineering. As a result, the IT and engineering departments are collaborating to provide the kind of employees ready for the integrated technology of tomorrow's grid. Fifth, SDG&E will implement tools to ensure an effective organizational shift from old practices and procedures into an evolved smart grid-ready program.[532]

This kind of focus on vocational training of its work force and collaboration with other community interests prepares SDG&E to deploy smart grid technology. SDG&E is wise to think ahead and have a work force prepared to handle the grid challenges posed by the "newer" grid technologies. This focus should keep workers safe and electric power service reliable.

Environmental Defense Fund Evaluation

In addition to its direct work with SDG&E, the EDF has been monitoring smart grid deployment in all of the California utilities under the jurisdiction of California Senate Bill 17, using the Evaluation Framework for Smart Grid Deployment Plans that it developed in consultation with national experts.[533] In August 2011, it issued "mid-term"[534] grades for the three investor-owned utilities in California, PG&E, SCE, and SDG&E.

The Evaluation Framework's guiding principles, based on the PUC decision and input from other stakeholders, were as follows:

- Smart grid deployments should seek to share costs between utilities and consumers and deliver benefits to consumers commensurate with investments.
- The smart grid should empower customers to make choices about their energy use, both to save money and to support clean energy.
- The smart grid should create a platform for a wide range of innovative energy technologies and management services.
- The smart grid should enable and support the sale of demand-side resources into wholesale energy markets, on equal footing with traditional generation resources.
- The smart grid should deliver environmental and public health benefits.

Based on these principles, EDF's framework identified eight criteria:[535]

- Asset utilization
- System losses
- Criteria pollutants
- Greenhouse gas emissions
- Renewables
- Water use
- Land use
- Solid waste

The EDF's midterm scores assigned to the California IOUs are based on the fund's evaluation of the IOUs' level of compliance with the stated goals of Senate Bill 17 in the following areas:

- Dynamic pricing options
- Demand management
- Plug and play, generation choice

- Consumer technologies
- Electric vehicles
- Information
- Customer service
- Customer bills
- Customer equity
- Data access and privacy
- Power quality and power reliability

This framework guided EDF's review of the California IOUs. Each of these criteria was discussed in at least one of the three California IOUs' deployment plans, and many were discussed in all three. However, according to EDF, creating downward pressure on customer bills, improving and supporting customer equity, reducing barriers to plug-and-play devices, expanding generation choice, expanding consumer technologies for net energy metering and expanding third-party access to data for demand-side resource sales were not discussed in any of the plans.[536] SDG&E does not fully agree with this conclusion since they believe projects within the plan, such as the Customer Energy Network, Community Solar, and Home Area Network Infrastructure and Lab, address issues such as sharing customer data with authorized third parties, expanding customer generation choices, and reducing barriers to plug-and-play devices.

Overall, EDF gave scores to PG&E, SCE, and SDG&E of C (72%), B- (80%), and B- (81%), respectively. Under EDF's framework, SDG&E and the other utilities lost points for the lack of strong environmental metrics and goals, though EDF found that the other sections of their plans were carefully thought out and well crafted. For example, according to EDF's analysis, "words such as 'more' and 'better' and 'most' were used rather than quantity words like 'all' or 'X %' or 'Y number of customers'— therefore it will be difficult to use the roadmap sections to inform actual deployments or track whether deployments are delivering the promised benefits."[537] SDG&E responded to its score saying, "We are currently reviewing the EDF scorecard and will be looking for ways that we can improve our score as we move forward with our smart grid Deployment Plans."[538] In a recent CPUC filing, EDF recommended adoption of SDG&E's and the other utilities' plans, with the understanding that the environmental metrics and goals would be developed under a different proceeding.[539, 540] Third parties who evaluate smart grid deployments for other utilities in the future can use a framework like this, which lets the utility clearly see what will be expected from the evaluation in advance. Then the utility can work with stakeholders and the third-party evaluators to increase positive performance on selected principles like safety, privacy, and environmental responsibility.[541]

In support of additional transparency on smart grid implementation, the CPUC has required that the California IOUs file annual reports on a variety of smart grid implementation metrics which were to be further developed in a series of technical working groups.

Observations and Lessons Learned

Focus on the Big Picture

The state of California is advanced in its deployment of smart grid technology. The elements of the smart grid are gears in a rather large machine that enable benefits for the utilities, customers, and the environment. But, the pieces individually are not worth the same as the sum of their parts. SDG&E has begun to assemble various parts of the smart grid such as time-of-use rates, plug-in electric vehicles, and automated demand response to work together to provide storage, decreased peak energy use, and energy efficiency in one package. According to analyses of smart grid benefits, a utility that deploys the smart grid successfully will see the potential for vast improvements for operations, reliability, and environmental improvement.[542]

For example, looking forward, the state of California and SDG&E both have placed importance on interoperability standards. This focus on standards has the potential to ensure that the smart grid investments made today are compatible with the investments other utilities will make all over the country, now and into the future. This will help ensure that customers have a smooth experience whether in California's service territories or elsewhere.

Clear Policies and Goals Lead to Innovative Results

San Diego Gas & Electric has benefitted from clear expectations and guidelines in its plans for the smart grid.[543] This is of course, part of the "big picture" mentioned above, but it is especially important for state legislatures and public utilities commissions to understand. Senate Bill 17 and the subsequent CPUC decision clearly set out for the California IOUs goals to plan how smart grid technology and services should follow. Similar to utilities across the country, the California IOUs must get CPUC approval to increase rates. The commission only approves rates that are prudent, just, and reasonable.[544] Smart grid investments are very capital intensive and a utility must obtain the approval of its public utility commission for cost recovery of smart grid investments in the rate base. A utility making smart grid investments must have clear policy goals and have a high level of assurance that they are making a prudent investment.

One primary reason why SDG&E has been able to develop and effectively begin to implement such a comprehensive smart grid deployment plan is because the state of California gave such clear guidance for the CPUC to follow to create an environment where the California electric corporations can be highly confident that they will be able to recover the costs of their smart grid investments.[545] The state of California passed a comprehensive law that set the clear expectations and smart grid goals.[546] Then, the CPUC followed up on this legislative policy with clear guidelines for what was expected from the IOUs in their smart grid deployment plans.[547]

These guidelines required very comprehensive plans from the utilities that would then be subject to review and approval by the CPUC. Once the utilities got this guidance from the CPUC, they were able to be innovative with their plans for smart grid deployment while understanding that their plans were consistent with state policy. They all submitted very comprehensive smart grid deployment plans for the commission's review and approval.[548] The California utilities are now able to make technology investments in the smart grid with little anticipation that their actions will be second guessed, especially in regards to policies and goals. This kind of leadership from the state government should ultimately result in earlier and more successful smart grid implementation; the example of SDG&E has begun to demonstrate clear benefits.

Advanced Customer Education Enhances Customer Acceptance

Smart grid implementation has not always been without controversy in California. For Pacific Gas & Electric, another California IOU, one of the biggest obstacles to its smart grid deployment has been the backlash of its customers. It has received so much public attention that there's a term for it—the "Bakersfield Effect"—which spawned from PG&E's first attempt at rolling out smart meters. Their initial installation was in the heat of the summer, so some customers believed they experienced higher bills once they installed smart meters. As an example the media reported that one seventy-one-year-old woman's bill shot up from $55.52 in April to $222.20 in July 2009.[549] A subsequent CPUC-required audit of the PG&E meters determined that the meters were accurate, but that did not prevent further complaints about health and privacy issues.

San Diego Gas & Electric is seemingly more fortunate because it has a customer base that is largely approving of, and willing to accept, its smart grid deployment goals. Because it has the highest penetration of EVs and rooftop solar in the country, SDG&E has both high customer acceptance of new technologies as well as special technical challenges. While, the SDG&E customer base has been mostly in favor of increased investments in the smart grid, SDG&E deserves some of this credit given that one of the key pieces of the SDG&E deployment plan is its communication with their customers and the communities that they operate within about the process and how it affects all stakeholders. Furthermore, SDG&E communicated with customers and community members in its service territory for years before filing their deployment plan with the CPUC.

Specifically, the utility worked to educate its customers about the environmental and cost benefits of smart meters well before they started to deploy them. SDG&E made an effort to communicate on an individual customer basis by sending out information and notification when the utility was preparing to install smart meters. The utility was careful to speak to customers about the issues that affect them closely and identify the issues customers are interested in. Not surprisingly, customers have not shown much interest in the synchrophasors on the electric lines, but they do care about reliability and functionality. One more important opportunity for the utility to communicate with customers is dynamic pricing. Customers who opt into time-of-use rates are best served by being educated about the ways dynamic pricing can benefit their pocketbook and the environment.[550] Likely because of its efforts to communicate and be transparent, SDG&E has not experienced significant customer backlash for the integration of smart grid technologies,[551] with the noted exception of building and siting larger scale projects such as the Sunrise Powerlink.[552]

Increased Transparency Through Third-Party Evaluation

The California IOUs have benefited by the third-party evaluation of the smart grid implementation plans by the Environmental Defense Fund. Having a credible, independent third party evaluate utility smart grid implementation plans is something that other regions should consider in order to both improve on implementation and increase customer acceptance of the plan. Building upon the work of the EDF in California, third-party evaluators can utilize a developed framework for evaluation of smart grid deployment plans, which can be modified to incorporate the state or regional goals for things like renewable energy portfolio standards, electric vehicle integration, reliability, and privacy. Independent third parties can provide the utility with useful feedback and at the same time it can also help educate and inform the public about the project's goals and utility's implementation plan.

San Diego Gas & Electric's implementation plan, coupled with clear state policy goals, place SDG&E in a national leadership role for comprehensive smart grid implementation. While SDG&E's experience to date represents significant progress, the Electric Power Research Institute has estimated that, nationally, fully implementing a smart electric grid will cost between $1.3 and $2.0 trillion, with benefits likely exceeding costs by a factor of three or more.[553] For SDG&E this suggests the opportunity for a significant amount of additional investment to be made in future years and will involve ongoing negotiation with regulators and other parties.

Research from Pacific Northwest National Laboratory has estimated that with full implementation of a smart electric grid by 2030 U.S. energy consumption and carbon emissions could be reduced by 12 percent.[554] Yet as noted previously, it will take time to develop and offer additional technologies and rates to customers. In some areas, however, the smart grid will likely spur greater electricity use, such as smart charging of electric vehicles, in order to achieve efficiencies in total energy use across the economy. Continued investment in automation of the utility distribution system will offer future opportunities for improving reliability and optimizing energy use. Furthermore, as renewable energy reaches higher levels of development across the utility service territory, greater investment in smart grid technologies will be needed in order to reliably and cost-effectively manage these resources.

APPENDIX II: A MODEL PRIVACY POLICY FOR SMART GRID DATA

INTRODUCTION AND USE OF THIS POLICY

Advanced metering infrastructure and other emerging Smart Grid technologies have the potential to revolutionize the ways in which Utilities provide services to their Customers. Such technologies can

- improve reliable electric service,
- reduce Utility operating expenses,
- reduce Customer cost, and
- help Customers make informed choices that could reduce their electricity consumption.

One of the advances of the Smart Grid is that it enables the collection and reporting of individualized granular data about Customer electricity demand. Despite these manifest benefits, however, electric Customers have legitimate concerns regarding the manner in which such data is collected and how it is used. They want to preserve the privacy of their personal information.

The goals of implementing a more intelligent and responsive electric infrastructure and maintaining Customer privacy are not mutually exclusive. What is required is a policy or set of rules and procedures that govern how information is used and collected, and which prevents misuse or public disclosure. Such a policy will act as a roadmap for Utilities responsibly to implement Smart Grid technology while providing their Customers with the assurance that concrete, identifiable safeguards are in place to protect personal information.

The authors hope that the following Model Privacy Policy will provide a foundation for Customer dialogue and a starting point for Utilities to develop their own policy, adapted to the needs of their Customers and the regulatory environment of their jurisdiction(s).[1]

§ I. Statement of Policy

It shall be the policy of the Utility to preserve the privacy of Customer personally identifying information (PII), as defined in § 2 below, to the maximum extent possible. The Utility shall use all reasonable means to ensure (1) that only that PII which is reasonably necessary for the Utility to provide services to Customers is collected and retained, (2) that any PII collected is accessed only by those Utility employees and Independent Contractors who have a legitimate business need connected to the provision of Utility services to Customers, for such data, (3) that PII is not disseminated outside of the Utility except to the extent necessary to provide Utility services to the Customers, (4) that prior written notification and, where possible, prior consent, be given to any Customer before his or her PII is released to a third party, (5) that Confidential Information, with or without PII, be kept confidential and released only to the extent necessary to provide Utility services, (6) that Confidential Information be made available to the Customer or the Customers for whom such data was collected, or to that Customer's designee upon reasonable notice and request, and (7) that appropriate safeguards, including technological/cybersecurity, employee screening, training and monitoring, and administrative procedures, be implemented to protect the privacy of Customer information, including PII, to the maximum extent possible.

§ II. Definitions

A. Confidential Information: Confidential Information consists of the following three groups of data:

1. **Anonymous Personal Usage Information:** Anonymous personal usage data is any information that is collected, received, and/or stored by the Utility regarding the electrical demand and/or usage habits of individual Customers or small groups of Customers that either explicitly or implicitly reveals details, patterns, or other insights into the personal lives, characteristics, or activities of individual Customers or members of the group but which does not reveal the identity of the consumer or group from whom the information was collected.

   Such information shall not be considered anonymous if it contains Personally Identifiable Information or any other information from which a third party could reasonably deduce the identity of the Customer or Customers for who such data is collected.

2. **Personally Identifiable Information:** PII includes specific items of information that reveal, or reasonably could be expected to reveal, the identity of an individual or small group of Utility Customers, including the following:

   i. Names
   ii. All geographic subdivisions smaller than a county, including street address, city, county, precinct, zip code, and their equivalent geo-codes
   iii. All elements of dates directly related to an individual
   iv. Telephone or fax numbers
   v. Electronic mail addresses
   vi. Social Security numbers
   vii. Account numbers (including energy bill account numbers, credit card numbers, bank account numbers, etc.)
   viii. Any information received in the credit check processes and any unique personally identifying information related to finances
   ix. Certificate and license numbers
   x. Network/Internet protocol address, LAN, and other unique digital networking information
   xi. Device identifiers and serial numbers
   xii. Biometric identifiers, including finger and voice prints
   xiii. Photographic images and any comparable images that could identify an individual Customer
   xiv. Any other unique identifying number, characteristic, or code

3. **Private Customer Information:** Any information that combines PII with Anonymous Personal Usage Information or which otherwise could allow individual Customer electricity usage data and/or behavioral habits to be attributed to an identifiable Customer or small group of Customers.

B. Non-Confidential Information: Confidential Information consists of the following two groups of data:

1. **Public Information:** Any nonprivileged or non–Personally Identifiable Information prepared, owned, used, or retained by the Utility that is required or intended to be disclosed or made available to the public. This information may include general characteristics of the Utility's total load and generation mix as well as general information regarding rates and programs.

2. **Aggregate Use Data:** Aggregate Use Data refers to information regarding the usage habits of utility Customers or broad categories of Customers (e.g., industrial business, residential) where the information is collected from a sufficiently large group of Customer so as to make it highly improbable that the person receiving such information could deduce the identities and/or electricity usage habits of individual Customers within the group for which the information has been aggregated.

C. Third Parties

1. **Vendors:** An entity selling products or services to the Utility's Customers that does not directly provide services to the Utility in the Utility's ordinary course of business.
2. **Independent Contractors:** An entity or person performing a function or service under contract with or on behalf of the Utility, such as billing, Customer service, demand response, payroll services, or other functions related to providing reliable electric service.

D. Customer(s): Customers means any person, corporation, government or other legal entity to which the Utility provides electricity and/or ancillary services or from whom the Utility collects Confidential Information. For purposes of this Policy, "Customer" includes person or entities that receive such services regardless of whether they have a contractual relationship with the Utility or pay compensation for the services received.

§ III. Customer Privacy and Other Rights

A. Collection of Customer Confidential Information

1. Before collecting any new confidential information from Customers or implementing any programs or systems that automatically collect Confidential Information, the Utility shall determine what Confidential Information is reasonably necessary to effectively implement Smart Grid technology.
2. Consistent with cost considerations and available technology, the Utility shall endeavor to collect only that Confidential Information identified as reasonably necessary in subparagraph A(1) above.
3. Before the Utility begins collecting any Confidential Information, the Utility shall make available to Customers a summary of the types of Confidential Information that will be collected and the reason(s). This summary shall be posted on the Utility's Internet site, updated

at regular intervals to reflect changes in technology or Confidential Information collection practices, and made available to Customers upon request.

B. Customer Right of Access

1. Customers shall be entitled to access their own Private Customer Information within a reasonable time after the Utility collects and verifies the data. This information will be presented in an easily readable format that is as detailed as the information that the Utility uses in providing its services to the Customer. The Utility will make reasonable efforts to ensure that Customers have options regarding how they receive such information from the Utility, such as postal mail, electronic mail, and so on.
2. The Utility will provide Customers with access to their own Confidential Information through a convenient, user-friendly Internet website interface.
3. Customers shall have the right to know what personal information the Utility maintains about the Customer. The Utility will make a reasonable effort to respond to requests for such information within five business days of being contacted by the Customer.

C. Customer Right to Accuracy

1. The Utility shall ensure that the information it collects, stores, uses, and discloses is reasonably accurate and complete and otherwise compliant with applicable rules and tariffs regarding the quality of energy usage data.
2. Customers shall have the opportunity to dispute the accuracy or completeness of Confidential Information, including Private Customer Information, that the Utility has collected for that Customer. The Utility will provide adequate procedures for Customers to dispute the accuracy of their Confidential Information, and request appropriate corrections or amendments.

D. Customer Right to Privacy

1. Except as provided in Section IV of this Model Policy, the Utility shall not disclose any Confidential Information (including Anonymous Personal Usage Information, Personally Identifying Information or Private Customer Information) to any person or entity, including Utility employees and Contractors.

E. Customer Right to Disclose Confidential Information

1. Notwithstanding any other provision of this Policy, Customers shall have the option to share their Confidential Information with third parties (e.g., service providers that facilitate compatible devices, technologies, and appliances that augment the visibility, understanding, and control of electricity consumption). The Utility shall implement procedures for allowing Customers to share such information, including electronic copies of their Private Customer information or through "click through" or "green button" technology.

2. Whenever a Customer requests access to their own Confidential Information, whether electronically or in writing, the Utility may require that the Customer agree that the Customer is solely responsible for the information that the Customer chooses to disclose any information that the third party thereafter makes of such information.

3. Whenever the Utility allows Customers to transfer information directly from the Utility to a third party through "click through" or "green button" technology, the Utility shall disclose to the Customer the specific elements of Confidential Information that are to be released in order to allow the Customer to make an informed decision prior to releasing such information to the third party.

F. Customer Right to Information Education

1. The Utility shall implement a continuing Customer education program. This program shall offer informational materials to Customers regarding Smart Grid technology, the ways in which Customer Confidential Information is being used, the procedures by which Confidential Information may be shared, and guidance for making informed and responsible decisions regarding information sharing with third parties.

2. The Privacy Officer designated by the Utility in accordance with § VI(A) of this Policy shall have primary responsibility for designing and overseeing the continuing Customer education program set forth in §III(F)(1) and shall have discretion in designing a program that is cost effective and tailored to the needs of the Utility's various Customer bases.

§ IV. Permitted Disclosure of Customer Information and Procedures

A. Disclosure to Utility Employees/Employee Access

1. The Utility will limit access by its officers and employees to Confidential Information so that each employee or Contractor has

access only to the information that is needed to perform their
assigned duties.

2. Prior to granting officers and employees access to Confidential Information, the Utility shall ensure that the employee or officer satisfied
all of the requirements of § 5(B). These requirements can be satisfied either as during a new employee or officer's hiring and orientation process or prior to an existing employee or, in the case of an
officer or employee whose previous duties did not involve access to
Confidential Information, prior to being assigned new duties that do
involve such access.

3. The Utility shall require officer and employees to surrender all Confidential Information, including duplicate or electronic copies, promptly
upon their departure from Utility employment or reassignment to position that does not require access to Confidential Information to perform their regularly assigned duties. The Utility shall implement and
the Privacy Officer shall enforce procedures sufficient to verify compliance with this paragraph.

B. Disclosure to Contractors and Vendors

1. The Utility may share Confidential Information with Contractors
and Vendors only to the extent necessary for such Contractor or
Vendor to carry out services requested by the Utility. Before sharing
such information, the Utility shall determine what information/type
of information is necessary for the Contractor or Vendor to provide
their service and limit disclosure to such information.

2. Before disclosing any Confidential Information to a Contractor or
Vendor, the Utility shall require the Contractor or Vendor to certify
in writing that they have read, understand, and will comply with all
requirements of this Privacy Policy in the same manner as if they
were employees of the Utility. As a precondition to disclosure, all
such Vendors and Contractors shall sign a nondisclosure agreement
that specifically provides that Utility Customers are intended third-
party beneficiaries of the nondisclosure agreement.

3. The Utility shall take the appropriate action, including considering
appropriate legal action, in the event of breach of contract by any
third party who violates any provision of the contract regarding Customer privacy.

4. The Utility shall require that all Contractors and Vendors who seek
access to Confidential Information have policies, procedures and
technological safeguards in place sufficient to prevent the misuse
and/or improper or unauthorized dissemination of Confidential

Information. The Utility shall verify the existence and efficacy of such procedures before first releasing confidential Information to the Contractor or Vendor and then at regular intervals thereafter.

C. Disclosure of Non-Confidential Information to Other Third Parties

1. When authorized, but not required, by law, the Utility may disclose Information, other than Confidential Information, to government agencies, researchers, or other entities who request access to such Information. To the fullest extent allowable by law, the Utility shall ensure that only Non-Confidential Information is shared without the prior written consent of the Customer or Customers.

D. Disclosures Required by Law

1. To the fullest extent allowable by law, the Utility will comply with all obligations to provide Information, including Confidential Information in the following manner:
   a. **General Information/Freedom of Information Act (FOIA):** The Utility will only respond to a request for Information made pursuant to a FOIA or analogous statute with Non-Confidential Information.
   b. **Customer Specific Confidential Information/Warrants:** The Utility shall comply with requests for Confidential Information when such information is demanded through valid legal process, such as through a warrant or subpoena. Upon receipt of a warrant, the Utility shall:

      i.   Notify the Customer(s) whose information has been demanded or requested of the demand or request and transmit to the Customer(s) a copy of the document containing the demand or request within three (3) days after first receiving it unless such notification is precluded by court order or other law.

      ii. Cooperate with the Customer(s) in seeking an extension of time to respond to the demand or request so that the Customers(s) can assert their interests through an appropriate hearing or motion.

      iii. Nothing contained in § IV(E)(1)(b)(i) and (ii) shall preclude or in any way diminish the right of the Utility to object to, move to quash, oppose or seek qualifications such as a protective order to the demand or request.

E. Disclosure to Other Third Parties/Customer Consent Required

1. The Utility shall not disclose Confidential Information to a third party other than those enumerated in § IV(A), (B), (C), and (D) of this Policy without the prior express consent of the Customer(s) from whom the Confidential Information was collected.

   a. **Form of Consent:** Customer consent shall be effective only if it is:

      i. given after a full disclosure of the material facts, specifically including the identity of the third party to which the information is disclosed, the use that third party intends to make of the Confidential Information, and any limits on the use and further disclosure of the Confidential information imposed by the Utility;

      ii. given in writing, including electronic approval, by the Customer; and

      iii. identifies by name the Third Parties to whom it applies.

   b. **Consent Forms Prepared by the Utility:** If the Utility uses its own form to obtain Customer consent, that form must be transmitted to the Customer separate from all other correspondence from the Utility, must specifically identify the name of the third party to whom the data will be disclosed, and must contain a statement advising the Customer of its right to revoke consent and the procedures for so doing.

   c. **No inference of Consent from Silence:** In no case shall silence by the Customer ever be construed to mean they are giving express or implied consent to a request by the Utility or third party.

   d. **No Penalty for Withholding Consent:** The utility shall not withhold any service, or impose any other penalty on a Customer based in whole or in part on that Customer's failure or refusal to provide the Utility with written consent to share Confidential Information with third-party Vendors.

   e. **Revocation:** Subject to agreements with third parties, a Customer has the right to revoke, at any time, any previously granted authorization to transfer Confidential Information to a third party.

   f. Upon receipt of revocation from a Customer, the Utility shall have a reasonable period of time, not to exceed one full billing cycle, to cease further disclosure of that Customer's Confidential information.

2. The Utility will be responsible for any breach of agreement with a third party that results from the Customer's decision to stop sharing Confidential Information with an authorized third party.

3. When a Customer is enrolled in a voluntary program wherein the Customer shares Confidential Information with the Utility or its Contractors, the Utility will contact the Customer once every calendar year to inform the Customer of the authorization granted and to provide an opportunity for revocation.

§ V. Privacy Safeguards

A. Comprehensive Information Technology Security Systems

1. Prior to implementing any plan that calls for the collection of Confidential Information, the Utility shall investigate options for deploying a Comprehensive Information Technology Security System (CITSS), which integrates hardware, software, and human resources at all points along the data lifecycle, to prevent the misuse or disclosure of Confidential Information.

2. Following completion of the investigation required by § V(A)(1) and prior to the collection of any Confidential Information, the Utility shall select a CITSS that is secure according to industry practices and best practices for data storage.

    a. Provided that any system selected meets industry standards and best practices, the Utility shall have discretion in selecting a CITSS and may balance costs against incremental improvements in information security.

    b. In selecting and implementing a CITSS, the Utility shall consider implementing the following features:

    i. Systems that store Confidential Information separately from other information possessed by the Utility.

    ii. Systems that store Confidential Information offline so as to prevent outside security breaches.

    iii. Systems that compartmentalize and separate Confidential Information in such a way that breach of one system, or access to one system, will not give access to all Confidential Information (i.e., systems that segregate and firewall either different type of confidential information, or which store Confidential Information from different regions separately).

    iv. Systems that employ a high level of encryption and require multiple-step authentication to access.

    v. Systems that can detect and respond to breaches rapidly.

    vi. Systems which are secure at all points in the data lifecycle, including at the point of collection on the Customer's premises.

     vii. Systems that securely dispose of, or securely transfer offline any Confidential Information no longer needed by the Utility to provide services.

    viii. Systems that incorporate any other features that either are considered standard in the industry, or which are recommended by the Utility's experts or consultants.

3. Following implementation of a CITSS, the Utility shall retain an independent consultant to test and make recommendations regarding the CITSS. The Utility shall correct any serious deficiencies in the CITSS identified by the consultant as potentially placing Confidential Information at risk and shall consider any recommended, non-essential improvements.

B. Employee/Third-Party Contractor Security

1. **Criminal Background Check:** Officers, employees, and Contractors whose job descriptions require access to Confidential Information shall undergo a criminal background check before gaining access to such Confidential Information. Any prior misdemeanor or felony violation related to privacy or which involved dishonesty or moral turpitude shall disqualify that Officer, employee, and Contractor from access. The Utility shall have discretion to refuse to grant access to any person regardless of criminal background.

2. **Training and Procedures:** The Utility shall implement procedures training protocols designed to maximize the security of Confidential Information at all points in the data lifecycle, including data collection, storage, use, retention and disposal and shall train all employees and third-party Contractors in these procedures prior to granting access to Confidential Information.

    a. The Utility shall evaluate and update its privacy procedures and training materials at regular intervals to account for new technologies and developments. When such updates or changes are made, the Utility shall require officers, employees, and Contractors who have been granted access to Confidential Information to familiarize themselves with the updates or changes as a condition to continued access.

    b. The Utility shall implement a procedure for the prompt initiation of an investigation and, if appropriate, discipline, of any officer, employee, or third party who causes Confidential Information to be disclosed to unauthorized individuals. The Utility's employee discipline policy, shall allow for, but need not require, the termination of any officer, employee, or third party found to have intentionally or recklessly disclosed Confidential Information to unauthorized persons. No provisions of this subsection shall preclude the Utility from handling negligent or inadvertent disclosures of Confidential Information through its existing employee discipline or performance review policies.

   c. The Utility shall inform officers, employees and Third Parties of potentially severe consequences of unauthorized disclosure of Confidential Information during training.

3. **Nondisclosure Agreement:** Prior to being granted access to any Confidential Information, all persons identified in §V(B)(1) shall be required to execute a nondisclosure agreement preventing that officer, employee, or Contractor from disclosing Customer Confidential information to third parties without authorization.

§ VI. Controls and Audits

A. Privacy Officer: The Utility will identify an officer or employee to be responsible for implementing and reviewing Utility privacy procedures. This may be a new employee or delegated to an existing employee.

1. The Privacy Officer shall have primary responsibility for all aspects of Information security, including
   a. overseeing the implementation, maintenance and improvement of the CITSS, described in § V(A);
   b. drafting security and training protocols and ensuring enforcement of their provisions;
   c. identifying officers, employees, and third parties subject to trainings and ensuring each are properly trained;
   d. ensuring the surrender of Confidential Information by officers, employees, and Contractors who no longer require access to such information;
   e. overseeing the secure destruction of obsolete or unnecessary Confidential Information;
   f. overseeing the Utility's response to any unauthorized access or use of Confidential Information or breach of the systems in which such information is stored;
   g. overseeing audits or inspections of the CITSS as provided for by this Policy; and
   h. performing any other duties deemed appropriate for this position as determined by the Utility.

2. The Privacy Officer shall report to the Utility's executive leadership or Board at periodic intervals not to exceed one year regarding the status of the Utility's privacy safeguards and CITSS and shall make recommendations and proposals regarding privacy improvement.
3. The Privacy Officer shall have overall responsibility for ensuring the timely provision of reasonably complete and accurate reports to Customers covering disclosures required by this Policy.

B. Privacy Impact Assessment (PIA) and Annual Review

1. **Privacy Impact Assessment:** The Utility shall complete a structured and reliable analysis of how the Utility handles information relating to or about individuals or groups of individuals. The assessment generates a report, similar to an audit report, describing the types of privacy risks discovered based upon each privacy category, documents the findings, and then provides recommendations for mitigating the privacy risk findings. Goals of the PIA include:
   a. Determining whether the Utility's information handling and use complies with legal, regulatory, and policy requirements regarding privacy
   b. Determining the risks and effects of collecting, maintaining, and disseminating information in identifiable or clear text form in an electronic information system or groups of systems
   c. Examining and evaluating the protections and alternative processes for handling information to mitigate the identified potential privacy risks

2. **Annual Review:** The Privacy Officer shall undertake an annual review of the Utility's information collection, storage, disclosure, and destruction procedures. The annual review will also take into account developments or advancements in security technology or practices. Copies of the PIA and annual review shall be presented to the Utility's executive leadership or Board and, after being edited to remove any information that could enable unauthorized access to or use of Confidential Information, shall be made available to Customers upon request.

C. Independent Audit

1. The Utility will establish a procedure for a bi-annual independent audit of its information collection, storage, disclosure, and destruction practices. The Utility will also require that Third Parties granted access to Confidential Information either participate in the independent

audit or follow similar, adequate, procedures for independent auditing of these practices.

2. Notwithstanding the provisions of § VI(C)(1), in the event of a breach of the Utility's CITSS or other unauthorized access to or disclosure of Confidential Information, the Utility shall within two weeks after discovering that a breach or unauthorized access/use has occurred, cause an independent audit to be conducted into the cause of the breach or unauthorized access/use and take corrective measures based on the conclusions of that audit.

D. Mitigation and Customer Notification in the Event of Breach

1. As soon as practicable, but no longer than within one week after discovering that a breach or unauthorized access/use of Confidential Information has occurred, the Utility shall notify all of its Customers of the breach and any information that may have been compromised or disclosed as a result thereof. The Utility also shall provide regular updates to its Customers regarding the status of mitigation efforts, including data recovery efforts and system strengthening until the problems that caused the breach have been identified and remedied.

2. In the event of a breach of the CITSS or unauthorized access to or disclosure of Confidential Information occurs, the Utility shall take all reasonable measures, including cooperating fully with law enforcement agencies, to recover lost information and prevent the loss of further Confidential Information.

NOTES

CHAPTER 1

1. Electric Power Research Institute, *Estimating the Costs and Benefits of the Smart Grid: A Preliminary Estimate of the Investment Requirements and Resultant Benefits of Fully Functioning Smart Grid* (Palo Alto, Calif.: EPRI, 2011), 4-3, http://www.epri.com/abstracts/Pages/ProductAbstract.aspx?ProductId=000000000001022519&Mode=download/ (accessed August 11, 2013).

2. Analysis Group for Advanced Energy Economy, *U.S. Electric Power Industry: Context and Structure*, 2011, 3, http://www.aee.net/4E9B6D20-9939-11E1-B2BB000C29CA3AF3/; Energy Information Administration, *The Changing Structure of the Power Industry 2000: An Update* (Washington, D.C.: Department of Energy, 2000), 109–17, http://www.eia.gov/cneaf/electricity/chg_stru_update/update2000.pdf/.

3. Richard Munson, *From Edison to Enron: The Business of Power and What It Means for the Future of Electricity* (Westport, Conn.: Praeger, 2005), 129.

4. Ibid., 152.

5. National Science Board, *Science and Engineering Indicators* (Arlington, Va.: National Science Foundation, 2012), appendix table 4-16, http://www.nsf.gov/statistics/seind12/pdf/seind12.pdf/.

6. David Fribush, Scudder Parker, and Shawn Enterline, *Electric Evolution: Issues Posed and Opportunities Presented by Emergence of the Smart Grid* (Burlington: Vermont Energy Investment, 2010), 9.

7. R. G. Pratt, P. J. Balducci, C. Gerkensmeyer, and S. Katipamula, *The Smart Grid: An Estimation of the Energy and CO_2 Benefits* (Richland, Wash.: PNNL, 2010), 2.2, http://www.veic.org/Libraries/Resumes/Smart_Grid.sflb.ashx/.

8. Energy Information Administration, *Annual Energy Review 2011* (Washington, D.C.: U.S. Department of Energy, 2013), 304, http://www.eia.gov/totalenergy/data/annual/pdf/aer.pdf/.

9. Department of Energy, *Smart Grid Investment Grant Program: Progress Report* (Washington, D.C.: Department of Energy, 2012), ii, http://energy.

gov/sites/prod/files/Smart%20Grid%20Investment%20Grant%20 Program%20%20Progress%20Report%20July%202012.pdf/.

10. Environmental Defense Fund, *Keys to Smart Grid Success: Lessons from Texas and California,* http://www.edf.org/sites/default/files/smart-grid-keys -to-success.pdf/ (accessed July 3, 2013).

11. Munson, *From Edison to Enron,* 3, 132.

12. Fribush, Parker, and Enterline, *Electric Evolution,* 1.

13. World Coal Association, "Coal Mining and the Environment," *World Coal Association,* http://www.worldcoal.org/coal-the-environment/coal-mining -the-environment/ (accessed August 9, 2013); J. Daniel Arthur, Brian Bohm, and Mark Layne, *Hydraulic Fracturing Considerations for Natural Gas Wells of the Marcellus Shale* (Tulsa, Okla.: ALL Consulting, 2008), 13–16, http://www.dec.ny.gov/docs/materials_minerals_pdf/GWPCMarcellus.pdf/.

14. Munson, *From Edison to Enron,* 133, 141; Energy Information Administration, *Annual Energy Review 2011,* 219. It should be noted that some cogeneration facilities—those that capture waste heat to warm buildings or for other industrial purposes—can achieve efficiencies of up to 80 percent. Munson, *From Edison to Enron,* 141.

15. Lisa Schwartz, *Smart Policies Before Smart Grids: How State Regulators Can Steer Investments Toward Customer-Side Solutions* (Montpelier, Vt.: Regulatory Assistance Project, 2010), 5–338; Electric Power Research Institute, *The Green Grid: Energy Savings and Carbon Emissions Reductions Enabled by a Smart Grid* (Palo Alto, Calif.: EPRI, 2008), 5-1, http://aceee.org/files/ proceedings/2010/data/papers/2070.pdf/.

16. Energy Information Administration, *Annual Energy Review 2011,* 224 (based on a ten-year average between 2000 and 2010).

17. Ibid., 309; Environmental Protection Agency, *Inventory of U.S. Greenhouse Gas Emissions and Sinks: 1990–2011* (Washington, D.C.: EPA, 2013), 2-1, http://www.epa.gov/climatechange/Downloads/ghgemissions/US-GHG -Inventory-2013-Main-Text.pdf/ (U.S. calculations are based on a ten-year trend between 2000 and 2010); T. A. Boden, G. Marland, and R. J. Andres, *Global, Regional, and National Fossil-Fuel CO2 Emissions* (Oak Ridge, Tenn.: Department of Energy, 2010), http://cdiac.ornl.gov/trends/emis/tre_glob.html/.

18. Intergovernmental Panel on Climate Change, *Climate Change 2007: Synthesis Report* (Valencia, Spain: IPCC, 2007), 37, http://www.ipcc.ch/pdf/ assessment-report/ar4/syr/ar4_syr.pdf/.

19. Ibid., 30–31.

20. Ibid., 39.

21. Alan S. Miller, Robert V. Percival, Christopher H. Schroeder, and James P. Leape, *Environmental Regulation: Law, Science, and Policy,* 6th ed. (New York: Aspen Publishers, 2009), 1137.

22. "A Sensitive Matter," *Economist,* March 30, 2013, http://www.economist .com/news/science-and-technology/21574461-climate-may-be -heating-up-less-response-greenhouse-gas-emissions/.

23. Ibid., 30.

24. Ibid., 45. This figure is relative to sea levels between 1980 and 1999.

25. Ibid.

26. Ibid., 46.

27. Energy Information Administration, *Emissions of Greenhouse Gases in the United States* (Washington, D.C.: Department of Energy, 2010), 41, 44; Energy Information Administration, *Annual Energy Review 2011*, 314–16.

28. Charles T. Driscoll, G. B. Lawrence, Art Bulger, Tom Butler, Chris Cronan, Chris Eagar, Kathleen Lambert, Gene Likens, John Stoddard, and Kathleen Weathers, *Acid Rain Revisited: Advances in Scientific Understanding Since the Passage of the 1970 and 1990 Clean Air Act Amendments* (n.p., N.H.: Hubbard Brook Research Foundation, 2001), 12–17, http://www.hubbardbrook .org/6-12_education/Glossary/AcidRain.pdf/.

29. American Lung Association, *Toxic Air: The Case for Cleaning Up Coal-Fired Power Plants*, 2011, 4, http://www.lung.org/assets/documents/healthy-air/ toxic-air-report.pdf/; National Ambient Air Quality Standards for Particulate Matter, 78 Fed. Reg. 3086, 3103–04 (January 15, 2013), http://www .gpo.gov/fdsys/pkg/FR-2013-01-15/pdf/2012-30946.pdf/; Environmental Protection Agency, *Regulatory Impact Analysis for the Final Mercury and Air Toxic Standards* (Research Triangle Park, N.C.: EPA, 2011), 5-29–5-36, http://www.epa.gov/mats/pdfs/20111221MATSfinalRIA.pdf/.

30. Environmental Protection Agency, *Regulatory Impact Analysis*, 5-83–5-89.

31. Regulatory Finding on the Emissions of Hazardous Air Pollutants from Electric Utility Steam-Generating Units, 65 Fed. Reg. 79,825, 79,827 (2000), http://www.gpo.gov/fdsys/pkg/FR-2000-12-20/pdf/00-32395.pdf/.

32. Electric Power Research Institute, *Green Grid*, 10-1.

33. Ibid., 9-1–9-4.

34. Pratt et al., *Smart Grid*, 2.2.

35. Ibid., 3.3.

36. Electric Power Research Institute, *Green Grid*, 10-4. This calculation (and all subsequent calculations associated with the EPRI study) assumes that total electricity sales in 2030 will be 4,276 billion kWh. Energy Information Administration, *Annual Energy Outlook 2013* (Washington, D.C.: Department of Energy, 2013), 138.

37. Energy Information Administration, *Annual Energy Outlook 2013*, 155. This calculation assumes that the electric power sector will emit 2,244 million metric tons of CO_2 in 2030.

38. Pratt et al., *Smart Grid*, 3.5; Electric Power Research Institute, *Green Grid*, 4-3, 5-3, 7-3, 8-4.

39. Electric Power Research Institute, *Green Grid*, 10-3.

40. Pratt et al., *Smart Grid*, 3.1.

41. Michael Reid, *The Smart Grid Is Not About Residential Energy Efficiency— Yet* (American Council for an Energy Efficient Economy, 2010), 5-325, http://www.esource.com/system/files/files/2010-12/ESource-WP-10 -SmartGrid_0.pdf/.

42. Fribush, Parker, and Enterline, *Electric Evolution*, 9.

43. Pratt et al., *Smart Grid*, 3.3.

44. Electric Power Research Institute, *Green Grid*, 10-4. This calculation relies on the assumption that in 2030 total electricity sales will be 4,540 billion kWh and that the electric power sector's CO_2 emissions will be 2,224 MMT. Energy Information Administration, *Annual Energy Outlook 2013*, 138, 155.

45. Pratt et al., *Smart Grid*, 3.24.

46. Electric Power Research Institute, *Green Grid*, 6-3.

47. Energy Information Administration, *Electric Power Annual 2011* (Washington, D.C.: Department of Energy, 2013), Tables 1.2, 10.1.

48. National Resources Defense Council and Electric Power Research Institute, *Environmental Assessment of Plug-in Hybird Electric Vehicles*, vol. 1, *Nationwide Greenhouse Gas Emissions* (Palo Alto, California: EPRI, 2007), 7.

49. Electric vehicles are still a more expensive capital investment, which is why they are not yet cost competitive on a lifecycle basis with conventional vehicles.

50. Pratt et al., *Smart Grid*, 3.25.

51. Ibid., 3.26.

52. Electric Power Research Institute, *Green Grid*, 10-4. This calculation assumes that in 2030 the electric power sector's CO_2 emissions will be 2,224 MMT. Energy Information Administration, *Annual Energy Outlook 2013*, 155.

53. Pratt et al., *Smart Grid*, 3.32.

54. Wendy Kaufman, "Utility's 'Voltage Reduction' Plan Saves Energy," *NPR*, February 28, 2006, http://www.npr.org/templates/story/story.php?storyId =5236858/.

55. Paul Mauldin, "Conservation Voltage Reduction: A No-Brainer Smart Grid Benefit?," *SmartEnergyPortal.Net*, October 12, 2010, http:// smartenergyportal.net/article/conservation-voltage-reduction-no-brainer -smart-grid-benefit/; Pratt et al., *Smart Grid*, 3.27.

56. Ibid.

57. Ibid., 3.27.

58. Ibid., 3.28.

CHAPTER 2

1. Electric Power Research Institute, *Estimating the Costs and Benefits of the Smart Grid*, 1-4.

2. Robert Bradley Jr., "The Insull Speech of 1898: Call for Public Utility's Regulation of Electricity (The Origins of EEI's Support for Cap-and-Trade in Today's Energy/Climate Bill)," *MasterResource*, Apr. 29, 2010, http:// www.masterresource.org/2010/04/the-insull-speech-of-1898/.

3. Electric Power Research Institute, *Estimating the Costs and Benefits of the Smart Grid*, 2-14.

4. Ibid., 5-5–5-27, 6-4–6-5.

5. Ibid.; National Energy Technology Laboratory, *Environmental Impacts of Smart Grid*, January 10, 2011, 6–7, http://www.netl.doe.gov/energy -analyses/pubs/EnvImpact_SmartGrid.pdf/.

6. Institute for Energy and the Environment, *San Diego Gas & Electric: The Smart Grid's Leading Edge* (South Royalton: Vermont Law School, 2012), 31, http://www.vermontlaw.edu/Documents/IEE/SDGandEFinal.pdf/.

7. Vermont Public Service Board, Order Approving Central Vermont Public Service's SmartPower Plan, Docket No. 7612, August 6, 2010, 17; Institute for Energy and the Environment, *CVPS SmartPower: A Smart Grid Collaboration in Vermont* (South Royalton: Vermont Law School, 2012), 14.

8. Institute for Energy and the Environment, *CVPS SmartPower*, 15.

9. Richard Miller, "Despite Bankruptcy Threats, Illinoisans Still Want Freeze," *CapitolFax.com*, October 30, 2006, http://capitolfax.com/2006/10/30/ depite-threats-illinoisans-still-want-freeze/.

10. Dale Righter, "Power Customers Need a Long-term Solution to Higher Costs," *Arthur Graphic-Clarion*, May 31, 2007, 11.

11. Illinois Commerce Commission, Petition to Approve an Advanced Metering Infrastructure Pilot Program and Associated Tariffs, Docket No. 09-0263 (Ill. C. C. Oct. 14, 2009), http://www.icc.illinois.gov/docket/files .aspx?no=09-0263&docId=137071/.

12. Ibid.

13. Ibid.

14. Illinois Statewide Smart Grid Collaborative, *Collaborative Report*, September 30, 2010, 25, http://www.ilgridplan.org/Shared%20Documents/ ISSGC%20Collaborative%20Report.pdf/.

15. *Commonwealth Edison v. Illinois Commerce Commission*, 405 Ill. App. 3d 389 (Ill. App. 2d 2010).

16. Ibid., 42–43.

17. ICC Order, Docket 10-0467, May 24, 2010.

18. Ray Long and Julie Wernau, "ComEd Scrambling to Get Its Smart Grid Plan through Legislature," *Chicago Tribune*, May 23, 2011.

19. Julie Wernau, "Lawmakers Override Quinn Veto: Smart Grid Becomes Law," *Chicago Tribune*, October 26, 2011.

20. Commonwealth Edison, *Smart Grid Advanced Metering Annual Implementation Report*, 2013, 1, http://blogs.edf.org/energyexchange/files/2013/04/ ComEd-2013-AIPR.pdf/.

21. Commonwealth Edison, Verified Application for Rehearing, ICC Docket No. 12-0298, July 6, 2012; Commonwealth Edison, "Petition for Statutory Approval of a Smart Grid Advanced Metering Infrastructure Deployment Plan Pursuant to Section 16-108.6 of the Public Utilities Act," April 23, 2012, p. 1-2.

22. Ibid.

23. Ibid.

24. *In Re Commonwealth Edison Co.*, 300 P.U.R. 4th 1 (Ill. C. C., October 3, 2012) (Docket 11-0721).

25. "News Release: ComEd Announces Delays to Grid Modernization Program Following ICC Rehearing Decision," *Commonwealth Edison*, October 3, 2012, http://www.comed.com/newsroom/news-releases/Pages/newsroomreleases_10032012.pdf/.

26. *In Re Commonwealth Edison Co.*, 300 P.U.R. 4th, at 13-15.

27. Julie Wernau, "ComEd: Rate Formula Ruling Puts Smart Grid, Jobs at Risk," *Chicago Tribune*, October 3, 2012.

28. Julie Wernau, "Ill. Senate Overrides Quinn Veto of Smart Grid Rate Hike," *Chicago Tribune*, May 21, 2013.

29. "By July 1, 2011, each electrical corporation shall develop and submit a smart grid deployment plan to the commission for approval," Cal. Pub. Util. Code § 8364 (West 2009).

30. Cal. Pub. Util. Code § 8360 (West 2009).

31. Cal. Pub. Util. Code § 8360-69 (West 2009).

32. CPUC D.10-06-047.

33. San Diego Gas & Electric, *Smart Grid Deployment Plan*, 2011, 34, http://www.sdge.com/documents/smartgrid/deploymentplan.pdf/.

34. Cal. Pub. Util. Code § 8360-69 (West 2009).

35. CPUC D.10-06-047.

36. San Diego Gas & Electric, *Smart Grid Deployment Plan*, 2011.

37. As noted in our Salt River Project case study, SRP is governed by landowners in its service territory. Institute for Energy and the Environment, *Salt River Project: Delivering Leadership on Smarter Technology and Rates* (South Royalton: Vermont Law School, 2012), http://www.vermontlaw.edu/Documents/SRP-Report-Final-120618.pdf/.

38. "Track the Money," http://www.recovery.gov/ (accessed September 9, 2013).

39. Institute for Energy and the Environment, *Salt River Project*, 13.

40. Institute for Energy and the Environment, *SMUD's SmartSacramento: A Clean Technology Pioneer* (South Royalton: Vermont Law School, 2011), 11, http://www.vermontlaw.edu/Documents/SMUD-Report-Final-120618.pdf/.

41. David Greising, "Promise and Peril in Utilities' Smart Grid," *New York Times*, May 28, 2011, http://www.nytimes.com/2011/05/29/us/29cncgreising.html/.

42. Personally identifiable information is information that can be used on its own or with other information to identify a single person.

43. Gerard Wynn, "Privacy Concerns Challenge Smart Grid Rollout," *Reuters*, June 25, 2010, http://www.reuters.com/article/2010/06/25/us-energy-smart-id USTRE65O1RQ20100625/.

44. Ibid.

45. Environmental Protection Agency, *Smart Grid's Potential for Clean Energy: Background and Resources*, 2010, 5, http://www.epa.gov/statelocalclimate/documents/pdf/background_paper_3-23-2010.pdf/.

46. Implementing the National Broadband Plan, 75 Fed. Reg. 26,203, May 11, 2010.

47. Office of the President of the United States, *Consumer Data Privacy in a Networked World: A Framework for Protecting Privacy and Promoting Innovation in*

the Global Digital Economy, 2012, 44, http://www.whitehouse.gov/sites/default/files/privacy-final.pdf/.

48. The social media site Facebook has proven the importance of privacy. The site has named a new chief privacy officer and faces a class-action lawsuit based on its alleged privacy violations. See *Fraley v. Facebook, Inc.* (No. 11-CV-01726 [N.D. Cal. 2011] and settlement agreement, http://www.fraleyfacebooksettlement.com/).

49. Facebook, Google, and Yahoo! have all faced customer privacy breaches.

50. Federal Trade Commission, "Fair Information Practice Principles," June 25, 2007, http://www.ftc.gov/reports/privacy3/fairinfo.shtm/.

51. Department of Energy, *Data Access and Privacy Issues Related to Smart Grid Technologies* (Washington, D.C.: Department of Energy, 2010), 15, http://energy.gov/sites/prod/files/gcprod/documents/Broadband_Report_Data_Privacy_10_5.pdf/.

52. Federal Trade Commission, "Fair Information Practice Principles."

53. Ibid.

54. Ibid.

55. Cal. Pub. Util. Code § 8380.

56. Information and privacy commissioner of Ontario, Canada.

57. See Information and Privacy Commissioner of Ontario, "Smart Grid Must be Built with Privacy Embedded as the Default," press release, Oct. 21, 2010, http://www.ipc.on.ca/english/Resources/News-Releases/News-Releases-Summary/?id=988/.

58. Institute for Energy and the Environment, *A Model Privacy Policy for Smart Grid Data* (South Royalton: Vermont Law School, 2011), http://www.vermontlaw.edu/Documents/Model%20Privacy%20Policy%20_%20APPA%20Legal%20Seminar%202011%20%5Bfinal%20draft%5D.pdf/.

59. Colo. Code Regs. § 3027(c)(VI).

60. Colo. Code Regs. § 3026(c) (2011).

61. Colo. Code Regs. § 3027(a)–(b).

62. Colo. Code Regs. § 3029(a). Utilities also disclose aggregate anonymous data. See § 3031(a).

63. Colo. Code Regs. § 3026(g).

64. Senate Bill 1476 (2010) (codified after further amendments as Cal. Pub. Util. Code § 8381 (2012).

65. Senate Bill 17, Cal. Pub. Util. Code § 8360-69 (West 2009).

66. *In Re Smart Grid Technologies*, 282 P.U.R. 4th 189, 189 (Cal. Pub. Util. Comm., June 24, 2010) (decision 10-06-047 in Rulemaking Proceeding 10-06-047).

67. Ibid.

68. Ibid., 196.

69. Cal. Pub. Util. Code § 8380(a) (2011).

70. Ibid., § 8380(b)(1).

71. Ibid., § 8380(b)(2)–(3).

72. Ibid., § 8380(e)(2).

73. Ibid., § 8380(e)(1). Identifiable information is considered "electrical or gas consumption data" and means data about a customer's electrical or natural gas usage that is made available as part of an advanced metering infrastructure, and includes the name, account number, or residence of the customer. Ibid., 8380(a).
74. Ibid., § 8380(f).
75. Ibid., § 8380(d).
76. *In Re Smart Grid Technologies*, 291 P.U.R. 4th 412 (Cal. Pub. Util. Comm., July 28, 2011) (decision 11-07-056 in Rulemaking Proceeding 08-12-009), http://www.smartgrid.gov/sites/default/files/doc/files/Decision_Adopting _Rules_Protect_Privacy_d_Security_Electric2.pdf/.
77. Ibid., 95.
78. Ibid., 87.
79. Privacy by Design, *Applying* Privacy by Design *Best Practices to SDG&E's Dynamic Pricing Project*, 2012, http://www.ontla.on.ca/library/repository/ mon/26003/316063.pdf/.
80. Ibid., 4.
81. Ibid., 5.
82. Ibid., 8.
83. Ibid., 9.
84. Ibid., 10.
85. Vermont Department of Health, *Radio Frequency Radiation and Health: Smart Meters*, 2012, 1, http://healthvermont.gov/pubs/ph_assessments/ radio_frequency_radiation_and_health_smart_meters.pdf/.
86. Ibid., 1.
87. Ibid.
88. Ibid.
89. California Council on Science and Technology, *Health Impacts of Radio Frequency from Smart Meters*, 2011, 1, http://www.ccst.us/publications/2011/ 2011smartA.pdf/.
90. Ibid., 26.
91. *In Re Pacific Gas & Electric Co.*, 2012 WL 503938 (Cal. Pub. Util. Comm., Feb. 1, 2012) (decision no. 12-02-014 on application no. 11-03-014), http://docs.cpuc.ca.gov/word_pdf/AGENDA_DECISION/158309 .pdf/.
92. Ibid.
93. "Consumer Concerns About Smart Grid," *Intelligent Utility*, July 12, 2010, http://www.intelligentutility.com/article/10/07/consumer-concerns-about -smart-grid/.
94. Smart Grid Consumer Collaborative, *Spotlight on Low Income Consumers*, 2012, 5–7, http://www.smartgridcc.org/research/sgcc-research/sgccs-spotlight -on -low-income-consumers/.
95. Christine Hertzog, *Smart Grid Dictionary* (Menlo Park, Calif.: GreenSpring Marketing, 2010), 151.
96. Ibid., 126–27.
97. Ibid., 129.

98. National Institute of Standards and Technology, *NIST Framework and Roadmap for Smart Grid Interoperability Standards, Release 2.0*, 2012, http://www.nist.gov/smartgrid/upload/NIST_Framework_Release_2-0_corr.pdf/.

99. This means that smaller units of information will be transmitted than usual and those smaller units will go to and from the utility far more frequently.

100. 47 U.S.C. § 1305(k)(2)(D) (2006).

101. See Federal Communications Commission, *National Broadband Plan*, 2010, 263–80.

102. Ibid., 273.

103. Ibid., 267.

104. "Narrowband networks in that broadband networks can be used for many different traffic characteristics, while narrowband networks are used for one." "Broadband Versus Narrowband," *Sun Microsystems*, August 9, 2000, http://www.informit.com/articles/article.aspx?p=28490&seqNum=3/.

105. Federal Communications Commission, *National Broadband Plan*, 269.

106. Ibid.

107. Ibid., 271.

108. Ibid., 269.

109. Charles M. Davidson and Michael J. Santorelli, *Realizing the Smart Grid Imperative: A Framework for Enhancing Collaboration Between Energy Utilities and Broadband Service Providers*, Washington, D.C., Summer 2011, 17, http://www.twcresearchprogram.com/pdf/TWC_Davidson.pdf/.

110. Ibid.

111. Ibid., 18.

112. Ibid.

113. Ibid., 14–15.

114. Ibid., 15, 18.

115. Federal Communications Commission, *National Broadband Plan*, 270; Davidson and Santorelli, *Realizing the Smart Grid Imperative*, 15–16, 18.

116. Davidson and Santorelli, *Realizing the Smart Grid Imperative*, 14.

117. Ibid., 16.

118. Ibid.

119. John M. Shaw, "NERC CIP and Smart Grid: How Do They Fit Together?" *Utility Automation & Engineering*, May 2009.

120. Federal Communications Commission, *National Broadband Plan*, 274.

121. Ibid.

122. Ibid. As noted, several states have opened inquiries into data access and privacy regulations.

123. Central Vermont Public Service was part of the collaboration, but it merged into Green Mountain Power in 2012.

124. "GMP, CVPS and VTel Reach Smart Grid-Broadband Operating Agreement," July 20, 2011, http://www.vermontel.com/news/118-gmp-cvps-and-vtel-reach-smart-grid-broadband-operating-agreement/.

125. Dave Gram, "Vt. Utilities Enter Smart Grid-Broadband Deal," *Bloomberg Businessweek*, July 20, 2011, http://www.businessweek.com/ap/financialnews/D9OJN2600.htm/.

CHAPTER 3

1. William Cleveland and Martin Bunton, *A Modern History of the Middle East*, 4th ed. (Boulder, Colo.: Westview Press, 2009), 338–40, 376.
2. Ibid.
3. Victor Zarnowitz and Geoffrey H. Moore, "The Recession and Recovery of 1973–1976," *Explorations in Economic Research* 4, no. 4 (October 1977): 473, 489.
4. Dan York, Patti Witte, Seth Nowak, and Mary Kushler, *Three Decades and Counting: A Historical Review and Current Assessment of Electric Utility Energy Efficiency Activity in the States* (Washington, D.C.: American Council for an Energy Efficient Economy, 2012), 2.
5. Energy Information Administration, *Annual Energy Review 2011*, 233 (author's calculations).
6. Ibid., 267; Energy Information Administration, *Electric Power Annual 2011*, 181.
7. Electric Power Research Institute, *Assessment of Achievable Potential from Energy Efficiency and Demand Response Programs in the U.S.: 2010–2030* (Palo Alto, Calif.: EPRI, 2009), 4-1.
8. Energy Information Administration, *Electric Power Annual 2011*, 181, 185 (author's calculations).
9. Energy Information Administration, *Levelized Cost of New Generation Resources in the Annual Energy Outlook 2013* (Washington, D.C.: Department of Energy, 2013), 4–5.
10. York et al., *Three Decades and Counting*, 1.
11. Kenneth Gillingham, Richard Newell, and Karen Palmer, *Retrospective Examination of Demand-Side Energy Efficiency Programs* (Washington, D.C.: Resources for the Future, 2004), 82, 84.
12. Reid, *Smart Grid Is Not About Residential Energy Efficiency*, 5-325.
13. Elizabeth Doris, Jaquelin Cochran, and Martin Vorum, *Energy Efficiency Policy in the United States: Overview of Trends at Different Levels of Government* (Golden, Colo.: National Renewable Energy Laboratory, 2009).
14. For the remainder of this chapter we will focus on energy efficiency and conservation and refer to them jointly as energy efficiency. We will pick up the discussion of demand response in chapter 3.
15. Amory B. Lovins, *Energy End-Use Efficiency* (Snowmass, Colo.: Rocky Mountain Institute, 2005), 5, http://www.rmi.org/Knowledge-Center/Library/E05-16_EnergyEndUseEfficiency/.
16. Ibid.
17. Energy Information Administration, *Annual Energy Review 2011*, 219; Eurelectric, *Efficiency in Electricity Generation* (Brussels: Eurelectric, 2003), 7–9.
18. Lovins, *Energy End-Use Efficiency*, 5.
19. Eric Hirst, "Electric Utilities and Energy Efficiency," http://www.ornl.gov/info/ornlreview/rev28_2/text/uti.htm/ (accessed July 5, 2013).
20. For public power utilities and cooperatives that are not subject to state regulation, their governing boards approve rates. In most jurisdictions, utilities

set different rates for different types (or classes) of customers (e.g., residential, commercial, or industrial). The following discussion of the development of rates is simplified to assume that there is one class of customers and one retail rate.

21. National Association of Regulatory Utility Commissioners, *Decoupling for Electric and Gas Utilities: Frequently Asked Questions* (Washington, D.C.: NARUC, 2007), 2–3, http://www.epa.gov/statelocalclimate/documents/pdf/supp_mat_decoupling_elec_gas_utilities.pdf/.

22. Ibid., 2.

23. Ibid., 4.

24. Ibid.

25. Gillingham, Newell, and Palmer, *Retrospective Examination*, 15.

26. Hirst, "Electric Utilities and Energy Efficiency."

27. Gillingham, Newell, and Palmer, *Retrospective Examination*, 15–16.

28. Ibid., 16.

29. Hirst, "Electric Utilities and Energy Efficiency."

30. Gillingham, Newell, and Palmer, *Retrospective Examination*, 18.

31. Ibid., 18.

32. Ibid., 20.

33. Ibid., 21.

34. Ibid., 22.

35. Bob Gohn, *Smart Meter Backhaul Communications and the Role of Broadband Satellite* (Boulder, Colo.: Pike Research, 2012), 3–4.

36. Bob Gohn and Clint Wheelock, *Smart Grid Network Technologies and the Role of Satellite Communications* (Boulder, Colo.: PikeResearch, 2010), 6–7, http://www.idirect.net/Applications/Energy-and-Utilities/~/media/Files/White%20Papers/Pike%20ResearchSmart%20Grid%20Networks%20FINAL%2020100920.ashx/.

37. Fribush, Parker, and Enterline, *Electric Evolution*, 9.

38. Recording data at fifteen-minute increments seems to be a popular choice by utilities.

39. Federal Energy Regulatory Commission, *Assessment of Demand Response and Advanced Metering* (Washington, D.C.: Department of Energy, 2008), 5.

40. Fribush, Parker, and Enterline, *Electric Evolution*, 9–10.

41. Rahul Tongia, "Can Broadband Over Powerline Carrier (PLC) Compete? A Techno-Economic Analysis," *Telecommunications Policy* 28 (2004): 560, DOI: 10.1016/j.telpol.2004.05.004.

42. Ibid.

43. Ibid., 561–62.

44. Ibid., 562.

45. Ibid., 563.

46. Chris King, *Advanced Metering Infrastructure: Overview of System Features and Capabilities*, eMeter Corporation, 2005, 8, http://sites.energetics.com/madri/toolbox/pdfs/background/king.pdf/.

47. Ibid., 11.

48. Gohn and Wheelock, *Smart Grid Network Technologies*, 9.

49. The RF from these wireless smart meters has generated some public health concerns which are discussed in more detail in chapter 7.

50. Ibid., 10; Corning, "Broadband Technology Overview: White Paper," 2005, 8.

51. Emma Ritch, "San Diego Cancels WiMAX Smart Grid Plans," October 10, 2012, http://www.greentechmedia.com/articles/read/san-diego-cancels-wimax -smart-grid-plans/.

52. Gohn and Wheelock, *Smart Grid Network Technologies*, 18.

53. These wireless communication chips have been somewhat less controversial since it is generally the customer's decision whether this communication technology is enabled.

54. Policies associated with these demand response initiatives are discussed in the next chapter.

55. John A. Laitner, *The Economy-Wide Impact of Feedback-Induced Behaviors that Drive Residential Electricity Savings* (Washington, D.C.: American Council for an Energy Efficient Economy, 2012).

56. Lou McClelland and Stuart Cook, "Energy Conservation Effects of Continuous In-Home Feedback in All-Electric Homes," *Journal of Environmental Systems* 9, no. 2 (1979): 169–73.

57. Ben Foster and Susan Mazur-Stommen, *Results from Real-Time Feedback Studies* (Washington, D.C.: American Council for an Energy Efficient Economy, 2012), 2.

58. Laitner, *Economy-Wide Impact of Feedback-Induced Behaviors*, 9.

59. Pratt et al., *Smart Grid*, A.1–A.2.

60. Laitner, *Economy-Wide Impact of Feedback-Induced Behaviors*, 11.

61. Ibid., 6.

62. Ibid.

63. Ibid., 7–8.

64. Pratt et al., *Smart Grid*, A.3.

65. Christopher Casey and Kevin Jones, "Customer Centric Leadership in Smart Grid Implementation: Empowering Customers to Make Intelligent Energy Choices," *Electricity Journal* 26, no. 7 (2013): 101.

66. Ibid., 4–5.

67. Electric Power Research Institute, *Paying Up Front: A Review of Salt River Project's M-Power Prepaid Program* (Palo Alto, Calif.: EPRI, 2010), 4-3, 6-1.

68. Casey and Jones, "Customer Centric Leadership," 101.

69. San Diego Gas & Electric, *Smart Grid Deployment Plan 2012 Annual Report* (San Diego Gas & Electric: 2012), 23.

70. Casey and Jones, "Customer Centric Leadership," 105.

71. Ibid., 10.

72. Pratt et al., *Smart Grid*, 3.9.

73. Laitner, *Economy-Wide Impact of Feedback-Induced Behaviors*, 16.

74. "Consumer Behavior Studies," http://www.smartgrid.gov/recovery_act/consumer_behavior_studies/ (accessed February 5, 2014).

75. Pratt et al., *Smart Grid*, 3.13–3.14.

76. Ibid., 3.14.

77. Ibid., 3.16.

78. Reid, *Smart Grid Is Not About Energy Efficiency*, 5-331.

79. Pratt et al., *Smart Grid*, 3.19.

80. Ibid., 3.20

81. Ibid., 3.20–3.21.

82. Electric Power Research Institute, *Green Grid*, 4-1.

83. Pratt et al., *Smart Grid*, 3.18.

84. Electric Power Research Institute, *Green Grid*, 4-1–4-2.

85. Ibid., 4-2

86. Ibid.

87. Pratt et al., *Smart Grid*, 3.18.

CHAPTER 4

1. Office of Technology Assessment, "Energy Efficiency: Challenges and Opportunities for Electric Utilities," September 1993, 101.

2. P.L. 102-486, 106 Stat. 2776 (October 24, 1992).

3. Energy Information Administration, "Electricity Generation and Environmental Externalities: Case Studies," September 1995, 1.

4. Office of the President of the United States, "A Policy Framework for the 21st Century Grid: Enabling our Secure Energy Future," June 2011, 31.

5. Maury Klein, *The Power Makers: Steam, Electricity, and the Men Who Invented Modern America* (New York: Bloomsbury Press, 2008), 406.

6. Doug Hurley, Paul Peterson, and Melissa Whited, "Demand Response as a Power System Resource," *Synapse Energy Economics*, May 2013, 2.

7. "PJM Load Shedding, Use of DR Examined," *Megawatt Daily*, September 16, 2013, 1, 20–21.

8. "PJM Sets Record Sept. Peak Power Use: Weather and Local Grid Conditions Require Load Reductions," PJM news release, September 11, 2013, http://www.pjm.com/~/media/about-pjm/newsroom/2013-releases/20130911-pjm-sets-record-september-peak-power-use.ashx/.

9. Ibid.

10. See NERC's "Data Collection for Demand-Side Management" or Federal Energy Regulatory Commission, *Assessment of Demand Response and Advanced Metering*, December 2012, http://www.ferc.gov/legal/staff-reports/12-20-12-demand-response.pdf/.

11. As a reference point, our definition of dynamic pricing programs would be included within NERC's and FERC's nondispatchable or time-based programs, respectively.

12. Federal Energy Regulatory Commission, *Assessment of Demand Response and Advanced Metering*, December 2012, 22.

13. Nancy Brockway and Rick Hornby, "The Impact of Dynamic Pricing on Low-Income Customers: An Analysis of the IEE Whitepaper," report to the Maryland Office of the People's Counsel, 20–21, http://www.synapse-energy.com/Downloads/SynapseReport.2010-11.MD-OPC.IEE-Low-Income-Customer-Report.10-042.pdf/.

14. Ahhmad Faruqui, "The Ethics of Dynamic Pricing," in *Integrating Renewable, Distributed, and Efficient Energy*, ed. F. P. Sioshansi (Oxford: Academic Press, 2012), 75–76.

15. Brockway and Hornby, "Impact of Dynamic Pricing," 4–9.

16. Ibid., 77.

17. S. D. Braithwait and D. G. Hansen, "How Large Commercial and Industrial Customers Respond to Dynamic Pricing—The California Experience," in *Integrating Renewable, Distributed, and Efficient Energy*, ed. F. P. Sioshansi (Oxford: Academic Press, 2012), 311.

18. Sacramento Municipal Utility District, *General Manager's Report and Recommendation on Rates and Services*, May 2, 2013, vol. 1, http://www.smud.org/en/about-smud/company-information/document-library/documents/2013-GM-Rate-Report-Vol-1.pdf/.

19. B. Hamilton, C. Thomas, S. J. Park, and J. Choi, "The Customer Side of the Meter," in *Integrating Renewable, Distributed, and Efficient Energy*, ed. F. P. Sioshansi (Oxford: Academic Press, 2012), 407.

20. American Home Appliance Manufacturers, "Smart Grid White Paper: The Home Appliance Industry's Principles & Requirements for Achieving a Widely Accepted Smart Grid," 2009, ii, http://www.aham.org/ht/a/GetDocumentAction/i/44191/.

21. Jeff St. John, "Whirlpool Launches the Wi-Fi Smart Appliance," *Greentech Media*, April 25, 2013, http://www.greentechmedia.com/articles/read/whirlpool-launches-the-wi-fi-smart-appliance/.

22. Whirlpool, http://www.whirlpool.com/smart-appliances/ (accessed August 10, 2013).

23. St. John, "Whirlpool Launches the Wi-Fi Smart Appliance."

24. Brian Steiner, "Smart Appliances Make Service a Snap," *Sacramento Bee*, August 10, 2013, http://www.sacbee.com/2013/08/10/5637389/smart-appliances-make-service.html/.

25. GE Appliances, http://pressroom.geappliances.com/news/smart_meter_pilot09/ (accessed August 10, 2013).

26. Silver Spring Networks, *Oklahoma Gas & Electric Co.: Case Study*, 2013, http://61827ea6031ff2e7a9bc6d82d48cc20ebafe1731d8b336d3561a.r18.cf2.rackcdn.com/uploaded/s/0e898315_silverspring-casestudy-oge.pdf/.

27. Jeff St. John, "Silver Spring's Energy-Saving Home Experiments," *GigaOM*, http://gigaom.com/2011/02/09/silver-springs-energy-saving-home-experiments/ (last modified February 9, 2011).

28. S. George, "Interim Load Impact Results from SMUD's Smart Pricing Options Pilot, " Freeman, Sullivan and Company presentation, July 11, 2013, http://www.demandresponsetownmeeting.com/wp-content/uploads/2012/03/1A-0830-GEORGE.pdf/.

29. "2012 California Statewide Non-residential Critical Peak Pricing Evaluation," Freeman, Sullivan, and Company, April 1, 2013, 2, http://goo.gl/rJKgB/.

30. *Demand Response Compensation in Organized Wholesale Energy Markets,* FERC Order 745, 134 FERC ¶ 61,187 (March 15, 2011), http://www .ferc.gov/EventCalendar/Files/20110315105757-RM10-17-000 .pdf/.

31. Ibid., 8–9.

32. Ibid., 9.

33. *Preventing Undue Discrimination and Preference in Transmission Service,* Order 890-A, 121 FERC ¶ 61,297 (December 28, 2007), http://www.ferc.gov/ whats-new/comm-meet/2007/122007/E-1.pdf/.

34. *Wholesale Competition in Resources with Organized Electric Markets,* Order No. 719, 125 FERC ¶ 61,071 (October 17, 2008), http://www.ferc.gov/ whats-new/comm-meet/2008/101608/E-1.pdf/.

35. FERC Order 745, 2-4.

36. Federal Energy Regulatory Commission, *Assessment of Demand Response and Advanced Metering,* December 2012, 24.

37. Casey and Jones, *Customer-Centric Leadership in Smart Grid Implementation,* 108.

38. "Retailers are Viewing DR as a 'Differentiator,'" *Megawatt Daily,* September 3, 2013, 17.

39. "SRP Partners with EnerNOC to Help Manage Peak Demand, EnerNOC Case Study," 2010, http://www.enernoc.com/utilities/.

40. Ibid., 110.

41. Ibid., 26.

42. Ibid.

43. Federal Energy Regulatory Commission, *Assessment of Demand Response and Advanced Metering,* December 2012, 63.

44. Ibid., 27, 110.

45. Theodore Hesser and Samir Succar, "Renewables Integration Through Direct Load Control and Demand Response," in *Integrating Renewable, Distributed, and Efficient Energy,* ed. F. P. Sioshansi (Oxford: Academic Press, 2012), 223.

46. Ibid.

47. Office of Technology Assessment, "Energy Efficiency: Challenges and Opportunities for Electric Utilities," 106–17.

48. "Firm Hit with Penalties Tied to DR Manipulation," *Megawatt Daily,* September, 3, 1014, 1.

49. Hesser and Succar, "Renewables Integration Through Direct Load Control," 231.

50. Greg Brinkman, Paul Denholm, Easan Drury, Robert Marolis, and Matthew Mowers, "Toward a Solar-Powered Grid," *IEEE Power and Energy Magazine* 9 (May/June 2011): 31.

51. Pratt et al., *Smart Grid,* 3.33–3.35.

52. Ibid., 3.35.

53. Ibid., 3.33.

54. Ibid., 3.24.

CHAPTER 5

1. Jim Motavalli, *Forward Drive: The Race to Build "Clean" Cars for the Future* (London: Earthscan Publications, 2000), 25.

2. Ibid., 52.

3. Ibid.

4. Ibid., 14, 22–23.

5. Richard Gilbert and Anthony Perl, *Transport Revolutions: Moving People and Freight Without Oil* (Gabriola Island, B.C.: New Society Publishers, 2010), 147.

6. "Table 1-11: Number of U.S. Aircraft, Vehicles, Vessels, and Other Conveyances," *Research and Innovative Technology Administration: Bureau of Transportation Statistics*, http://www.rita.dot.gov/bts/sites/rita.dot.gov.bts/files/publications/national_transportation_statistics/html/table_01_11.html/ (accessed May 25, 2013).

7. Fifty-three percent of consumers ranked having a battery range equal to the full tank of a conventional car as "very important." Accenture, *Plug-In Electric Vehicles Changing Perceptions, Hedging Bets: Accenture End-Consumer Survey on the Electrification of Private Transport*, 2011, 15, http://www.accenture.com/SiteCollectionDocuments/PDF/Resources/Accenture_Plug-in_Electric_Vehicle_Consumer_Perceptions.pdf#zoom=50/.

8. Gilbert and Perl, *Transport Revolutions*, 147–48.

9. California Air Resources Board, *Staff Report: 2000 Zero Emission Vehicle Program Biennial Review* (2000), iv, http://www.arb.ca.gov/msprog/zevprog/2000review/staffreportfinal.pdf/.

10. Comptroller General of the United States, *Electric Vehicles: Limited Range and High Costs Hamper Commercialization* (Washington, D.C.: Government Accountability Office, 1982), 9–11, http://www.gao.gov/assets/140/137043.pdf/.

11. Ibid., 15–16.

12. Ibid., 13.

13. Department of Energy, Alternative Fuels Data Center, "U.S. HEV Sales by Model," table, http://www.afdc.energy.gov/data/tab/vehicles/data_set/10301/ (accessed May 23, 2013); Department of Energy, Alternative Fuels Data Center, "Light Duty Vehicles Sold in U.S.," http://www.afdc.energy.gov/data/tab/vehicles/data_set/10314/ (accessed May 23, 2013).

14. Electrification Coalition, *Electrification Roadmap: Revolutionizing Transportation and Achieving Energy Security*, 2009, 71; Jinming Liu and Huei Peng, "Modeling and Control of a Power-Split Hybrid Vehicle," *IEEE Transactions on Control Systems Technology* 16, no. 6 (November 2008): 1242–43, http://dx.doi.org/10.1109/TCST.2008.919447/.

15. Benjamin K. Sovacool and Richard F. Hirsch, "Beyond Batteries: An Examination of the Benefits and Barriers to Plug-In Hybrid Electric Vehicles (PHEVs) and a Vehicle-to-Grid (V2G) Transition," *Energy Policy* 37, no. 3 (March 2009): 1096, http://dx.doi.org/10.1016/j.enpol.2008.10.005/.

16. Sovacool and Hirsch, *Beyond Batteries*, 1096; Vincent Freyermuth, Eric Fallas, and Aymeric Rousseau, *Comparison of Powertrain Configuration for Plug-In HEVs from a Fuel Economy Perspective*, Argonne National Laboratory, 2008, 2, http://www.autonomie.net/docs/6%20%20Papers/HEVs%20 &%20PHEVs/Powertrain%20Configurations/comparison_of_powertrain .pdf/.

17. P. Denholm and W. Short, *An Evaluation of Utility System Impacts and Benefits of Optimally Dispatched Plug-In Hybrid Electric Vehicles* (Golden, CO: National Renewable Energy Laboratory, 2006), 2, http://www.nrel.gov/ docs/fy07osti/40293.pdf/.

18. Danielle Changala and Paul Foley, "The Legal Regime of Widespread Plug-In Hybrid Electric Vehicle Adoption: A Vermont Case Study," *Energy Law Journal* 32, no. 99 (2011): 101.

19. Ibid., 102. Under the ARRA, the federal government is offering a tax credit of seventy-five hundred dollars to consumers who purchase these vehicles (ibid.)

20. Denholm and Short, *Evaluation of Utility System Impacts*, 2.

21. Department of Energy, Alternative Fuels Data Center, "Alternative & Advanced Vehicles: Plug-In Hybrid Electric Vehicle Basics," http://www.afdc .energy.gov/afdc/vehicles/electric_basics_phev.html/ (accessed May 23, 2013).

22. Ibid.

23. Changala and Foley, "Legal Regime of Widespread Plug-In Hybrid Electric Vehicle Adoption," 102.

24. Department of Energy, Alternative Fuels Data Center, "Alternative & Advanced Vehicles."

25. Ibid.

26. Changala and Foley, "Legal Regime of Widespread Plug-In Hybrid Electric Vehicle Adoption," 103.

27. Ibid.

28. Electrification Coalition, *Electrification Roadmap*, 55.

29. Bill Canis, *Battery Manufacturing for Hybrid and Electric Vehicles: Policy Issues*, Congressional Research Service, 2011, 2, http://assets.opencrs.com/ rpts/R41709_20110322.pdf/.

30. Electrification Coalition, *Electrification Roadmap*, 74; Canis, *Battery Manufacturing for Hybrid and Electric Vehicles*, 2.

31. Power density and energy density are calculated using different metrics because power and energy are different concepts altogether. Whereas a kilowatt is a unit of power that measures the rate of energy transfer at a single moment, a kilowatt-hour is a unit of energy that measures power used over a period of time.

32. Comptroller General of the United States, *Electric Vehicles*, 10; Marcy Lowe, Saori Tokuoka, Tali Trigg, and Gary Gereffi, *Lithium-Ion Batteries for Electric Vehicles: The U.S. Value Chain* (Durham, N.C.: Duke University Center on Globalization, Governance, and Competitiveness, 2010), 13,

http://www.cggc.duke.edu/pdfs/Lowe_LithiumIon_Batteries_CGGC_10
-05-10_revised.pdf/.

33. Electrification Coalition, *Electrification Roadmap*, 76; Lowe, Trigg, and Gerreffi, *Lithium-Ion Batteries*, 13.

34. Lowe, Trigg, and Gerreffi, *Lithium-Ion Batteries*, 11. Car manufacturers use
NiMH technology in hybrid electric vehicles such as the Toyota Prius and
the Honda Insight. Canis, *Battery Manufacturing for Hybrid and Electric
Vehicles*, 4–5.

35. Lowe, Trigg, and Gerreffi, *Lithium-Ion Batteries*, 11.

36. Electrification Coalition, *Electrification Roadmap*, 76.

37. Canis, *Battery Manufacturing for Hybrid and Electric Vehicles*, 6; "Nissan
Leaf," *Nissan USA*, http://www.nissanusa.com/leaf-electric-car/ (accessed
May 26, 2013).

38. Andreas Dinger, Ripley Martin, Xavier Mosquet, Maximilian Rabl, Dimi-
trios Rizoulis, Massimo Russo, and Georg Sticher, *Batteries for Electric Cars:
Challenges, Opportunities, and the Outlook to 2020*, Boston Consulting
Group, 2010, 4, http://www.bcg.de/documents/file36615.pdf/.

39. Gilbert and Perl, *Transport Revolutions*, 147–48.

40. Canis, *Battery Manufacturing for Hybrid and Electric Vehicles*, 21.

41. Dinger et al., *Batteries for Electric Cars*, 4.

42. Electrification Coalition, *Electrification Roadmap*, 77.

43. Dinger et al., *Batteries for Electric Cars*, 4.

44. Department of Energy, *The Recovery Act: Transforming America's Transportation Sector*, 2010, 2, http://www.whitehouse.gov/files/documents/Battery
-and-Electric-Vehicle-Report-FINAL.pdf/. The American Recovery and
Reinvestment Act of 2009 provided $2.4 billion to establish thirty electric
vehicle battery and component manufacturing plants. The DOE Advanced
Research Projects Agency–Energy has provided more than $80 million to
battery and electric drive research. Electric Power Research Institute,
Transportation Electrification: A Technology Overview (Palo Alto, Calif.:
EPRI, 2011), 1-1–1-5.

45. Lowe, Trigg, and Gerreffi, *Lithium-Ion Batteries*, 23.

46. Department of Energy, *Transforming America's Transportation Sector*, 2.

47. Ibid., 4.

48. "New MIT Battery Could Make Charging as Quick as Pumping Gas,"
ElectricCarsReport.com, http://electriccarsreport.com/2011/06/new-mit-battery
-could-make-charging-as-quick-as-pumping-gas/ (accessed May 26, 2013).

49. "New Battery Technology Allows Electric Vehicles to Recharge in Two
Minutes," *ElectricCarsReport.com*, http://electriccarsreport.com/2011/03/
new-battery-technology-allows-electric-vehicles-to-recharge-in-two
-minutes/ (accessed May 26, 2013).

50. "Toyota Partners with WiTricity for Wireless Electric Car Charging,"
ElectricCarsReport.com, http://electriccarsreport.com/2011/05/toyota
-partners-with-witricity-for-wireless-electric-car-charging/ (accessed May 26,
2013).

51. Gabriel Nelson, "DOE Offers $12M for Research on Wireless Charging," *E&E Publishing*, Apr. 10, 2012, http://www.eenews.net/.

52. Lowe, Trigg, and Gerreffi, *Lithium-Ion Batteries*, 13. However, the average costs for small rechargeable NiMH batteries have fallen from $1,000/kWh in 1999 to around $700/kWh today, and costs for lithium-ion batteries have fallen from $1,600/kWh to about $500/kWh in that same period. Haresh Kamath, *Lithium-Ion Batteries for Electric Transportation: Costs & Markets* (Palo Alto, Calif.: Electric Power Research Institute, 2009), 7, http://www.arb.ca.gov/msprog/zevprog/2009symposium/presentations/kamath.pdf/.

53. Lowe, Trigg, and Gerreffi, *Lithium-Ion Batteries*, 17.

54. Energy Information Administration, "Crude and Petroleum Products Explained: Use of Oil," http://www.eia.gov/energyexplained/index.cfm?page=oil_use/; Texas Alliance of Energy Producers, "The Many Uses of Petroleum," 2008, http://www.texasalliance.org/wp-content/uploads/2013/01/Uses-of-Petroleum.pdf/.

55. Energy Information Administration, *Annual Energy Review 2011*, 145, 148.

56. Gilbert and Perl, *Transport Revolutions*, 112.

57. The United States accounted for about 21 percent of total global oil consumption in 2010. British Petroleum, *Statistical Review of World Energy*, 2010, 9, http://www.bp.com/statisticalreview/.

58. America's net petroleum imports fell from 60 percent of total consumption in 2005 to about 44 percent in 2011. This trend is expected to continue for the next fifteen years. Energy Information Administration, *Annual Energy Review 2011*, 120; Energy Information Administration, *Annual Energy Outlook 2013*, 83.

59. David L. Greene, "Fact #522: Costs of Oil Dependence 2008," Department of Energy, last updated June 9, 2008, http://www1.eere.energy.gov/vehiclesandfuels/facts/2008_fotw522.html/.

60. David L. Greene and Sanjana Ahmad, *Costs of U.S. Oil Dependence: 2005 Update* (Oak Ridge, Tenn.: Oak Ridge National Laboratory, 2005), 1, http://cta.ornl.gov/cta/Publications/Reports/ORNL_ TM2005_45.pdf/.

61. David L. Greene, "Measuring Energy Security: Can the United States Achieve Oil Independence?" *Energy Policy* 38 (2010): 1614.

62. Greene, *Costs of U.S. Oil Dependence*, 45.

63. Ronald E. Minsk, Sam P. Ori, and Sabrina Howell, "Plugging Cars in to the Grid: Why the Government Should Make a Choice," *Energy Law Journal* 30 (2009): 336; Nouriel Roubini and Brad Sester, *The Effects of the Recent Oil Price Shock on the U.S. and Global Economy*, New York University Stern School of Business, 2004, 1, http://people.stern.nyu.edu/nroubini/papers/OilShockRoubiniSetser.pdf/.

64. Electrification Coalition, *Electrification Roadmap*, 38.

65. Energy Information Administration, "Electricity Explained: Factors Affecting Electricity Prices," http://www.eia.gov/energyexplained/index.cfm?page=electricity_factors_affecting_prices/.

66. Electrification Coalition, *Electrification Roadmap*, 38

67. Energy Information Administration, *Annual Energy Review 2011*, 173 (author's calculations).

68. Ibid., 255. The average retail price has fluctuated between a low of 7.0 cents/kWh (in 1970) to a high of 10.5 cents/kWh (in 1981). Yearly prices fluctuated by more than 10 percent only once—in 1973, when the Arab oil embargo sent shocks across energy markets (my calculations) (ibid.).

69. Ibid.

70. Ibid., 173, 255 (author's calculations).

71. Department of Energy, "Comparing Energy Costs per Mile for Electric & Gasoline-Fueled Vehicles," http://avt.inl.gov/pdf/fsev/costs.pdf/ (accessed May 26, 2013).

72. Mamdouh G. Salameh, "Oil Crises, Historical Perspective," in *Encyclopedia of Energy*, vol. 4, ed. Cutler J. Cleveland et al. (New York: Elsevier Science, 2004), 633–34.

73. Keith Crane, Andreas Goldthau, Michael Toman, Thomas Light, Stuart E. Johnson, Alireza Nader, Angel Rabasa, and Harun Dogo, *Imported Oil and U.S. National Security* (Santa Monica, Calif.: RAND Corporation, 2009), 9–11, http://www.rand.org/pubs/monographs/2009/RAND_MG838.pdf/.

74. Energy Information Administration, "Crude Oil & Total Petroleum Imports Top 15 Countries," http://www.eia.gov/pub/oil_gas/petroleum/data_publications/company_level_imports/current/import.html/.

75. Crane et al., *Imported Oil and U.S. National Security*, 27; Greene, *Measuring Energy Security*, 1616.

76. Crane et al., *Imported Oil and U.S. National Security*, 43.

77. Benjamin K. Sovacool, *The Dirty Energy Dilemma: What's Blocking Clean Power in the United States* (Westport, Conn.: Praeger, 2008), 35.

78. Crane et al., *Imported Oil and U.S. National Security*, 61–62.

79. Energy Information Administration, *Annual Energy Review 2011*, 199.

80. Ibid., 179.

81. Ibid., 182.

82. More than 78 percent of these imports come from Canada, Australia, Russia, Kazakhstan, and Uzbekistan. Energy Information Administration, *Uranium Marketing Annual Report* (Washington, D.C.: Department of Energy, 2011), 1, http://www.eia.gov/FTPROOT/nuclear/umar2010.pdf/.

83. Paul Gipe, "Opportunities Forsaken: The Iraq War & Renewable Energy," *Wind-Works.org*, April 8, 2013, available at http://www.wind-works.org/cms/index.php?id=496&tx_ttnews[tt_news]=2319&cHash=1af0d1c40ad89f3c76d47128ec3ade01/.

84. Energy Information Administration, *Emissions of Greenhouse Gases in the United States* (Washington, D.C.: Department of Energy, 2009), 26, http://www.eia.gov/environment/emissions/ghg_report/pdf/0573(2009).pdf/.

85. Ibid., 2.

86. See International Panel on Climate Change, "Summary for Policymakers," in *Climate Change 2007: The Physical Science Basis*, ed. S. Solomon et al.,

2007, 7–9, http://www.ipcc.ch/pdf/assessment-report/ar4/wg1/ar4-wg1 spm .pdf/.

87. Ibid., 64.

88. Ibid.

89. Ibid.

90. Mike Soraghan, "U.S. Well Sites in 2012 Discharged More than Valdez," *EnergyWire* (blog), July 8, 2013, http://www.eenews.net/stories/10599 83941/.

91. Environmental Protection Agency, draft of "EPA Final Rule on National Ambient Air Quality Standards for Ozone," 40, 201–8, http://www.epa .gov/glo/pdfs/201107_OMBdraft-OzoneNAAQSpreamble.pdf/.

92. National Ambient Air Quality Standard for Particulate Matter, 78 Fed. Reg. 3086, 3103–4 (January 15, 2013).

93. "Oil sands are deposits of bitumen, viscous oil that must be treated in order to convert it into an upgraded cruel oil before it can be used in refineries to produce gasoline and other fuels." World Energy Council, "Oil Sands & Heavy Oil," in *Encyclopedia of Energy*, vol. 4, ed. Cutler J. Cleveland et al. (New York: Elsevier Science, 2004), 731.

94. Ibid., 731, 733.

95. Oil shale is sedimentary rock that contains organic matter called kerogen that releases a substance similar to oil when heated. Kristie M. Engemann and Michael T. Owyang, *Unconventional Oil Production: Stuck in a Rock and a Hard Place*, Regional Economist, St. Louis, Mo., July 2010, 14–15, http:// research.stlouisfed.org/publications/regional/10/07/oil.pdf/.

96. John R. Dyni, "Oil Shale," in *Encyclopedia of Energy*, vol. 4, ed. Cutler J. Cleveland et al. (New York: Elsevier Science, 2004), 739, 742.

97. Ibid., 739.

98. James T. Bartis, Tom LaTourrette, Lloyd Dixon, D. J. Peterson, and Gary Cecchine, *Critical Policy Issues for Oil Shale Development* (Santa Monica, Calif.: RAND Corporation, 2005), 36–37, http://www.rand.org/pubs/ monographs/2005/RAND_MG414.pdf/; Department of Energy, "Fact Sheet: Oil Shale & the Environment," 2011, http://fossil.energy.gov/ programs/reserves/npr/Oil_Shale_Environmental_Fact_Sheet.pdf/.

99. World Energy Council, "Oil Sands & Heavy Oil," 734.

100. Ibid.

101. Energy Information Administration, *Annual Energy Outlook 2013*, 3–4, 39, 71.

102. Ibid., 39–41, 60, 71.

103. Ibid., 71, 140.

104. Ibid., 4–6, 21.

105. Electrification Coalition, *Electrification Roadmap*, 87.

106. Natural Resources Defense Council and Electric Power Research Institute, *Environmental Assessment of Plug-In Hybrid Vehicles* 1:7–8.

107. Pratt et al., *Smart Grid*, 3.25.

108. Ibid.

109. Denholm and Short, *Evaluation of Utility System Impacts*, 3–4.

110. Capacity factor measures the productivity of an electrical generating unit by comparing its actual power output to the amount of power it could have produced operating at nameplate (i.e., maximum) capacity. Generating units with a high capacity factor—for instance, coal and nuclear units—are designed to meet base-load demand because they operate constantly. Those with a lower capacity factor—for instance, natural gas or petroleum-driven units—are designed to meet peak demand because they are only brought online during peak hours.

111. Energy Information Administration, *Electric Power Annual 2009* (Washington, D.C.: Department of Energy, 2011), 48, http://www.eia.gov/electricity/annual/archive/03482009.pdf/.

112. Denholm and Short, *Evaluation of Utility System Impacts*, 5.

113. Rebecca Wigg, "Realizing the Promise of Electric Vehicle Adoption: Sending the Right Price Signals," 13, unpublished ms., Vermont Law School Institute for Energy and the Environment, 2011, on file with authors.

114. Edison Electric Institute, *The Utility Guide to Plug-In Electric Vehicle Readiness* (Washington, D.C.: EEI, 2012), 23.

115. Ibid.

116. Ibid.

117. Ibid., 24.

118. San Diego Gas & Electric, *Smart Grid Deployment Plan*, 2011, 236–38.

119. "EV Rates," *San Diego Gas & Electric*, http://www.sdge.com/ev-rates/ (accessed May 27, 2013).

120. Commonwealth Edison, *Initial Assessment of the Impact of the Introduction of Plug-In Electric Vehicles on the Distribution System*, 2010, 46, http://switchboard.nrdc.org/blogs/rstanfield/CCCLGLP2-148080-ComEd%20PEV%20Initial%20Assessment_1012151.pdf/.

121. "Electric Rate Options," *Commonwealth Edison*, https://www.comed.com/technology/electric-vehicles/Pages/rate-options.aspx/ (accessed May 27, 2013).

122. Commonwealth Edison, *Initial Assessment*, 47–48.

123. "Price Plans," *Salt River Project*, http://www.srpnet.com/electric/home/cars/pricing.aspx/ (accessed May 27, 2013).

124. "Frequently Asked Questions About EZ-3," *Salt River Project*, http://www.srpnet.com/prices/home/ez3faq.aspx/ (accessed May 27, 2013).

125. "Price Plans," *Salt River Project*.

126. Scott Shepard, "How Deregulated Electricity Markets Spark EV Infrastructure Development," *Navigant Research Blog*, February 23, 2012, http://www.navigantresearch.com/blog/how-deregulated-electricity-markets-spark-ev-infrastructure-development/.

127. "Charging Plans," *eVgo*, https://www.evgonetwork.com/Charging_Plans/ (accessed March 12, 2012).

128. Sovacool and Hirsch, *Beyond Batteries*, 1096.

129. SP Innovation, *Using Fleets of Electric Vehicles for Electric Vehicle Power Grid Support*, 2008, 10, http://www.lifepo4.info/Battery_study/V2G_memo_Senter_V01.pdf/.

130. Ibid.
131. Sovacool and Hirsch, *Beyond Batteries*, 1096.
132. Ibid., 1097.
133. Matthew Wald, "In Two-Way Charging, Electric Cars Begin to Earn Money from the Grid," *New York Times,* April 25, 2015, http://www.nytimes.com/2013/04/26/business/energy-environment/electric-vehicles-begin-to-earn-money-from-the-grid.html?_r=0/; Katherine Tweed, "Electric Vehicles Start Selling Power into PJM Grid," May 2, 2013, Green Tech Media, http://www.greentechmedia.com/articles/read/electric-vehicles-start-selling-power-into-pjm/.
134. Electrification Coalition, *Electrification Roadmap*, 12.
135. Michael Kintner-Meyer, Kevin Schneider, and Robert Pratt, *Impact of Plug-In Hybrid Vehicles on Electric Utilities and Regional U.S. Power Grids Part 1: Technical Analysis* (Richland, Wash.: PNNL, 2007), 11.
136. Ibid.
137. Jeff Pilcher, Kathy Lindquist, and Michel Wendt, *Electric Vehicle Technology, Sales, Taxation & State Laws: Synthesis* (Olympia: Washington Department of Transportation, 2010), 2, http://www.wsdot.wa.gov/NR/rdonlyres/5F116B79-741D-4DD0-8D02-218BF50CBEC3/0/ElectricVehicleTechnologySalesTaxesandStateLawsSynthesisJDoyle110W07.pdf/.
138. Edison Electric Institute, *Utility Guide*, 34.
139. Ibid., 35.
140. Ibid.
141. Ibid.
142. San Diego Gas & Electric, *Smart Grid Deployment Plan*, 2011, 77.
143. Ibid.
144. Response and Opening Comments of the Sacramento Municipal Utility District, 4, Order Instituting Rulemaking on Alternative-Fueled Vehicle Tariffs, Infrastructure and Policies to Support California's GHG Emissions Reduction Goals, No. D.11-07-029 (Cal. Pub. Util. Comm., August 24, 2009).
145. Ibid.
146. Electrification Coalition, *Electrification Roadmap*, 90–91.
147. Assuming, of course, that the Volt's 16-kWh battery is fully depleted.
148. Robert Bruninga, "At Work: Where Speed Hardly Matters," *Charged Electric Vehicles Magazine*, June/July 2012, http://www.chargedevs.com/content/features-inside/where-speed-hardly-matters-level-1-charging-opportunities/.
149. Electrification Coalition, *Electrification Roadmap*, 92.
150. While level 2 charging may be practical for certain uses from an electric efficiency perspective, it is important that these stations be subject to appropriately structured TOU rates.
151. Pratt et al., *Smart Grid*, 3.26.
152. Larry Butkovich, "A Case for 25 kW DC Quick Chargers," *Charged Electric Vehicle Magazine*, June/July 2012, http://www.chargedevs.com/content/features-inside/case-25-kw-dc-quick-chargers/.

153. Peter Kelly-Detwiler, "Electric Cars and the Power Grid: How are They Coming Together?" *Forbes*, January 28, 2013, http://www.forbes.com/sites/peterdetwiler/2013/01/28/electric-cars-and-the-power-grid-how-are-they-coming-together/.

154. The obvious exception to this is the Tesla Supercharger network, which is being developed privately by Tesla and will be free to Tesla owners whose cars are capable of supercharging.

155. Electrification Coalition, *Electrification Roadmap*, 95–98.

156. Electric Power Research Institute, *Transportation Electrification*, 3–18.

157. Michael J. Kearney, "Electric Vehicle Charging Infrastructure Deployment: Policy Analysis Using a Dynamic Behavioral Spatial Model" (master's thesis, MIT, 2011), 21.

158. Ibid., 24

159. Ibid., 25.

160. Ibid., 24–25.

161. Mark Salisbury, *What Can Cities and Counties Do to Promote the Deployment of Electric Vehicles?* Southwest Energy Efficiency Project, 2011, 12, http://www.swenergy.org/publications/documents/SWEEP%20Electric%20Vehicle%20Infrastructure%20Report2.pdf/.

162. Michael Kent, "Workplace Charging: Employers Face a Maze of Issues When Considering EV Charging," *Charged Electric Vehicle Magazine*, January/February 2013, http://www.chargedevs.com/content/features-inside/workplace-charging-employers-face-maze-issues-when-considering-ev-charging/.

163. Alana Chavez-Langdon and Maureen Howell, *Lessons Learned: The EV Project, Regulatory Issues and Utility EV Rates* (Phoenix: EcoTality, 2013), 2, http://www.theevproject.com/cms-assets/documents/103425-835189.ri-2.pdf/.

164. Michael Kent, "Proceed with Caution," *Charged Electric Vehicle Magazine*, August/September 2012, http://www.chargedevs.com/content/features-inside/proceed-caution-charging-ev-charging/.

165. Kent, "Proceed with Caution."

166. Re Alternative-Fueled Vehicle Tariffs, 283 P.U.R. 4th 361, 361–62 (Cal. P.U.C., 2010); Cal. Pub. Util. Code § 216(i) (West 2012).

167. "Coulomb Technologies, California Charging Up for Electric Vehicles: Governor Brown Signs Assemblywoman Ma's AB 631 to Increase the Number of Charging Stations in CA," press release, October 6, 2011, http://www.coulombtech.com/blog/ev-charging-stations/press-release-gov-brown-signs-ab-631-increase-number-charging-stations-in-ca/.

168. Chavez-Langdon and Howell, *Lessons Learned*, 4–6.

169. Eurelectric, *Market Models for the Roll-Out of Electric Vehicle Public Charging Infrastructure* (Brussels: Eurelectric, 2010), 13.

170. Chavez-Langdon and Howell, *Lessons Learned*, 6–9.

171. 220 Ill. Comp. Stat. 5/16–103(a), (b), (e) (2010).

172. Illinois Commerce Commission, *Initiative on Plug-In Electric Vehicles, Report and Recommendations*, 9.

173. Commonwealth Edison, *Initial Assessment*, 26.

174. Illinois Commerce Commission, *Initiative on Plug-In Electric Vehicles: Report and Recommendations*, 9, 14, 2012, https://www.icc.illinois.gov/electricity/pev.aspx/.

175. Order Instituting Rulemaking on the Commission's Own Motion to Consider Alternative-fueled Vehicle Tariffs, Infrastructure, and Policies to Support California's Greenhouse Gas Emissions Reduction Goals, R.09-08-009, San Diego Gas & Electric Co., Comments on Proposed Decision, 5–9, August 20, 2009.

176. *In Re Electric Vehicle Charging*, 295 P.U.R. 4th, 7 (Ore. P.U.C., January 19, 2012).

177. Ibid., 10.

178. Ibid., 8.

179. Chavez-Langdon and Howell, *Lessons Learned*, 2–3.

180. Order Instituting Rulemaking on Alternative-Fueled Vehicle Tariffs, Infrastructure and Policies to Support California's GHG Emissions Reduction Goals, No. D.11-07-029, slip op. at 49 (Cal. Pub. Util. Comm., July 25, 2011).

181. "The EV Project," *EcoTality*, http://www.theevproject.com/overview.php/ (March 12, 2012); Jim Motivalli, "E.V.s Are Here, but Expect Wait for Charging Stations," *Wheels* (blog), December 20, 2010, http://wheels.blogs.nytimes.com/2010/12/20/e-v-s-are-here-but-expect-wait-for-charging-stations/.

182. "Simply Smarter Charging Wherever You Go," *Blink*, http://www.blinknetwork.com/network.html/ (accessed March 11, 2012).

183. Ibid.

184. "Frequently Asked Questions," *Coulumb Technologies*, https://www.chargepointportal.net/index.php/general/uri/faq.html/ (accessed March 12, 2012).

185. Bruninga, "At Work," 83.

186. Edison Electric Institute, *Utility Guide*, 27.

CHAPTER 6

1. Note that there are essentially two types of solar power installations. Solar photovoltaic power is generated from the sort of panels that you see on houses and businesses throughout the country. These panels "directly convert solar energy into electricity using a PV cell made of a semiconductor material." By contrast, with concentrated solar power (CSP), a series of mirrors or lenses redirects sunlight to a receiver, which uses the heat to create mechanical energy that is later converted to electricity. "Topic: Solar (PV and CSP)," *International Energy Agency*, http://www.iea.org/topics/solarpvandcsp/.

2. Peter Kind, *Disruptive Challenges: Financial Implications and Strategic Responses to a Changing Retail Electric Business Model* (Washington, D.C.: Edison Electric Institute, January 2013), 3, http://www.eei.org/ourissues/finance/Documents/disruptivechallenges.pdf/.

3. Will McNamara, "Comparison Shopping: Distributed vs. Central Station," *Power Engineering*, August 1, 2005, http://www.power-eng.com/articles/print/volume-109/issue-8/features/comparison-shopping-distributed-vs-central-station.html/.

4. Herman K. Trabish, "Wellinghoff: Solar Is Going to Overtake Everything," *Green Tech Media*, August 21, 2013, http://www.greentechmedia.com/articles/read/ferc-chair-wellinghoff-sees-a-solar-future-and-a-utility-of-the-future/.

5. Solar Energy Industries Association, *U.S. Solar Market Insight Report, Q2 2012, Executive Summary*, 2, http://www.seia.org/research-resources/solar-market-insight-report-2013-q2/.

6. Benjamin Kroposki, Robert Margolis, and Kevin Lynn, "Power to the People," *IEEE Power and Energy Magazine* 9 (May/June 2011): 18.

7. Trabish, "Wellinghoff."

8. Graham Sinden, "Assessing the Costs of Intermittent Power Generation," Environmental Change Institute, University of Oxford, 2005, http://www.ukerc.ac.uk/Downloads/PDF/05/050705TPASindenpres.pdf/.

9. Farid Katiraei and Jolio Romero Aguero, "Solar PV Integration Challenges," *IEE Power and Energy Magazine* 9 (May/June 2011): 69.

10. Brinkman et al., "Toward a Solar-Powered Grid," 39.

11. Ibid., 40.

12. Pratt et al., *Smart Grid*, H.5.

13. Jeff St. John, "The Solar Inverter—Smart Grid Connection," *Greentech Media*, April 5, 2012, http://www.greentechmedia.com/articles/read/the-solar-inverter-smart-grid-connection/.

14. Brinkman et al., "Toward a Solar-Powered Grid," 57.

15. Ibid., 31.

16. Accenture, *Achieving High Performance with Solar Photovoltaic (PV) Integration*, 2011, 13, http://www.accenture.com/SiteCollectionDocuments/PDF/Accenture-Achieving-High-Performance-Solar-Photovoltaic-Integration.pdf/./

17. Policy and Planning Division, California Public Utility Commission, *Electric Energy Storage: An Assessment of Potential Barriers and Opportunities*, July 9, 2010, 3.

18. "What Is an Ancillary Services Market," *EnerNOC*, http://www.enernoc.com/our-resources/term-pages/what-is-an-ancillary-services-market/ (accessed September 29, 2013).

19. Electric Power Research Institute, *Electricity Energy Storage Technology Options*, December 2010, 1–3.

20. Ibid., 6–7.

21. Merrill Smith and Dan Ton, "Key Connections: The U.S. Department of Energy's Microgrid Initiative," *IEEE Power and Energy Magazine* 11 (July/August 2013): 22.
22. Michael T. Burr, "Economy of Small: How DG and Microgrids Change the Game for Utilities," *Public Utilities Fortnightly* 151, no. 5 (May 2013): 21.
23. Terry Mohn, "In the Wider World, Microgrids Will Flourish," *Electricity Journal* 25, no. 8 (October 2012): 17.
24. Burr, "Economy of Small," 21.
25. Byron Washom, John Dilliot, David Weil, Jan Kleissl, Nataha Balac, William Torre, and Chuck Richther, "Ivory Tower of Power: Microgrid Implementation at the University of California San Diego," *IEEE Power and Energy Magazine* 11 (July/August 2013): 28–29.
26. Bobby Magill, "Microgrids: Sandy Forced Cities to Rethink Power Supply," *Climate Central*, September 9, 2013, http://www.climatecentral.org/news/microgrids-in-nyc-connecticut-a-new-kind-of-power-struggle-16451/.
27. San Diego Gas & Electric, *Smart Grid Deployment Plan*, 2011, 48.
28. Katherine Thomas and Kevin Jones, "San Diego Gas and Electric: The Smart Grid's Leading Edge," Institute for Energy and the Environment, Vermont Law School, April 2013, http://www.vermontlaw.edu/Documents/IEE/SDGandEFinal.pdf/.
29. Mark Rawson, "SMUD PV and Smart Grid Pilot at Anatolia," 2011, http://www1.eere.energy.gov/solar/pdfs/highpenforum1-14_rawson_smud.pdf/.

CHAPTER 7

1. Energy Information Administration, *Annual Energy Review 2011*, 219.
2. Department of Energy, "Application of Automated Controls for Voltage and Reactive Power Management—Initial Results," 2012, 13, http://www.smartgrid.gov/sites/default/files/doc/files/VVO%20Report%20-%20Final.pdf/.
3. "Guidelines for Evaluating Distribution Automation," Electric Power Research Institute, November 1, 1984, http://www.epri.com/abstracts/Pages/ProductAbstract.aspx?ProductId=EL-3728/.
4. *Electricity's Journey: Anatomy of a Transmission System Explored*, American Electric Power Ohio, https://www.aepohio.com/global/utilities/lib/docs/safety/transmissionsystem/PublicSafety_FactSheet_Anatomy-TransmissionSystem-AEPOhio.pdf/.
5. "Current Electricity: Lesson 3," *Physics Classroom*, http://www.physicsclassroom.com/class/circuits/U9L3a.cfm/ (accessed September 18, 2013); "The Physics of Everyday Stuff: Transmission Lines," *Bsharp.org*, http://www.bsharp.org/physics/transmission/ (accessed September 18, 2013).
6. Pierre Cugnet, "Confidence Interval Estimation for Distribution Systems Power Consumption by Using the Bootstrap Method—Chapter 2" (master's thesis, Virginia Polytechnic Institute, 1997), 5–6, http://scholar.lib.vt.edu/theses/available/etd-61697-14555/unrestricted/Ch2.pdf/.

7. American Electric Power Ohio, *What's on an Electric Power Pole?* https://www.aepohio.com/global/utilities/lib/docs/safety/whatsonpole/WhatsonPole_AEPOhio.pdf/.

8. Siemens, *Power Engineering Guide: Version 7.0* (Erlangen, Germany: Siemens Aktiengesellschaft, 2012), 95, http://www.energy.siemens.com/hq/pool/hq/energy-topics/power%20engineering%20guide/PEG_70.pdf/.

9. Marshall Brain, "How Power Grids Work," *How Stuff Works*, http://science.howstuffworks.com/environmental/energy/power5.htm/ (accessed September 19, 2013).

10. Siemens, *Power Engineering Guide*, 95–96.

11. Warren Causey, "Getting Smarter: New Approaches to Distribution Automation," *EnergyBiz Magazine*, January/February 2006, 52.

12. Charles W. Newton, "Technology Transforming Distribution," *EnergyBiz Magazine*, January/February 2006, 55.

13. Ibid., 55.

14. Ibid.

15. Shalini Sumil Kumar, Birtukan Teshome, Samrawit Bitewlgn Muluneh, and Bitseat Tadesse Aragaw, "Working Phases of SCADA System for Power Distribution Networks," *International Journal of Advanced Research in Electrical, Electronics, and Instrumentation Engineering* 2, no. 5 (2003): 2038, http://www.ijareeie.com/upload/may/46_H.pdf/.

16. "The Evolution of SCADA/EMS/GMS: Managing the World's Power Networks," *ABB.com*, http://www.abb.com/cawp/db0003db002698/b372f131c1a54e5fc12572ec0005dcb4.aspx/ (accessed September 23, 2013).

17. Siemens, *Power Engineering Guide*, 444.

18. Tim Taylor, "Integrated SCADA/DMS/OMS: Increasing Distribution Operations Efficiency," *ElectricEnergyOnline.com* (last accessed September 22, 2013), http://www.electricenergyonline.com/?page=show_article&article=389; Department of Energy, *Reliability Improvements from the Application of Distribution Automation Technologies- Initial Results* (2012), 4.

19. Taylor, *Integrated SCADA/DMS/OMS*.

20. Ibid.

21. Siemens, *Power Engineering Guide*, 445–46.

22. John Tengdin, PSRC Working Group D15, et al., *High Impedance Fault Detection Technology*, Power Systems Relaying Committee, 1996, 2, http://www.pes-psrc.org/Reports/High_Impedance_Fault_Detection_Technology.pdf/.

23. Department of Energy, *Reliability Improvements from the Application of Distribution Automation Technologies*, 8.

24. Ibid., 10.

25. Ibid., 11.

26. Tengdin et al., *High Impedance Fault Detection Technology*, 2; Fabian Marcel Uriarte, "Modeling, Detection, and Localization of High-Impedance Faults in Low-Voltage Distribution Feeders" (master's thesis, Virginia Polytechnic Institute, 2003), 2, http://scholar.lib.vt.edu/theses/available/etd-01052004125535/unrestricted/ThesisMasterFabianUriarte.pdf/.

27. Uriarte, "Modeling, Detection, and Localization of High-Impedance Faults," 1; Tengdin et al., *High Impedance Fault Detection Technology*, 1.

28. Ibid., 2.

29. Department of Energy, *Reliability Improvements from the Application of Distribution Automation Technologies*, 8.

30. Ibid., E-2.

31. Ibid., E-2–E-3.

32. Ibid., 9.

33. Ibid., 12–13.

34. Pratt et al., *Smart Grid*, 3.27.

35. Department of Energy, "Application of Automated Controls for Voltage and Reactive Power Management," 4.

36. Ibid., 8.

37. Sierra Energy Group, *AMI & DA Convergence: Enabling Energy Savings through Voltage Conservation* (2010), 6, http://hoffmanpower.com/docs/Energy-Savings-Voltage-Conservation.pdf/.

38. Department of Energy, "Application of Automated Controls for Voltage and Reactive Power Management," 8.

39. Stephen David Hearn, *Does Power Factor Correction Save Money?* Hearn Engineering, 2009, 2, http://www.hearneng.com/WhitePapers/Does%20Power%20Factor%20Correction%20Save%20Money.pdf/.

40. Environmental Potentials, *Power Factor in the Digital Age* (Carson City, Nev.: 2010), 1; Hearn, *Does Power Factor Correction Save Money?* 1, http://ep2000.com/uploads/EP_WhitePaper_PowerFactor.pdf/.

41. Hearn, *Does Power Factor Correction Save Money?* 1.

42. Department of Energy, "Application of Automated Controls for Voltage and Reactive Power Management," 11–12.

43. Will Gifford, "Is Conservation Voltage Reduction Truly Energy Efficiency?" DNV KEMA, July 23, 2013, http://www.dnvkemautilityfuture.com/is-conservation-voltage-reduction-truly-energy-efficiency/.

44. Department of Energy, "Application of Automated Controls for Voltage and Reactive Power Management," 12.

45. Hearn, *Does Power Factor Correction Save Money?* 2.

46. Phillip Anderson, Conservation Voltage Reduction, Idaho Power, https://www.idahopower.com/pdfs/AboutUs/PlanningForFuture/irp/2013/DecMtgMaterials/ConservatioVoltageReduction.pdf/.

47. Kelly Warner and Ron Willoughby, "Voltage Management: A Hidden Energy Efficiency Resource," *Greentech Media*, May 7, 2013, http://www.greentechmedia.com/articles/read/Voltage-Management-A-Hidden-Energy-Efficiency-Resource/.

48. Robert Fletcher, "Conservation Voltage Reduction: A Chance for T&D and Energy Efficiency to Team UP," Utility Energy Efficiency Summit, Portland, Ore., March 17, 2009, 12, http://www.bpa.gov/Energy/N/utilities_sharing_ee/Utility_Summit/Workshop2009/pdf/BobFletcherSnohomishPUD.pdf/.

49. Warner and Willoughby, "Voltage Management," 2013.

50. Barbara Vergetis Lundin, "SMUD Unlocking Smart Grid's Promise," *Fierce Smart Grid,* September 25, 2013, http://www.pnl.gov/main/publications/external/technical_reports/PNNL-19596.pdf/.

51. San Diego Gas & Electric, *Electric Distribution System Interconnection Handbook,* rev. September 16, 2013, 26, https://www.sdge.com/sites/default/files/documents/DistributionInterconnectionHandbook.pdf/.

52. Pratt et al., *Smart Grid.*

CHAPTER 8

1. "Wired: The First 20 Years," *WIRED,* May 2013, 25.

2. Amory B. Lovins, *Reinventing Fire: Bold Business Solutions for the New Energy Era* (White River Junction, Vt.: Chelsea Green, 2011), 166.

3. Ibid., 167.

4. Dieter Helm, *The Carbon Crunch: How We're Getting Climate Change Wrong and How to Fix It* (New Haven: Yale University Press, 2012), 213–14.

APPENDIX I

1. Green Mountain Power, Vermont's second largest utility, and Central Vermont Public Service merged in 2012. CVPS was acquired by GMP's parent company Gaz Metro and they merged into one utility called Green Mountain Power.

2. Vermont Electric Cooperative, which is also a member of the Vermont smart grid partnership, has previously installed smart meters for their customers.

3. Vermont Public Service Board, Order Approving Advanced Metering Infrastructure Plan, Docket No. 7612, August 6, 2010.

4. "CVPS, State, Announce New 'Smart' Grid Plans," press release, August 1, 2008, http://www.cvps.com/AboutUs/news/viewStory.aspx?story_id=190/.

5. See Vermont Public Service Board, Proposal for Decision Recommending Approval of Memorandum of Understanding, Docket No. 7307, August 3, 2009 (hereafter cited as MOU Order); "CVPS, MOU in Hand, CVPS Moves toward 'CVPS SmartPower,'" press release, February 2, 2009, http://www.cvps.com/AboutUs/news/viewStory.aspx?story_id=210/ (accessed February 2, 2009).

6. "CVPS, MOU in Hand, CVPS Moves toward 'CVPS SmartPower.'"

7. "CVPS, Vermont Seeks $66 Million in Stimulus Funds for 'Smart Grid,'" press release, August 7, 2009, http://www.cvps.com/AboutUs/news/viewStory.aspx?story_id=232/.

8. Ibid.

9. Central Vermont Public Service, *2009 Annual Report: Ushering in a New Era of Opportunity* 8, 2009.

10. Ibid.
11. See Vermont Public Service Board, Order Approving Advanced Metering Infrastructure Plan.
12. Terri Hallenbeck, "Vermonters Feel Boost from Stimulus," *Burlington Free Press*, Aug. 16, 2009, 1A.
13. Central Vermont Public Service, *2009 Annual Report*, 4.
14. Nancy Remsen, "State Wins $69 Million 'Smart Grid' Grant," *Burlington Free Press*, Oct. 28, 2009, at 1A.
15. Central Vermont Public Service, SmartPower Plan, April 2010, 24 (hereafter cited as SmartPower Plan).
16. See Vermont Public Service Board, Order Approving Updated Business Case, Docket No. 7612 Order, September 1, 2011), 7 (describing the utility's intent to complete the installations within thirteen rather than eighteen months).
17. Vermont Public Service Board, Order Approving CVPS SmartPower Plan, Docket No. 7612 (Aug. 6, 2010), 14 (hereafter cited as SmartPower Order).
18. Vermont Public Service Department, *2011 Comprehensive Energy Plan*, vol. 1, p. 11.
19. SmartPower Plan, 82.
20. SmartPower Order, 6–7.
21. SmartPower Plan, 83.
22. SmartPower Order, 14.
23. SmartPower Plan, 28.
24. Ibid.
25. Ibid.
26. Ibid., 21.
27. Amanda Beraldi, "Introduction to CVPS Smart Grid Project," 2010 Renewable Energy Vermont Distributed Generation Northeast Conference, May 19, 2010.
28. SmartPower Plan, 37.
29. Remsen, "State Wins $69 Million 'Smart Grid' Grant," 14.
30. SmartPower Plan, 13.
31. Ibid., 21.
32. SmartPower Order, 8.
33. One Public Service Board order describes that the Department of Public Service "recogniz[es] that government policy-makers have been encouraging rapid development of smart-metering systems." MOU Order, 34.
34. See Vermont Public Service Board, Proposal for Decision Recommending Approval of Memorandum of Understanding.
35. Vermont Energy Efficiency and Affordability Act § 10, Act 92 (2008).
36. Ibid., § 10 (requiring the scope of the board's investigation to include current status of implementing AMI in Vermont, experience from other states, opportunities for pilot programs and sharing experience in Vermont, analysis of cost/benefits, opportunities to reduce rates or mitigate rate impact,

and analysis of supporting/ancillary equipment and efficiency programs needed).

37. Ibid.
38. Ibid.
39. An Act Relating to Renewable Energy §13b, Act 159, 30 V.S.A. § 8008(b)(2)(F) (amending the state's legislation regarding renewable energy programs and authorizing the board to invest revenues from the transfer of certain renewable energy certificates in integrating electric vehicles into Vermont's smart grid infrastructure).
40. An Act Relating to the Vermont Recovery and Reinvestment Act of 2010, Act 78, 30 V.S.A. § 218(b)(3) (providing "an applicant may propose and the board may approve or require an applicant to adopt a rate design that includes dynamic pricing, such as real-time pricing rates").
41. See Vermont Public Service Board, Order Authorizing VT Utilities to Pledge Assets for a Smart Grid Investment Grant, Docket No. 7610, August 13, 2010 (approving Vermont utilities' petition to pledge assets in order to supplement funding from a smart grid investment grant from the U.S. Department of Energy).
42. Ibid., 2.
43. The board granted the petition within four days.
44. 30 V.S.A. § 202a.
45. 30 V.S.A. § 202a(1).
46. Vermont Public Service Department, *2011 Comprehensive Energy Plan*, 11.
47. SmartPower Order, 2.
48. MOU Order, 34.
49. Ibid.
50. SmartPower Order, 17–18. CVPS's SmartPower plan proposed that any material changed to the plan that had the support of the Department of Public Service would be filed with the board and take effect thirty days later unless the board took action. The board rejected CVPS's proposal based on four rationales: It would create additional reviews, complicate annual reviews, and lack a clear benefit to the utility; and the utility can protect itself by proposing modified plan if subsequent changes occur.
51. MOU Order, 35.
52. Ibid., 35–36.
53. Ibid., 36.
54. Ibid.
55. Vermont Public Service Board, Order Clarifying the "Used and Useful" Test for Smart Grid Investments, Docket No. 7307, November 16, 2009, 2.
56. Ibid.
57. Ibid.
58. Ibid., 3.
59. SmartPower Order, 17.
60. SmartPower Plan, 79 (identifying major milestone financial commitments, including Backhaul System, Meter Data Management System, Advanced

Metering Infrastructure and Meters, and Master Station and Meter Install).

61. Central Vermont Public Service, *2009 Annual Report*, 6.
62. Department of Energy, Office of Electricity Delivery and Energy Reliability, Smart Grid Investment Grant Project Description, 2011.
63. Central Vermont Public Service, *2009 Annual Report*, 8.
64. SmartPower Plan, 81.
65. Ibid., 6.
66. Ibid., 29.
67. Ibid., 35, 81.
68. SmartPower Order, 3.
69. Ibid.
70. Ibid.
71. Ibid., 4.
72. Vermont Public Service Board, Order Approving Updated Business Case 8.
73. SmartPower Plan, 5, 18 (CVPS sees these investments as "necessary prerequisites to the introduction of a fully functional Smart-Metering system").
74. Ibid., 41.
75. Ibid., 79.
76. Vermont Public Service Board, Order Approving Updated Business Case, 2.
77. "State of Vermont, GMP, CVPS and VTel Reach Smart Grid-Broadband Operating Agreement," press release, July 20, 2011.
78. Ibid.
79. Ibid.
80. Ibid., 3.
81. Ibid., 8.
82. Amanda Beraldi, manager, Market Research and Strategic Planning; Jeff Monder, chief information officer; et al., CVPS, interview with author, March 17, 2011, Rutland, Vt. (hereafter cited as CVPS Interview).
83. Beraldi, "Introduction to CVPS Smart Grid Project," 10.
84. CVPS Interview.
85. SmartPower Plan, 20.
86. Ibid., 24.
87. Ibid., 29.
88. CVPS Interview.
89. SmartPower Plan, 6.
90. CVPS Interview.
91. SmartPower Plan, 30–34.
92. Central Vermont Public Service, *Glossary of Terms*, http://www.cvps.com/ CustomerService/Glossary.aspx/.
93. Beraldi, "Introduction to CVPS Smart Grid Project," 8.
94. CVPS Interview.
95. Central Vermont Public Service, *General Service Rates*, http://www.cvps .com/CustomerService/BusRates.aspx/.

96. SmartPower Plan, 32.

97. SmartPower Order, 8.

98. Ibid.

99. Stephen S. George et al., MW Consulting, *Final Workshop on Benefit-Cost Analysis for Advanced Metering and Time-Based Pricing*, January 15, 2008, slides at 30.

100. SmartPower Plan, 24.

101. Opponents to smart meters in Vermont launched a campaign in January 2012 under the name "Wake Up, Opt Out!" This campaign warns CVPS customers of privacy and other concerns related to smart meters. The campaign aired radio advertisements challenging CVPS's trustworthiness in securely managing customers' data. Bruce Edwards, "Smart Meter Opponents Take to the Air," *Rutland Herald*, January 30, 2012, http://www.vermonttoday.com/apps/pbcs.dll/article?AID=/RH/20120130/BUSINESS/701309949/.

102. eEnergy Vermont, "Guiding Principles," https://www.burlingtonelectric.com/ELBO/assets/smartgrid/Guiding%20principles.pdf/.

103. SmartPower Order, 7.

104. SmartPower Plan, 37. In addition, the Vermont Public Service Board has previously noted that its contract with Efficiency Vermont requires that all customer data be kept confidential and prohibits the use of the data "for purposes other than providing Board-approved energy efficiency utility services." Vermont Public Service Board, Order *In Re Village of Hyde Park Electric Department*, Docket No. 6379, June 23, 2000, 1.

105. Hallenbeck, "Vermonters Feel Boost from Stimulus," 1A.

106. Central Vermont Public Service and Green Mountain Power, Jt. Reply Comments, Investigation into Vermont Electric Utilities' Use of Smart Metering and Time-Based Rates, Docket No. 7307, December 16, 2011, 15.

107. Central Vermont Public Service, *The Facts: Answers to Your Questions*, http://cvps.com/ProgramsServices/smartpower/TheFacts/AnswersToYourQuestions/index.asp#answerSix/.

108. Central Vermont Public Service and Green Mountain Power, Jt. Reply Comments, 15.

109. Scudder Parker and Bruce Bentley, *Using the Smart Grid Intelligently*, 2010 ACEEE Summer Study on Energy Efficiency in Buildings, 7, http://www.eec.ucdavis.edu/ACEEE/2010/data/papers/2057.pdf/.

110. Ibid., 3.

111. Ibid., 5.

112. Vermont Public Service Department, *2011 Comprehensive Energy Plan*, 3.

113. Ibid., 10.

114. SmartPower Plan, 34.

115. Ibid., 4; Parker and Bentley, *Using the Smart Grid Intelligently*, 11.

116. Hallenbeck, "Vermonters Feel Boost from Stimulus," 1A.

117. Electric Power Research Institute, *Estimating the Costs and Benefits of the Smart Grid*, 1-4 (2011).

118. Pacific Northwest National Laboratory, *The Smart Grid: An Estimation of the Energy and CO$_2$ Benefits*, January 2010, http://www.pnl.gov/main/publications/external/technical_reports/PNNL-19112.pdf/.

119. M. Granger Morgan, Jay Apt, Lester B. Lave, Marija D. Ilic, Marvin Sirbu, and Jon M. Piha, *The Many Meanings of "Smart Grid,"* Carnegie Mellon University Department of Engineering and Public Policy, July 2009.

120. "Salt River Project Profile," *SmartGridNews*, May 11, 2011, http://www.smartgridnews.com/artman/publish/Key_Players_Utilities/Salt_River_Project_Profile-1095.html/.

121. Ibid.

122. Salt River Project, *Building a Legacy: The Story of SRP*, 2006, 12.

123. Salt River Project, *A History of the Salt River Project*, May 11, 2011, http://www.srpnet.com/about/history/legacy.aspx/.

124. The ACC is similar to Public Utility Commissions or Public Service Commissions in other states, except that the ACC also has authority of corporations, securities regulation, and railroad/pipeline safety. See http://www.azcc.gov/Divisions/Administration/about.asp/.

125. "SRP Elected Officials," May 11, 2011, http://www.srpnet.com/about/elected.aspx/.

126. The board is composed of ten district representatives and four at-large members. District representatives are elected by acreage-based voting system. This acreage-based system dates back to the origination of SRP, when landowners pledged private property for collateral on government loans. The system was upheld by the U.S. Supreme Court in 1981. At-large members have a one-landowner, one-vote system. See http://www.srpnet.com/about/governing.aspx#district/, and Salt River Project, *Building a Legacy: The Story of SRP*, 8.

127. "SRP Governance," May 11, 2011, http://www.srpnet.com/about/governing.aspx#district/.

128. Salt River Project, *Building a Legacy: The Story of SRP*, 8.

129. "Facts About SRP," May 11, 2011, http://www.srpnet.com/about/facts.aspx/.

130. Ibid.

131. Salt River Project, *Renewable Energy*, May 11, 2011, http://www.srpnet.com/environment/renewable.aspx/.

132. *SmartGridNews*, "Salt River Project Profile," 2011, http://www.smartgridnews.com/artman/publish/Key_Players_Utilities/Salt_River_Project_Profile-1095.html/ (accessed May 11, 2011).

133. 16 U.S.C. § 2621(d) (2010).

134. Joe Nowaczyk, telephone interview with author, December 6, 2010.

135. The plan was primarily rejected because the Maryland PSC would not approve a cost recovery customer surcharge, would not impose mandatory time of use rates, was concerned with educational components of the plan, and did not want customers to face the full economic risk of smart meter technology. Maryland Public Service Commission Order No. 834102-3, June 21, 2010; see also http://www.greentechmedia.com/articles/read/baltimore-gas-electrics-smart-meter-plan-is-rejected/.

136. Maryland Public Service Commission Order No. 83531, August 13, 2010.
137. Frederick Butler, "A Call to Order: A Regulatory Perspective on the Smart Grid," *IEEE Power and Energy Magazine*, March/April 2009, 16–25, 93.
138. Joe Nowaczyk, presentation of SRP Smart Grid Roadmap Validation Review, April 8, 2009 (hereafter cited as Smart Grid Roadmap).
139. IntelliGrid seeks to link the communications and safety systems of modern grids together to create a central management system for a quicker healing grid. "The Case for Use Cases," *Smart Grid Newsletter*, 2006, available at http://intelligrid.epri.com/docs/SRP_use_cases.pdf/.
140. Electric Power Research Institute, *EPRI Smart Grid Demonstration Initiative Two Year Update*, 2010.
141. Transmission and Distribution World, *EPRI Green Circuits Project Launched*, May 1, 2010, http://tdworld.com/overhead_distribution/epri-green-circuits -project/.
142. Salt River Project presentation to the National Science and Technology Council Subcommittee on Smart Grid, August 23, 2010.
143. Ibid.
144. Ibid.
145. Ibid.
146. Smart Grid Roadmap.
147. Joe Nowaczyk, presentation of SRP Smart Grid Implementation, December 15, 2009.
148. Smart Grid Roadmap.
149. Nowaczyk, presentation of SRP Smart Grid Implementation, December 15, 2009.
150. Smart Grid Roadmap.
151. Jeff Younger, telephone interview with author, February 21, 2011.
152. Smart Grid Roadmap.
153. Salt River Project presentation to the National Science and Technology Council Subcommittee on Smart Grid, August 23, 2010; Younger telephone interview.
154. Ibid.
155. Nowaczyk telephone interview.
156. Ibid.
157. Younger telephone interview.
158. Ibid.
159. Smart Grid Roadmap.
160. IEC 61850 is the International Electrotechnical Commission standard design for substation automation. See http://seclab.uiuc.edu/docs/iec61850 -intro.pdf/.
161. Smart Grid Roadmap.
162. Ibid.
163. Younger telephone interview.
164. Smart Grid Roadmap.
165. Ibid.

166. Ibid.
167. Joe Nowaczyk and Jeff Younger, interview with author, March 21, 2011.
168. Smart Grid Roadmap.
169. Ibid.
170. Presentation to National Science and Technology Council Subcommittee on Smart Grid, August 23, 2010.
171. Smart Grid Roadmap.
172. Nowaczyk and Younger interview.
173. Ibid.
174. Ibid.
175. Smart Grid Roadmap.
176. Ibid.
177. Nowaczyk and Younger interview.
178. Ibid.
179. Smart Grid Roadmap.
180. Ibid.
181. Ibid.
182. Ibid.
183. See http://www.smartgrid.gov/project/salt-river-project-smart-grid-project.
184. Ryan Randazzo, "SRP Gets $56.9M Boost from Feds for Customer 'Smart Meters'" *Arizona Republic,* October 27, 2009, http://www.azcentral.com/business/articles/2009/10/27/20091027biz-srp1028.html/.
185. See http://www.srpnet.com/electric/home/smartmeterfaqs.aspx
186. Salt River Project, 2010 Annual Report, 6.
187. Ibid.
188. See http://www.smartgrid.gov/projects/investment_grant/.
189. Patrick O'Grady, "Salt River Project Buys Smart Meters for Stimulus Package, American City Business Journals," May 18, 2010.
190. Salt River Project, 2010 Annual Report, 6.
191. O'Grady, "Salt River Project Buys Smart Meters for Stimulus Package."
192. See http://www.srpnet.com/electric/home/smartmeterfaqs.aspx.
193. Ibid.
194. Scott Trout, interview with author, March 21, 2011.
195. Ibid.
196. Ibid.
197. Smart Grid Roadmap.
198. Ibid.
199. Nowaczyk and Younger interview.
200. Smart Grid Roadmap.
201. Trout interview.
202. Younger telephone interview.
203. Michael T. Burr, "Middleware Mashup: Smart Grid and the Back Office," *Public Utilities Fortnightly* 65, no. 3 (2007): 145.
204. Ibid.
205. Younger telephone interview.

206. See http://www.srpnet.com/electric/home/smartmeterfaqs.aspx#7/.

207. See http://www.srpnet.com/prices/home/basicfaq.aspx#1/ (listing the exact rates of the Basic Plan).

208. Salt River Project, "E-26 Standard Price Plan for Residential Time of Use Service," http://www.srpnet.com/prices/pdfx/ResTOU0111.pdf/.

209. Ibid.

210. Trout interview.

211. See Salt River Project, "E-21 Price Plan for Residential Super Peak Time-of-use Service," http://www.srpnet.com/prices/pdfx/EZ3Jan2011.pdf/.

212. See http://www.srpnet.com/prices/home/ez3faq.aspx#5 (describing how to pre-cool in this program).

213. Nowaczyk telephone interview.

214. Scott M. Gawlicki, *Got Prepaid?* 148 No. 7 Pub. Util. Fort. 10, 2 (2010).

215. Electric Power Research Institute, *Paying Upfront: A Review of Salt River Project's M-Power Prepaid Program,* 2010, 1-2, http://www.srpnet.com/environment/earthwise/pdfx/spp/EPRI_MPower.pdf/.

216. Ibid., 2-2.

217. Ibid., 3-2.

218. Ibid., 2-4.

219. Ibid., 1-4.

220. Ibid., 2-1.

221. Ibid., 1-3.

222. Ibid., 2-3.

223. Ibid., 3-6.

224. Ibid., 1-1

225. Ibid., 4-6.

226. Gawlicki, *Got Prepaid?*

227. Electric Power Research Institute, *Paying Upfront,* 5-4.

228. Ibid., 4-3.

229. Ibid., 1-1.

230. Gawlicki, *Got Prepaid?* (noting over eighteen U.S. utilities have visited SRP in 2010 alone regarding M-Power).

231. Ibid.

232. Salt River Project, 2010 Energy Efficiency Report.

233. Nowaczyk and Younger interview.

234. Presentation to National Science and Technology Council Subcommittee on Smart Grid, August 23, 2010.

235. Electric Power Research Institute, *Estimating the Costs and Benefits of the Smart Grid,* 2011, 1-4.

236. Pacific Northwest National Laboratory, *Smart Grid: An Estimation of the Energy and CO_2 Benefits.*

237. Title XIII of the Energy Independence and Security Act of 2007 (EISA).

238. While the title of this case study references SMUD's SmartSacramento, a number of SMUD's related smart grid and clean energy initiatives are discussed throughout the report.

239. Sacramento County residents originally voted to establish SMUD in 1923 as a customer-owned utility, but due to legal controversy with Pacific Gas & Electric Company of San Francisco, it did not start providing power for two decades. Additionally, it needed to build an organization of engineers, electricians, managers, and office workers to take over Sacramento's old electric system before supplying electricity to Sacramento customers. See http://www.smud.org/en/about/Pages/history-1940s.aspx/ (accessed June 15, 2011).

240. See http://www.smud.org/en/about/documents/reports-pdfs/draft-time-based-electricity-and-smart-grid.pdf/.

241. Sacramento Municipal Utility District, company profile, https://www.smud.org/en/about-smud/company-information/company-profile.htm/ (accessed January 20, 2012).

242. Timothy N. Tutt, SMUD's government affairs representative, presenting SMUD's comments regarding implementing the proposed goal of 12,000 mW of clean local distributed generation using smart grid solutions to the California Energy Commission, July 20, 2011, http://www.energy.ca.gov/2011_energypolicy/documents/2011-06-22_workshop/comments/SMUD_comments_TN-61471.pdf/ (accessed August 10, 2011).

243. SMUD's energy efficiency programs have already resulted in customer savings of more than $550 million over the last thirty-five years.

244. SMUD comments on "Renewable Power in California: Status and Issues," October 5, 2011, http://www.energy.ca.gov/2011_energypolicy/documents/2011-09-14_workshop/comments/SMUD_Comments_on_Draft_Renewable_Power_in_California_TN-62550.pdf/ (accessed January 18, 2012).

245. Ibid.

246. See video presentation, November 2010, http://www.smud.org/en/about/Pages/index.aspx/; video presentation, http://www.smartgridnews.com/artman/publish/Video-Education-and-Information/Smart-grid-implementation-at-SMUD-3304.html/.

247. Many "clean technology" websites have highlighted SMUD's focus on clean technology, such as Pike Research, CleanTech Market Intelligence, http://www.pikeresearch.com/blog/articles/will-utilities-such-as-smud-develop-microgrid-models-for-the-developing-world/ (accessed June 30, 2011).

248. Sacramento Municipal Utility District, 2008 Annual Report.

249. Jim Parks, presentation to the CPUC Smart Grid Workshop, March 18, 2010; "Smart Grid Implementation at the Sacramento Municipal Utility District," http://www.cpuc.ca.gov/NR/rdonlyres/D25C3103-D534-4F19-B267-823FD40C9C20/0/CPUCWorkshop31810SMUDParks2.pdf/.

250. Ibid.

251. Sacramento Municipal Utility District and the American Recovery and Reinvestment Act of 2009, http://www.smud.org/en/about/grants/Pages/default.aspx/ (accessed June 20, 2011).

252. Jim Parks, energy presentation, November 2010, http://www.youtube.com/watch?v=RyKVm078cJ4&feature=player_embedded/.

253. In August 2011, SMUD became the twelfth host site project in EPRI's smart grid demonstration initiative.

254. Jim Parks, presentation to the CPUC Smart Grid Workshop; "Smart Grid Implementation at the Sacramento Municipal Utility District," http://www.cpuc.ca.gov/NR/rdonlyres/D25C3103-D534-4F19-B267-823FD40C9C20/0/CPUCWorkshop31810SMUDParks2.pdf/.

255. Communication with SMUD's Smart Grid Core Team, April 1, 2011.

256. Communication with SMUD's Smart Grid Core Team, February 14, 2012, updating the data from published presentation by Tutt, SMUD's government affairs representative, commenting on SMUD's implementation of the proposed goal of 12,000 mW.

257. Public Utility Regulatory Policies Act of 1978 as Amended by the Energy Independence and Security Act of 2007: "Staff Report and Proposed Board Determination on the Information on Time-Based Electricity Prices and Sources of Power Standard Smart Grid Information," July 15, 2011, http://www.smud.org/en/about/Documents/reports-pdfs/draft-time-based-electricity-and-smart-grid.pdf/.

258. Sacramento Municipal Utility District, *General Manager's Report and Recommendation on Rates and Services: SmartSacramento Pricing Pilot*, vol. 2, April 7, 2011, https://www.smud.org/en/about-smud/company-information/document-library/documents/GMRateReport-Vol2-04-07-11.pdf/.

259. Jaspal Deol, "Transmission and Distribution Substation Design, Construction, and Maintenance," SmartSacramento presentation, March 23, 2011, http://www.usea.org/Programs/EUPP/SouthCentralAsiaTDWorkshop/DAY3PRESENTATIONS-DISTRIBUTION/5_-_SMUD_SmartSacramento_March_2011.pdf/.

260. As of January 31, 2012; Jaspal Deol, "Transmission and Distribution Substation Design, Construction, and Maintenance."

261. Ibid.

262. Ibid.

263. Ibid.

264. *Draft Staff Report and Proposed Board Determination on the Rate Design Modifications to Promote Energy Efficiency Investments Standard*, https://www.smud.org/en/about-smud/company-information/document-library/documents/draft-rate-design-mod-EE-invest-standard.pdf/ (accessed January 20, 2012).

265. Sacramento Municipal Utility District, *Consumer Behavior Study*, SmartSacramento, http://www.smartgrid.gov/sites/default/files/pdfs/cbs/smud-cbs-description-final_0.pdf/ (accessed April 2011).

266. Karen Herter, *SMUD's Residential Summer Solutions Study*, August 26, 2011, http://eetd-seminars.lbl.gov/seminar/smud%E2%80%99s-residential-summer-solutions-study/.

267. Deol, "Transmission and Distribution Substation Design, Construction, and Maintenance."

268. Sacramento Municipal Utility District, *Consumer Behavior Study.*

269. *Draft Staff Report and Proposed Board Determination on the Rate Design Modifications.*

270. Ibid.

271. Communication with SMUD's Smart Grid Core Team, April 5, 2012.

272. Tutt, SMUD's government affairs representative, presenting SMUD's comments regarding implementing the proposed goal of 12,000 mW.

273. Deol, "Transmission and Distribution Substation Design, Construction, and Maintenance."

274. Tutt, SMUD's government affairs representative, presenting SMUD's comments regarding implementing the proposed goal of 12,000 mW.

275. Sacramento Municipal Utility District and the smart grid video, http://www.smud.org/en/video/Pages/cc_tabbed.html?bclid=769701255&bctid=930929496001/ (accessed August 10, 2011).

276. Tutt, SMUD's government affairs representative, presenting SMUD's comments regarding implementing the proposed goal of 12,000 mW.

277. Ibid.

278. Ibid.

279. Deol, "Transmission and Distribution Substation Design, Construction, and Maintenance."

280. SMUD has received funding from the federal government and other sources to advance transportation through vehicle electrification and to advance SMUD's strategy to accelerate the transition to electric vehicles. Sacramento Municipal Utility District, "Our Stimulus Grants," https://www.smud.org/en/about-smud/company-information/grants.htm/.

281. "SMUD Leading Local Plug-In Electric Vehicle Wave," November 15, 2011, https://www.smud.org/en/about-smud/news-media/news-releases/2011-11-15.htm/ (accessed January 22, 2012).

282. "Sac State, Sacramento Municipal Utility District Formalize Energy Partnership," (June 9, 2011, http://www.csus.edu/sacstatenews/articles/2011/06/SacStateSMUD06-09-11.html/.

283. Deol, "Transmission and Distribution Substation Design, Construction, and Maintenance."

284. Communication with SMUD's Smart Grid Core Team, April 5, 2012.

285. Some SMUD presentations suggest $5.3 million.

286. Deol, "Transmission and Distribution Substation Design, Construction, and Maintenance."

287. "SMUD's Smart Meters Frequently Asked Questions," http://www.smud.org/en/smartmeter/pages/smartmeter-faq.aspx/ (June 30, 2011).

288. "Staff Report and Proposed Board Determination on the Information on Time-Based Electricity Prices and Sources of Power Standard Smart Grid Information."

289. SMUD received one of the top ten largest grants in the country.

290. Jim Parks, I 4 Energy Presentation, November 2010, http://www.youtube .com/watch?v=RyKVm078cJ4&feature=player_embedded/ (July 20, 2011).

291. Communication with SMUD's Smart Grid Core Team, April 5, 2012.

292. Ibid.

293. Ibid.

294. Tutt, SMUD's government affairs representative, presenting SMUD's comments regarding implementing the proposed goal of 12,000 mW.

295. See http://www.usea.org/Programs/EUPP/SouthCentralAsiaTDWorkshop/ DAY3PRESENTATIONS-DISTRIBUTION/5_-_SMUD_SmartSacramento_March_2011.pdf/.

296. Jim Parks I 4 Energy Presentation, November 2010, http://www.youtube .com/watch?v=RyKVm078cJ4&feature=player_embedded/.

297. Rick Daysog, "SMUD Selling Wind Energy Project to Gain Stimulus Funds," *Sacramento Bee*, September 13, 2011, sec. B, p. 6.

298. Rawson, "SMUD PV and Smart Grid Pilot at Anatolia."

299. Erik Krause, SMUD's project development manager, communication with author, January 31, 2012.

300. Sacramento Municipal Utility District, "Our Stimulus Grants."

301. Communication with SMUD's Smart Grid Core Team, April 5, 2012.

302. Communication with SMUD's Smart Grid Core Team, March 23, 2012.

303. SMUD has not had any public opinion issues other than with a very small percentage of customers (about 0.45 percent) who have asked not to receive a meter. According to communication with SMUD's Smart Grid Core Team, January 31, 2012.

304. Michael Gianunzio to the author, e-mail, November 15, 2010.

305. John J. Fitzgerald, "Public Utility Corporations," in *Burham's Manual of Chicago Securities* (Chicago: John Burnham, 1918), 173.

306. Hoover's Commonwealth Edison Company Profile, 2010, http://www .hoovers.com/company/Commonwealth_Edison_Company/rfsftri-1.html/.

307. Exelon Corporation Summary Annual Report, 2010, http://www.exeloncorp .com/assets/newsroom/downloads/docs/Financial/dwlnd_annualreport .pdf/.

308. Anne Pramaggiorre, "ComEd Smart Grid," presentation, January 8, 2010, slide 2.

309. Illinois Commerce Commission, Docket No. 07-0566, Commonwealth Edison Company, September 10, 2008.

310. Val Jensen, "The ComEd Customer Applications Program (CAP): Customer Engagement in a Smart Grid World," *ComEd Report*, December 14, 2010, 3.

311. Illinois Commerce Commission, Petition to Approve an Advanced Metering Infrastructure Pilot Program.

312. Pramaggiorre, "ComEd Smart Grid," slide 5.

313. Ibid., slide 12.

314. Illinois Commerce Commission, Petition to Approve an Advanced Metering Infrastructure Pilot Program, 11.

315. Jensen, "ComEd Customer Applications Program (CAP)," 11.
316. Electric Power Research Institute, "The Effect on Electricity Consumption of the Commonwealth Edison Customer Application Program Pilot: Phase 1—Draft Report," EPRI Report No. 1022703, draft, March 2, 2011, 1-1.
317. Illinois Commerce Commission, Petition to Approve an Advanced Metering Infrastructure Pilot Program, 12.
318. Electric Power Research Institute, "Effect on Electricity Consumption," draft report, 1-2.
319. Ibid., 6-15.
320. Ibid., 6-16.
321. Electric Power Research Institute, *The Effect on Electricity Consumption of the Commonwealth Edison Customer Applications Program: Phase 2 Final Analysis*, Technical Report 1023644 (Palo Alto, Calif.: Electric Power Research Institute, 2011).
322. Ibid., 7-1.
323. Ibid., 7-2.
324. Ibid., 4-4.
325. Ibid., 4-3.
326. Ibid., 4-6.
327. Ibid., 4-6.
328. Ibid., 4-8.
329. Jensen, "ComEd Customer Applications Program (CAP)," 15.
330. Miller, "Despite Bankruptcy Threats, Illinoisans Still Want Freeze."
331. Righter, "Power Customers Need a Long-term Solution to Higher Costs," 11.
332. Illinois Commerce Commission, Petition to Approve an Advanced Metering Infrastructure Pilot Program.
333. Illinois Statewide Smart Grid Collaborative, *Collaborative Report*, 25.
334. Ibid.
335. Illinois Commerce Commission, Petition to Approve an Advanced Metering Infrastructure Pilot Program.
336. Appellate Court of Illinois, Second District (2010), Order No. 07-0566, *On Petition of Administrative Review from the Illinois Commerce Commission*, September 30.
337. Ibid., 42–43.
338. ICC Order, Docket 10-0467, May 24, 2011.
339. Long, and Wernau, "ComEd Scrambling."
340. Wernau, "Lawmakers Override Quinn Veto."
341. Richard D. O'Toole, direct testimony, in Illinois Commerce Commission, Petition to Approve an Advanced Metering Infrastructure Pilot Program, 5.
342. Ibid., 3.
343. Ibid.
344. Ibid., 4.
345. Ibid., 4.

346. Ibid.
347. Ibid.
348. Ibid., 7–8.
349. Ibid., 5.
350. Illinois Commerce Commission, Petition to Approve an Advanced Metering Infrastructure Pilot Program, 8.
351. O'Toole, direct testimony, in Illinois Commerce Commission, Petition to Approve an Advanced Metering Infrastructure Pilot Program, 9.
352. Black and Veatch, *Advanced Metering Infrastructure (AMI) Evaluation Final Report* (Overland Park, Kans.: Black & Veatch Holding), Version 1.0, July 2011.
353. Ibid., 1.
354. Ibid.
355. Ibid., 62.
356. Ibid., 47.
357. Ibid., 65.
358. Ibid., 47.
359. O'Toole, direct testimony, in Illinois Commerce Commission, Petition to Approve an Advanced Metering Infrastructure Pilot Program, 61.
360. Illinois Statewide Smart Grid Collaborative, *Collaborative Report*, 165.
361. Ibid., 89.
362. Ibid., 161.
363. Ibid., 150.
364. Ibid., 146.
365. Greising, "Promise and Peril,"
366. Ibid.
367. Illinois Statewide Smart Grid Collaborative, *Collaborative Report*, 146.
368. Greising, "Promise and Peril."
369. Commonwealth Edison "Frequently Asked Questions," https://www.comed.com/technology/smart-meters/Pages/smart-meter-faqs.aspx/.
370. Commonwealth Edison, "Privacy Policy," https://www.comed.com/Pages/privacy-policy.aspx/.
371. Illinois Statewide Smart Grid Collaborative, *Collaborative Report*, 153.
372. Illinois Commerce Commission, Petition to Approve an Advanced Metering Infrastructure Pilot Program, 34.
373. Commonwealth Edison, AMI Plan, 1.
374. Commonwealth Edison Company, Application for Rehearing, in Docket No. 12-0298 of the Petition for Statutory Approval of a Smart Grid Advanced Metering Infrastructure Deployment Plan, 1.
375. Ibid., 2.
376. Illinois Commerce Commission, Order on Rehearing in Docket No. 11-0721, October 3, 2012, Commonwealth Edison Company, formula rate tariff and charges authorized by Section 16-108.5 of the Public Utilities Act.
377. Commonwealth Edison, press release, October 3, 2012.

378. Illinois Commerce Commission, Order on Rehearing in Docket No. 11-0721, 16–17.

379. "ComEd: Rate Formula Ruling Puts Smart Grid, Jobs at Risk," *Chicago Tribune*, October 3, 2012.

380. Electric Power Research Institute, "Plug-In Electric Vehicle Adoption Forecasts," EPRI Report 101992, December 2010, 4-1–5-2.

381. Ibid.

382. Commonwealth Edison Company, "ComEd Electric Vehicle Strategy," presentation, November 15, 2009, slide 6.

383. Illinois Commerce Commission, Commonwealth Edison Company Petition to Approve an Advanced Metering Infrastructure Pilot Program and Associated Tariffs, Docket No. 09-0263, October 14, 2009, 5.

384. Ibid., 12.

385. Ibid., 14.

386. Ibid., 54.

387. Ibid., 41.

388. Ibid., 42.

389. Ibid., 43.

390. Julie Wernau, "Electricity Prices Could Be Impacted by When Electric Vehicles Charge Up," *Chicago Tribune*, March 10, 2011.

391. Edison Electric Institute, *Industry-Wide Plug-In Electric Vehicle Market Readiness Initiatives*, August 2009, 9.

392. Commonwealth Edison Company, Docket No. 09-0263, October 14, 2009, 25.

393. Commonwealth Edison Company, Illinois Commerce Commission Initiative on Plug-In Electric Vehicles: Supplemental Comments 3, 2011, http://www.icc.illinois.gov/Electricity/PEV.aspx/.

394. Kathleen Davis, "The Knowledge Foundation of a Good Substation," *POWERGRID International*, April 29, 2011, http//www.vision-systems.com/content/up/en/articles/print/volume-8/issue-1/product-focus/substation-management-maintenance/the-knowledge-foundation-of-a-good-substation.html/.

395. Pramaggiorre, "ComEd Smart Grid," slide 21.

396. Ibid., slide 18.

397. We assume that ComEd does not intend to continue the "hold harmless" variable with its system-wide AMI rollout.

398. Julie Wernau, "For Many, ComEd's Smart Grid Needs an Explanation," *Chicago Tribune*, April 24, 2012. Several states, including New York, Ohio, and Maryland, have mandated that utilities visit a home before disconnection.

399. Ibid.

400. Electric Power Research Institute, *Estimating the Costs and Benefits of the Smart Grid*, 1-4 (2011).

401. Pacific Northwest National Laboratory, *Smart Grid: An Estimation of the Energy and CO2 Benefits.*

402. Austin Energy is the City of Austin's largest single source of revenue (Working Group Recommendations, 15).

403. Working Group Recommendations, 4.

404. Working Group Recommendations, 2, 4.

405. Working Group Recommendations, 6.

406. Working Group Recommendations, 10.

407. See http://www.earthtechling.com/2012/01/austin-fires-up-largest-solar-farm -in-texas/.

408. "LIGHTSON: Austin Energy Delivers First Smart Grid in the US," Electric Energy Online.com, http://www.electricenergyonline.com/?page=show _article&mag=60&article=451/.

409. Ibid.

410. Pecan Street, Inc., "Pecan Street Project Energy Internet Demonstration: Project Narrative, Proposal to Department of Energy, from Pecan Street Project, Inc., Austin Energy, University of Texas, Environmental Defense Fund, and City of Austin," 5.

411. Available at http://www.austinenergy.com/energy%20efficiency/Programs/ Green%20Choice/index.htm/.

412. Available at http://www.austinenergy.com/Energy%20Efficiency/Programs/ Rebates/solar%20rebates/index.htm/.

413. Proposal to Department of Energy, 11.

414. Pecan Street, Inc., Pecan Street Project Energy Internet Demonstration Project Management Plan, Cooperative Agreement DE-OE0000219, Department of Energy, February 24, 2011, 5.

415. DOE PMP, 5.

416. DOE PMP, 5.

417. "LIGHTSON: Austin Energy Delivers First Smart Grid in the US."

418. Proposal to Department of Energy, 3.

419. DOE PMP, 14.

420. Pecan Street Project Energy Internet Demonstration, project narrative, 8.

421. Ibid.

422. Pecan Street Project, Request for Information, Customer Side of the Meter, May 17, 2011, 39.

423. See http://perfectpowerinstitute.org/apply-seal/evaluate-projects-0/.

424. Proposal to the Department of Energy, 41.

425. See Electric Rate Schedule and http://www.austinenergy.com/About%20Us/ Rates/Fuel%20Adjustment%20Factors.htm/. Calculations assume standard summer residential rate, monthly consumption equal to 1,000 kWh, and use 2012 fuel adjustment factor.

426. "Austin Energy Rate Analysis and Recommendations Summary Report," December 19, 2011, 25.

427. Under the proposed rate, residential customers would pay in inclining rate per kWh consumed. The proposed residential rates are discussed in more detail in section X.

428. "Austin Energy Rate Analysis and Recommendations Summary Report," 185.

429. A smaller, three-thousand-dollar incentive is available for households that choose to lease instead of purchase the Volt.

430. See http://www.austinenergy.com/About%20Us/Environmental%20Initia tives/plug-in%20Partners/index.htm/.

431. See http://energy.gov/sites/prod/files/SGDP%20Awards%20Combined% 20%202011%2011%2008%201353.pdf/.

432. San Diego Gas & Electric, "San Diego Gas & Electric—About Us," http:// www.sdge.com/aboutus/ (accessed August 3, 2011).

433. Sempra Energy, "The Sempra Energy Story," September 17, 2011, http:// www.sempra.com/about/.

434. San Diego Gas & Electric, *Smart Grid Deployment Plan, 2011–2020*, Rep. 2011, 57, http://www.sdge.com/documents/smartgrid/deploymentplan.pdf/.

435. Steve Pullins and John Westerman Sr., *San Diego Smart Grid Study Final Report*, Energy Policy Initiatives Center University of San Diego School of Law, 84, 2006, http://www.sandiego.edu/epic/research_reports/documents/ 061017_SDSmartGridStudyFINAL.pdf/.

436. San Diego Gas & Electric, *Smart Grid Deployment Plan, 2011–2020*, 60.

437. Ibid., 64 (citing "PA Consulting Group recognizes North American Utilities for excellence in reliability and customer service at the 2010 ReliabilityOne and ServiceOne Awards," November 18, 2010).

438. "New Safety Concerns Raised After Powerlink Tower Mishaps," *10News .com*, June 15, 2011, http://www.10news.com/news/28253731/detail.html/.

439. San Diego Gas & Electric, *Smart Grid Deployment Plan, 2011–2020*, 60.

440. Onell R. Soto, "Governor Calls Sunrise Powerlink Example to Nation," *San Diego Union-Tribune*, http://www.signonsandiego.com/news/2010/ dec/09/governor-to-attend-sunrise-groundbreaking-today/ (accessed August 4, 2011).

441. Protect Our Communities Foundation, http://protectourcommunities.org/ poc-blog/ (accessed August 10, 2011).

442. See http://recovery-and-reinvestment-act.theblaze.com/q/526170/7357/ How-much-did-the-San-Diego-Gas-And-Electric-Company-Smart-Grid -Investment-Grant-Program-EISA-1306-in-San-Diego-CA-receive-from -the-ARRA/.

443. "By July 1, 2011, each electrical corporation shall develop and submit a Smart Grid Deployment Plan to the commission for approval." Cal. Pub. Util. Code § 8364 (West 2009).

444. Senate Bill 17, Cal. Pub. Util. Code § 8360 (West 2009).

445. Cal. Pub. Util. Code § 8360-69 (West 2009).

446. CPUC D.10-06-047.

447. San Diego Gas & Electric, *Smart Grid Deployment Plan, 2011–2020*, 34.

448. Ibid., 17.

449. Michael R. Niggli to Michael R. Peevey, President, California Public Utility Commission, in San Diego Gas & Electric, *Smart Grid Deployment Plan, 2011–2020*.

450. Ibid., 69.

451. San Diego Gas & Electric, *Smart Grid Deployment Plan 2012 Update*, 1, http://www.sdge.com/sites/default/files/documents/1138900767/SDGE_Annual_Report_Smart_Grid_Deployment.pdf/.

452. San Diego Gas & Electric, *Smart Grid Deployment Plan, 2011–2020*, 69.

453. Tom Brill, San Diego Gas & Electric, e-mail to the author, September 9, 2011.

454. Ibid.

455. Ibid.

456. San Diego Gas & Electric, *Smart Grid Deployment Plan 2012 Annual Report*, 20–21.

457. San Diego Gas & Electric, *Smart Grid Deployment Plan, 2011–2020*, 50.

458. Ibid., 51.

459. Department of Energy, "Federal Tax Credit for Electric Vehicles Purchased on or after 2010," http://www.fueleconomy.gov/feg/taxevb.shtml/ (accessed September 18, 2011); Plug in America, "State & Federal Incentives," http://www.pluginamerica.org/why-plug-vehicles/state-federal-incentives/ (accessed September 18, 2011).

460. San Diego Gas & Electric, *Smart Grid Deployment Plan, 2011–2020*, 70.

461. San Diego Gas & Electric, "The Cost of Charging Your Electric Vehicle," http://www.sdge.com/environment/cleantransportation/evRates.shtml/ (accessed September 15, 2011).

462. At http://sdge.com/electric-tariff-book-commercialindustrial-rates/.

463. At http://sdge.com/low-income-home-energy-assistance-program-liheap/.

464. Ibid.

465. San Diego Gas & Electric, *Smart Grid Development Plan 2012 Annual Report*, 7, http://www.sdge.com/sites/default/files/documents/1138900767/SDGE_Annual_Report_Smart_Grid_Deployment.pdf/ (accessed October 1, 2012).

466. San Diego Gas & Electric, *Smart Grid Deployment Plan 2012 Update*, 21.

467. Ibid., 2.

468. Neighborhood Electric vehicles are like golf carts. They can usually only go low speeds like thirty miles per hour.

469. California Environmental Protection Agency, Air Resources Board, *Staff Report: Initial Statement of Reasons for Proposed Rulemaking, Public Hearing to Consider Adoption of Regulations to Control Greenhouse Gas Emissions from Motor Vehicles*, http://www.arb.ca.gov/regact/grnhsgas/isor.pdf/ (accessed September 10, 2011).

470. Federal Power Act, 16 U.S.C. § 796(24) (1935).

471. Ibid., § 796(15).

472. Ibid., § 824(d), E.g., Electrical corporations; procurement plans, Cal. Pub. Util. Code § 454.5 (West 2008).

473. *Re: Alternative-Fueled Vehicle Tariffs*, 283 P.U.R. 4th 361 (Cal. P.U.C., 2010).

474. Ibid., 361.

475. Public Utilities—Electric Vehicles, Cal. Pub. Util. Code § 216 (West 2009).

476. 283 P.U.R. 4th at 361, 362.

477. Ibid., at 361.
478. 2011 California Assembly Bill No. 631, California 2011–2012 Regular Session.
479. San Diego Gas & Electric, *Smart Grid Deployment Plan, 2011–2020*, 237.
480. "California State Assembly Passes Energy Storage Bill AB 2514," *PR News-wire*, http://www.prnewswire.com/news-releases/california-state-assembly-passes-energy-storage-bill-ab-2514-95656959.html/ (accessed September 22, 2011).
481. CPUC D.96-09-045.
482. San Diego Gas & Electric, *Smart Grid Deployment Plan, 2011–2020*, 216–17.
483. D.98-07-097, adopting General Order 166, D.00-05-022 adding Standards 12 and 13 to GO 166, pertaining to the Restoration Performance Benchmark for a Measured Event.
484. Scott DiSavino, "Insight: Power Reliability Will Cost Americans More," *Reuters*, http://www.reuters.com/article/2011/09/13/us-utilities-sandiego-blackout-idUSTRE78C4UG20110913/ (accessed September 15, 2011).
485. Hertzog, *Smart Grid Dictionary*, 151.
486. San Diego Gas & Electric, *Smart Grid Deployment Plan, 2011–2020*,125.
487. Ibid., 126–27.
488. Ibid., 129.
489. See http://www.cpuc.ca.gov/PUC/energy/Renewables/index.htm/.
490. See http://www.cpuc.ca.gov/PUC/energy/Solar/aboutsolar.htm/.
491. San Diego Gas & Electric, *Smart Grid Deployment Plan 2012 Update*, 2.
492. See http://www.cpuc.ca.gov/PUC/energy/Renewables/feedintariffssum.htm/.
493. San Diego Gas & Electric, *Smart Grid Deployment Plan, 2011–2020*, 214–15.
494. See http://www.epa.gov/cleanenergy/energy-resources/calculator.html/.
495. Ibid., 48.
496. San Diego Gas & Electric, *Smart Grid Deployment Plan, 2011–2020*, 129.
497. See http://docs.cpuc.ca.gov/efile/RULC/157634.pdf/, 8.
498. Application of Pacific Gas and Electric Company to Revise Its Electricity Marginal Costs, Revenue Allocation, & Rate Design, including Real Time Pricing, to Revise Its Customer Energy Statements, & to Seek Recovery of Incremental Expenditures (U 39 M), 10-03-014, 2011, WL 2246067 (May 26, 2011).
499. See http://docs.cpuc.ca.gov/efile/A/157735.pdf/.
500. "In Middle of Desert, SDG&E Will Explore Solar Smoothing," *Smart Grid Today*, July 2, 2012.
501. San Diego Gas & Electric, *Smart Grid Deployment Plan, 2011–2020*, 265, FN 44.
502. Ibid., 268.
503. San Diego Gas and Electric, *Smart Grid Deployment Plan, 2012 Annual Report*, 19.
504. San Diego Gas & Electric, *Smart Grid Deployment Plan, 2011–2020*, 289.
505. San Diego Gas and Electric, *Smart Grid Deployment Plan 2012 Annual Report*, 20.

506. San Diego Gas & Electric, *Smart Grid Deployment Plan, 2011–2020*, 295.

507. Ibid., 292.

508. Ibid., 296.

509. Jesse Berst, "Smart Transformer Breakthrough—but Will We Be Too Slow to Take Advantage?" *Smart Grid: Smart Grid News—Grid Modernization and the Smart Grid*, http://www.smartgridnews.com/artman/publish/Delivery _Grid_Optimization/Smart-transformer-breakthrough-but-will-we-be-too -slow-to-take-advantage-3764.html/ (accessed September 13, 2011).

510. Vermont Law School's Institute for Energy and the Environment's model privacy policy can be found at http://www.vermontlaw.edu/smartgrid/.

511. Ann. Cal. Pub. Util. Code § 8380, http://docs.cpuc.ca.gov/published/ Graphics/140370.pdf/.

512. San Diego Gas & Electric, *Smart Grid Deployment Plan, 2011–2020*, 120.

513. National Institute of Standards and Technology, "Guidelines for Smart Grid Cyber Security: Vol. 2, Privacy and the Smart Grid," August 2010, 1, http://csrc.nist.gov/publications/nistir/ir7628/nistir-7628_vol2.pdf/.

514. Tom Brill, San Diego Gas & Electric, e-mail to author, September 16, 2011.

515. San Diego Gas & Electric, *Smart Grid Deployment Plan, 2011–2020*, 121.

516. Ibid., 78-85.

517. Ibid., 83.

518. San Diego Gas & Electric, *Smart Grid Deployment Plan, 2011–2020*, 83–84.

519. There is a model privacy policy in the appendix to this report. It is also available at http://www.VermontLaw.edu/smartgrid/.

520. San Diego Gas & Electric, *Smart Grid Development Plan 2012 Annual Report*, 8.

521. Ibid., 8.

522. CPUC Agenda ID #11156, *Application 11-03-015* (filed March 24, 2011), http://docs.cpuc.ca.gov/efile/PD/161677.pdf/.

523. Jeff St. John, "SDG&E, SoCal Edison Get Smart Meter Opt-Out Orders," *GreenTechGrid*, http://www.greentechmedia.com/articles/read/sdge-socal -edison-get-smart-meter-opt-out-orders/ (accessed April 1, 2012).

524. CPUC Agenda ID #11156, *Application 11-03-015* (filed March 24, 2011) p. 2.

525. CPUC (D.) 07-04-043.

526. St. John, "SDG&E, SoCal Edison Get Smart Meter Opt-Out Orders."

527. Lauren Steussy, "Smart Meter Customers Must Pay to Opt Out: SDG&E," *NBC San Diego*, http://www.nbcsandiego.com/news/local/Customers— 138805844.html/ (accessed April 1, 2012).

528. Utility Consumers' Action Network, "UCAN to PUC: Smart Meters Shouldn't Be Forced Upon SDG&E Customers," *Energy*, http://www.ucan .org/energy/electricity/advanced_metering/ucan_puc_smart_meters _shouldnt_be_forced_upon_sdge_customers/ (accessed April 1, 2012).

529. The commission authorized San Diego Gas & Electric's AMI Project in 2007, and SDG&E has almost completed its deployment of smart meters. Consequently, the standard for metering in SDG&E's territory is now a wireless smart meter. Requiring SDG&E to provide an option that deviates from the standard will require the company to incur additional costs, as identified in the November 28, 2011, filing. CPUC Agenda ID #11156, Application 11-03-015 (filed March 24, 2011), 18.

530. San Diego Gas & Electric, *Smart Grid Deployment Plan, 2011–2020*, 20.

531. Ibid., 20.

532. Ibid., 260–62.

533. Cal. Pub. Util. Code § 8360-69 (West 2009).

534. *Reply of Environmental Defense Fund Regarding the Consolidated Applications of San Diego Gas & Electric Company, Southern California Edison, and Pacific Gas & Electric Company, for Adoption of Smart Grid Deployment Plans*, 4, http://www.edf.org/sites/default/files/A1106006%20EDF%20Reply%20to%20Application%20-%20August%2011.pdf/.

535. Ibid., 8.

536. Presentation of EDF at a CPUC smart utility hearing on January 30, 2012, http://www.cpuc.ca.gov/NR/rdonlyres/891330EE-60FD-4E92-84EC-7F467E5C9CAD/0/Smart_Customer_Jan30_Panel3_EDF.pdf/.

537. *Reply of Environmental Defense Fund Regarding the Consolidated Applications of San Diego Gas & Electric Company, Southern California Edison, and Pacific Gas & Electric Company, for Adoption of Smart Grid Deployment Plans*, 10, http://www.edf.org/sites/default/files/A1106006%20EDF%20Reply%20to%20Application%20-%20August%2011.pdf/.

538. Leslie Guevarra, "Smart Grid Report Card Finds CA Utilities Barely Average," *GreenBiz.com*, http://energynow.com/energypanel/2011/08/17/smart-grid-report-card-finds-ca-utilities-barely-average/ (accessed August 3, 2011).

539. See http://docs.cpuc.ca.gov/EFILE/CM/162090.htm/.

540. Thomas Brill, San Diego Gas & Electric, telephone interview, August 22, 2011.

541. Image source: *Reply of Environmental Defense Fund Regarding the Consolidated Applications of San Diego Gas & Electric Company, Southern California Edison, and Pacific Gas & Electric Company*, 4.

542. Pacific Northwest National Laboratory, *The Smart Grid: An Estimation of the Energy and CO_2 Benefits*, http://energyenvironment.pnnl.gov/news/pdf/PNNL-19112_Revision_1_Final.pdf/ (accessed February 25, 2012).

543. Thomas Brill, San Diego Gas & Electric, telephone interview with author, August 22, 2011.

544. Cal. Pub. Util. Code § 451 (West 1977).

545. Brill telephone interview, August 22, 2011.

546. Cal. Pub. Util. Code § 8360-69 (West 2009).

547. CPUC D.10-06-047.

548. San Diego Gas & Electric, *Smart Grid Deployment Plan, 2011–2020*; Pacific Gas and Electric, smart grid deployment plan: http://docs.cpuc.ca.gov/efile/A/138415.pdf/; SCE, smart grid deployment plan: http://docs.cpuc .ca.gov/efile/A/138423.pdf/.

549. John Cox, "PG&E Explains Soaring Bills." *Bakersfield Californian*, October 4, 2009, A1.

550. Brill telephone interview with author, August 22, 2011.

551. Ken Stone, "(Update) SDG&E: Few Have Health Complaints About Smart Meters—La Mesa, CA Patch," *La Mesa, CA Patch*, http://lamesa .patch.com/articles/sdge-says-only-a-handful-of-la-mesans-have-health -complaints-about-smart-meters/ (accessed September 10, 2011).

552. "New Safety Concerns Raised After Powerlink Tower Mishaps," *10News .com*, http://www.10news.com/news/28253731/detail.html/ (accessed August 4, 2011).

553. Electric Power Research Institute, *Estimating the Costs and Benefits of the Smart Grid*, 1-4.

554. Pacific Northwest National Laboratory, *The Smart Grid: An Estimation of the Energy and CO_2 Benefits*.

APPENDIX II

1. The authors do not in any way warrant or present that this model policy will be compliant with the laws of the jurisdiction in which the utility operates. Before implementing any new rules or policies, the utility should consult with legal counsel to ensure compliance with applicable state and federal laws.

INDEX

About the Authors

KEVIN B. JONES, PH.D., is deputy director and senior fellow for energy technology and policy at the Institute for Energy and the Environment at Vermont Law School, where he also leads the Smart Grid Project. Jones previously served as director of power market policy with the Long Island Power Authority, associate director with Navigant Consulting, and director of energy policy for the city of New York. He received his doctorate from the Lally School of Management and Technology at Rensselaer Polytechnic Institute, a master's degree in public affairs from the Lyndon B. Johnson School of Public Affairs at the University of Texas at Austin, and a bachelor of science degree from the University of Vermont.

DAVID ZOPPO, J.D., is a junior associate with Foley & Lardner, LLP, in Madison, Wisconsin, where he practices in the areas of environmental law and energy regulation. He was a research associate at Vermont Law School's Institute for Energy and the Environment between 2011 and 2013. In 2012, he worked as a legal extern for the Hon. Judge Richard Clifton, who sits on the Ninth Circuit Court of Appeals. Zoppo received a bachelor's degree in political science from the University of North Carolina at Chapel Hill and a juris doctor degree, summa cum laude, from Vermont Law School.